# MOTIVATION AND
# CONTROL IN
# ORGANIZATIONS

# THE IRWIN-DORSEY SERIES IN
# BEHAVIORAL SCIENCE

EDITOR     JOHN F. MEE     *Indiana University*

ARGYRIS   *Interpersonal Competence and Organizational Effectiveness*

ARGYRIS   *Organization and Innovation*

CARZO & YANOUZAS   *Formal Organization: A Systems Approach*

CUMMINGS & SCOTT   *Readings in Organizational Behavior and Human Performance*

DALTON & LAWRENCE (eds.)   *Motivation and Control in Organizations*

DALTON & LAWRENCE (eds.) WITH GREINER   *Organizational Change and Development*

DALTON & LAWRENCE (eds.) WITH LORSCH   *Organizational Structure and Design*

GUEST   *Organizational Change: The Effect of Successful Leadership*

KELLY   *Organizational Behaviour*

KUHN   *The Study of Society: A Unified Approach*

LAWRENCE & SEILER, WITH BAILEY, KATZ, ORTH, CLARK, BARNES, & TURNER   *Organizational Behavior and Administration: Cases, Concepts, and Research Findings*   rev. ed.

LORSCH & BARNES (eds.)   *Managers and Their Careers: Cases and Readings*

LORSCH & LAWRENCE (eds.)   *Managing Group and Intergroup Relations*

LORSCH & LAWRENCE (eds.)   *Organization Planning: Cases and Concepts*

LORSCH & LAWRENCE (eds.)   *Studies in Organization Design*

LYNTON & PAREEK   *Training for Development*

MASLOW   *Eupsychian Management: A Journal*

MASSARIK & RATOOSH   *Mathematical Explorations in Behavioral Science*

O'CONNELL   *Managing Organizational Innovation*

ORTH, BAILEY, & WOLEK   *Administering Research and Development: The Behavior of Scientists and Engineers in Organizations*

PORTER & LAWLER   *Managerial Attitudes and Performance*

PRICE   *Organizational Effectiveness: An Inventory of Propositions*

RUBENSTEIN & HABERSTROH (eds.)   *Some Theories of Organization*   rev. ed.

SCOTT   *The Management of Conflict*

SCOTT & MITCHELL   *Organization Theory: A Structural and Behavioral Analysis*   rev. ed.

SEILER   *Systems Analysis in Organizational Behavior*

WHYTE   *Organizational Behavior: Theory and Application*

WHYTE & HAMILTON   *Action Research for Management*

# MOTIVATION AND CONTROL IN ORGANIZATIONS

Edited by

## GENE W. DALTON, S.M., D.B.A.

Professor of Organizational Behavior
College of Business
Brigham Young University

## PAUL R. LAWRENCE, M.B.A., D.C.S.

Wallace Brett Donham Professor of
Organizational Behavior
Graduate School of Business Administration
Harvard University

1971

RICHARD D. IRWIN, INC.
and
THE DORSEY PRESS    Homewood, Illinois  60430
IRWIN-DORSEY INTERNATIONAL London, England   WC2H 9NJ
IRWIN-DORSEY LIMITED Georgetown, Ontario  L7G 4B3

*First Printing, January, 1971*
*Second Printing, January, 1972*
*Third Printing, August, 1972*
*Fourth Printing, January, 1973*
*Fifth Printing, June, 1973*

Case material of the Harvard Graduate School of Business Administration is made possible by the cooperation of business firms who may wish to remain anonymous by having names, quantities, and other identifying details disguised while basic relationships are maintained. Cases are prepared as the basis for class discussion rather than to illustrate either effective or ineffective handling of administrative situations.

*Library of Congress Catalog Card No. 75–138418*

*Printed in the United States of America*

*To the Original Teachers of*
*Administrative Practices*
*Professors* Learned
Roethlisberger
Hower
Lombard
*and*
Glover

# Acknowledgments

THE AUTHORS wish to acknowledge their indebtedness to the following persons who, as staff members of the Harvard Business School, played a role in preparing some of the cases in this book: John D. Donnell (Empire Glass Company B); Gerald Leader (Lewis Equipment Company); A. B. C. Raj (Olympic Foods Inc.); Jean Deschamps (Seneca Steel Corporation); Andre Reudi (Pennsylvania Metals); D. Booz (Flint Electric Company); H. Braig (Hampton Shipyard); and D. Ulrich and Harriet Ronken (Marshall Company).

We are also indebted to Eric Trist, H. Murray, and K. Bamforth for permission to convert some research reports from the Tavistock Institute ("Some Social and Psychological Consequences of the Longwall Method of Coal-Getting," *Human Relations*, 1951, Vol. 4–1, and "Work Organization at the Coal Face," Doc. No. 506, Tavistock Institute, London, England) into case material (British Coal Industries).

We are likewise indebted to several of our faculty colleagues, present and past, for valuable direct contributions they have made to the materials in this book, especially David Hawkins (Empire Glass Company A) and Edmund P. Learned (Flint Electric Company and Marshall Company).

We are especially grateful to the following men for the direct contributions they have made to the materials in this book and, even more importantly, for the indirect contributions they have made over the years to the development of the Organizational Problems course here at the Harvard Business School: Joseph C. Bailey, Louis B. Barnes, Gerald Bell, Stanley M. Davis, Ronald J. Fox, Ralph M. Hower, J. B. M. Kassarjian, Alva F. Kindall, Paul R. Leitch, Harry Levinson, George H. Litwin, Jay W. Lorsch, David Moment, George A. Von Peterffy, John A. Seiler, James R. Surface, Richard E. Walton, and John R. Yeager.

We thank the many publishers and authors who have granted us permission to quote copyrighted material. The source of each of these quotations is indicated in the appropriate place. With only a few exceptions, all cases in this book have been individually copyrighted by the President and Fellows of Harvard College. They are reprinted here by special permission

vii

and may not be reproduced in whole or in part without written permission.

Finally, we wish to acknowledge the invaluable help of Mrs. Sherrill Kobrick in the preparation of this manuscript.

Even though we gladly acknowledge the many contributions of others to this book, we, the authors, are fully responsible for the book and accept any and all of its faults.

Boston, Massachusetts                                          G.W.D.
*December, 1970*                                                P.R.L.

# Contents

## CASES

# READINGS

# Motivation and Control in Organizations

## GENE W. DALTON

THERE are few activities in an organization which have greater importance to its performance than those which are included in the goal setting, measurement, and reward cycle. The decisions about how individual, departmental, and division performance objectives are to be established, the methods by which actual performance is measured against these objectives, and the means by which individuals are rewarded for their part in that performance are central to the viability of the firm. However, few things have been more baffling to managers than the results of some of their attempts to develop workable performance measures and controls, thus channeling the energies of their employees toward the firm's objectives. Often when they least expect it, they encounter restriction of output or departmental in-fighting. On one hand they find what seems to be apathy, and indifference; yet on the other hand, they keep discovering remarkably ingenious methods developed by their subordinates for beating the system.

## STANDARDS, INCENTIVES, AND SCIENTIFIC MANAGEMENT

American management history has been marked by a number of phases during which certain practices have been widely used; the imprint of these phases is evident in many of the systems of control and reward in use today. One of the earliest and the most widely heralded of these was the period when scientific management made itself felt. Although by no means originated by the advocates of scientific management, the notions of measured output and monetary incentives have come to be largely associated with this movement. The function of the industrial engineer, a product of this period, was to establish standard methods of performance standards. Quotas and budgets for departments and divisions were established by similar but less precise methods and the function of the manager was to act as a thermostat, taking corrective action only when performance moved

1

more than a certain number of degrees from standard. This made management by exception possible. The concept was clearly applicable to departmental budgets, plant production quotas, etc., but it found its greatest acceptance in individual production standards. Here the industrial engineer developed scientific ways of the most efficient methods of performing work and for each task calculated hourly and daily standards which an average worker could perform with normal effort. To provide motivation for above-standard performance, individual monetary incentives were developed whereby the worker could share in the benefits of the increased productivity. Wherever possible, individual duties and responsibilities were completely specified and his performance measured. Frederick Taylor laid down the dictum that managers should "deal with only one person at a time." It also became a well accepted truism that "a man should be held accountable for only that which he alone can control," and hence, there should be a correspondence between authority and responsibility. The manager's job, succinctly summarized by Koontz and O'Donnell[1] was to: (1) plan, (2) organize, (3) motivate, and (4) control. If production was low, it was the manager's job to redesign the jobs and/or the incentive and control system to insure adequate motivation and production.

## HUMAN RELATIONS AND THE "DISCOVERY OF COLLUSIVE RESISTANCE"

The book which signalled the launching of the "human relations" phase of management history was, in part, a documentation of the resistance of employees to influence by the controls described above. *Management and the Worker*[2] contained a careful description of the process by which rate restriction was practiced and the informal organization which grew up around the enforcement of group-established norms about a fair day's work.

During this phase a large number of the unanticipated consequences of control and incentive schemes were documented. Behavior with which nearly every manager had become familiar was finally described in print. Budgets designed to set an upper limit on expenditures were transformed into a minimum target as departments, fearful of cuts, hastened to completely spend their entire budget as the end of the period neared. Individual standards and performance measures fostered competition and blocked the necessary coordination among the members of a department to the detriment of overall performance.[3] Budgets being used as pressure devices

---

[1] H. Koontz and C. O'Donnell, *Principles of Management* (3d Ed.; New York: McGraw-Hill, 1964).

[2] F. J. Roethlisberger and W. J. Dickson, *Management and the Worker* (Cambridge, Mass.: Harvard University Press, 1939). (See section describing the Bank-Wiring Room.)

[3] Peter Blau, *The Dynamics of Bureaucracy* (Chicago: University of Chicago Press, 1955).

increased tension, pitted some groups against others and made people parochial in their thinking.[4] Sales were maximized at the expense of profit; departments concealed valuable information from each other; and perhaps worst of all, the efforts of individuals and groups to protect themselves from, or to "beat" the system distorted the performance information itself to the point that it had become unreliable. Most of what has been written by those interested in the behavioral side of management has focused on the dysfunctional behavior which has resulted from the control systems in organizations, looking only at its ill effects, particularly on motivation.

## THE NEED FOR UNDERSTANDING

However, managers have made increasing use of measurement and control systems in attempting to carry out their functions, in spite of the many problems they raised. These pragmatic managers realized better than many theorists that organizations, after all, are the largest assemblages in our society that have anything resembling a central coordinating system. Organization implies control, and control is an inevitable correlate of organization. As Tannenbaum points out, "The coordination and order created out of the diverse interests and potentially diffuse behaviors of members is largely a function of control.[5] Organizations are purposive, hence managers need feedback to guide their acts toward the achievement of these purposes. Standards play a vital role in the planning, coordination, and problem location which make that feedback useful.

Measurement, moreover, has powerful motivational effects. As Galbraith has pointed out, its motivational impact is so strong that we often devote our time working on those objectives which lend themselves to quantification, to the exclusion of those objectives we acknowledge to be of equal or greater importance but where progress cannot be so easily measured.[6] The use of measurable intermediate goals has a potent motivational effect, especially among individuals with a high "need for achievement." (Such individuals, according to McClelland, Litwin, and others,[7] perform most effectively when concrete and immediate feedback on results is available). Measurement and incentives can focus attention on the achievement of specific goals. Quantification helps reduce the amount of stress felt by those who must evaluate performance and allocate rewards in the face of

---

4 Chris Argyris, "Human Problems with Budgets," *Harvard Business Review,* January/February, 1953.

5 Arnold Tannenbaum, "Control in Organizations: Individual Adjustment and Organizational Performance," *Administrative Science Quarterly,* September 1962.

6 John Kenneth Galbraith, *The New Industrial State* (Boston: Houghton Mifflin Company, 1967).

7 David McClelland, *The Achieving Society* (Princeton, N.J.: D. Van Nostrand Co., 1961). George Litwin and Robert Stringer, Jr., *Motivation and Organizational Climate* (Boston: Division of Research, Harvard Business School, 1968).

ambiguity. Moreover, quantification ties directly into the money system. It is not surprising that measurement and control occupies such a central role in management life in spite of the problems encountered.

The surprising thing is that those men in companies and universities who have devoted their primary attention to the behavioral and motivational aspects of management have had so little to say about the design and administration of control and management information systems. Because of the pervasiveness of these systems, the controller and the management information systems designer must often make the very decisions which have the greatest impact on motivation and behavior. This comes as no surprise to those who understand the nature and function of control systems well; Robert Anthony makes the point that: "The central function of a management control system is motivation: the system should be designed in such a way that it assists and guides operating management to make decisions and to act in ways that are consistent with the overall objectives of the organization."[8]

But he also points out that the designers of these systems have received little help from their behaviorally oriented critics. Anthony further makes the important distinction between operational control (the process of assuring that specific operations are carried out) and management control (the process by which managers assume that resources are obtained and used effectively in the accomplishment of the organization's objectives). He also states that while the designer of an operational control system can draw on knowledge from the mathematical and physical sciences to arrive at models and decision rules, "the designer of a management control system has no comparable body of knowledge to guide him. The relevant concepts stem from social psychology which so far have little to say on the subject."[9]

In my opinion, Anthony is correct both in saying that the relevant underlying concepts are social and psychological in nature, and that the behavioral disciplines have had too little to say explicitly on the subject of formal management controls. There are a number of concepts, studies, and ideas from these fields. These have important implications for an understanding of the general topic of control in organizations, which includes formal and informal controls and their interaction. The following is an attempt to present some of these in a framework which will be useful both to managers and students of management.

## THE PARADOX OF CONTROL

Probably the most important thing to understand about control in organizations, and the most difficult to explain, is the paradox that managers and researchers so frequently encounter:

---

[8] Robert Anthony, *Planning and Control System: A Framework for Analysis* (Boston: Division of Research, Harvard Business School, 1965), p. 113.

[9] *Ibid.*, p. 82.

In many circumstances the more managers attempt to obtain and exercise control over the behavior of others in the organization, the less control they have. Furthermore, often the less control they have, the more pressure they feel to exert greater control, which in turn often decreases the amount of control they have, etc., etc.

Perhaps the best place to begin an explanation of this paradox is by describing the work of three sociologists, who devoted a considerable amount of attention to the study of "bureaucracies" (their use of the term bureaucracy is closer to our use of the term modern formal organizations than to the general, newspaper usage of the term bureaucracy, which connotes inefficiency and rigidity). These three men, Merton, Selznick, and Gouldner[10] all noted that efforts to control the activities of members of the organization have both intended and unintended consequences and that these consequences tended to lead managers toward further use of controls.

## Merton

Merton's[11] propositions begin with top management's attempt to obtain control over the behavior of the members of the organization as the organization grows larger and more complex. This attempt takes the form of an increased emphasis on the reliability of behavior within the organization. Standard operating procedures are instituted and emphasized, while control consists largely in checking to insure that procedures are followed. The consequences are: (a) Relationships become less personalized and are more prescribed by the position people hold. Evaluation and reward become less closely tied to individual achievement. (b) The rules of the organization become internalized and adherence to rules becomes valued even when it no longer results in the outcome for which the rule was originated. (c) Finally, decision making evolves into a process of sorting questions that arise into a restricted number of categories and applying the rule connected with the first formally applicable category rather than searching for more appropriate alternatives. As a result, behavior becomes increasingly rigid and defensible. Behavior also becomes less responsive to customer or client needs and more responsive to internal organization standards. As trouble with outside parties arise, individuals feel an even stronger need to be able to defend their actions and so place an even higher premium on following prescribed rules. Management's efforts to prescribe behavior (to assure that the customer or client's needs are served) actually results in the loss of the organization's power to serve their needs. As a con-

---

[10] An excellent summary of the theories of these three men can be found in J. G. March and H. A. Simon, *Organizations* (New York: John Wiley & Sons, 1958), pp. 33–82. The simplified diagrammatic models that follow were taken in a modified form from March and Simon's summary.

[11] R. K. Merton, "Bureaucratic Structure and Personality," *Social Forces*, 1940, 18, pp. 560–68.

## FIGURE 1

The Simplified Merton Model

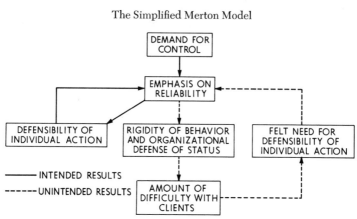

sequence, management feels an even greater need for control and issues new rules and procedures, etc. Thus management efforts to control not only have dysfunctional unintended consequences, but also a tendency to perpetuate the consequences.

### Selznick

Where Merton emphasized rules as a response to the need for control, Selznick[12] emphasized delegation of authority and its unintended consequences. In Selznick's model, management's response to the need for better

## FIGURE 2

The Simplified Selznick Model

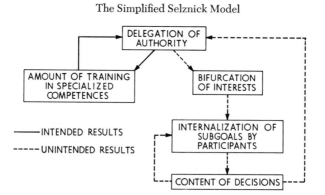

---

[12] P. Selznick, *T.V.A. and the Grass Roots* (Berkeley: University of California Press, 1953).

control, as the organization grows, is departmentalization and increased delegation of authority. This results in increased specialization and an increased ability to deal with problems in limited areas. But it also brings about a bifurcation of interests among the subunits of the organization and commitment to the subunit goals over and above their contribution to the goals of the total organization. Individuals come to internalize the goals of the subunits. Increasingly, the criteria for decision making are based on the subunit goals, in spite of the fact that these may be suboptimum for the total organization. Delegation, like rules, has both intended and unintended consequences and, interestingly, Selznick reports that the response to both types of consequences is a further increase in delegation.

## Gouldner

Gouldner's[13] model of the dilemma of control in organizations begins, like Merton's, with top management's use of enforcement of general and impersonal rules regulating work procedures as a means of maintaining control over operations. These work rules provide the intended guides for the behavior of the members of the organization, but they also have the unintended effect of signaling minimum acceptable behavior. In situations where there is not a high level of internalization of the organization's goals, signaling a minimum level of permissible behavior tends to depress performance to the minimum level. Management sees this as a failure and responds with closer supervision, which increases the visibility of power

**FIGURE 3**

The Simplified Gouldner Model

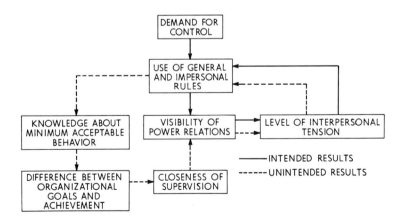

---

[13] A. W. Gouldner, *Patterns of Industrial Bureaucracy* (Glencoe, Ill.: Free Press, 1953).

and authority differences, which raises the tension level in the organization, which elicits even closer enforcement of formal rules, etc., etc.

### Control Problems Arising from Compliance and Resistance

Each of these sociological models is somewhat different in some ways, but it is their similarities that are important here. One of the things they all point to is that the problem with management's efforts to control is *not* that their efforts don't affect behavior. Almost invariably they do have effect. The problem is the unanticipated effects. Interestingly enough, these unanticipated consequences sort themselves into two types: those arising out of compliance and those from resistance.

Problems from compliance arise when people follow the prescribed behavior even when it becomes inappropriate. The effort to control has worked too well, in a sense. In his preoccupation with following the procedure, or meeting the budget, quota, or standard, the employee becomes unresponsive to the unanticipated needs of a customer or of other persons or departments in his own company. Sometimes, of course, these ought to be ignored, but not indiscriminately. The employee's attention has been narrowed to a far greater extent than the originator of the measure had in mind. This has both an overt and a covert aspect to it. The overt signal is that the individual *should* follow the rule or maximize the performance of his subunit and he will be reinforced for doing so. The covert signal is that no more is expected of him. The power of these covert signals has been dramatically demonstrated by the research being done on the "Pygmalion Effect," wherein students have been shown to comply to a remarkable degree with the unspoken expectations of their teachers,[14] and employees with those of their superiors.[15]

The source of resistance to control has been probably best illustrated by Elizabeth Converse, managing editor of the *Journal of Conflict Resolution*, in her review of the material published in that journal in the previous 12 years. To summarize this material she made use of a simple "control paradigm":

In the famous film *High Noon*,—one cuts the dusty street in half between the sheriff and the outlaw, and finds that the two pieces resemble each other in certain basic analytical respects. Each centers on an actor involved in a situation which he is tryng to control and which notably includes another human being. The action involved a control plan, a control attempt and an outcome.[16]

---

[14] R. Rosenthal and L. Johnson, *Pygmalion in the Classroom* (New York: Holt, Rinehart and Winston, Inc., 1968).

[15] S. Livingston, "Pygmalion in Management," *Harvard Business Review*, July/August, 1969, pp. 81–89.

[16] Elizabeth Converse, "The War of All Against All," *The Journal of Conflict Resolution*, 1968, 12, pp. 471–532.

The simple point of Converse's apt illustration is that each individual is involved in an attempt to try to gain control over the major elements in his environment. But, as was the case for the two characters in *High Noon*, Person's efforts to obtain control over his environment is often experienced by Other as a reduction or a threatened reduction in the amount of control

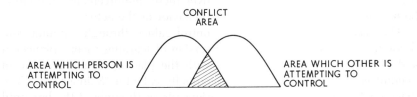

he has. The result is conflict and resistance. Neither party is seeking conflict; each is "minding his own business," but his business intersects with that of another. Management is only trying to control the relevant parts of its environment by setting up a budgeting system. A department head is only trying to gain some control over his environment by providing in his budget request the 10 percent that he anticipates management will cut out of his request. But the efforts of one works against efforts of the other. This problem is magnified by the fact that when an individual finds himself unable to maintain control in important areas of his life, he may join his efforts with those of others, in either a formal or informal grouping to try to gain this control. Soon the conflict and resistance is institutionalized and becomes harder and harder to resolve.

## THE ELUSIVE SYNERGY

The logic of the above analysis would, of course, lead to far more conflict and far less management control over operations than we experience in the organizations we observe and inhabit. In fact, there is far more intelligent compliance than resistance to management direction and more cooperation than conflict. Actually, it is the large amount of control in modern organizations, rather than its absence, that begs for explanation and understanding. There are many writers who have sought to explain the dynamics of this control, and we shall have space to refer to only a few of them here. But first, it may be most helpful to begin with a simple metaphor.

### The Reciprocity of Control

We mentioned earlier the basic tendency in nearly all living creatures to find ways to control their environment as a means of fulfilling their needs. Both men and animals spend much of their time and energy testing their environment, experimenting by acting in different ways, to draw from their environment those things which satisfy their needs. When some act or series of acts results in the desired outcome, the actor learns to repeat that act in order to fill that need in the future. B. F. Skinner and other learning theorists would say he has been reinforced; both their theory and their empirical findings say that behavior which is reinforced tends to be repeated. If someone else has control over these reinforcements, therefore, he has some potential to control the behavior of the actor.

The classical illustration of this control gained through "operant conditioning" (which is that particular version of learning theory pioneered and developed by Skinner) begins with the placing of a pigeon in an operant conditioning apparatus, colloquially called a "Skinner-box." The pigeon, which is hungry, pecks in various places throughout the box until he pecks a red button. At that point, Professor Skinner, via the conditioning apparatus, reinforces that behavior by giving the pigeon a piece of corn. The pigeon pecks the red button again and again receives the corn. The corn is fed only when the pigeon pecks the button. Soon, the pigeon is observed to peck the red button frequently. By a similar procedure, the pigeon can be brought to peck a red button and then a green button.

We could say that Professor Skinner is controlling the pigeon. But the pigeon is also controlling Professor Skinner! All the pigeon has to do to get Professor Skinner to give him a piece of corn is to peck the buttons.

Strangely, this simple metaphor illustrates what is more important about control in human organizations. In order for either the pigeon or the experimenter to control, he must be controlled. If either refuses to be controlled by the other, he loses the control he has. It is the reciprocal nature of the exchange that gives the control its effectance. Note the powerful synergy that is built into this simple model. Each of the parties has found a way to increase his control of the other. The amount of control was not zero-sum in its nature; both gained control.

Now, this is a simple illustration and its limits are obvious. We will not even discuss the problems of satiation, or power differentials. If someone is interested in these, he should read Homans[17] or someone else who has examined the process of social exchange. But the central points are valid and are applicable far beyond this illustration to help us think about control in the complex organizations we seek to understand. In some sense, each person can be viewed as acting, reacting, and testing to find ways to obtain greater control over his environment, or to maintain the control he has. Where his actions are valuable or potentially valuable to others, they may act (or promise to act) in such a way that rewards or reinforces his acts. Humans, of course, can anticipate rewards, and work long periods for un-

---

[17] G. C. Homans, *Social Behavior: Its Elementary Forms* (New York: Harcourt, Brace and World, Inc., 1961).

certain and delayed gratifications. In fact, it is the anticipated rewards, and not the current rewards, which have the greatest motivating effect. In the process, each party has increased the amount of control he has over his environment, and with such a profitable exchange, each party is inclined to continue what he is doing in order to maintain this control.

## The Expansibility of Control

Arnold Tannenbaum of the University of Michigan has been one of those who has recognized the synergistic nature of control in organizations. He maintains that control in organizations is a variable rather than a constant commodity and that it can expand or contract.[18] To demonstrate this, he came up with the ingeniously simple device of asking people at each level of the organization how much influence he and others at each level have over the operations of the firm. Tannenbaum can then plot a curve showing not only the relative differences in perceived influence between levels in the heirarchy, but also the absolute amount of control at work.

The essential elements of our example and the way they can work together in human organizations have been reported and discussed by a number of those studying management and organizational life. One of the best known examples is the famous set of experiments which concluded with the study conducted in the relay-assembly room at the Western Electric Hawthorne Works.[19] In this study, which was begun as a test of the effects of physical working conditions on productivity, the potential for mutual and expanding control was demonstrated almost by inadvertence. The experimenters were interested in finding ways to increase productivity. To do so, they set aside a small group of workers and prepared to measure the effect on performance of various changes in lighting, rest periods, and working hours. In trying to set up the necessary conditions to conduct a "scientific" experiment, the researchers inadvertently created a situation which, for themselves and the girls, was reciprocal and the amount of control expanded. Before each change in working conditions, the supervisor discussed proposals with the girls, listened and responded to their suggestions, and generally showed a genuine and sustained interest in the girls and their work. Seeing that the researchers were obviously interested in performance, and not being afraid that high output records would be used coercively to raise standards later, the girls proceeded to increase output nearly each period, whether the lights and working hours went up or down. Stuart Chase, articulating what many felt at the time, reported that "there is an idea here so big it leaves one gasping." Here was the synergistic para-

---

[18] Arnold Tannenbaum, *Control in Organizations* (New York: McGraw-Hill Book Co., 1968).

[19] This study was also reported by F. J. Roethlisberger and W. J. Dickson in *Management and the Worker* (Cambridge, Mass.: Harvard University Press, 1939).

dox, the more control the girls came to have, the more their supervisor seemed to have.

Vast distances stretch between insights and their successful application, however, and the potential in this idea which so excited Stuart Chase has been illusive. For decades both researchers and managers who have sought to study or utilize the insights they have gained from this study or from similar experiences have found themselves grappling with a host of thorny complications.

The difficulty in making the insights operational has not prevented their having persuasive and imaginative advocates. Probably one of the most imaginative and certainly one of the most persuasive has been Douglas McGregor. McGregor has also centered on the control paradox; he begins by establishing that a manager does not "motivate" anyone.[20] Motivation is built into each of us. Each of us has pressing and unsatiated needs which we are constantly trying to fill. The opportunity and the responsibility of the manager, then, if he is going to operate under the assumptions of this theory (Y) of motivation, is to "create conditions where his men can fulfill these needs through effectively advancing the organization's aims."

McGregor repeatedly affirms that this is not management control, but instead, management through self-control. His point is well made, and because of the connotations that the word control carries in our society, his wording is perhaps less likely to be misunderstood than my own. But if the manager has been successful in this, and his subordinate has achieved greater self-control in this way, what has happened to the control of the manager and the company? If the superior and subordinate jointly set goals and the subordinate is committed to those objectives, if he has come to "own" them, what has happened to the control of the manager? Hasn't it increased?

Robert Anthony, a man whose interests and experience grow out of financially based management control systems, has also built his management framework on the ubiquitous tendency of individuals to seek ways to control their environment.[21] Anthony is less inclined to see the parallel increase of company and employee control as a paradox, but we find him advocating that managers, in building their measurement and control systems, constantly strive for "goal congruence." When goal congruence is achieved, the aims of the organization are best served and its control over its environment is served as the individual strives toward his goals and finds better ways to control his environment. Again, the organization's control is extended not only by the success of his efforts, but by the very fact that those efforts are being made.

---

[20] See the article by McGregor in this book, p. 304. For a fuller statement of McGregor's position, see his two books cited in the suggested list for further reading at the back of this book.

[21] See works by Anthony listed in the suggested list for further reading at the back of this book.

## TYPES OF CONTROL

One way to simultaneously clarify some of the things we have been saying about the relationship among such things as management control, self-control, and total control, is to distinguish among some of the types of control at work in an organization. The word control is one of the most broadly used terms in the English language. It is a central concept in engineering, management, sociology, psychology, and in many other disciplines and applied sciences. In each, it has come to have its own particular meanings and connotations, but there are common elements. Control implies that (a) there is some standard or set of standards, (b) that performance is compared against the standard(s) on a continuous or frequency basis, and (c) that corrective action is taken when there is a deviation from the limits defined by the standard.

There are three major types of controls over behavior in organizations. Each has its own standards, its own monitoring system, and its own system for corrective action when behavior does not meet standards. We will call these: organizational controls, group or social controls, and individual or self-controls.

### Organizational Controls

The direction for organizational controls comes from the plans and purposes of the organization. In a business organization, this direction is often expressed in terms such as share of market, cost reductions, earnings growth, or rate of return on investment. In a reciprocally interactive way, these are translated into specific performance measures such as budgets, standard costs, and sales quotas. The signal for corrective action is a variance from standard in any one of these measures. Rewards for meeting or exceeding standards may range from a word of praise from your boss to a salary increase or a promotion. The sanctions in this formal system may range from a request for explanation all the way to dismissal from employment.

### Social Controls

Social control does not have the explicit written form nor the authority of the formal organization behind it, but it is a very real and often powerful form of control over behavior in organizations. Anyone that has seen a child teased for being a teacher's pet or an adult "razzed" for being a rate-buster or a tail-dragger has seen these controls at work.

The direction for these controls derives from the mutual commitments of members of the group to each other and the shared ideals of the members. From these come the "group norms" about sharing, helping, work performance, etc. When someone deviates from these norms, he may be good-naturedly kidded about it at first, but if it is an important norm to the other members of the group, the kidding will get a sharp edge to it and may be escalated into ostracism and hostility if the deviator doesn't swing back into line. At a time when individualism is verbally honored so much, few of us think of ourselves as being influenced by social controls. But a big part of the power of social controls derives from the fact that they are so naturally and widely accepted in a group. Compliance to these controls is easier to see in others than in yourself, and in groups to which you do not belong than in groups whose standards you have come to think of as normal. Rewards for compliance include approval, membership, and even informal leadership.

**Self-Control**

The third type of control is self-control or self-regulation. These are not popular terms in management or psychological literature. The popular term is motivation. If someone is directing his energies toward certain accomplishments, we say he is highly motivated. But whatever the terminology, individuals can be described as controlling their acts. They make decisions and act to carry these out; they become committed to certain objectives and often work tirelessly to accomplish them. The direction for this control derives from individual goals and aspirations. The standards become expectations about one's own performance, and certain intermediate targets we set for ourselves. The signal for corrective action is any indication that we may not achieve our goal or meet the deadline to which we have psychologically committed ourselves. The rewards for compliance to these self-administered controls include satisfaction, elation, and sense of self-mastery. The sanctions in this system for noncompliance range from a mild sense of disappointment to a deep sense of failure and inadequacy.

Table 1 summarizes the comparison of these three types of control.

**The Interactive Effect of Different Types of Control**

The reader can quickly see that these controls are not independent. If one type of control is working at counter-purposes with another, one can readily see the effect. If there is an incentive or a bonus program to promote high productivity, but the group norms set a "fair day's work" at a moderate level of output, each type of control is likely to be less than optimally effective. If a new budget is introduced, but the department managers do not come to view the budget targets as their own, the amount of actual control may be small. On the other hand, if all of these three controls are working in the same direction, the total amount of control acting in that direction is considerable. If the management is calling for improved

**TABLE 1**

Types of Control in Organizations

| Controls Administered By: | Direction for Controls Deriving From: | Behavioral and Performance Measures: | Signal for Corrective Action | Reinforcements or Rewards for Compliance: | Sanctions or Punishments for Noncompliance |
|---|---|---|---|---|---|
| Organization | Organizational plans, strategies, responses to competitive demands | Budgets, standard costs, sales targets | Variance | Management commendation → Monetary incentives, promotions | Request for explanation → Dismissal |
| Informal group | Mutual commitments, group ideals | Group norms | Deviance | Peer-approval, membership, leadership → | Kidding, → Ostracism, hostility |
| Individual | Individual goals, aspirations | Self-expectations, intermediate targets | Perceived impending failure, missed targets | Satisfaction of "being in control" → Elation | Sense of disappointment → Feeling of failure |

quality and has set new quality goals for a department, and the expectations are that meeting these goals will be recognized and eventually rewarded by management; if group norms call for members to always be looking for ways to improve quality, and if genuine respect goes to those who find ingenious methods of doing so; if individuals in the department have internalized these quality goals and have set even higher goals for themselves; then total control is high, even if no one *feels* controlled. In fact, control is usually highest when it *is* least apparent. Do we have more control in our communities now that there is so much talk about "law and order" and more policemen on the payroll than there was a decade ago when less effort and money for police control was being called for or expended? Vigorous apparent efforts to achieve control often signal a deterioration or a lack of it.

These controls have not only a reenforcing, but a mutually determining effect on each other. We all know instances where an individual was regulating his own behavior toward a certain end, but when required by an external set of controls to work toward that goal, perhaps in a different way, came to feel less personal concern about meeting the total objective. His energies have been diverted into coping with the organizational controls in an effort to regain control over his own activities.

## THE CAPACITY TO CONTROL

Earlier, we postulated a tendency in living creatures, within the limits of their capabilities, to act in a way which will control certain parts of their environment to satisfy their needs. Stated in varying ways, these postulates have been consistent with a wide variety of motivational theories, ranging from Hull's learning theory to Freud's dynamic theory of motivation. Hullian, Freudian, and many other approaches to motivation have shared a reliance on the homeostatic concept that drive or motivation for action derives from a tendency in the individual to act to reduce the tension which arises from an unsatisfied need within himself. According to Miller and Dollard, a drive is a "strong stimulus which impels action."[22] Physiological needs such as hunger or sex provided the prototype. The explicit or implicit assumption has been that all activity expended on the environment is in the service of internal tension reduction, and that if all such biologically based needs were to be satiated at some point the individual would be behaviorally quiescent.

This model is being challenged by what a number of writers have termed a "new look" in motivation theory which has arisen from a number

---

[22] N. E. Miller and J. Dollard, *Social Learning and Imitation* (New Haven, Conn.: Yale University Press, 1941).

of different sources. There is considerable evidence that organisms, human and nonhuman, under many conditions, do not always seek to avoid stimulation, but in some cases search for it. Sensory deprivation studies show that humans find very low levels of stimulation intolerable. People actually seek situations where there is at least a possibility that they will not be completely in control. To take such observations into account, McClelland et al.[23] have suggested that the satisfying and dissatisfying properties of any stimulus are dependent on the size of the discrepancy between the stimulus and the individual's adaptation level, which has been acquired as a result of coping with past stimulation. People may tend to try to avoid great discrepancies between expectations and occurrences but find small discrepancies between expectations and occurrence interesting and generally pleasant.

In the 1950s, experimental psychologists working with animals began to report that higher level animals apparently found it rewarding just to have the opportunity to explore and manipulate their environment. Harlow and his associates, for example, found that monkeys would repeatedly solve a mechanical problem, apparently just for the pleasure of solving the problem; they were not rewarded for doing so in any other way.[24] Later Harlow and Butler were able to show that monkeys will learn discrimination problems when the sole outcome is the opportunity to inspect new territory.[25] These findings, along with developments in personality theory and general psychology led Robert White to propose the concept of effectance motivation. Effectance (he also uses the terms competence and mastery), argues White, is innately satisfying and is not necessarily learned through association with some primary drive reduction.

Effectance motivation must be conceived to involve satisfaction—a feeling of efficacy—in transactions in which behavior has an exploratory, varying experimental character and produces changes in the stimulus field. Having this character, the behavior leads the organisms to find out how the environment can be changed and what consequences flow from these changes.[26]

Finally, Dember and Earl have proposed that a major aspect of stimulation which makes it attractive or not is its information value or its complexity. Each new situation or problem has a certain complexity level. The

---

[23] D. C. McClelland, et al., The Achievement Motive (New York: Appleton-Century-Crofts, 1953).

[24] H. F. Harlow, M. K. Harlow, and D. R. Meyer, "Learning Motivated by a Manipulation Drive," Journal of Experimental Psychology, 1950, 40, pp. 228–34.

[25] R. A. Butler and H. F. Harlow, "Discrimination Learning and Learning Sets to Visual Exploration Incentives," Journal of General Psychology, 1957, 57, pp. 257–64.

[26] Robert W. White, "Motivation Reconsidered," Psychological Review, 1959, 66, pp. 329. (See also R. W. White, "Ego and Reality in Psychoanalytic Theory," Psychological Issues, 1963, 3.)

model also assumes that each individual, in principle, has an attained complexity level for coping with various types of problems. This level changes, with maturation, but more importantly as a function of the person's experience with stimulation of varying levels of complexity.[27] Earl found that individuals will voluntarily spend the greatest amounts of time with problems which are within a small range of complexity values just above their attained level.[28] Hyperattractive stimuli—those that are a little more complex than the person's attained level—are called "pacers" and they perform the function of helping to raise a person's complexity level. As a result of the processes that occur while the individual is actively engaged in making sense of, solving, and in general coping with pacers, he himself eventually takes on their complexity value.

We may say, therefore, that not only is there a tendency for individuals to act to control parts of their environment to fulfill their needs, but there is a tendency to explore, to find answers, to develop new skills, even when no other end is expected to be served (no incentive bonus, no promotion, no need satiation, unless we think of need for effectance). Working on a challenging task, an intriguing problem, or a new territory has value in and of itself, *if* the task is within that band of tasks or problems which lies just beyond the individual's present attained capacity. The consequential effect of this tendency, of course, is to enhance an individual's capacity to control parts of his environment in the future. Again, this is a set of activities, potentially valuable to the organization, which, under certain conditions, the individual is led to engage in himself without being coerced, persuaded, or bargained into it.

As much as any other writer on the subject of motivation, Herzberg[29] has argued the motivating effect of a challenging task and new responsibilities. Herzberg has divided a number of factors which affect job attitudes into what he calls Hygiene Factors and Motivators. Hygiene factors tend to be those things affecting a man's work life such as company policy, supervision, and working conditions, which are not directly a part of the work itself. These, according to Herzberg's research, can lead to dissatisfaction if they are not properly handled, but when they are well handled, their presence does not contribute importantly to satisfaction or to the motivation to work. Of the six factors which *do* contribute to job satisfaction (Herzberg calls them motivators) five are challenges which derive from the content of the work itself or to increased responsibility. Herzberg and those who have been strongly influenced by his research (notably Robert Ford at A.T.&T.) have been strong advocates of job enrichment as a means of achieving greater motivation, productivity, and satisfaction.

---

[27] W. N. Dember and R. W. Earl, "Analysis of Exploratory, Manipulatory, and Curiosity Behaviors," *Psychological Review*, 1957, 64, pp. 91–96.

[28] R. W. Earl, *A Theory of Stimulus Selection*. Hughes Ground Systems, 1961.

[29] See his reading in this book beginning on page 313.

## MOTIVATION THEORY: PRACTICE AND RESEARCH

As we have noted, two of the best-known and most influential writers on the subject of motivation in organizations are McGregor and Herzberg.[30] Both of them advocate positions which have a great deal of face-validity. Intuitively, anyone who has worked in organizations knows that they are pointing to something important. Both are trying to make use of the insight that organizational and individual control can work synergistically. Although this is more true of McGregor, both have a somewhat humanistic, inspirational message which has fitted the times. Both speak in a language which communicates readily to practicing managers and to students of management, and both have had an effect on the vocabulary and the practice of management.

Among those currently engaged in organizational research and theory-building, however, the utility of the constructs of both men have been raised into question. McGregor's constructs make heavy use of Abraham Maslow's "need hierarchy" which even Maslow admits is almost impossible to test operationally, for all its apparent face-validity. Moreover, the dramatic dichotomy which McGregor uses to communicate his ideas, oversimplifies and polarizes some things which are not discontinuous, but fall on an underlying continuum. Herzberg's work has come under question partly because of the nature of his research methods. His data is obtained via retrospective reports on satisfaction rather than on performance. Moreover, retrospective reports may elicit a respondent's statements of what he thinks he *should* say about his behavior and attitudes, rather than the behavior and attitudes themselves. Recent in-company studies have begun to provide some performance data to demonstrate the utility of job-enrichment in certain instances, however. More importantly, it is theoretically possible to explain the phenomena Herzberg is pointing out in terms of expectancies. In our society, when a person is given a more challenging job or more responsibility, he is called on to make a greater investment of energy and involvement. Greater investments have usually been associated, in the person's past, with commensurate rewards such as advancement, remuneration, formal recognition, or status. The increased satisfaction and energy may derive from these expectancies, which unless ultimately realized may lead to disillusionment.

Some researchers and theorists in the field of management are therefore turning to constructs which are more limited in their explanatory scope, but whose variables are more readily made operational. Hunt and Hill, in the reading beginning on page 337, describe their reservations about the

---

[30] A third writer who might be placed in the same category is Rensis Likert, who is not discussed here. For a discussion of Likert's position, see his books listed in the recommended reading list at the back of this volume.

use of McGregor's and Herzberg's constructs for research and advocate the use of Vroom's expectancy model as an alternative. Nord suggests that learning theory and operant conditioning, with their solid base of experimental methodology and body of findings, have been too long ignored in organizational research and practice (p. 352). Stringer's is an attempt to apply the findings and insights derived from the years of imaginative research on achievement motivation to the problem of management control (p. 329). Since all three of these approaches tie in directly with the issues of evaluation, feedback, and reward, they will have strong implications from management control where they can be found applicable.

## THE PROBLEM OF FIT

Interesting and useful as some of the foregoing ideas about motivation and control may be, their direct application to the problems of designing and administering management controls is not obvious. Not only are there a number of interacting types of control potentially at work, but the type of work to be performed varies, the kinds of people will vary, and the nature of the relationships which have been built up in the past will have an effect and must be taken into account. The problem, therefore, is not to find some optimal approach to management and management control for all organizations, but in each situation to find a workable "fit" among: (a) the task of this organization (what it must be able to do well to cope effectively with its environment), (b) the people making up the organization (their capabilities, backgrounds, and expectations), (c) the existing social system (the informal statuses and relationships), and (d) the formal methods and systems for setting objectives, measuring performance and taking action to reward or improve performance.

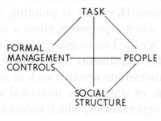

For several decades, writers concerned with the behavioral side of management have been saying, in various ways and using various terms, that the central human problems have arisen because managers have not clearly understood the paradoxes we discussed earlier, and more importantly, that they haven't seen the possibilities for synergy that can come by bringing self-control and social control into line with organizational needs. McGregor and Herzberg are good examples. To a degree, most managers have been able to agree. (Of course, even where there has been complete acceptance of this diagnosis, there remains the awesome task of making use of that insight in daily practice.)

But there have often been those who have had their reservations, saying, "but my situation is different." Many of us have come to feel that often they have also been right. Situations do differ! The tasks differ, the people differ, the existing relationships differ. Unless this fact is recognized, often the wrong questions are asked. The general question, "How tightly or loosely should men be measured and supervised?" is often not helpful. One of the most practical guidelines for a manager is that the measurements he uses and the supervision he gives should help each of his men address the realities and complexities of his job. To follow that guideline, a good analysis of that job is needed.

### An Analysis of the Task

One of the most important parts of men's jobs is the decision making they do. Often the decisions may be small but their cumulative effect is critical. One of the chief tasks of top management and of the management control system is to increase the likelihood that those decisions will be made in a way that will best contribute to the organization's performance. If these decisions really need to be made jointly, because several men have the information necessary to make a good decision or because several men must carry it out, no artificial barriers should be erected to make it difficult for them to work together on these decisions. A man should also be aware of the general effect his decisions will have on the company's performance. A man should not be placed in a position where he is rewarded in the short run for making decisions which will work to the company's long-term detriment. The utilization of these criteria requires hard thinking and a careful analysis of the task to be performed.

### An Understanding of the People Involved

As Vroom[31] and others have shown, individuals also differ in the amount of direction they both desire and need. Some people have been trained for years to direct most of their own activities; others have had almost the opposite experience. For years, researchers have been finding a relationship between high performance and supervisory practices which allow high autonomy and have assumed that the leadership these high performers received was the causal factor. But the findings might be explained even more economically by postulating that much of the causation flows in the

---

[31] V. Vroom, *Some Personality Determinants of the Effects of Participation* (Englewood Cliffs, N.J.: Prentice-Hall, 1960).

reverse direction; high performers tend to be given more autonomy by their supervisors.

## A Recognition of the Existing Social System

Finally, the nature of the existing relationships and their history can be ignored only at one's peril. How much trust presently exists between management and those that report to them? The same action taken in two different firms will be accepted enthusiastically in one and resisted with suspicion in another. How have they been trained to act and respond? In two companies I have studied, the management had, for years, dealt with the work force in a very directive and authoritarian way. After a bitter strike in one company and the arrival of a new management in another, both top managements adopted a more consultative approach to the union and the members. But in both cases this sudden shift left the foremen feeling bewildered and frustrated. They had built a relationship with the men built on management's prior approach. The foremen needed both time and aid to accommodate their thinking and their relationships to this shift.

## TASK ANALYSIS

The general objective of obtaining a "fit" among these factors will find few opponents. If an advocate of such an approach stays at a high enough level of generality, he can get agreement from everyone. The problem, of course, is to move it toward being something more than a platitude. Applying a situational approach to organizational problems requires analysis, judgment and skill. No complete set of decision rules is available. On the other hand, there are certain dimensions of the task, of the people, of the relationships which are generally useful to consider. To illustrate, let us examine three dimensions of the task which should not be overlooked by anyone designing or utilizing a system for assessing and rewarding performance. These are:

1. The programmability of the task.
2. The amount of required interdependence.
3. The time span of the performance cycle.

## Programmability

We will begin with the questions surrounding performance standards. Performance standards serve a great many functions. Of course, they serve an almost indispensable role in planning and coordination. Beyond that, however, they have important psychological effects. They help provide targets, and in general, people respond favorably to targets and feedback on performance. We have a need for feedback, which gives us a sense of progression. As McClelland has pointed out, one of industry's great attractions for persons with a high need for achievement (and we all have some of this need) is the fact that concrete measures of accomplishment are available. To use an admittedly simple illustration, high-jumping or pole-vaulting loses much of its zest and appeal when there is no bar to leap over and to measure the outcome of our efforts. Performance standards act as an attention-centering device, helping us to focus our efforts. Specific individual and organizational accomplishments are seldom achieved without a concentration of attention and effort. Probably the major contribution of scientific management, along with its focus on rationalization and planning, was the means it provided for limiting and focusing attention and effort. As March and Simon have pointed out, one of the aims of the time-study man was to restrict the behavioral alternatives with which the worker was faced.[32]

The kinds of tasks with which the scientific management group primarily concerned itself were those jobs on the factory floor and in the clerical offices where the task could be broken down into small repetitive segments which required no complex problem-solving activities. They were able to describe these tasks in terms of overt behavior, without explicit reference to the mental processes of the worker, or without giving overriding concern to his emotional states or commitments. The assembly line, one of the brilliant products of this era, has been castigated by (some) psychologists, sociologists, and humanists. But with all the alienation, rate restriction, worker noninvolvement, and lack of identification with the product or the company, which have attended its use, the assembly line with externally determined work standards has remained a central part of modern industrial organizations. Among a number of possible, known, alternative means of producing goods, it has been the most economically efficient method. Moreover, as Drucker has noted, it raised the standard of living of millions of semiskilled workers to levels very close to that of the men in skilled trades.[33] (The real challenge to the assembly line has come only from the use of the automated line and the computer, which are taking over some of the repetitive tasks.)

The dilemma posed by Gouldner has been a problem, of course. Externally determined standards and impersonal rules *have* signalled minimum acceptable standards. There *has* been conscious individual and group rate restriction, stemming partly from the fear that higher output will just bring higher standards. This sometimes *has* brought close supervision, greater visibility of power relations, increased interpersonal tension, greater use of rules, etc., etc. But the needed activities from the workers on an assembly line are so circumscribed and programmable that machine-pacing and close

[32] March and Simon, *Organizations*, p. 15.
[33] Peter Drucker, *The Age of Discontinuity* (New York: Harper & Row, 1968).

supervision have been effective in keeping performance within acceptable limits. The plant has not depended on workers for ideas on how to increase productivity, since that function is primarily assigned to industrial engineers. Moreover, the foreman has acted as a buffer, developing personal loyalties, often absorbing the pressure, and eliciting the cooperative efforts of his crew.

This is not to say that there have not been untapped energies and ideas. Ingenious experiments such as the Scanlon plan have, in some small plants, been able to realize the kind of synergy among organizational, group, and self controls we described earlier, and have gotten an outpouring of spontaneous cooperative effort and cost-saving ideas. A large number of industrial firms today such as Procter and Gamble, Texas Instruments, Maytag, and others are also experimenting with other ways to achieve some of these benefits without losing the efficiencies of programmed tasks. But on balance, the close structuring, performance standards, and supervisory enforcement of rules and standards must be given credit as a success in dealing with tasks where the desired repetitive behavior can be specified in advance, closely observed and measured for compliance. This approach is now being introduced into service industries, such as the fast-service food business, with some of the fascinating cost-saving economies of scale that so revolutionized production.

The real problems with close structuring and imposed standards have come more with those jobs that are not so programmable. Staying, for a moment, with individual and group tasks, let us consider a scale along which tasks of different types might be ordered. At the "hard" end of this scale are the types of tasks I have described above. A manager or a staff man can specify, in advance, the precise behaviors he wants, and can measure or monitor to assure that the specifications are being followed. He can teach anyone how to perform the task successfully if that person will only follow instructions. At the other end, the "soft" end of this scale, are those jobs where the manner of doing the job cannot be prespecified. In these tasks there are constant new problems to be solved, and the worker or the group performing them must constantly improvise, experiment, and innovate. Very often, even the ends to be accomplished must be stated only in very general terms, because they will be partly determined by events. There also is a large learning component to these tasks.

At the hard end of this scale, the training can be specific, concrete, and usually brief (although it can be fairly long and exacting if there are a large number of contingencies, each with specified alternative responses). At the soft end, the training must be general, focused on approaches and strategies for problem solving. Tasks can be at the soft end of this scale when the technology is new and little is known about it, but as more knowledge and experience is acquired, parts of the task can be moved toward the hard end of the scale. Mark Twain once said that life is a storm of thought. Successful performance of tasks at the hard end of this scale require that more of this storm be kept separate from performance and that only a small and closely specified segment of that thought be allowed to influence task performance. At the soft end, this storm is essential, and it is from this rich but sensitive source that much of the direction for specific actions must come.

Moderate to high performance can be obtained from most persons performing jobs at the hard end of this scale, through the use of fairly directive supervision, performance standards, and adequate compensation. However, at the other end of the scale, high performance is usually obtained only when the person performing the task feels personally responsible for the contribution his efforts will make in reaching the organization's objectives. External pressure for performance may have different effects at the two ends of this scale. If it is directed at specific behaviors or ends, as pressure often is, it may have a positive effect at the hard end by concentrating attention where attention is needed. Since all other activities are specified, they are less likely to suffer from neglect at this end of the scale. At the soft end, however, we run into the problem Merton described. Pressure applied for behavior in a specific direction will bring a concentration of that behavior, often to the detriment of other equally important activities. As this failure in performance makes the person more anxious, he is likely to concentrate even more on the part of the job receiving the pressure, making him even less responsive to other needs, etc., etc.

External pressure also has different effects on the *ability* of individuals to perform at the two ends of the scale. When pressure for higher performance is placed on a person who already knows how to perform a task well, performance can increase for some time as additional pressure is exerted. But when the task involves learning, performance rises only slightly as greater pressure is applied, then falls off rapidly. Related, of course, is the effect of the feelings aroused. Positive emotions are less likely to have an effect at the hard than at the soft end, partly because there is less leeway for such an effect. Negative emotions, such as fear or resentment, are most likely to interfere at the soft end where so much of the behavior is unprogrammed.

There is a danger of misapplying the above reasoning which should be noted. If a job is still being performed by human hands, it is probably far from the extreme hard end of this scale. Unless a job has been completely automated, human skill, discretion, and judgment are still depended on. A sense of involvement and personal responsibility for performance outcomes (or the lack thereof) can make important differences in performance. Relative to most jobs, those performed in the Relay-Assembly Room Experiments were somewhat routine, but the attitudes of the women had a consistent and measurable effect on performance.

We have been talking about individual performance, but much of what has been said applies to departments and divisions. Performance standards here are most often expressed in terms of budgets, budgeted volumes, costs, and profits. But the tasks these units perform can also be ordered roughly along the scale described above. Tasks where the amount of uncertainty is low, where changes come slowly, where much is known about the technology or the market, these can be described as more programmable, and at the harder end of this scale. Directive management, structured budgets with close attention to variances, and frequent budget reviews will be more likely to affect performance positively in departments and divisions where the task falls at the hard end of the scale. This kind of management behavior is more likely to have an opposite effect at the opposite end of the scale.

Most individual or departmental tasks do not fall at the extremes of this scale we have conceived, of course. They fall in between; and the performance measures and the way they are administered must take that into account. Nor are we implying that no measures should be used near the soft end of the scale. Wherever appropriate measures can be found, they should be utilized, but the typical accounting measures are less likely to reflect all that is important in the complex tasks. Care should be exercised to obtain the fit that is being aimed for, to keep from narrowing an individual's or a department's focus too much, and to avoid false specificity and concreteness. Quantitative measures have an elegance and an appearance of objectivity that is seductive. In evaluating performance, those areas where quantitative measures are available are often given greater weight than they deserve in relation to those areas where only unquantified and subjective judgments are available. Essentially subjective judgments are sometimes quantified also and then erroneously treated as if they had a precision unjustified by their source. Individuals resent being measured by standards which take into account only part of the elements of their job. They resent being torn between "doing a good job" and maximizing a number or series of numbers which do not fully reflect what is required for successful performance.

Before leaving this section, it is important to note that effective measurement systems, used effectively, have as great a potential for facilitating self control as for organizational control. With an adequate set of measures available to him, an individual can set objectives, test himself, see how he is doing, experiment with new methods, and test their effects. He can evaluate his own performance as well or better than can his superior and can take informed steps to improve it. As a rapid and discriminating feedback on the effects of man's work, the computer has the potential for enhancing the development and use of skill and judgment to an extent unprecedented in history.

The development of sophisticated control and measurement systems has also made possible the widespread decentralization of decision making in organizations. By providing adequate and discriminating aggregate performance measures, control systems have freed top management from having to look over their subordinates' shoulders on specific decisions or transactions in order to know what is going on and feel that they are doing their jobs.

Management by objectives, when used intelligently instead of mechanically, utilizes this potential for men to help set targets for themselves and their departments, monitor their performance, and learn from the results. (See readings by McGregor, Meyer-Key-French, and Thompson-Dalton in this volume, which all relate to management by objectives in different ways.) Again, used intelligently, it can enhance the control of both the subordinate and the superior.

## Interdependence

One of the clearest dictums of scientific management was that each man should be given a definable and distinct responsibility wherever possible and that his performance in meeting that responsibility should be measured in some objective way. The individual, knowing that he is being held accountable, will, according to the theory, take this responsibility seriously and perform his work better. This principle has been extended to departments, plants, and divisions through the use of cost and profit centers. The unit being measured has a cost (or a profit) budget and is held responsible for meeting it. To accumulate the separate expenditure and revenues of a number of subunits of the organization is a complex and expensive task. Costs of equipment, materials, and labor have to be allocated to departments. When the finished products of one unit become the raw materials of another unit, the problems of cost and profit allocation become complex and are often computed only by the use of transfer prices which perform the function that buying and selling prices perform on the outside. Since failure or success in meeting budgets can be determined by such factors as raw materials cost or production volume that are beyond the control of the individual manager, accounting procedures are usually prepared to factor out that part of the variance from budget which can be attributed to these factors. All this collection and analysis of data is performed in order to identify problem areas and to fix responsibility. The wide and accelerating use of such centers attests to the fact that managers believe that the cost and time required to measure performance in this way is more than offset by its motivating effect. Those who design such centers go to great lengths to distinguish between those costs and revenues which a manager can and cannot control. As was mentioned earlier, a guiding principle often used is that "a man should be held accountable for only that which he alone can control."

There are other, often hidden, costs associated with such measurements, however, which far outshadow the costs of collecting, analyzing, and reporting the data. These costs are best illustrated by an apocryphal story about a high-school track team.

It seems a small high school had a winning track relay team which had been operating thus far without a coach. Finally, a local businessman, and controller of his corporation, was persuaded to coach the team. He immediately saw that this had parallels with his business enterprise, so he proceeded to bring the principles of his own work to the problem of improving the team's performance. First, he decided a system of measurement was needed so that improvement or deterioration in performance could be detected. His second rule was that men should be held responsible for performance. Thirdly, a man should be held responsible only for that which he alone can control. So he proceeded to set up a system of clocking each man's running time. Criteria were set for determining when each man's measured time would begin and end. Moreover, each man's running time was posted in the locker room and the coach made sure that he praised each man when he was able to cut a second off his time. The men worked hard and things went very well, except for one small difficulty, which had a rather unfortunate effect on their win-lose record. The baton kept being dropped! Each man, now concentrating on improving his own measured time, was anxious to delay getting the baton till the last possible second and to hand it off as soon as possible in order to stop the clock on his own recorded time.

Whose job is it, on a relay team, to pass the baton? It is a joint responsibility! Baton passing is essentially a cooperative task, and there are a great many responsibilities in modern business firms which, like baton passing, cannot be divided and assigned to separate persons or subunits. They must remain a joint responsibility.[34] When this fact is ignored by those measuring performance, it can result in significant and often unrecognized costs. As was mentioned earlier, one of the major functions which people (and particularly managers) perform in organizations is that of decision making. Some decision making is a joint responsibility by its very nature. Often two or more people have the information necessary to arrive at an adequate decision. But if, like the members of the relay team, each is forced by the measurement system to concentrate on the performance of his own subunit, effective information-sharing and joint problem solving may be seriously blocked. Often such decisions require the weighing of a number of trade-offs, open sharing of information, and an overall perspective. If each party must constantly be concerned with protecting his interests, bargaining becomes subordinate to problem solving.

---

[34] There may be those who are disturbed by this idea because they have been taught that "authority must always match responsibility." But one of the clearest, if not well-advertised, facts about modern complex organizations is that they contain innumerable situations where authority and responsibility cannot be matched. The aerospace industry with its extensive use of the matrix form of organization is an excellent case in point. Complex, highly interdependent tasks do not lend themselves to such tidy distinctions.

This is close to the dilemma posed by Selznick; management's efforts to maintain control and to improve performance lead them to develop measurements which foster a strong sense of personal responsibility for subunit performance. This very tendency, however, can block joint decision making and promote suboptimization.

William James used to advocate that, faced with an apparent dilemma or contradiction, one should make a distinction. The rule holds good here, and again the distinction comes from an analysis of the organization's task. There are a great many individuals and units in organizations the performance of whose tasks are not highly interdependent with that of others. Where that is the case, an evaluation system which tends to focus attention narrowly on individual and subunit performance can elicit the high energy expenditure which derives from a direct personal sense of responsibility and from the effects of intracompany competition, with not much danger that overall organization goals will be subverted. But when the task is highly interdependent in nature it becomes a serious threat with the result that subunit measurement centers and comparative measures fostering competition should be established with caution.

The powerful effect of competition on behavior had an interesting history in management literature. A few decades ago internal competition was celebrated as a management tool for motivating workers by such stories as the following:

Andrew Carnegie, hearing of a problem of low productivity in a section of one of his mills, went to one of the crews as they were finishing the shift and asked how many units they had poured. When they replied six, he wrote it on the floor with chalk. When the next shift came on, they asked what the six was and were told. They said, "We can beat that," and did. Their seven went on the floor, only to be erased by the eight of the next crew, etc., etc.

As the years have gone by, the dysfunctions of such competition (fighting over who gets credit, refusing to share information and ideas, mutual stereotyping, and so on) have been given much more attention along with strategies for developing bases for cooperation. But the facts of organizational life are that both internal competition and cooperation can be useful. A manager needs to be able to ascertain where and to what degree each is appropriate. A close analysis of task interdependencies provides one useful criterion.

An important and a valid rationale for setting up profit and cost centers is that they help move decision making downward in the organization to levels where much relevant detail can be considered in a way which retains a proft focus. Far-flung decentralized organizations seem almost inconceivable without them, but without a thorough analysis of the interdependencies involved in overall company performance, such centers are likely to be set up where they are not only inappropriate but dysfunctional. The psychological pressures on managers to establish them are sometimes unusually strong. One of the effects of such centers is to push profit responsibility downward and that responsibility carries with it a built-in pressure which is not always comfortable. A natural tendency for a manager carrying this load is to try to divide it up and pass it down to those reporting to him in the same way it was passed to him. But while the overall task he supervises may be relatively separable from that of other groups in the company, the work of his subordinates within his department, plant, or division may require shared efforts and joint decision making which such centers would impair. Often a difficult but useful decision for a manager is to decide that he will carry the responsibility for profit and develop a team which can work together to do the work.

In closing the discussion on this variable, a word should be said about management by objectives. Much that has been said about profit centers applies, to a lesser degree, to management by objectives. One of the great strengths of management by objectives is the strong personal responsibility a man feels for goals he has helped set. But that very strength can be a liability if it fixes his attention on objectives for which he alone is responsible to the point where joint responsibilities are neglected. This is a problem which companies planning to use management by objectives extensively must consider seriously. Simply having each man include in his objective that he will "work with Smith" or "coordinate with Department A" does not resolve this problem.

### Time Span

It goes without saying, perhaps, that a measure which provides feedback soon enough so that corrective action can make a difference is more useful than a measure which comes too long after the fact. Periodic measures can also serve the very important function of providing intermediate goals which help us to focus our energies. Long-term general goals, by themselves, fail to provide most of us with the structure and immediacy which enable us to sustain a high level of interest and effort. One of the potentially most helpful roles of a manager is to help those under him to devise and utilize measures as guides toward increasing their own effectiveness.

The other side of the time aspect of measurement, however, is that an imbalanced emphasis on short-term measures can reinforce behavior which is harmful to the organization's interests. Developmental expenditures may be curtailed to minimize current costs at the expense of future market position, current maintenance costs may be limited at the expense of future sales, or high pressure to meet current sales quotas may prevent the establishment of customer confidence in an industry where long-term relationships are the key to successful marketing. Short-term sales contests, in markets where long-term relationships are vital, may result in salesmen playing an "end game," milking a territory, then leaving the company.

John Dearden, writing about some of the pitfalls of R.O.I. management,[35] has recently pointed out that the annual accounted profit can be a very poor measure of what has been accomplished during any relatively short period of time. A new product could have been developed, or a major organization change implemented, either of which could affect future performance. But neither would be reflected in current profitability, Dearden points out. He advocates that when evaluation requires a period longer than a year, management should consider extending the accounting time period in even their formal control system.

Likert and Seashore[36] have also argued that present accounting procedures reinforce certain management practices which appear profitable in the short run but are profit-reductive in subsequent periods. Cost reduction drives, they argue, are typically characterized by the following management action: personnel is reduced (especially in staff departments); standards are introduced or extended to more jobs; increased pressure is applied to get performance up to standard; budgets are tightened and subjected to closer control; maintenance and supply activities are often curtailed; and activities with uncertain or distant values such as R.&D. are cut back. The results, they argue, are that in the first year or two scrap losses will go down, costs will be lowered, productivity measures will go up, and profits will improve. But during this period the interesting variables of attitudes, motivation, and communication will deteriorate. The net result is that in subsequent periods other negative signs will appear. Turnover and absences will increase; labor relations and product quality will deteriorate; and customers will begin to complain and take business elsewhere.

Unfortunately, the data upon which Likert and Seashore drew their data were inferential, fragmentary, and anecdotal. Some of the measures they would have needed for more direct evidence of their conclusions were not being kept on a continuing basis (Likert has been working in recent years to see that companies do make such measurements). Our own analysis and experience suggests that if more complete findings were available, they would follow lines less global and more differentiated than these authors suggest. Likert and Seashore did not differentiate between the *kinds* of jobs on which standards were being introduced or where pressure for performance is applied. (They do acknowledge that "this cycle would not apply in all situations where jobs are timed and standards set. It refers

---

[35] John Dearden, "The Case Against ROI Control," *Harvard Business Review,* May/June, 1969.

[36] R. Likert and S. E. Seashore, "Making Cost Control Work," *Harvard Business Review,* November/December, 1963.

only to those situations where top management is felt to be changing its behavior substantially.") We would predict that the negative results they have noted will not be universal but will be found to center in those situations where the management actions described are inappropriate, either in view of the programmability of the tasks or the required interdependencies of the time cycle required for task completion.

What we have said about aligning measurement and evaluation periods with the time cycle of the task will provide no rules that can be applied mechanically. In many cases, for example, the increased energy flow which more frequent evaluation periods can elicit will offset the negative effects resulting from a focus on inappropriately short-term measures. In many cases too, the existing measurement period can be too long (rather than too short), failing to focus attention on certain issues and details frequently enough. The concept of time span can overlap our analysis of interdependencies. If the measurement unit isolates only part of a whole task, needed cooperation may be prevented. But even though the issues surrounding the relationship between time span and measurement are not easily resolved, a critical look at the time variable can be very fruitful in designing and administering controls.

### Formal Rewards and Incentives

We have been discussing measurement; but one of the major reasons why measurements are such a critical issue in organizations is that they are used in evaluation and evaluation determines the dispensing of rewards. The topic of rewards is too vast to attempt to treat here, but a few words relating what has been said above to the subject of rewards is in order. We mentioned that measures are in large part attention-centering devices. Relating a reward to the outcomes of the measure magnifies this effect, and tying it directly centers attention even more. As we have seen, this potentially has both positive and negative outcomes. Learning theory would also tell us that all other things being equal, the behavioral and cognitive effects of rewards are greatest when rewards are specific and immediate. This would argue for a system of direct incentives—but therein lies the problem area. As March and Simon have pointed out, the effectiveness of a system of incentives depends on the precision of the standards on which they are based.[37] Even when the standards seem clear-cut, the problems of justice and equitable administration connected with incentives are formidable. When the standards lack precision, direct incentives raise even more difficult problems. Moreover, managers often find themselves rewarding unproductive behavior.

Monetary incentives tied directly to performance standards also intro-

---

[37] March and Simon, *Organizations*.

duce a rigidity into operations and methods that is sometimes intolerable. In the past decade many companies have bought their way out of financial incentive systems and have gone to day rates just to have greater freedom to make technological and methods changes without protracted negotiations.

One of the other reasons why companies have been willing to give up their incentive systems is that the systems have not been unusually successful. In their enthusiasm for the potential "motivation" their systems would produce, it has been easy for the designers of these systems to forget that men and women (even those with blue collars) are complex beings with a multiplicity of needs, and that they are capable of time-binding. Employees, from top managers to production-floor workers, have generally taken a longer term view of rewards than the designers of these schemes expected. Many incentive schemes have failed in their intent simply because employees have refused, and often rightfully so, to believe that their long-term interests would be best served by maximizing current rewards available under these systems.

Managers' sublime faith in the power of monetary incentives to motivate other people (not themselves) has led them to quickly resort to monetary incentives or commissions as a frontal attack on problems which could be better and more inexpensively handled other ways. Often a careful analysis of the determinants of a "problem" will suggest effective ways to eliminate the inertia or reluctance which the incentives are designed to overcome. This faith in direct incentives has also led managers to move increasingly into the impoverished condition of having only one *kind* of reward (monetary) which has meaning in the organization.

Managers have a natural reluctance to make subjective judgments about reward allocations. Thus they are attracted by schemes which promise to prevent them from having to make these judgments. They are also easy prey for experts who imply that managers should tell a man in advance exactly how everyone is to be judged and rewarded. In truth, there is much to be said for that much maligned word, ambiguity, in such matters. In evaluating performance, in allocating rewards, and in deciding on promotions, it is almost impossible to state beforehand all the criteria that will eventually be used. Certain factors will come to play a more important part than was anticipated. A number of intangibles will inevitably play a part in decisions. Unless management retains the right to exercise judgment, it forfeits its ability to respond flexibly to a complex and changing world and to ameliorate the inequities which any formula will create. Unless managers acknowledge this subjectivity and ambiguity to themselves and others, they will misrepresent a concrete reality. Their fairness and the appropriateness of their methods will best be established by the quality of the decisions, not usually by a detailed explication of the method by which the decisions will be (or were) made.

## PARTICIPATION AND OWNERSHIP OF GOALS

Much was said earlier about the importance and the possibility of a synthesis between organizational control and self-control. This comes into being primarily when individuals feel a personal ownership in the vital goals and subgoals of the organization. Probably with justification, participation in goal setting is mentioned most frequently as the key means of promoting this sense of ownership. It is mentioned so frequently that a few words of caution seem necessary. Since the imaginative and influential research studies of Kurt Lewin,[38] writers have come to accept that a person's participation in setting a goal increases the likelihood that he will act to insure that the goal is met. The importance of this insight cannot be overstated—but the most effective means of utilizing this insight is far from obvious. One of the misconceptions of students and new managers is that participation will somehow solve most management problems. If a manager will only allow his men to participate with him in setting objectives, and in solving problems, he will be on the royal road to success. Subordinates, however, are often new, inexperienced, and lacking in the background to make skillful judgments; they are also not always fully aware of this lack. They may not agree with each other about what should be done. They may be competing with each other for influence with management the critical target of the battle. Their positive experiences in the past may have been with authorities who set goals for them as a framework within which to operate. The managers failure to do so could be seen as confusing at best and incompetent at worst. Sometimes they may perceive more clearly than the manager that he actually has a preferred solution or a target which he is likely to keep advancing till accepted. The manager may feel participative after this target or solution is adopted, but subordinates may feel only that their time and energy was wasted. On the other hand, their participation does not absolve the manager from using judgment; both his superior and his subordinates will hold him accountable for doing so. Finally, there is considerable evidence that superiors with high expectations and who set high standards have more productive units than those with moderate expectations or standards.

The above statements are not made to deny the utility of an approach to management such as management by objectives which recognizes the importance of goal ownership. They are made to point out that it must be used with flexibility and judgment. Like any approach to management, if it is codified to the point where it becomes a set of rules to follow, it

---

[38] Kurt Lewin, "Group Decision and Social Change," in T. M. Newcomb and E. L. Hartley (eds.), *Readings in Social Psychology* (New York: Holt, 1947), pp. 330–44.

treats the manager's job (a very complex task at the "soft" end of the scale) as if it were programmable.

## ORGANIZATIONAL TASKS AND SYSTEMS OF CONTROL

Despite all the problems it has engendered, the formal organization is one of the most important inventions in modern history. It ranks with the great technological inventions in having transformed human experience. It is through these organizations that we feed ourselves, produce our goods, communicate with one another (except face-to-face) and move from city to city. Their ubiquitous nature prevents us from seeing our modern organizations for the remarkably productive entities that they are. But some sense of it can be obtained by going through a modern paper mill or steel mill. When one sees the immense quantity of sophisticated materials produced and realizes that no one man in the plant possesses even a small part of the knowledge and skill needed to produce those goods, he can get some sense of what an organization does. These intricate complexes of human capability and patterned relationships are entities and they perform tasks which are more than the sum of the individuals' duties within them. Management's function is to conceptualize these organizational tasks, build and maintain viable organizations to perform them, and to develop and administer the systems of control which effectively bring the capabilities of the organization to bear on these tasks. These interactive systems go well beyond the formal systems which appear in the company procedure manuals.

The cases which follow pose some of the problems facing managers as they attempt to perform their function. If the cases seem thorny at times and do not lend themselves to tidy solutions, if the readings are helpful in addressing only part of the issues in these situations, the student can take some faint comfort in knowing that he is dealing with problems in one of the most difficult (but interesting) areas in corporate life.

# CASES

## Flint Electric Company (A)*

WHEN RICHARD MATHEWS, a case writer from the Harvard Business School, first visited the Providence branch of the Flint Electric Company, he was impressed with the rapid rate of change that was apparently plant-wide. The Flint Company was a leading manufacturer of radios, electric appliances, cable conduit, and electrical testing equipment. The Providence branch specialized in advanced types of electrical apparatus, such as special types of electronic tubes.

The Flint Company had been founded twenty-five years ago as a result of a merger of several small manufacturers of electrical products. The merger had prospered and sales had expanded in spite of strong competition in the electrical field. Over the years the company had gradually moved into the development of special electrical apparatus, but only two and one-half years ago it had established the Providence branch as a separate operating unit for the engineering and manufacturing development of special apparatus. It was anticipated that any product which had reached profitable, high-volume production would be moved out of the Providence branch.

The Providence plant occupied a two-floor concrete and steel-girdered factory building in the industrial section of the city. The plant operated on shift, five days a week. The hourly employees reported for work at 8:00 A.M. and left at 4:30 P.M. Some 46 percent of the plant's 500 employees were classified as indirect labor. A year earlier, 57 percent of the employees had been classified as indirect labor. Thirty percent of the plant's 500 employees had previously worked in Flint plants in Attleboro and Fall River, Massachusetts, transferring to Providence when the work of their departments was transferred there. Many of them still commuted between these towns and Providence. Most of the other employees of the branch lived in Providence and its suburbs.

During the first year of operations the Providence branch was under the managership of an old-time Flint engineer. Engineering developments caused a constant change in products, methods, and work layouts. The

_____
* All names have been disguised.

36

branch lost over a million dollars during its first year and a half. At that time Mr. Charles W. Cox was brought in as manager of the Providence branch. Mr. Cox was 45 years old and had spent most of his life in the electrical apparatus field. During his business career Mr. Cox had worked for several companies and had risen steadily to positions of ever greater responsibility, often involving a change of residence. He had developed a wide circle of acquantainces and friends in his business and had acquired firsthand familiarity with working conditions and markets for electrical apparatus in several areas of the United States. Just before Mr. Cox was employed by the Flint company as manager of the Providence branch, the Flint headquarters management had placed a new controller, a sales manager, a purchasing and production control man, and an industrial engineering manager in the branch. Two of the previous men had been discharged and two had been transferred. (For an organization chart of the branch, see Exhibit 1.)

Richard Mathews' first contact with the Flint Company was made after Mr. Cox had been manager of the plant for one year. Mathews wanted to

**EXHIBIT 1**

Providence Branch Organization Chart

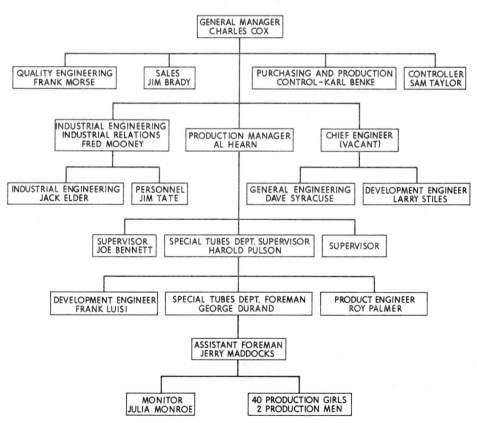

obtain Mr. Cox's permission to spend several months in the plant observing human aspects of the organization for the purpose of securing teaching case material. Mr. Cox met Mathews at the receptionist's desk and took him into the office. His office was a simple glass-enclosed room on the first floor of the plant, containing two plain wooden tables and eight straight-backed chairs. There were neither rugs on the floor nor curtains at the windows (see Exhibit 2).

Mr. Cox was about six feet tall, slim, with slightly thinning hair, and smartly dressed. He walked with a slight stoop. His face had a few heavy lines which were accentuated when he smiled, as he frequently did. Mr. Cox welcomed Mr. Mathews and, after discussing possible sources of case material, suggested that Mathews would be interested in a brief history of the branch and its problems as Cox saw them. The manager added, "Where I come from, they call me Charlie. They call you Dick where you come from, don't they?"

Mathews replied, "That's right, Charlie," and they were on a first-name basis thereafter.

Charlie Cox explained,

When I used to walk into the office in my first days here, no one would smile or speak to me or anyone else. No one really felt they belonged to the team here. That was my first job, to get the members of our employee family to work together.

My other job was to try to straighten out our product lines. Our branch produces approximately 30 different product lines. We had been trying to put equal emphasis on all of them. I saw that I had to choose certain products as bread-and-butter items and push those to give us income with which we could develop the newer product lines which would be coming along. One of the biggest problems was the fact that we had not done a very good job of market analysis. We would run up development costs and start making products before we were sure they could be sold. The result was that we had a tremendous inventory of parts on hand for products which would go into inventory. One of the reasons we rushed into production was that we wanted to keep our war-time work force employed.

Of the 30 product lines, 50 percent of our sales income has been from development contracts with the armed services. These contracts have enabled this branch to maintain a relatively large research staff. Of our 500 employees, over 90 are engineers. Service contracts are usually signed on a cost-plus-fixed-fee (CPFF) basis and frequently call for the production of 10 to 20 pilot models on any device which we develop. Another 25 percent of the branch's income is from the sale of special radio tubes and apparatus. The final 25 percent has been from the sale of special test apparatus and miscellaneous items in the early developmental stages.

By breaking our product lines into these categories and assigning definite responsibility to indivduals for profitable results on these various lines, we were able to make some real progress in raising our production volume and avoiding costly oversights. We had to drop a number of product lines that did not appear

**Exhibit 2**

Providence Branch Floor Plan
(scale ⅟₃₂″ = 1′—0″)

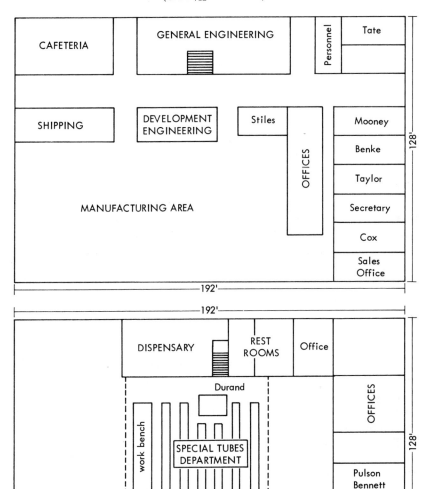

CAFETERIA

GENERAL ENGINEERING

Personnel

Tate

SHIPPING

DEVELOPMENT
ENGINEERING

Stiles

OFFICES

Mooney

Benke

Taylor

Secretary

Cox

Sales
Office

MANUFACTURING AREA

128'

192'

192'

DISPENSARY

REST
ROOMS

Office

Durand

work bench

SPECIAL TUBES
DEPARTMENT

OFFICES

Pulson
Bennett

Hearn

Ind. Eng.

128'

MANUFACTURING AREA

2nd Floor

to offer profit possibilities in the near future. Naturally, men who had worked long and hard on a product did not like to give up an incomplete job.

Every research contract we negotiate with the armed services calls for new products we have never made before. New products often require new skills and new methods. We often have to change our ideas after we have started production.

We've lost a lot of money during the year I've been here, but it was only half as much as during the first year of postwar operation. Now I think we have turned the corner at last and should be in the black for the first time.

When Mr. Cox talked about the product lines and profit potentials of his branch, he sketched briefly on a large scratch pad the amount of money which he expected his branch to make during the coming year. After the loss of the previous years Mr. Cox expected his branch to make nearly half a million dollars. This was the total of his profit estimates by product lines.

Another of Mr. Cox's first acts upon assuming control of the Providence branch was to call a meeting for the purpose of acquainting the employees with his plans and the branch's prospects. He gave the employees the same report he had given the president of the Flint Company on his size-up of the plant.

Mr. Cox continued by explaining to Mathews that shortly after he assumed his duties, a large international union, which had unionized other branches of the Flint Company, began a membership drive in his plant. Mr. Cox held meetings with his entire supervisory force during the period of negotiations with the union and at the time of the NLRB elections. Mr. Cox believed that these meetings of supervisors to keep them specially informed through management channels had done much to promote teamwork and morale of the supervisory force. During union negotiations Mr. Cox was insistent on informing his supervisors of developments before the union issued its interpretations of negotiations.

The eligible employees decided they did not want to join the union and the Providence branch became the only nonunion branch of the Flint Electric Company. Shortly after the election, Mr. Cox learned that several workers who had been prominent in organizing activities were planning to leave the company because they felt that they would be discriminated against in the future. He called these workers into his office and told them that he hoped they would stay with the company and that he would do his best to see that no reprisals were taken against them. All the workers he talked to were still with the company a year later.

Mr. Cox continued to talk to all his workers personally at three-month intervals, meeting with them in the company cafeteria. At these meetings he reviewed the company profit picture and told them of intended changes. Each quarterly talk also was built around a single theme which he hoped to convey to the workers.

During the nine months following the union negotiations, Mr. Cox had no occasion to speak to his supervisors as a separate group. He realized, he hold Mathews, that the team spirit which had developed at the time of the union crisis was ebbing away.

Mr. Cox concluded this first meeting by enthusiastically agreeing to have Dick Mathews spend some time making observations throughout the organization to collect teaching material. "I don't know if you can help us handle some of our problems around here, but I'd like to get any suggestions you might have that won't destroy confidences. You'll find that we believe in getting quite a bit of help from outside the company from different consulting firms as well as from staff specialists at Philadelphia. There are normally a lot of outsiders around the plant so your addition to the group won't surprise people too much." Finally, Mr. Cox suggested that he arrange for Dick to meet the top officials of the branch on his next visit.

## THE MANAGEMENT TEAM

On a second visit to the Flint plant Dick Mathews talked briefly with several top officials of the branch. He first met Jim Tate, the personnel director. Jim was 28 years old and had been with Flint six years. Tate, in turn, introduced Dick to Sam Taylor, controller. Taylor was 33 years old, but he appeared to be slightly older. He had been at the branch for two years, having come from an accounting job at the Philadelphia headquarters. Dick next met Karl Benke, purchasing agent and production control manager. These two functions had been combined under Benke when he had started work for Flint at the Providence branch two years previously. Benke was a former college teacher of business subjects and had also worked for other electrical product companies before coming to the Flint Company. Benke introduced the casewriter to Al Hearn, the production manager. Al was a heavy-set man of about 40. Dick learned later that Al's fellow employees considered him an old-timer since he had been with the Flint Company for many years and had worked in a number of branches. He had been working at the Providence branch since it was started. Finally, he met Larry Stiles, one of the branch's top engineers. Larry was a man of about 50 who had been with Flint for many years. He spent considerable time during his first talk explaining the use of some of the special devices the branch produced.

On subsequent trips to the Flint plant Dick Mathews became interested in the way Mr. Cox and his group of subordinate department managers worked with each other. In a later conversation, Mr. Cox referred to these men as "a great team." He continued,

We have a great group here. Take Sam Taylor. He's as smart as they make them and he has the courage of a lion. Sam hits them right on the head. Karl

Benke has done a great job here. He has a great sense of humor. In one year he has got a bad inventory condition under control. Al Hearn is a real tough guy. He was brought up in the old foremen school. He's coming along well. He's a swell guy and gets the work out.

As Dick had subsequent talks with the various department heads he found a consensus that during the year Mr. Cox had been on the plant he had substantially improved cooperation among his department heads. To develop management teamwork, Mr. Cox spent much of his time talking to his department heads individually and as a group. He called frequent meetings of all department heads. When executives from the Philadelphia headquarters were at the plant he brought all of his department heads into his office for joint discussions of such problems as priorities of projects and the plant budget. Mr. Cox often said, "I believe in using my team and following their advice. There's no point in having staff unless you use it." It was a common experience for others in the plant to look through the glass partitions of Mr. Cox's office and see "management" in session.

The members of this "management team" tended to share common experiences and attitudes. They had all had extensive executive experience in the industry and were almost all college graduates. They felt qualified to pass on a wide range of management subjects. They all shared an interest in the general administrative and policy issues that confronted the plant. They were all concerned with and talked about "return on investment" and other management concepts that cut across departmental lines. All of the department heads had some contacts with people at the Philadelphia headquarters. They saw their future as dependent on these contacts as well as contacts within the plant.

Once Mr. Cox and his department heads had reached a decision in one of their meetings they seemed to expect each other to secure the support of their respective subordinates in carrying out the decision. For instance, in regard to a decision that Mr. Cox and his department heads had reached to effect a cutback in the work force, Mr. Cox commented to Dick,

> I called my department heads in this morning. I told them this was the day for carrying out our cutback decision. I asked them to go back and tell their people who were not being affected that we had made the move for greater efficiency and that we didn't plan any further cuts in the foreseeable future. I proposed to them that I also give a speech to the hourly paid people on this subject. They objected to this quite strenuously so I agreed to postpone any decision on a speech until we had more time to think about it.

As one result of his talks with Mr. Cox and the other top officials, Dick decided that he would like to continue his investigation by learning more about a single department. At Mr. Cox's suggestion he decided to study the special tubes department.

## BACKGROUND FACTS ABOUT THE SPECIAL TUBES DEPARTMENT

On his next visit to the plant, Dick arranged to meet Harold Pulson, the special tubes department supervisor, who reported directly to Al Hearn. He later learned that Pulson was a 27-year-old engineer who had joined the Providence branch four months earlier after working for a year in the photographic supply business. Mathews opened the conversation by explaining his research work to Pulson and asked if Harold could give him any pointers on the department. Harold Pulson said, "Well, I will certainly help you as much as I can, but I have only been on this job a few months, so I am not too well acquainted here myself. I really know more about the engineering problems of the photographic supply business that I worked in before."

Pulson then offered to show Dick around the production floor. The tour took about 15 minutes. Dick obtained a general idea of how the work in the department was performed. The department produced five similar types of small electronic tubes. Most of the work was of an assembly nature, and this assembly work was performed by approximately 40 girls and 2 men who worked at 6 long benches. Three-fourths of these employees worked on one type of tube, the argon tube, while the rest of them worked on a separate "F line" or on a few individual assignments. The work of the special tubes department was performed in a 70 by 50 foot area of the second-floor production space (see Exhibit 2).

The assembly operations were simple, repetitive hand operations in which the girls assembled very small tube parts. The girls handled many of these fine parts with tweezers. They passed the partially assembled tubes to one another along the benches in trays of 50. The quantity of work-in-process inventory waiting to be processed beside each girl varied considerably at the different work positions.

After taking Dick around the production floor, Pulson introduced him to George Durand, the foreman who supervised the production operations of the department and reported to Pulson. Dick Mathews later learned that George Durand had been with Flint for eight years. Before that time he had been a mountain climber and a salesman. He was about 43 years old. He had worked in the special tubes department in two different plants during his time with Flint.

Later in the day while conversing individually with Dick, both George Durand and Harold Pulson talked at length about the chief problem bothering the department at the time. Dick found out that a rare gas, argon,[1] that was used in the prinicpal product of the department, presented a number of unsolved engineering problems. The preliminary

---

[1] The term argon is a disguised name for the actual substance used in this tube.

processing of argon took place in another department, where several Flint engineers were experimenting with new methods of preparing it for use. In the special tubes department itself, there were 22 operations performed in the production of the complete argon tube. These 22 operations did not form a single continuous production line. Three stages of argon processing occurred, four operations on an assembly incorporating argon, and five operations on a separate subassembly, before these two units were assembled and subjected to preliminary tests where a large proportion of the total rejection rate occurred. The tubes were then put through eight additional processing stages including final tests and packing. The most critical operations, at which bottlenecks sometimes developed, were the processing or argon and the preliminary testing. The effectiveness of the argon used could not be tested until the preliminary testing. When the rejection rate ran high from preliminary testing, the girls who performed the following operations were occasionally idle; on the other hand, when a large number of units came through at once bottlenecks sometimes developed at these positions. To maintain a steady work flow, Pulson and Durand usually tried to keep at least one half hour's work before each girl. Pulson commented,

We're having all kinds of trouble with argon. No one knows much about the properties of it or how to control it, so that everything is being done on an empirical basis. We're trying to get some help from a number of sources. This gas is only a side line to our supplier, so they can't spend much effort on basic research. Our company laboratory is working on it, but they are a bunch of "long hairs" and very theoretical with no interest in getting a job done now. We won't get anything from them for a year or so. It's really a headache when we can't get any pure argon to use and have to have 40 girls that are either idle or are working on tubes that prove to be useless.

George Durand said,

Our big problem is argon. We don't know much about the stuff and all we know is that the gas we're using now is not as good as the stuff they were sending us last fall. We have to test every individual batch of argon that comes in by producing a few tubes and checking the results. Then we can estimate how many good tubes we will get when we use that batch and what percent will be duds. We used to discard the batch unless the test indicated it would make 85 percent acceptable tubes, but now we have to settle for 75 percent. With bad argon our rejection rate increases terrifically. The trouble doesn't show up until late in the operations, and then we lose all of the work that has gone into the tubes up to that point. If we could get good argon, and enough of it, we could fill the pipelines, like Harold says. Then the girls' work would improve. Now, when they know we don't have enough good argon to keep them busy, they slow down. They get inefficient. During the war, when they all saw work pile up in front of them, they did 50 percent more work and never complained. They get into bad habits when they don't have enough work to do.

Then when they get more work, they are not used to working faster and can't catch up with their old rate.

The tubes produced in the department required argon in their manufacture with the exception of one product of similar construction which offered no unusual engineering problems. A separate assembly line operated by five girls known as the "F line" made this product. Transfers of personnel between the two lines were extremely frequent, and the girls working on the two lines regarded themselves as a single work group.

The employees of the special tubes department were receiving hourly rates determined by a number of factors. The industrial engineering department had established a base pay rate for each operation depending on the degree of skill required to perform it. They had also, about a year prior to Mathews' study, set hourly output standards for each operation on the argon line. When an employee averaged 90 percent of the standard output figure for ten consecutive days, she became eligible for a pay increase to the maximum for the job. This rate was substantially above her base rate. Standards of this kind had not been set for the "F line." On the latter line, the engineers had informally set an hourly "quota" for each job, but these quotas were not used as a basis for pay raises. Instead, the employees of this line were eligible for a series of merit raises of approximately two cents per hour apiece based on length of service, increase in output above standard, good attendance records, and other similar factors. The personnel department considered requests for merit raises. Although a number of employees had requested such raises in the last few months, personnel records indicated that only one of the girls had received a merit raise during the first five months of 1948. Ten merit raises were given in 1947.

After having secured this background information, Dick Mathews decided to concentrate his attention on the human factors affecting the production problems of the special tubes department. With this in mind he spent time talking with Durand about his employees and then proceeded to interview most of the girls in the department. What follows are representative excerpts from these conversations.

## COMMENTS BY DURAND ABOUT THE PRODUCTION WORKERS

George Durand said of his department,

We have the best group of girls in the plant in my department, but girls coming in from another department don't like the work. They get in the rest room and start talking over their jobs, and someone tells them the special tubes department has a bunch of slave drivers in it. We don't work the girls very hard, but we do expect them to make bogey and we are the only department using output standards.

Durand was assisted in his work by Jerry Maddocks, assistant foreman, and Julia Monroe, shop clerk.[2] Durand said of Maddocks, "Jerry is a good boy—clean, does his work neatly and thinks about it a lot, not only on the job, but at home. Many times he comes in in the morning and tells me what he has thought to help our work. We have a good team here. Jerry gets along with the girls and helps me a lot." Speaking of Julia Monroe, Durand said, "She keeps records at the desk and goes around once an hour picking up work slips. It's good to have someone like that. She can find out things that the girls would never tell a man. When two girls are fighting with each other, she can let you know about it and you can see it if you watch them."

On another occasion Durand commented to Mathews about his work.

My job could be too much for some people. There was a time when I found myself worrying about it. I lost 35 pounds in two months last fall. I finally analyzed myself and decided I had to stop worrying. That's why I like to live out in the country so I can get away from all this in the evening. I have a nice place out in East Greenwich and a house and my family to go home to every night. I enjoy it very very much out there, and there is always something to do. Of course, when you're on the job you have to be constantly vigilant. I could get sore at these girls. You have to watch each one of them closely to make sure that they are doing their job right and getting it out on time.

I have to act in a businesslike manner myself. I get here about twenty of eight on Mondays, which is earlier than other mornings, and get everything ready. When the girls start work (eight o'clock) I walk around them and say hello to them like I always try to do. I speak to two or three of them and say things like, "Is your jig working all right?" or "That order you are working on is one we are trying to rush." If I just wandered around and made a lot of small talk with them, they would slack off right away. It's the same way with tardiness. You have to notice which girls are tardy and speak to them about it so that they will know that you are conscious of it, and they will have it in their minds.

Last Friday I told Louise Dumont that she might as well get used to producing more before next month comes around, because the production schedule for next month was going to call for a higher output in her job. I told her, "You are aware that you can do more than the standard on this job, and I am aware of it, too." When Louise came in this morning she said, "Well, how many do you want me to do?" I told her, "Well, I would like you to do 240, but you should bear in mind that if you put out 240, that is the figure you will be expected to make next month. You had better experiment around and see how much you think you can do."

## COMMENTS BY THE PRODUCTION WORKERS

In Mathews' talks with the girls on the production line of the special tubes department, he was particularly interested in picking up comments

---

[2] Prepared reports for production control and cost accountants; assigned work to operators; handled special tests.

about their foreman, their productivity, their job, and their relations with one another.

The following are typical of their comments about Durand:

George is O.K. He has always treated me well and as long as he does, I won't have anything to say about him. . . . All the girls like him—he doesn't bother us. . . . Yesterday George asked me to do another job as well as my own, and I told him, "You've got plenty of healthy girls around here. Why don't you get one of them who isn't busy on this job?" And he did, too. He is very fair that way. . . . George is very congenial and very fair, and he will do anything he can to help, too. . . . He gives everything he has to his job all the time. I have always enjoyed working for him. It makes a great deal of difference whether you have good supervisors or not. I like my job here.

The following are some comments on the girls' attitudes towards their work standards and their productivity.

SUE CORONA:   (Argon line.) The standard on my job is 420 an hour, but I have never been able to make it. I don't worry much about it; I guess I like to talk too much, like now! One day I tried real hard to make it and wasn't able to. We used to work harder toward making the standard when there was more work to be done, but right now, there isn't so much so we don't try so hard.

JEAN LARSON:   I'm only working on this job (testing on the "F line") for a month while this girl's out. This job hasn't been time-studied yet, so there are no standards. You just sit and work along. This job is easier than my regular one. My regular job is testing on the other line. It's the same kind of work, but you have to get out 87 units every hour. That job is kind of nerve-wracking.

BEATRCE PERKINS:   (Argon line.) Well, I like the job and there is a good crowd of girls here. The only complaint we have is that we can't hear the music over the loudspeaker. We are in a corner of the room and the equipment makes a lot of noise. I have worked in several sections of the factory, but this is the job I like best. It is monotonous, but it is easy. You don't have to think much about it, and there is a nice crowd of girls here. My hands are naturally quick and I work lots faster than most of the girls. I just can't help working fast. But I couldn't just sit and work eight hours a day on this job. You have to talk and kid around a little. If I didn't, I would go out of my head. If I make more than the quota they will raise the standard on the job. I figure I will be on this job for several years. There is no use breaking my neck on it. There isn't much prospect for a raise in pay. The work is monotonous. The girls here don't have any better kind of job to look forward to. They would need a college education or something to go higher than this. There are one or two interesting jobs, like testing, but there are so many girls waiting in line for those that most of us know we haven't got a chance of getting it. There is a quota on most jobs and the girls figure that is all they are supposed to do and that is all they are going to do. The job is monotonous and you cannot expect a couple of cents raise after you make standard and the girls are not going to knock themselves out to produce more than the standard. The standards are set on some of the jobs so that the girls have to work pretty steadily, anyway.

RUTH CRAWFORD:    ("F line.") Raises are one thing the company doesn't believe in. There's been a lot of talk about merit increases, but the girls haven't seen any. The girls are supposed to be rated every three months, but they just haven't got around to it. It just went up in smoke. The personnel department just had other things to do.

The following are some typical comments of the girls about their jobs and their relations to one another.

JANET BURR:    (In response to Mathews' question about seeing other girls in the department outside of work.) No, I don't and I don't care too much about it. I think it is enough to see them in the daytime. I have my own friends outside. They are all very fine girls in here, though. On this job (testing on the "F line") I don't get much chance to talk to them but I could just sit by the hour and watch them and I know pretty well what is going on.

DICK MATHEWS:    Would you like to try some of these other jobs?

JANET BURR:    No, I don't want to change jobs. I don't want to do one of those routine jobs. This job I am on gives me a lot of variety. I am sort of my own boss. Nobody tells me what do. I can do things when I want to. I wouldn't want any of the other jobs even if I can't talk to anybody on this job.

MARGARET FORD:    (After explaining to Mathews the manner in which she performed her work—preliminary testing.) That is all I know about it. When they teach you this job they don't explain anything about how the machine works. This tube I'm working on is no good. We're having a very bad time today. They want us to get out 83 tubes an hour and we have not found more than 60 good tubes all day.

ANN HALEY:    (Argon line.) As soon as I get some tubes, I will show you what my job is like. You know nobody likes this job. I have to work with acetone and nobody likes the fumes. They say it is a simple job for an imbecile and that it doesn't require any brains. Well, I asked for this job (assembly) because nobody else wanted it. I'm older than the rest of the girls and I don't care what they think. They all know I can do a job requiring more brains than this one. I used to do testing and then I was doing some other work, but nobody wanted this job so I asked for it. That was after I had trouble on this job on my right, filling the tubes. I worked on that job for a year and then they told me I didn't know how to do it. I made some suggestions on how to improve that job. I didn't expect to get credit for it but maybe a pat on the back or some thanks. Nobody thanks you around here for things like that. They kept raising the standard. They told me I had to make 849 an hour. I figure that's 15 a minute. When I told the other girls that, they called me crazy.

The job isn't going any faster now than it did before. All I wanted was two cents an hour more. The two cents doesn't make much difference, but it's nice to know you're getting ahead. I guess I'm too apt to blow up and get excited. I can't express myself very well. I can't explain to them what's wrong. If I could, I think maybe they might understand. Say, I bet you've talked to all the other girls in this department already, haven't you?

DICK MATHEWS:    No, I haven't talked to quite all of them yet.

ANN HALEY:    I thought sure you had. I was sure that they weren't even going to send you to me. At least I was last. They were afraid I was going to tell you too much. I'm surprised they sent you at all. You have to be awful careful about what you say around here. This place is full of spies. A lot of stool pigeons. You can't tell who your friends are. I test the girls around here sometimes by telling them a story and then if it comes back in a couple of days, then I know who my friends are.

BETTY O'KEEFE:    ("F line.") Did you know that Ruth Crawford's mother died recently? Marie Florek is taking Ruth's place while she is out and Carol Ripley is taking Marie's place. We consider Carol the baby around here—she's only 20. She really knocks your eyes out when she gets all dressed up. (Pause.) Did Ann Haley ask you a while ago if you were a stool pigeon?

DICK MATHEWS:    I believe she did ask something like that a while ago.

BETTY O'KEEFE:    Well, that's what she told me. You know, you don't want to take her too seriously. One day she'll sound off like that and the next day she's very friendly. She's sort of peculiar. I more or less leave her alone. When I first came here I went up to her one day out on the steps and because I thought I recognized her, I asked her if she came from Pawtucket. She said, "I don't like nosy girls like you. The next thing you'll want to know is how much rent I'm paying. You're just another one of those nosy Irish — —." I was certainly amazed. I was just trying to be friendly. It made me feel like a fool so I just left. We didn't speak to each other for a long time, but since then we've gotten fairly friendly. I try and take people as they come and don't worry too much about it. Most of the girls around here are very nice; there are only a few that are hard to get along with.

(Betty then went on to tell Dick that the day before they had taken a collection to send flowers to Mrs. Crawford's funeral.) Ruth is an awfully nice girl. She does thoughtful things for people. Last Wednesday she had a shower for Jean Larson at her house. She went to considerable trouble; she got all the food and made all the arrangements, just because Jean doesn't have a family to do things like that for her. I gave Jean a waffle iron. Sue Corona gave her a beautiful set of glassware. Edith Riordan gave her a set of towels, Martha Grant gave her a nightie. Margaret Ford wasn't there. She's sort of funny to get along with. There are only a few girls here that are sort of hard to get along with.

DICK MATHEWS:    Didn't she use to be a record clerk here?

BETTY O'KEEFE:    Yes, she used to have a job like Julia Monroe's. I've known and worked with Margaret a long time; she's sort of funny.

Dick Mathews also had a conversation about the special tube department with Fred Mooney, head of the industrial relations and industrial engineering departments. Mooney commented,

I did quite a bit of work in the special tube department when I first came here, two years ago. In that department some of the girls have ideas in their heads about how much work they should do and they just don't work any faster than that. The employees have been promised great things by the suggestion program and the program for merit pay raises, but both of these programs have bogged down during the past winter because of lack of staff personnel to keep them going. Our personnel policies are excellent ones, but they bog down in day-to-day administration because the budget is so limited.

Starting about the middle of March, a month after Mathews first contacted the company, the management of the Providence branch, from Mr. Cox on down, began putting pressure on the special tube department to improve its performance by increasing its output and cutting its unit costs.

# Flint Electric Company (B)*

STARTING ABOUT the middle of March, the special tube department of the Providence branch of Flint Electric Company[1] began to receive a considerable amount of pressure from higher management to improve its performance. This pressure started with a general cutback in indirect labor costs and built up toward something of a peak in early June. Dick Mathews, a research worker from the Harvard Business School, became interested in these developments and kept track of the major events that affected the special tube department during this time period. He was particularly interested in the way the supervisory hierarchy and the production employees responded to these pressures and the light this threw on the strengths and weaknesses of the organization.

Mathews first heard about the impending cutback in a conversation with Charles Cox, general manager of the branch. Mr. Cox commented,

Well, I'll be perfectly frank with you. This branch lost a helluva lot of money in the last two years. Philadelphia[2] is interested in making money and they are at least as interested as I am. We are really a glorified job shop and there are a lot of things here you can't run like some of the other branches. Our personnel that were trained in other branches have a lot to learn about this kind of work. (He got up while talking and closed the door to his office.) I said that I would be frank with you and I will. There are going to be a lot of heads rolling around here. Our overhead is too high. On about Friday we are going to release about 15 percent of indirect personnel and save about $125,000 in salaries.

As one consequence of this cutback, Jerry Maddocks, assistant foreman of the special tube department, was transferred out of the department. At this time George Durand, the department foreman, said,

---

* All names have been disguised.
[1] For background information on the branch and the special tube department, see Flint Electric Company (A).
[2] Philadelphia was the location of the home office of Flint.

51

When they came to ask me about Jerry, I told them they couldn't fire him. I told them they could fire me if they wanted to, but he was a young kid who has always done a good job. I asked them if I quit if Jerry would take my place. When they said yes, I said, "Then if you want to keep me you'd better find another place for him. And when orders pick up again, we will need him back here."

I've been in the electrical field for five years, and I know that there are a lot of things that we don't know—we have to try—and we make errors. The only thing permanent about Flint is change. And there isn't a clear market for this stuff. So I have seen several of these cutbacks. It's all right, Dick, so long as it's fair—I believe that if cuts are made with justice, then there can be no argument.

You know what all workers want is security. They—all Americans—want security so they can plan. I saw this cutback coming and I talked it over with my wife. I'm older and I made a living before I ever got into this. We made plans for what I could do when the time came that I would be through here, so I wouldn't waste too much time between jobs. If that time ever comes, I'll be ready. I don't think there will be many more changes. I don't know about them yet, anyway.

In early April, Harold Pulson, the special tubes department supervisor, commented on how his thinking was changing:

PULSON:   You know, this shop has been run rather loosely and now we are going to tighten up on some of our practices. We are not doing it abruptly or harshly but we do have to eliminate some of the waste. I have been cutting down on lost time in this department. A couple of months ago when the work went slack we had a lot of lost time. I have cut it down to almost nothing now by transferring girls out of the department. Also some of the girls have been getting away with coming in late consistently, and we're going to watch the offenders and speak to them about it. We are going to do it very fairly, but we will take note. Another thing, some of the standards around here are too low. There's a job over here where the standard is 150 per hour, and I am sure the girls could do more because they have been consistently making 150 hour after hour and never going over 150. I am planning to make a new time study on that job, and then get engineers in here to make some simple methods changes so we can get that standard up to 200. Also, some of the girls around here need closer supervision. A lot of the girls could make standard, but they won't exert themselves. In some cases they just don't know they could make standard if they tried.

One thing you will probably hear complained about a lot is the fact that we work the girls harder than a lot of the departments here. We are the only ones that have a production type of job. We have standards and line production. We have to keep pressing for output. This isn't true of the other departments. I think it would be better if we had an incentive system in here so that the girls would learn to work harder. A lot of the standards we have here are kind of low. They did some rather sloppy time-standard work when they put them in. As soon as the industrial engineering department gets some free time they are going to come up and regulate the jobs. On a few of them the standards will be lower because no one has ever been able to make that standard, but on most of them the standard will have to go up.

George Durand, meanwhile, was seeing the situation somewhat differently.

DURAND:   Most of this work is simple. I can handle the girls. When I get a new one I explain what we are trying to do here. I first take her through the line showing her the various steps in our operations, and then I point out what her job will be. I sit right down and do her job to show her how, or sometimes my shop clerk, Julia, shows her the work. Then I work with her for the first week off and on and don't push her. Usually by the third week she can make bogey.

Of course, when you're on the job you have to be constantly vigilant. I could get sore at these girls. You have to watch each one of them closely to make sure that they are doing their job right and getting it out on time. Some of them are in the habit of coming in a little late or sitting idle, and you have to watch them. If I had 40 really good workers, I could keep this place running like a top. As it is, I have about 25 good workers and 15 of those are really damn good. You have to keep after the others to make them carry their weight in the outfit.

There is certainly a difference in points of view. The engineers go on the idea that no worker is a good worker. They have the point of view that they want to set the goal very high and make it difficult to achieve so that the girls will always be trying harder. When you're living with the work, you realize that the girls like the standards, but there is no use setting them so high that it is impossible and laughable to try to make them. There are some standards that no girl has approached yet. Some girls who hit standard on one job are unable to hit it on another.

In April, a short while after the cutback, Mathews watched a small fragment of Durand's day. Durand was hurrying down the aisle when the head of the plant maintenance department stopped him and thrust a jig in his hands.

DURAND:   Is this done?

MAINTENANCE MAN:   What are we supposed to do with this?

DURAND:   We want a plastic base on that to insulate it.

MAINTENANCE MAN:   We don't need the whole jig. Just give us the specifications.

DURAND:   And we need two more made up like that.

MAINTENANCE MAN:   (Taking back the jig.) Why didn't you say so? We'll have to copy it. Do you have any?

Durand moved to a cabinet and looked through some boxes. While he was looking, the maintenance man was paged on the plant-wide call system. The maintenance man was phoning nearby when Durand turned around. Roy Palmer joined Durand and began talking earnestly. The maintenance man hung up the phone and waited impatiently for Palmer to conclude. They started a heavy three-way discussion. An engineer from the experimental section called Durand away to get some tubes. The maintenance man left; Palmer waited impatiently. Before Durand could get the requested tubes, Julia Monroe stopped him to ask about some paper work. An industrial engineer joined Palmer and they talked briefly until Durand returned with the tubes. The experimental section engineer left with his tubes, and the remaining two men turned to ask Durand a series of technical questions. A girl from the production line called Durand away to answer another question and a foreman from another department came up to ask Durand for some personnel to do some special packing. Through all of this Durand kept smiling, thanking people for their work, and remaining pleasant and apparently unruffled.

Two weeks later Durand told Mathews,

I am doing the work of two men. I am getting fed up with this. There is more work than I can do and I'm getting fed up. I sure wish I had Jerry Maddocks back. There's a great deal of detail work to do, and Jerry used to help me with it. Harold does the planning, but he doesn't do any of the work.

During one of the afternoon ten-minute rest periods, Mathews watched one of the two men on direct labor in the department walk between the aisles spreading green sweeping compound on the floor. By the end of the break, he had swept only two of the eight aisles. Girls who worked in the other aisles were delaying their return to work until their aisles had been swept. Durand had been talking to Mathews but excused himself saying, "Hearn said that we had to keep this place swept now and said that I looked like a good man with a broom. The dirt comes in here from the factory next door, and it's very difficult to keep the place clean." Durand started sweeping the remaining aisles and grew red-faced as the girls kidded him about his new job.

In early May higher management began to increase the output goals of the special tube department. An output goal of 35,000 good tubes was set for May and 45,000 for June. These goals had been set following several weeks of satisfactory results in the processing of argon and hence these goals were originally based on expectations of a continuing satisfactory supply. As early as May 4, Mathews recalled, Pulson and Durand had prepared plans in detail for the June labor layout and for the hiring and training of new workers.

To plan the next month's labor layout, Pulson and Durand computed the number of units that would have to be put through each of 22 operations hourly to make the month's production goal, taking the probable rejection rate at each operation into account. The next step in planning the labor layout was to take the known average hourly output for each employee and calculate how many employees would be needed full or part time for each operation. Most of the girls could perform a variety of the unskilled operations, and a few of the girls performing unskilled work had some training in the positions requiring skill. After some discussion, Durand and Pulson decided on the distribution of personnel among jobs that would take the individual operator's training, abilities, preferences, and physical handicaps into account as much as possible and would leave vacancies at positions where new operators could most readily be trained. They then decided on the number of new operators necessary to fill these positions and submitted the completed layout to the industrial engineers for their approval. The final step was a request to the personnel office to recruit new employees soon enough so that they could have about two weeks of on-the-job training. Experience had shown that this was enough time to allow new employees to acquire enough proficiency to carry a full work load at the least skilled positions. To date the personnel office had been able to meet recruitment requests without difficulty.

By May 13, however, a sharp decline in the quality of argon gas had occurred. Harold Pulson told Dick Mathews,

It is very frustrating to have your plans interrupted by something like this. We have only a two weeks' supply on hand, and we don't know where next month's material is coming from. It is doubtful whether the output in June can be increased or not. We may not have anything at all to work with. This argon is interesting stuff. We are keeping our research staff on it, but nobody knows what is wrong with it yet. It's a matter of engineering; once we get the engineering problem licked, we will have only the ordinary production problems to bother with.

MATHEWS:    Does this mean you won't be taking on any more new girls in the near future?

PULSON:    Well, we have got one new girl already, but we are not going to take on any more until we get our schedule straightened out. I'd like to be in a business making some sort of standardized product on a large-volume basis—no problems, but just get the stuff out.

During a dinner held in the middle of May for the purpose of acquainting all the production and engineering supervisors of the Providence factory with the operations of the tube department, various members of the company discussed technical and sales problems. Jim Brady, head of the sales department, emphasized the point that if tubes could be sold for 60 percent of their present cost, the annual sales would rise by more than 400 percent. In the following speech, Mr. Cox said:

I'm going to be a mighty hard guy to convince that these tubes cannot be made for less than half of their present cost. I am going to be just as mean as I can be to get them made at that price. Everyone has done a swell job, but we need a better job and more teamwork to reach this goal.

During the same week, the engineering personnel introduced a new experimental procedure for processing argon. The first few batches from this process proved satisfactory.

On May 21, when Durand talked to Mathews about this development, he said,

You know, Al Hearn (the production manager) came up to me this morning and asked me how the argon was going. I told him it had been quite bad for a while, but since Wednesday we have had a series of good batches. I told him I thought we would make our schedule of 25,000 tubes. He said that he thought the schedule was 35,000. You know, it had been 35,000 but we had to reduce it because of the bad argon we have been getting up till this week. I thought Harold Pulson had told him about the reduction, but I guess he hadn't. You know Pulson is inclined to set our goals a little too high. I've been working with him to get him to see that we can't do too much and to make reasonable estimates. He's beginning to see now that I am informing him correctly when I tell him that we can't do too much.

MATHEWS:   What are you scheduled to produce in June?

DURAND:   Thirty-five thousand . . . no, it's 45,000. By the time we get started, I think I'll tell them I'll be able to get out about 25,000. I can't afford to kid myself about what I can do. If I'm not able to do better than I told them, at least I can always point out that I never promised that I would be able to make the big estimate in the first place.

On May 28, Mathews was in Al Hern's office when the telephone rang, and Hearn talked briefly to Fred Mooney, head of the industrial relations and the industrial engineering departments:

Yes, Fred. What? No, I told Pulson definitely 45,000. He knows it. We talked it over a long time. That's right. Let me talk to him, and I'll call you back.

Hearn then asked the operator to page Harold Pulson, and shortly afterwards Pulson came in.

HEARN:   What's this about 35,000? I thought we agreed that you would set up for 45,000 in June. I just talked to Mooney and he said you were talking in terms of 35,000. Now we're straight on this point, aren't we?

PULSON:   I have Jack Elder (member of the industrial engineering department) on the floor making some studies of several jobs, and he agrees with me that we can get 100 percent more production out of the girls. In some places where the standards are too low, we're planning to set up the new production records by girls so that we will have . . .

HEARN:   I don't care about that. Are you going to be set up to handle 45,000 units in June?

PULSON:   Well, if we can raise the standards and the argon is all right. . . .

HEARN:   Don't worry about that. With this new process, you'll have good material. Can you turn out 45,000 with your present force?

PULSON:   We have three girls already requisitioned, and I think we can do it with these girls and the raised standards.

HEARN:   All right, then, that's agreed. You will be set up for 45,000. Mooney just called and said you had mentioned 35,000 to him.

PULSON:   Well, that's a big jump to 45,000.

HEARN:   That is our goal for the month, and I want to make sure that everyone is clear on that. Now what is this other thing you're talking about?

PULSON:    We have been making time studies, and there's too much wasted time and talking going on. Jack Elder agrees we can raise the standards, and we're going to start that next month.

HEARN:    Well, that department has been running for three years. Why don't you have correct standards already?

PULSON:    There have been a lot of changes, and we couldn't get the industrial engineers. Jack has worked out some new tentative standards which we will put into effect next week.

HEARN:    When are they going to be permanent standards?

PULSON:    It takes a lot of study and time. . . .

HEARN:    I know that, but when are they going to have permanent standards?

PULSON:    That will take several months.

HEARN:    By September, then, you ought to have new standards established. Is that right?

PULSON:    It depends on how much help we get from industrial engineering.

HEARN:    If you have any trouble, let me know.

On the morning of June 3, Mathews talked to Harold Pulson and then to George Durand about the labor and materials situation. Pulson told Mathews that the argon had taken another serious drop in purity. It had been good for several days, but the last two or three batches had been very poor. The research laboratory had abandoned the experimental process and was planning a new program of investigation to try to locate the source of trouble. Pulson said also that the production for the current month would be 35,000 units and that it would be necessary to get the girls to increase their efficiency considerably to meet this figure.

Durand told Mathews: "The current month's production figure has been set up to 35,000, but I will be lucky if I get out half that much. Boy, have I got troubles!" George then told Mathews in detail about eight of the girls. Two were sick; two were about to "get through" for personal reasons; one wanted a transfer to another department; one had just been forced out by strenuous objections of the other girls to the quality of her work. Another girl had just accused her job partner of not doing a fair share of the work and had requested a transfer unless the situation were straightened out. Finally, one girl was about to leave for a week on her honeymoon.

During a talk late in the day on June 3 Dick Mathews learned from Mr. Cox that he had decided to effect a major change in policy regarding the output of special tubes made by the company. Until this time the management had placed primary emphasis on cost reduction, with increased output a secondary objective. By June, however, the salesmen, with numerous unfilled orders on their books, were virtually begging for a substantial rise in output. A sudden increase of competition in the field, which threatened to jeopardize not only Flint's future sales but also unfilled orders already booked, led Mr. Cox to decide that output had to be doubled in spite of impure argon and regardless of the effect on production costs.

Mr. Cox explained that the company would have to throw enough labor into the line to get out 45,000 special tubes in June, even with argon that tested 60 percent good. If the argon improved, they could then produce 75,000 units per month. Mr. Cox said, "I have had a lot of resistance on this from the cost boys. They tell me our costs will be terrific, but it's a gamble we have to take."

This conversation took place on June 3 after the plant had closed for the day. At that time Mr. Cox had not informed his production staff of his decision to make this change in policy.

On the morning of June 4, Mr. Cox informed Al Hearn of his decision to obtain higher output in spite of the effect on costs and in spite of bad argon. Hearn called Luisi and Palmer (engineers without supervisory duties who were working on the tube problem), Pulson, Durand, and Elder together in his office to acquaint them with the situation. During the morning break immediately following this meeting, Dick Mathews listened to a discussion between Luisi and Durand in the cafeteria.

DURAND:    Hearn says the tube department is expected to produce 45,000 units this month. We only got 21,000 last month. That means doubling our output.

LUISI:    How many new girls are you taking on?

DURAND:    I've got two or three coming in.

LUISI:    But some of those are replacements. I should think you would need six new girls before you could double your output.

DURAND:    I got two new girls without going to the personnel department. Two of my girls brought in their friends whom I interviewed and hired. I think they will both be all right. If the personnel office can't get girls for me, I will recruit them myself.

When the group broke up, George returned immediately to the tube department and began work on the day's routine. Once, as he passed Dick Mathews at a fast walk, he grinned and said, "Nonstop day!"

Since Mathews had arranged with Pulson and Durand to call the tube department together for a meeting at 12:45 on June 4 to discuss certain aspects of his research with them, Pulson decided to use this occasion to make some remarks to the girls about the importance of greater efficiency and increased output. He talked over what should be said with Durand, and Durand spoke to the employees. He began with the fact that competition in the industry was increasing, and he told the group that an increase in production to 35,000 units during the current month would be necessary to meet it. He explained that the department would add about six new girls. Argon was going to be approved for use at 65 percent instead of the previous 70 or 75 percent. "I know," he said, "this will be difficult and our rejection rate will go up." Durand finished by saying that it would be necessary for the girls to come in on time, be there every day, and work hard. At this there was some whispering. One employee said to Dick Mathews: "Who are those competitors? I want to go to work for one!"

# Flint Electric Company (C)*

ON JUNE 3, Mr. Cox, general manager of the Providence branch of the Flint Electric Company, decided he needed a crash program to increase the output of the special tube department.[1] This decision was conveyed to Mr. A. Hearn, production manager, on June 4, but no dramatic shift in the affairs of the department followed immediately. Between June 4 and June 10, six new girls started work in the tube department. The personnel office did not actively recruit any outside labor. Two of the six new girls were those mentioned by Durand, the departmental foreman, as being sent to him by other girls in the department.[2] One entered the personnel office and asked for employment. Three were transferred from another department of the factory.

On the eighth of the month, Dick Mathews, a researcher from the Harvard Business School, talked to Durand about some of the new and transferred workers. Durand said,

We're sure having a time around here with so many people absent. I didn't realize how much I depended on Ruth Crawford until she didn't come in yesterday. I'm not ashamed to admit we really miss her, and it looks as if she'll have to be out all week. You know, the way things are going, I think we'll be lucky if we get 15,000 output this month, and I had hoped to make this month our very best one.

Mathews knew that Ruth Crawford performed one of the few skilled operations in the department—putting the argon through certain processes prior to its use in tubes. He knew also that she was generally regarded as one of the department's most responsible employees.

Later in the day Pulson remarked to Mathews,

Sometimes I get pretty discouraged. I guess we'll just keep plugging along. Maybe we'll lick this argon problem, but we still don't know how to do it right.

---

* All names have been disguised.
[1] See Flint Electric Company (A) and (B) for background on this situation.
[2] See Flint (B).

The girls are pretty lax, but you can't blame them for being discouraged when the gas is so poor.

On the afternoon of June 10, when Mathews arrived at the plant, he found that Hearn had called the tube production supervisors and engineering personnel together with some of the sales personnel in his office. Immediately following this meeting Durand told Mathews:

We just had a big meeting with some of the sales people. Brady, the sales manager, talked to us. I realize now that we've got to get out a lot more tubes if we are going to stay in this business. We have to get out 150,000 tubes in the next three months or we'll be out of the tube business by fall. That means we'll have to get production up to 50,000 a month. It will be tough going around here for a while, but we have to do it. It looks like we'll have to put on a second shift. We'll have to get more engineering on this job, get more girls in here and get them trained and get their efficiency up. We've only been shipping about 20,000 a month, so it means raising our production two and one-half times. The story is that some of our big customers, who put in really substantial orders, have a lot of equipment ready to ship except that they don't have the tubes to put in it. We have to get deliveries to them or we will lose their business. One of our competitors is willing to ship them cheaper tubes on time. For a long time we sort of had this business to ourselves. We didn't have to worry about competition. Now we've really got competition, and we are going to meet it. We've got to get the tubes out regardless of cost. Our costs may go up, but we will have to do it. Now I just need to be sure I've got Cox's O.K. to do what is necessary to get out the tubes.

As a result of this meeting on June 10 all management personnel involved in the production of special tubes had established a June and July production goal of at least 45,000 units per month, to be met regardless of the quality of argon available and regardless of cost. This goal was more than double the May output of 21,000 units.

In preparing to meet the new production schedule, the supervisors of the special tubes department faced a number of difficult problems such as recruiting and training new employees, improving productivity of regular employees, maintaining line balance, dealing with fluctuating argon quality, etc. To help with these problems Mathews knew that Jack Elder and some other members of the industrial engineering staff under Fred Mooney had been assigned to do part-time work in the department. Mathews became interested in following the events around the efforts of the production supervisors and the industrial engineers to solve these problems.

One of the primary problems was the number of new employees to be added to the production line. As Harold Pulson explained to Dick Mathews, "We are going to fill up the extra positions in the line with new girls and try to run as much through as we can, even if we have to work with poor argon."

On June 11, the industrial engineering department made a study of the work flow through the special tubes department. A few hours after this study was completed, Jack Elder took the results to Harold Pulson. Elder pointed out that there was an insufficient backlog of work at several positions in the line, adding,

It's obvious that you have to take care of these later positions by getting a flow of work started through from the beginning. What you want to do is to get at least two people on this job and get a lot more done here and here.

(He indicated the first three operations on the production line.)

PULSON: I don't want to give you a string of apologies, but there are some explanations for what you see. Ruth Crawford (who performed the first operation) is out this week, and her substitute, the only girl we have available with any experience on that type of work, cannot keep up with the schedule very well. Ruth has never been out before, and we did not realize how difficult a job she was doing. You know we also have a serious personnel problem on our hands with the two fellows working next to Ruth. Besides that, we have four or five people out this week. You have not picked a typical time.

ELDER: You have four or five people out every week.

PULSON: No, you are wrong. It is unusually heavy this week.

The conversation continued for several minutes. Mathews felt that Elder's tone of voice was consistently critical, while Pulson's was defensive.

On June 14, Fred Mooney, head of the industrial engineering and industrial relations departments, commented to Mathews,

You know Jack Elder made a study here on Friday of the work flow. He found that there was not enough work by some girls, and some of them had no work at all. Now you can see that the girls are just sitting there idle, but you can't tell me it's all their fault. It shows that the supervisors are just not doing enough planning. You can't blame the girls if the work isn't coming through for them. Harold Pulson thinks the answer is to load up the line with a lot of girls. That doesn't make sense to me. The bottleneck is at the beginning of the line. Until you get work flowing through the line, there's no use loading up with a lot of girls in the later positions. Harold Pulson ought to take care of that bottleneck first. Those two guys in front there are not even getting their work done. Supervision has fallen down on that one. Pulson and Durand have been lax with the girls in general. Then they say the girl who is working there is having trouble. If necessary, they should get two girls.

I have laid the facts before Al Hearn, and I am very much interested in seeing what he does with them. Jack Elder says he just couldn't get anywhere with Harold and George. They won't listen to him. They have concluded that the answer is to load up the line with girls. I told Al Hearn what had to be done was to get people in there to break that bottleneck at the first three positions. If there's no extraordinary change in the next few days, we're going to have to take action.

Ruth Crawford returned to work on June 15 and the problem of line balance became somewhat less critical.

Mathews knew that during the month of June, Jack Elder and other time study men, in addition to the other work they were doing in the special tube department, were active in the department obtaining data which would provide a basis for the new hourly output standards which Harold Pulson had wanted for some time as a means to increase productivity.

About June 1, Pulson had commented on this subject,

Jack Elder made some preliminary studies and he thinks the bogeys on some of these jobs are two or three times below what the girls can produce. They just make their standard and then they stop work and start talking. We have to cut out this fooling around. The girls are loafing and Durand is too easygoing. I've been too easygoing, too, but now we're going to get tough about this. The girls are going to be unhappy because they've had it too easy. There are so many things that should be done around here that we haven't done. We are going to stop crying "argon" and do the things we can do something about. If a girl isn't doing her work, I'm going to get rid of her. That will show them that the party is over. We have been too easygoing for too long. We couldn't raise bogeys without a methods change if this were a union shop—but so long as we're not, we'll try to get away with it. It won't affect the pay, at least at first, until we get permanant time studies made on the job. Oh, they'll holler, but it will quiet down and if these girls can't do the job, we will get some who will.

MATHEWS:  Do you have any idea as to what are the obstacles in the way of their wanting to put out more work?

PULSON:  Well, I don't know. Perhaps it's a resistance to being pushed.

On June 14, Pulson explained that he was putting in the new output quotas.

We're going to throw out the old standard system completely. It won't affect the pay and we will go back to merit increases. Jack Elder has made some studies around here and has found out that the girls could do from 100 to 150 percent more work than they're doing now if they just used the time that they spend now talking and running around. We have set up new standards for the jobs and we are going to introduce them on about Wednesday. Elder cut back his standards by 25 percent and I have cut his figures by 10 or 20 percent more and we still get figures running 25, 50, or 100 percent over what the girls are doing now. When we set these new standards, the girls will have to meet them or we will get girls who can. We are operating under a new management philosophy now. The idea is to get production. The sales force is really screaming for more deliveries. That was the decision that Charlie Cox had to make himself.

In the next few days Mathews picked up several comments from the girls about the industrial engineers and production quotas.

MATHEWS:  That was one of the industrial engineers I was talking to.

PERKINS:  (Argon line.) He's a nice guy. A lot of the girls have him wrong.

MATHEWS:  What do you mean?

PERKINS:    He is just timing them, but they are so afraid of losing their jobs.

PERKINS:    I understand we are supposed to work harder now. Didn't you hear Durand's speech? But they are not going to get any more work out of me. I am doing 20 pieces an hour more than the quota now, and that's all they can expect. If they want me to work more, they will have to give me a raise in pay.

MATHEWS:    Durand mentioned competition in his speech. What did you think of that?

PERKINS:    Every place you work has competition. The more you give them, the more they want. If they raise the rate on this job for me, I am going to change jobs.

MARGARET FORD:    (Argon line.) We used to be able to make standard on this job (testing) but it's been a long time since we've been able to. We heard they're going to raise the standard on this job to 125 an hour. They had a time study man in the department who timed us to see how long we talked and then he estimated how many more units we could test if we worked all the time and didn't talk, so they are going to say that 125 is the rate. Can you imagine that? How could we make a standard like that? Very few units are any good when you first test them. We save them by making slight adjustments in them. If we tried to make that standard, we'd have to stick a unit in the jig and if it didn't work the first time we'd have to reject it. No fiddling with it. We'd have about 100 percent shrinkage that way.

On June 23 a meeting of all the employees of the special tube department was called by Pulson and Durand. At this meeting the changes in the output quotas and in the pay system were announced. The following are some of the comments Mathews heard about this event.

PULSON:    We had a meeting with the girls yesterday afternoon. We explained to the girls that the standards are out and that we are going to set up new production bogeys. Raises will be determined by the new bogeys. We have a merit raise system here, you know. The raises will be determined mainly by the girls' production.

DURAND:    You have probably heard about the meeting we had yesterday down at the cafeteria. All the old standards are out. We are going to give the girls merit raises from now on. I told Harold we are going to have to get going on these or the girls will really be on our necks. A lot of them think they deserve merit raises. Even the bad ones will be asking for raises.

JANET BURR:    ("F line.") Did you hear about the meeting yesterday? They told us they are throwing out the old standards and setting up bogeys. If you make the bogey, you get a raise. They are going to study each girl individually and set a bogey for her job. It seems to me that is the fair way to do it because there is such a difference in the ability of various girls.

MATHEWS:    There will be raises if the girls make the new standards?

BURR:    Yes, merit raises. I could get a merit raise, but I have been working here two years now and I haven't. I don't understand it. I have asked Harold and George for raises, but they just tell you that everything is going to be changed around in a little while and they will see about it. I don't think they know what they're doing. The pay system here is all mixed up. Now that they have set up new bogeys I probably never will get my raise.

LILA TOUCHETTE: (Argon line.) Here I am turning out 175 an hour on this job (grinding) and I thought I was doing real good. I could never turn out 600. I dont know how they could expect me to. After six hours you can't see what you're doing anyway. Your eyes begin to blur up on you. I've been in a place where the girls had to work at top speed all the time. They were out about one day a week resting up so they didn't really get any more done. And the quality suffers when you have to work that fast.

BETTY O'KEEFE: ("F line.") They gave us a speech about standards yesterday. They gave us a lot of baloney. All I heard was that the old standards were "obsolete." Obsolete, that's all they talked about.

LOUISE MARSHARD: They told Betty she's going to get a merit raise.

O'KEEFE: Yeah, I'll get a merit raise when I've been here ten years. Louise has been here nine years, so she has only one year to go. I have not had a merit raise since I got here. I don't know of anybody who has had one. I have asked George for a raise and all he says is, "Well, I'll see."

MATHEWS: What did they say about the standards?

O'KEEFE: They got rid of all the old standards yesterday. We are going to have new standards. You have to make the new standards to get a raise. I think it's very unfair to me because there isn't any standard on my job so I can't make a raise. The only way I can get a raise is on merit. That means you have to be in here every day, on time, and get out your work. I have gotten out my work and I am never late or absent, but I haven't had a merit raise. It looks like you would have to stand on your head. Sometimes you wonder what's the use. You wonder whether it pays to do your work. Do you know what I think? I think the girls are going to have to get their merit raises before the new standards are set up or they never will get them. They are going to put the new standards so high that nobody will be able to make them. They didn't say that, but that's what I think. The only ones who will be able to get a raise anyway are the new girls who haven't already made the standard on their job. The old girls who have already made standard and gotten their raise will not be able to get any more. I have a suggestion I would like to make. Why can't they give the girls who have already made standard and keep making standard a bonus and why can't they give me a standard?

MARSHARD: I made the standard a long time ago and earned my top rate. I have been putting out on standard ever since. I could have slacked off but I didn't. Why can't they give me a bonus every three months if I stay on standard?

In addition to working in the special tube department on line balance and output quotas during June, Jack Elder also prepared an "evaluation sheet" which was intended to help the foreman improve the performance of his employees. During June, Elder had secured from Durand a list of the department employees and their principal work assignments. At this time Durand had commented to Mathews about the evaluation sheet, "They have a method which only they can understand and that is the way they want it. When they come in they usually try to devaluate the jobs."

On July 2, Mathews learned that Elder had completed his evaluation sheet and returned it to Durand. By comparing a girl's output per hour on her principal job with the new standard set for the job, Elder had reached a percentage of labor efficiency for each girl.

When Mathews stopped by Betty O'Keefe's work place later that day, she started talking to him heatedly.

Myrtle Haines is very mad at George. George has a new list of some sort and he has been talking to the girls individually telling them whether or not they are efficient. He told Frances Nadell that she was very efficient. That's all right. But he went on and said that some other girls around here weren't efficient and he mentioned them by name. Don't you think he should know better than that? He told Frances that Myrtle wasn't efficient and Frances told Myrtle what he said. Myrtle was furious. She said, "He's only a stupid necktie salesman!" Isn't that a scream? It's all right to tell people when they do a good job, but you shouldn't tell other people about it when some girl is not doing a good job. It gets all over the plant. Myrtle works hard and doesn't waste much time, and I don't see where George gets off telling Frances that Myrtle isn't efficient. . . . He's two-faced. He will tell you one thing to your face and something else behind your back. I think he should be honest. If he doesn't tell you when you're doing a bad job, then you never know. If you can't have confidence in your boss, you start to wonder.

Durand was continuing his individual conferences with the girls about their rating on the industrial engineering evaluation sheet. Mathews listened to Durand's talk with Beatrice Perkins.

DURAND:   Beatrice, I would like to talk to you about your work. We have a sheet here which shows the findings of a special study which was made during the last five days of last month. This shows your standard, how many you produced, and the percent of your labor efficiency. Your standard is 133 an hour. It shows that you produced 117 an hour. Now that's 88 percent efficient. That's pretty good. That's better than the department average, which is 71 percent efficient. But I'm sure it is not as good as it could be.

PERKINS:   What do you mean my standard is 133 an hour? That only started this week. When this study was made, my standard was 115 and I made that.

DURAND:   Well, er, that's true, yes. Your old standard was 115.

PERKINS:   How am I supposed to know that I should do 133 an hour if no one tells me about it?

DURAND:   Well, this shows that you weren't up to full efficiency when the study was made.

PERKINS:   That's silly. If they want me to make 133, why don't you tell me? If they tell me 115, they can't say I'm inefficient because I don't make 133.

DURAND:   Well, you have a point there. Don't worry about it. You're doing a good job and I appreciate your work.

At the end of the day, Jack Elder stopped by Durand's desk as he was leaving the plant.

ELDER:   What do you think of our study?

DURAND:    It's very good. I'm really talking seriously to the girls about it.
ELDER:    You believe it?
DURAND:    Yes, it's a very good study and it gives me something definite to work on.

Elder smiled and left.

On July 3, Mr. Cox asked Dick Mathews into his office and said he wanted to tell Mathews about a new idea. Mr. Cox explained that he wanted the girls in the special tubes department to select two representatives from their group to take a short, informal course in time study work. The course would be given by the industrial engineers on company time. Then these girls would hold a meeting with the special tubes employees to explain how time study worked and how standards were established. Mr. Cox said,

You see, what I want to do is get as much overlap as possible between management thinking and employee thinking. I believe there are differences, but I want to do my best to put the employees' thinking in management terms. I think they will accept an explanation of time study better from the girls than they would from the industrial engineers.

Later that day Mathews learned from Harold Pulson that the special tube department had produced 30,000 tubes during June. Pulson told Mathews,

We're doing the best we can, but we're having a lot of problems, and we can't make the schedule they expect of us. It's very frustrating. Production has come up some, but we will not be able to produce what they want.

# The Hampton Shipyard

THE HAMPTON SHIPYARD near Philadelphia, Pennsylvania, was situated on a land-locked harbor which connected with the sea through a channel deep enough to float the largest battleship. Covering an area of 120 acres, the shipyard had 12 building ways, or slips, the biggest of which would accommodate ships up to 1000 feet in length and 150 feet in beam. Outfitting was carried out on five large piers built on water having an average depth of 30 feet below mean low water level.

Established in 1890, the shipyard was well known for its output of naval and commercial vessels of every type and size. The naval vessels ranged in type and size from small ones to battleships and aircraft carriers. The commercial vessels ranged in type and size from trawlers to luxury liners.

In 1954 the shipyard employed about 3000 employees and was the largest employer in the surrounding locality. The employees of the shipyard had been unionized first in 1938, and in 1946 they had been organized by a national union. Prior to 1946, industrial relations had been fairly harmonious; there had been a low turnover of labor, and the apprentice school system had led to many sons of old-time employees being employed. In 1946 the national union called a strike on a national issue which was not settled for five months.

The majority of employees of the shipyard were skilled tradesmen. The trades represented included welding, burning, ship fitting, drilling, chipping, pipe fitting, electrical, sheet metal, painting, carpentering, riveting, and rigging. Operations such as riveting and rigging were carried out by gangs, but most of the other operations were performed by individual tradesmen under the supervision of leading men.

In June 1954, Mr. James Ambrose, the general superintendent of the shipyard, was reminded that recently layoffs in manpower which had been made necessary by the recent decline in the volume of operation of the shipyard, had reduced the numbers of supervisors available for the daily "roving committee." Mr. Ambrose knew that on some days the roving committee had been reduced in number to two or three supervisors. He felt that he would have to rearrange the groups and reassign some supervisors or let the daily patrol of the roving committee expire.

The roving committee at the Hampton Shipyard had first been instituted in August 1949. At the time, Mr. Ambrose was dissatisfied with the behavior of employees in that he felt that a number of men were ceasing work before the whistle sounded for lunch at 12:00 noon, and for quitting time at 4:00 p.m. Mr. Ambrose was particularly dissatisfied with the lines which formed at the eight banks of timekeepers' clocks prior to the blowing of the whistle. For the plant layout, see Exhibit 1. Mr. Ambrose reasoned that the

## EXHIBIT 1

### Plant Layout

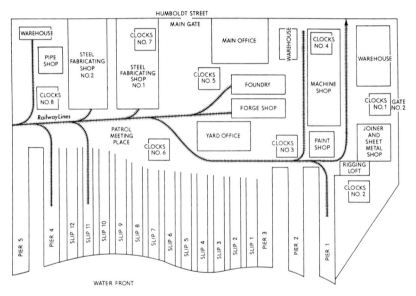

men would have to leave their jobs on the ships being built on the slips and being outfitted at the piers several minutes prior to the time when they lined up at the timekeepers' clocks, and he knew that at some shipyards this practice had ballooned to the point where men stopped work half an hour and more before the whistle sounded. To force the men to work full time, Mr. Ambrose formed a roving committee of divisional superintendents, foremen, and assistant foremen,[1] and required this committee to patrol specific areas of the yard daily at 15 minutes prior to the sounding of the whistle. Mr. Ambrose set up a fixed schedule and required

---

[1] For the case writer's concept of the formal relationships at the shipyard, see Exhibit 2.

## EXHIBIT 2

Partial Organization Chart*

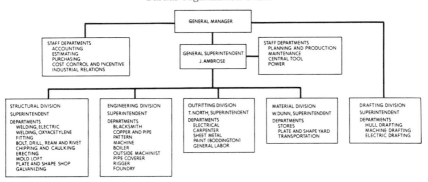

Note: The supervisory force in each department of the five divisions consisted of a foreman, an assistant foreman, quartermen, and leading men. Quartermen supervised from 5 to 10 leading men. Leading men supervised from 10 to 15 men on ships and as high as 35 men in the shops.

* The shipyard did not ordinarily make use of a formal organization chart. This chart is the case writer's concept of the formal relationships.

the rotation of assigned areas so that all the areas of the yard were somewhat covered each day by the patrols. To enforce his wishes, Mr. Ambrose instructed the patrol to take badge numbers for subsequent issue of chits wherever offenses warranted such issue. Chits in books had been issued to supervisors previously, and consisted of a notification in triplicate of the offense, together with the penalty for the offense. Exhibit 3 shows a chit.

The formation of the roving committee was designed to serve as an additional supervision of the men working on the ships. Mr. Ambrose thought that this additional supervision was necessary for a number of reasons. He knew, for instance, that supervisors below the rank of superintendents would never cross the departmental lines in order to question a man about the reason for his presence in any particular locality. Mr. Ambrose thought this questioning of individuals who had left their jobs on the ships without permission was necessary in order to tighten the discipline of working until the whistle sounded. The daily patrol of the roving committee was instructed to take the badge numbers of men not on jobs and to report these numbers through Mr. Ambrose's office to the foreman of the department concerned. The foremen were instructed to notify him of action taken on these reports and if a man did not have a good reason for being away from his job, the foremen were to issue chits.

Mr. Ambrose thought that the roving committee was successful in improving conditions at quitting time because he did not observe as many infractions of the rule after the patrol had been instituted. After several weeks, Mr. Ambrose thought that conditions had improved considerably and that the patrol was no longer necessary, so he gave instructions for the patrol to be discontinued.

## EXHIBIT 3

### The Hampton Shipyard

| Chit Stub | Chit |
|---|---|
| Serial No. 23575 | Employee's Name _____ Serial No. 23575 |
| Badge No. | Employee's Badge No. _____ |
| Name | 1 ☐ Loafing |
|  | 2 ☐ Losing time |
| Hull No. | 3 ☐ Leaving job early |
|  | 4 ☐ Arriving on job late without reason |
|  | 5 ☐ Off job without permission |
| Date | 1 ☐ First offense—*warning* |
|  | 2 ☐ Second offense—*one week off* |
|  | 3 ☐ Third offense—*discharge* |
| Time | The infraction of some company rules and regulations will result in *immediate discharge.* |
|  | Some, but not all, of these rules are: |
| Offense      Offense No. | 6      ☐ Employee found sleeping in the yard |
| 1 ☐      1 ☐ | 6(a) ☐ Intoxicated |
| 2 ☐      2 ☐ | 6(b) ☐ Gambling |
| 3 ☐      3 ☐ | 6(c) ☐ Stealing |
| 4 ☐ | 6(d) ☐ Defacing or destroying property |
| 5 ☐ | 6(c) ☐ Horseplay |
|  | 6(f) ☐ Other |
|  | Hull _____ Date _____ Time _____ |
|  | _____ |
|  | Supervisor's Signature |
| Immediate Discharge Offenses | First copy to industrial relations department |
| 6      ☐      6(d) ☐ | Second copy to employee |
| 6(a) ☐      6(e) ☐ | Third copy to department office |
| 6(b) ☐      6(f) ☐ |  |
| 6(c) ☐ |  |

Note: The local of the national union "went along" with this chit system of issuing written warnings of offenses.

In June 1950, a few months after the patrol had been discontinued, the work force of the shipyard had increased to 6000 employees and there were indications that the buildup would continue, although Mr. Ambrose did not envisage the buildup reaching the proportions of the wartime force of 30,000 unless the United States became involved in another world war. During June, Mr. Ambrose had occasion to visit some other shipyards, and during those visits he noticed a great deal of laxity at the other shipyards regarding the enforcement of the rule of working until the whistle sounded. At his next weekly meeting with the foremen, Mr. Ambrose brought up the problem of men quitting early. He said that if they allowed laxity in enforcing this rule they would soon find the men disregarding all rules. After some discussion wherein the foremen admitted that some men were inclined to quit early, Mr. Ambrose arranged for the timekeeping department to provide him with a list of all employees who punched out at 4:00, 4:01, and 4:02 p.m.

The timekeeping department kept a record of the men who punched out at these times for the next several weeks, and each foreman was notified of the badge numbers of the men in his department who appeared on this list of "early birds." Mr. Ambrose noticed that an excessive number of the men listed were employed by the paint department, so he questioned Mr. Boddington, the foreman of the paint department, about the reason for the excessive number of his men listed on the "early bird" list. Mr. Boddington defended his men and attributed the fact that they appeared on this list to the approved practice of allowing painters to leave their jobs on the ships five minutes before the quitting time so that they could return brushes and pails to the paint shop. Mr. Boddington pointed out that this approved practice was the only exception to the rule that all men should stay on the job until the whistle sounded, and he claimed that this accounted for the fact that his men were often the first to clock out.

In July 1950, Mr. Ambrose was dissatisfied with the record of "early birds," so he called a meeting with the officers of the Supervisors' Association.[2] At this meeting with the officers of the Supervisors' Association, Mr. Ambrose, the general superintendent, said that it was the responsibility of the immediate supervisors to keep the workmen on the job until quitting time. The officers of the S. A. immediately agreed that this was the responsibility of the immediate supervisors and they went on to express their view that the supervisors could do a better job of keeping their men working until quitting time if management people of the foremen and superintendent level made it a habit to be present in the slipways and on the piers just before quitting time. They also suggested that the situation was not as bad as the general superintendent had reported and they invited him to take a walk around any part of the yard he chose with representatives from the S. A. to see for himself that the supervisors were on the job.

After some discussion, it was decided that a roving committee should be set up to patrol the yard daily at 11:45 to 12:00 noon and 3:45 to 4:00 p.m. Mr. Ambrose requested the foremen of departments to assign their supervisors to patrol on different days so that each patrol group contained ten supervisors from ten different departments. He decided to leave the assignment of foremen to the patrol to the discretion of the divisional superintendents because he felt that the foremen might have more important things to do around quitting time. When the patrol was first instituted, Mr. Ambrose went with each patrol every day. Subsequently, when he found this assignment interfering with his other work, Mr. Ambrose assigned the divisional superintendents to take charge of the patrol each day, with the exception that he retained one day each week when he took charge

---

[2] The Supervisors' Association was a social organization of the supervisory personnel below the rank of assistant foreman. These supervisors were not organized for bargaining purposes, and the traditional role of the association was social in nature, with the specific job of organizing social activities such as yearly picnics. From time to time, the general superintendent had used the officers of the association as a means of conveying information of a general nature concerning all members of the association, and in particular the president of the S.A. often spent considerable time answering questions regarding the group bonus scheme of incentive payment for supervisors.

himself. From that time on, the patrol met each day at the head of slip 9 and, fair weather or foul, patrolled portions of the yard each day. The portion of the yard to be patrolled was selected by the superintendent in charge of the patrol without notice. The supervisors accompanying the superintendent had no prior knowledge of the area to be patrolled on any particular day.

In October 1951, when employment at the shipyard had decreased to approximately 4000 employees, the groups of supervisors forming the patrols were rearranged to accommodate some changes which had occurred in personnel. In 1953, when employment at the yard had increased to 6000 employees, the groups were again rearranged and at that time Mr. Ambrose decided to reduce the patrol from ten to eight supervisors.

During the period in which this regular patrol operated, the supervisors were well aware that the men had set up some countermoves of their own. A very efficient warning system had been organized by the men to alert areas of the yard which were directly in the path of the patrol, and conversely areas which did not appear to be covered on any one day were informed that they could relax. The men had named the patrol "The Gestapo" and often made unflattering comments to supervisors about the patrol.[3] Most of the supervisors thought that the patrol did assist in keep-

**EXHIBIT 4**

Excerpts from Two Union Fliers

GESTAPO

It is to be noted that Ambrose and his roving crew are still hard at work, checking on men off the job. It is my understanding that starting Monday morning they will check all men off the job at all times. WELL a word to the wise is sufficient.
. . . . . . . . . . . . . . . . . . . . . . . . . . . . . . . . . . . . . . . . . . . . . . . . . . . . . . . . . . . . . . . .

AS YOU HAVE NOTICED LEADING MEN—SUPERVISORS, FOREMEN, & HIGH YARD OFFICIALS ARE CRUISING THE YARD BEFORE THE LUNCH PERIOD & QUITTING TIME CHECKING UP ON EMPLOYEES THAT ARE NOT ON THEIR JOBS. THIS IS A FUNCTION OF MANAGEMENT & YOUR UNION HAS NOTHING TO DO WITH IT.

MANY OF THE BOSSES DISLIKE THIS JOB THEY HAVE TO DO—"ACTING AS A POLICE FORCE." BUT THEY TOO HAVE TO TAKE ORDERS. SO BOYS PROTECT YOURSELF & STAY OUT OF THE TOILETS & DON'T GIVE THEM A CHANCE TO PASS OUT CHITS.

ing men working until the whistle sounded. During this period a number of chits, averaging one per day, were issued. The threat of the issue of a chit, however, was used much more often than the actual issue. From August 1949, to June 1954, 1601 chits were issued, 1408 being first offense, 161 second offense, and 32 third offense or immediate discharge chits.

The pay system in force at the shipyard during this period was a complicated one. The company policy was to encourage the achievement of

---

[3] Excerpts from the Union flier are shown in Exhibit 4.

maximum production for the mutual benefit of the employees and the company. In line with this policy the company had established, in addition to hourly base rates of pay, an incentive pay system based on standard piece work rates. On the average, about 60 percent of the employees were employed from time to time on contract work offering this incentive pay. The contracts for work on the ships varied in size from one day's work to three or four weeks' work. The contracts were written by rate setters employed in the cost control and incentive department. Men working on the ships moved back and forth, sometimes employed on hourly pay and sometimes on incentive contract pay. According to observations of Mr. Ambrose and some other supervisors, men on incentive contract pay were just as prone to quit work before the whistle sounded as were men on hourly pay.

During discussions about the patrol the supervisors admitted that they felt they needed some assistance in stopping men from quitting early, because often a supervisor, such as a leading man electrician, would be responsible for men working throughout an entire ship or even for men working on two different ships and he could not possibly maintain a surveillance of his men all at once. The supervisors working on the ships often compared their problem of supervision with the easy task of supervision in the machine and fabricating shops where men were under the immediate eye of their supervisors. Mr. Ambrose had also required his own staff assistants to form and man patrols near the gangways of ships tied up at the piers and to maintain a surveillance of areas near the time clocks but he felt that these measures and the listing of badge numbers by the guard at the gangways of men leaving the ship 15 minutes before quitting time were not sufficient to enforce the rule of working until the whistle sounded.

The supervisors, individually, did not like the job of going on the daily patrol, particularly on days when the weather was bad, and they did not like the unflattering comments which were made about "the Gestapo."

In June 1954 employment at The Hampton Shipyard was at the low point of 3000 employees. Many of the employees who remained were old-timers, and a number of the men in some of the departments had been supervisors at some previous time. Mr. Ambrose, the general superintendent, found some of the patrol groups of the roving committee had been reduced by layoffs and demotions to two or three supervisors.[4] He felt that he would have to rearrange the groups once more or let the roving committee expire. He was not sure whether the patrol was still needed during this period of minimum man power employed and he knew that some people were critical of the usefulness of the patrol. However, Mr. Ambrose did not consider that the old-timers were immune to the temptation of quitting a few moments before the whistle sounded, though he did wonder whether the patrol served to keep them working on the job, and he was well aware of the unflattering references such as the use of the name "Gestapo." One

---

[4] Layoffs and demotions during slack periods were administered in order of seniority.

day when he was discussing the patrol with some of his subordinates, Mr. Ambrose said, "I know that conditions at lunch time and quitting time in other shipyards are much worse than this yard. I know also that the patrol is criticized, and perhaps it only keeps the fellows out of sight, but can you show me a better system? If anybody comes up with a better answer, I'll certainly give it a try."

On June 15, 1954, Joe Campbell, an engineer in the planning department, had occasion to accompany Mr. North, the superintendent of the outfitting division, on a trip to Trenton to a competing shipyard. Mr. North had noticed and had commented to Mr. Ambrose later that at Trenton there were at least 1000 men gathered at the main gate, which was 200 to 300 yards from the ships, five minutes before the whistle had sounded. Mr. North remarked that Mr. Welch, the general superintendent of the Trenton shipyard, had been with them when they had encountered this crowd waiting at the main gate and Welch had thought nothing of it. Welch had merely apologized to Mr. North because the crowd of men was blocking Mr. North's car from leaving by the main gate. Mr. North went on to say that in comparison he thought the behavior of their men at The Hampton Shipyard regarding quitting early was remarkably good.

A few days after his visit to the Trenton yard, Campbell happened to stop in at a small stores department shack at the head of slip 10 to get out of the rain. Mr. North was also present sheltering from the rain when the daily patrol under the supervision of Mr. Dunn, the superintendent of the material division, formed at the head of slip 9 and proceeded toward Pier 5. As the direction in which the patrol was headed became apparent, Joe Campbell heard Fred Cernot, the store man in charge of the shack, pick up the telephone and call another store man in a shack on slip 11. Campbell distinctly heard Cernot say into the telephone, "Say Ted, Dunn's got the 'Gestapo' today and he's headed your way." Mr. Dunn was the superintendent of the Material Division which included the stores department. Campbell was not sure, but he thought that North must have heard Cernot warning Ted, the store man on slip 11, that the "Gestapo" was headed in that direction. Campbell was sure that Cernot knew North was present, because North, who was well known to the men throughout the yard, was standing right next to the telephone.

The general superintendent's office and those of his divisional superintendents were all situated on the second floor of the yard office. Mr. Ambrose and his divisional superintendents often contacted one another on matters of mutual interest when they were in their offices around about quitting time. About quitting time on the day that North had heard Cernot warning the store man on Pier 11, he related the incident to Mr. Ambrose. "I was amused," said North, "to see their efficient warning system in action. That store man at the head of slip 10 lost no time in warning the guy on slip 11 that the 'Gestapo' was headed his way."

# Hovey and Beard Company*

## PART 1

THE HOVEY AND BEARD Company manufactured wooden toys of various kinds: wooden animals, pull toys, and the like. One part of the manufacturing process involved spraying paint on the partially assembled toys. This operation was staffed entirely by girls.

The toys were cut, sanded, and partially assembled in the wood room. Then they were dipped into shellac, following which they were painted. The toys were predominantly two-colored; a few were made in more than two colors. Each color required an additional trip through the paint room.

For a number of years, production of these toys had been entirely handwork. However, to meet tremendously increased demand, the painting operation had recently been re-engineered so that the eight girls who did the painting sat in a line by an endless chain of hooks. These hooks were in continuous motion, past the line of girls and into a long horizontal oven. Each girl sat at her own painting booth so designed as to carry away fumes and to backstop excess paint. The girl would take a toy from the tray beside her, position it in a jig inside the painting cubicle, spray on the color according to a pattern, then release the toy and hang it on the hook passing by. The rate at which the hooks moved had been calculated by the engineers so that each girl, when fully trained, would be able to hang a painted toy on each hook before it passed beyond her reach.

The girls working in the paint room were on a group bonus plan. Since the operation was new to them, they were receiving a learning bonus which decreased by regular amounts each month. The learning bonus was scheduled to vanish in six months, by which time it was expected that they would be on their own—that is, able to meet the standard and to earn a group bonus when they exceeded it.

* This case is taken from Alex Bavelas and George Strauss, *Money and Motivation* (New York: Harper Brothers, 1955), chap. 10, and was based on Dr. Bavelas' experience as a consultant. Reproduced by permission.

## PART 2

By the second month of the training period trouble had developed. The girls learned more slowly than had been anticipated, and it began to look as though their production would stabilize far below what was planned for. Many of the hooks were going by empty. The girls complained that they were going by too fast, and that the time study man had set the rates wrong. A few girls quit and had to be replaced with new girls, which further aggravated the learning problem. The team spirit that the management had expected to develop automatically through the group bonus was not in evidence except as an expression of what the engineers called "resistance." One girl whom the group regarded as its leader (and the management regarded as the ringleader) was outspoken in making the various complaints of the group to the foreman: the job was a messy one, the hooks moved too fast, the incentive pay was not being correctly calculated, and it was too hot working so close to the drying oven.

## PART 3

A consultant who was brought into this picture worked entirely with and through the foreman. After many conversations with him, the foreman felt that the first step should be to get the girls together for a general discussion of the working conditions. He took this step with some hesitation, but he took it on his own volition.

The first meeting, held immediately after the shift was over at four o'clock in the afternoon, was attended by all eight girls. They voiced the same complaints again: the hooks went by too fast, the job was too dirty, the room was hot and poorly ventilated. For some reason, it was this last item that they complained of most. The foreman promised to discuss the problem of ventilation and temperature with the engineers, and he scheduled a second meeting to report back to the girls. In the next few days the foreman had several talks with the engineers. They and the superintendent felt that this was really a trumped-up complaint, and that the expense of any effective corrective measure would be prohibitively high.

The foreman came to the second meeting with some apprehensions. The girls, however, did not seem to be much put out, perhaps because they had a proposal of their own to make. They felt that if several large fans were set up so as to circulate the air around their feet, they would be much more comfortable. After some discussion, the foreman agreed that the idea might be tried out. The foreman and the consultant discussed the question of the fans with the superintendent, and three large propeller-type fans were purchased.

## PART 4

The fans were brought in. The girls were jubilant. For several days the fans were moved about in various positions until they were placed to the satisfaction of the group. The girls seemed completely satisfied with the results, and relations between them and the foreman improved visibly.

The foreman, after this encouraging episode, decided that further meetings might also be profitable. He asked the girls if they would like to meet and discuss other aspects of the work situation. The girls were eager to do this. The meeting was held, and the discussion quickly centered on the speed of the hooks. The girls maintained that the time study men had set them at an unreasonably fast speed and that they would never be able to reach the goal of filling enough of them to make a bonus.

The turning point of the discussion came when the group's leader frankly explained that the point wasn't that they couldn't work fast enough to keep up with the hooks, but that they couldn't work at that pace all day long. The foreman explored the point. The girls were unanimous in their opinion that they could keep up with the belt for short periods if they wanted to. But they didn't want to because if they showed they could do this for short periods they would be expected to do it all day long. The meeting ended with an unprecedented request: "Let us adjust the speed of the belt faster or slower depending on how we feel." The foreman agreed to discuss this with the superintendent and the engineers.

The reaction of the engineers to the suggestion was negative. However, after several meetings it was granted that there was some latitude within which variations in the speed of the hooks would not affect the finished product. After considerable argument with the engineers, it was agreed to try out the girls' idea.

With misgivings, the foreman had a control with a dial marked "low, medium, fast" installed at the booth of the group leader; she could now adjust the speed of the belt anywhere between the lower and upper limits that the engineers had set.

## PART 5

The girls were delighted, and spent many lunch hours deciding how the speed of the belt should be varied from hour to hour throughout the day. Within a week the pattern had settled down to one in which the first half hour of the shift was run on what the girls called a medium speed (a dial setting slightly above the point marked "medium"). The next two and one-half hours were run at high speed; the half hour before lunch and the half hour after lunch were run at low speed. The rest of the afternoon was run at high speed with the exception of the last forty-five minutes of the shift, which was run at medium.

In view of the girls' reports of satisfaction and ease in their work, it is interesting to note that the constant speed at which the engineers had originally set the belt was slightly below medium on the dial of the control that had been given the girls. The average speed at which the girls were running the belt was on the high side of the dial. Few, if any, empty hooks entered the oven, and inspection showed no increase of rejects from the paint room.

Production increased, and within three weeks (some two months before the scheduled ending of the learning bonus) the girls were operating at 30 to 50 percent above the level that had been expected under the original arrangement. Naturally the girls' earnings were correspondingly higher than anticipated. They were collecting their base pay, a considerable piece rate bonus, and the learning bonus which, it will be remembered, had been set to decrease with time and not as a function of current productivity. The girls were earning more now than many skilled workers in other parts of the plant.

# PART 6

Management was besieged by demands that this inequity be taken care of. With growing irritation between superintendent and foreman, engineers and foreman, superintendent and engineers, the situation came to a head when the superintendent revoked the learning bonus and returned the painting operation to its original status: the hooks moved again at their constant, time-studied designated speed, production dropped again, and within a month all but two of the eight girls had quit. The foreman himself stayed on for several months, but, feeling aggrieved, then left for another job.

# The White Company*

## PART 1[1]

THE WHITE COMPANY was one of some 80 electroplating plants in the city of Detroit which applied nickel and chrome plating to automobile parts. Price competition among these eighty plants was very intense.

The company had a nonunion work force which fluctuated between 15 and 50, depending on orders from the auto manufacturers. Few personnel records were kept. There was a standard policy of firing anyone who showed any interest in unionism. Hiring and training practices were not formalized, and the number of workers varied widely from day to day, depending upon immediate contracts. There was practically no job training. No more than a few minutes was spent in pointing out workers' duties and in introductions to co-workers.

The work was mostly unskilled, and the company employed many manual work methods instead of the semiautomatic equipment found in other companies. It used a number of practices designed to cut costs: (1) repairs were neglected and workers were expected to make up for this mechanical ineffectiveness, (2) personal (work) equipment was not quickly replaced . . . , (3) many safety practices were neglected . . . , (4) hiring and training were fitted with a situation of high turnover, so that new workers were given little training, and fired if they did not quickly learn to turn out a standard amount of production . . . , (5) overall wages were so low that the most highly paid workers received only average union wages for the industry and the workers did not receive the usual union fringe concessions.

The workers in the plant could be categorized into two main groups:

---

* Information for this case was taken from W. F. Goode and Irving Fowler, "Incentive Factors in a Low Morale Plant," *American Sociological Review,* Vol. XIV, No. 5 (1949).

[1] This is a sequential case. Your instructor may want you to discuss Part 1 before reading Part 2 or to answer the questions at the end of Part 1 and then go right on to Part 2.

high-turnover personnel, and long-service employees. The backgrounds of the workers in the plant were quite different for longer service people as compared to high-turnover workers. High-turnover personnel tended to be either part-time workers, such as students, or relatives and friends of long-service workers; experienced workers who were on strike elsewhere or temporarily laid off; or finally, young newcomers to the labor market. The five longer service personnel were different in many respects but had in common a quite desperate need for a job, either because they had physical handicaps which would make them unemployable in many places or, in the case of women, because they had to support dependent husbands. Some of the long-service workers had been with the plant since its beginnings. Almost all of them could perform nearly every task and could substitute for an absent worker.

## PREDICTIONS

From what I know about the White Company, I would predict that:

a) Worker productivity would be (high) (moderate) (low). Explain the reasons for your prediction.
b) Satisfaction in the plant would be (high) (moderate) (low). Explain the reasons for your prediction.

# PART 2

The long-service employees under pressure from management initiated a work pace which the high-turnover group had to follow. Those who did not follow such a pace were exposed to reprimand by word, gesture, or look from the long-service workers. If they continued this lack of cooperation, informal pressures on the foremen by the key workers would eventually cause their discharge. Because of the timing aspects of electroplating, frequent bottlenecks occurred. However, these bottlenecks did not necessarily mean delays in production. They rather meant that at such times the key workers would attack the bottleneck with increased energy and, with the spontaneously induced help of the high-turnover personnel, would erase the difficulty. If this in turn produced a piling up of units at a later phase of the plating process, then the key personnel utilized the same practices and again the bottleneck was relieved. According to an expert in the industry, the White Company's level of worker productivity was running only 12 to 14 percent below those firms that had invested in semiautomatic equipment. The company was "financially successful against strong competition."

Morale in the plant was low. "Workers exhibited considerable animosity toward the owners as well as the production manager," and "among the workers themselves."

## POSTPREDICTION ANALYSIS

Refer to your predictions at the end of Part 1. How closely do they match the information above? Do inaccuracies in your predictions reflect inadequate analysis? If so, explain the analytical failure. If not, what additional information would you have needed in Part 1 to improve your predictive accuracy and how would you have used that information?

# Disarmament Exercise*

## INSTRUCTIONS

YOU AND YOUR team are going to engage in a disarmament exercise in which you can win or lose points. In this exercise your objective, as a team, is to win as many points as you can. The other team has received identical instructions.

### THE EXERCISE

1. Each team will be given 20 cards or "weapons." Each card will be marked on one side with an × to designate armed condition. The blank side of the card signifies that the weapon is unarmed. To begin the exercise each of the two teams will place each of the 20 weapons in an armed condition. During the course of an exercise, these weapons will remain in your possession and out of the sight of the other team.
2. Each "set" consists of no more than ten moves for each team. Each move may consist of changing two, one, or none of the weapons from armed to unarmed status or vice versa. Each team has two and one-half minutes to make a move and thirty seconds between moves. At the end of two and one-half minutes, you must have decided to turn two, one, or none of the weapons from armed to unarmed or from unarmed to armed status. If you fail to decide on a move in the allotted time, none will be turned.
3. There will be two or more sets depending on the time. Scores will be calculated after each set.

### THE POINTS

Each team will consist of approximately nine players. If there is an uneven number of players, an additional referee will be designated,

---

* This exercise was developed by Norman Berkowitz and Harvey Hornstein and is reprinted here with their permission.

making equal the number of players on each team. Each player will then furnish two hundred points to the "world bank," to be allocated in the following manner:

1. One third will be returned to your team to be used in the exercise. Your team may diminish or supplement the points during the course of the exercise. At the end of the exercise the points remaining in your team's treasury will be divided among members of your team.
2. One third will be returned to the other team to be used in the same fashion.
3. One third will be donated to the world bank, managed by the referees.

## THE SCORE

1. "Attack."
   a. Each team may announce an attack on the other team during the thirty seconds following *any* two and one-half minute decision period (including the last one). The choice of each team made during the previous decision period counts as a move. You may not attack during "negotiations" (see below).
   b. If there is an attack, the set ends. The team with the greater number of armed weapons will win five points (per member) for each armed weapon it has *over and above* the number of armed weapons of the other team. These points will be paid directly from the treasury of the losing group to the treasury of the winning team.
2. If there is no attack.
   a. At the end of each set, your team's treasury will *receive* from the world bank two points per member for each unarmed weapon and your treasury will *pay* to the world bank two points per man for each armed weapon.
   b. If both teams win points, they will be awarded by the world bank. If both teams lose points, they will be awarded to the world bank.
   c. If one team wins while the other team loses, the winning team will receive points from the world bank while the losing team will give points to the world bank, thus in effect making up for part or all of the losses to the other team.

## NEGOTIATIONS

1. Between moves you will have the opportunity to communicate with the other team through negotiators.
2. You may call for negotiations during the thirty seconds between any decision period. The other team may accept or reject your initiation. Negotiations can last *no longer* than three minutes.
3. When the negotiators return to their teams, the two and one-half minute decision time will start again.

4. Negotiators may say whatever is necessary to most benefit their team.
5. The team is not bound by agreements made by their negotiators, even when made in good faith.
6. Your negotiators *must* meet with those of the other team after the *third, sixth,* and *ninth* moves.

## SPECIAL ROLES

You will have fifteen minutes to discuss and plan your team strategy. During this time before the exercise begins, you must select persons to fill the following roles. The persons can be changed at any time by a majority of the group.

1. Two negotiators—activities stated above.
   A group spokesman—to communicate group decisions to references regarding initiation and acceptance of negotiations, moves in game, attacks, etc.
   a. You *must* elect a spokesman.
   b. Referees will listen only to the spokesman.
   c. Spokesmen cannot be negotiators.
3. One recorder—to record moves of team.

## REMINDERS

1. At each move you may turn over two, one, or zero of your weapons to the unarmed side—or back again to the armed side.
2. You have two and one-half minutes to decide which of the above you will do.
3. If there is no attack at the end of the set you will receive two points for each unarmed weapon and lose two points for each armed weapon.
4. If there is an attack the team with the greater number of armed weapons wins five points for each armed weapon it has over the number that the other team has.
5. You should immediately elect two negotiators, a team spokesman, and a recorder.
6. You may call for negotiations after each move, if you want. Mandatory meetings of negotiations will occur after moves 3, 6, and 9.
7. The negotiators will meet to do whatever you and they think will most benefit your group.

# British Coal Industries (A)*

INTRODUCTION OF mechanized equipment into British coal mines in recent decades brought substantial changes in the methods of coal getting. Traditional hand-got methods were largely replaced by the newer "longwall" techniques. Recently, however, there has been a search for some modifications to the longwall method which might help to alleviate the problems of low productivity and dissatisfaction among the face-workers. Consequently, there has been a serious reexamination not only of the current longwall method of coal getting but also the former hand-got methods.

## HAND-GOT METHODS OF COAL GETTING

Prior to the changes which accompanied mechanization, it was common practice for two colliers—a hewer and his mate—to make their own contract with the colliery management and to work their own small face with the assistance of a boy "trammer." Sometimes this working unit extended its number to seven or eight, when three or four colliers with their attendant trammers would work together. These small groups tended to become isolated from each other even when working in the same series of stalls, the isolation of the group being intensified by the darkness. There was no possibility of continuous supervision from any individual external to this small work group.

This type of work organization placed the responsibility for the complete coal-getting task squarely on the shoulders of a single small face-to-face group which experienced the entire cycle of operations. Each collier

* The data reported in the case have been secured with permission from the following published source: E. L. Trist and K. Bamforth "Some Social and Psychological Consequences of the Longwall Method of Coal-Getting," *Human Relations*, 1951, vol. 4–1. The material has been prepared in case form by Gene W. Dalton under the direction of Professor Paul R. Lawrence. Revised 1968.

was an all around workman usually able to substitute for his mate. He had craft pride and artisan independence.

Choices of work mates were made by the men. Work mate teams frequently endured over many years. In circumstances where a man was injured or killed, it was not uncommon for his work mate to care for his family.

These groups, being able to work their own short faces continuously, could stop at whatever point may have been reached at the end of a shift. The work pace was flexible; when bad conditions prevailed, the extraction process could advance according to the degree of difficulty encountered. Under good conditions, groups of this kind were able to set their own targets which could be adjusted to the age and stamina of the individuals concerned.

Earning a living under hand-got mining conditions often entailed physical effort of a formidable order and possession of exceptional skill in order to extract a bare existence from a hard seam with a bad roof. Trammers were commonly identified by scales, called "buttons," on the bone joints of their backs caused by catching the roof while pushing and holding tubs on and off the "gates," or passageways leading to and from the working faces. Yet anyone who has listened to the talk of older miners who have experienced in their work-lives the changeover to the longwall cannot fail to be impressed by their mourning for the past together with a feeling of indignation and dismay regarding the present.

## THE LONGWALL METHOD

With the advent of coal cutters and mechanical conveyors, the degree of technological complexity of the coal getting task was raised to a higher level. Mechanization made possible the working of a single long face in place of a series of short faces. In thin seams, short faces increase costs since a large number of gates (see Figure 1) have to be "ripped" up several feet above the height of a seam to create haulage and traveling facilities. Thus, in coal beds where seams less than four feet thick are common, there has been a tendency to make full use of the possibility of working optimally long rather optimally short faces.

The longwall method of coal getting was developed to realize this possibility. It enabled a pit, containing three or four seams of different thickness, to work its entire coal economically, to develop its layout, and to organize its production in terms of a single self-consistent plan. In the longwall method, a direct advance is made into the coal on a continuous front, faces of 180 to 200 yards being typical, though longer faces are not uncommon. The coal getting is broken down into a standard series of component operations which constitute a coal getting cycle; an undercut is made along the bottom of the face of the coal seam, holes are drilled along

FIGURE 1

Layout of a District, Longwall Method

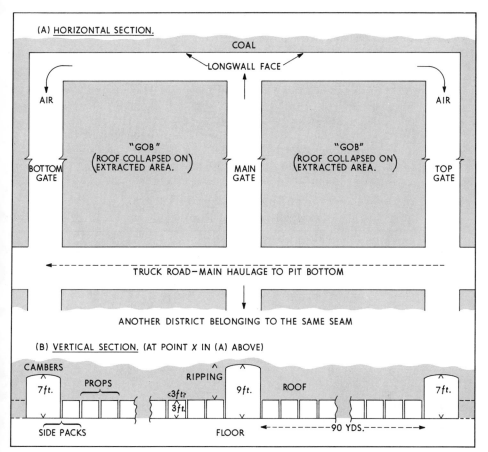

the top of the seam, and explosives are placed in the holes and "shot," loosening the coal. A conveyor is moved in place parallel to the coal face, while the gates are moved ahead to correspond with the advance of the longwall. The loosened coal is then removed (filled) and placed on the conveyor which carries it out to the gates.

A medium-size pit with three seams would have 12 to 15 longwall faces in operation simultaneously. These faces are laid out in districts as shown in Figure 1. Since the longwall method is specially applicable to thin seams, Figure 1 has been set up in terms of a three-foot working. The face extends 90 yards on either side of the main gate. The height of the face area—that of the three-foot seam itself—may be contrasted with the nine feet and seven feet to which the main and side gates have been ripped and built up as permanent structures with cambers (arched beams) and side-packs. By regulation, props must be placed every three feet, and the line of props, shown in Figure 1(b), is placed immediately against a coal-face waiting to be filled off. The area marked "Gob" (to use a term common in mining vernacular) indicates the expanse from which the coal has already been extracted. On this area the roof is left to collapse; only the tunnels made by the main and side gates, which are used for ventilation, haulage, and traveling, are kept open. These tunnels may sometimes extend for distances of two miles from the pit bottom.

In each coal getting cycle the advance made into the coal is equal to the depth of the undercut. A cut of six feet represents typical practice in a thin seam with a good roof. All equipment has to be moved forward as each cycle contributes to the advance. The detail in the face area is represented in Figure 2, where the coal is shown cut and waiting for the

FIGURE 2

Coal Face as Set for Filling Shift

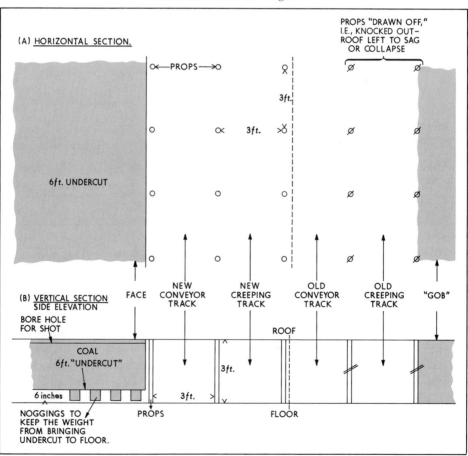

shot-firer, who performs the last task before the fillers come on. The combined width of the lanes marked new creeping track and new conveyor track equal the depth of six feet, from which the coal had been removed by the fillers on the last shift of the previous cycle. As part of the preparation work of the current cycle (before the fillers can come on again), the conveyor has to be moved from its previous position in the old conveyor track to its present position, shown in Figure 2, in the new conveyor track, against the face. At the same time the two lines of props on either side of the old creeping track are withdrawn (allowing the roof to sag or collapse) and thrown over beside the conveyor for the fillers to use in propping up their roof as they get into the next six feet of coal. The term "creeping track" refers to the single, propped, three-foot lane adjacent to that occupied by the conveyor but on the side away from the coal. It allows free passage up and down the face, and is called a creeping track since in thin seams the low roof makes it necessary for all locomotion to take the form of creeping, i.e., crawling on the hands and knees.

## ORGANIZATION OF THE CYCLE GROUP

The work is so organized that the component operations follow each other in rigid succession over three shifts of seven and one-half hours each, so that a total coal getting cycle may be completed in each twenty four hours of the working week. The overall tasks which must be performed in a cycle fall into four groups, concerned with (a) the preparation of the coal face for shot firing, (b) shifting the conveyor, (c) ripping and building up the main and side gates, and (d) moving the shot coal onto the conveyor.

The men are organized into a cycle group of approximately 40 men: 10 each to the first (cutting) and second (ripping) shifts; 20 to the third (filling) shift. The shot firer and the shift deputies are responsible to the pit management as a whole. The artisan type of pair, composed of a skilled man and his mate and assisted by one or more laborers, was out of keeping as a model for the type of work group required by the longwall cycle method.

Each of the workers belongs to one of seven different job categories: borer, cutter, gummer, belt breaker, belt builder, ripper, or filler. (See Table 1 for the functions and relationships of these seven categories.) Face workers have usually been trained for only one of the seven job categories and expect to spend all or most of their underground life in this one occupation.

The face preparation tasks are all performed on the first shift. They include boring holes for the shot firer, with pneumatic or electrically operated drills, near the roof of the seam through to the depth of the undercut, at short distances (within each filler's "lengths") along the entire expanse of face; driving the coal cutter so that the blade or "job" makes an even undercut into the coal some six inches from the floor to whatever depth has been assigned, again along the entire expanse of face; taking out the six inches of coal (called the "gummings") left in the undercut, so that the main weight of coal can drop and break freely when the shots are fired; placing supporting "noggings" underneath the coal so that this weight does not cause it to sag down to the floor while the "cut" is standing during the next shift. These tasks are performed in the order given. Three of the seven work roles are associated with their execution, two men being fully occupied in boring the holes, a further two in managing the coal cutter, and four in clearing out the undercut.

The success of the shots fired at the end of the second shift to make the coal finally ready for the filler depends on the efficiency with which each of these interdependent preparation tasks has been carried out. Bad execution of any one of them diminishes, and may even cancel out, the effect of the shots, with consequent havoc in the lengths of the particular fillers where such breakdowns have occurred. Holes bored too low leave a quantity of coal, difficult to extract, clinging to the roof after the shots have been fired. If the roof is sticky, this gives rise to "sticky tops." Holes not bored through to the full depth of the undercut create the condition of "hard backs," the shots having no effect on this part of the coal. The coal cutter only too frequently has a tendency to leave the floor and "get up into the coal," producing an uneven cut. This means less working height for the filler, and also less wages, since his tonnage is reduced. When the gummings are left in, the shot is wasted; the coal has nowhere to drop and the powder blows out of the hole (usually up the "cutting break" in the roof) so that the mass to be extracted is left solid. Failure to insert noggings, which leads to the cut sagging down, also renders useless the services of the shot firer.

The group of operations concerned with the conveyor involves—since forward movement is blocked by props which must be left standing—breaking up the sections of belt in the old conveyor track and building them up in the new. Each of these tasks requires two men: the belt breakers and belt builders. The dismantling part is done on the first shift in the wake of the cutting operation. The reasons for this include the necessity of shifting belt engines and tension ends out of the gate areas (where they are positioned when the conveyor is working) in order to allow the ripping operation of the second shift to proceed. The reassembly of the conveyor is the only task performed in the face area during the second shift. Unless the conveyor is properly jointed, set close to the new face, and accurately sighted in a straight line, a further crop of difficulties arises, and frequent stoppages may interfere with filling. The most modern types of belt, e.g., floor belts, avoid the labor of breaking up and reassembling plates. Belt engines and tension ends are cumbersome equipment, but they must nevertheless be shifted every day. Similarly, the last two lines of props have to be taken down and thrown forward.

The third group of tasks entails ripping up the roof of the main and side gates to the depth of the undercut, and building them with a stable roof and firmly packed sides so that haulage and air ways can advance with the face. Unless this work is expertly done, the danger of roof falls is acute, with the likelihood of both men and equipment being blocked in the face. The work is carried out by a team of seven or eight rippers.

Only when all these operations have been completed can the shots be fired and the fillers come on. (The culminating activity of moving the coal onto the conveyor is known as "filling off.") For the filling operation, the entire face is divided up into equal lengths, except that the corner positions are somewhat shorter in view of difficulties created by the proximity of belt engines and tension ends. In a 3-foot seam, lengths would be 8–10 yards, and some 20 fillers would be required, 10 in each half face of 90–100 yards. Each filler is required to extract the entire coal from his length, going back to the depth of the 6-foot undercut. As he progresses into his coal, he has the further task of propping up his roof every 3 feet. When he has thrown his last load onto the conveyor he has "filled off," i.e., finished his "length" or "stint." In addition to a hand pick and shovel, his tool kit includes an air pick, used for dealing with some of the difficulties created by bad preparation or hard coal.

## ISOLATION AND INTERDEPENDENCE OF THOSE PERFORMING THE VARIOUS TASKS

So close is the task interdependence that the system becomes vulnerable from its need for 100 percent performance. Yet the segmentation of the work cycle makes it difficult for workers to feel responsible for the completion of the total task or even responsible to the workers in the other shifts. As can be seen from the shift timetables (Table 1), the three shifts never meet on the job. Moreover, the two preparation groups alternate on the so-called back shifts while the fillers alternate on days and afternoons so that the fillers never meet the preparation groups even in the outside community.

It is upon the work of the cutting team, containing the front and the back man on the cutter and the four gummers, that the filling shift is most dependent. But the cutting team does not exist officially as a group since the cutters are responsible for, and paid for, their cutting alone. The gummers are not under their authority, and only the deputy can take responsibility for any tendency they may have to leave some or all of the gummings in as they traverse the face. As they are on day wage, they have nothing to lose unless they go too far—so, at least, the fillers feel on this score.

Performing the least skilled task, the gummers are the lowest paid and the lowest prestige group on the face. Their work is arduous, dangerous, dusty, and awkward. Hostility in them toward "the system" or toward

## TABLE 1

Occupational Structure in the Longwall System

| Shift Sequence | Job Categories | No. of Men | Methods of Payment | Group Organization | Tasks | Skills |
|---|---|---|---|---|---|---|
| First (usually called "cutting" shift). Either night, 8 p.m.–3:30 a.m., or afternoon, 12 noon–7:30 p.m. (borers start an hour earlier). Though alternating between night and afternoon, personnel on the cutting shift are never on days. | Borer | 2 | Per hole | Inter-dependent pair on same note. | Boring holes for shot-firer in each stint to depth of under-cut. | Management of electric or pneumatic drills, placing of holes, judgment of roof, hard-ness of coal, etc. |
| | Cutter | 2 | Per yard | Inter-dependent pair on same note, front man and back man. | Operating coal-cutter to achieve even cut at assigned depth the entire length of the face; knocking out (front man), re-setting (back man) props as cutter passes. Back man in-serts noggings. | Requires rather more "engineer-ing" skill than other coal-face tasks. Mining skills in keeping cut even under changing conditions, watching roof control. |
| | Gummer | 4 | Day Wage | Loose group attached to cutters, though front man with-out supervisory authority. | Cleaning out undercut, so that clear space for coal to drop and level floor for filler. The coal between undercut and floor is called "the gummings." | Unskilled, heavy manual task, which unless conscientiously done creates difficulties for filler, for when gummings left in, the shot simply blows out and coal is left solid. |
| | Belt-breaker | 2 | Per yard | Inter-dependent pair on same note. | Shifting belt-engine and tension-end into face clear of rippers; breaking up conveyor in old track, placing plates, etc., ready in new track, drawing off props in old creeping track; some packing as required. | Belt-breaking is a relatively simple engineering task; engine shifting is awkward and heavy; drawing off and packing involve responsibility for roof control and require solid underground experience. |
| Second (usually called the "ripping" shift). Either night or after-noon alternating with cutting shift. Rippers may start rather later than builders. None of these personnel go on day shift proper. | Belt-builder | 2 | Per yard | Inter-dependent pair on same note. | Reassembling conveyor in new track; positioning belt-engine and tension-end in line with this testing running of reassembled conveyor; placing chocks; pack-ing as required. | As with breaking, the level of engineering skill is relatively simple; inconvenience caused to fillers if belt out of position. The roof control responsibilities demand solid underground experience. |
| | Ripper | 8 | Cubic measure | Cohesive functionally interrelated group on same note. | To "rip" "dirt" out of main and side gates to assigned heights; place cambers and build up roof into a solid, safe and durable structure; pack-up the sides. The ripping team carries out all operations necessary to their task, doing their own boring. The task is a com-plete job in itself, seen through by the group with-in the compass of one shift. | This work requires the highest degree of building coal face tasks. Some very heavy labour is entailed. Since the work is relatively permanent there is much pride of craft. On the ripper depends the safety of all gates and main ways. |
| Third (usually called "filling" shift). Either day, 6 a.m.–1:30 p.m., or after-noon, 2 p.m.–9:30 p.m. Never night. | Filler | 20 | Weight-tonnage on con-veyors. | Aggregate of individuals with equal "stints" all on same note; fractioned relation-ships and much isola-tion. | The length of the "stint" is determined by the depth of the cut and the thickness of the seam. Using hand or air pick and shovel, the filler "throws" the "shot" coal on to the conveyor until he has cleared his length, i.e., "filled off." He props up every 2 ft. 6 in as he works in. | The filler remains in one work place while conditions change. Considerable underground experience is required to cope with bad conditions. Each man is responsible for each section of roof. Bad work on other shifts makes the task harder. It is heavy in any case and varies in different parts of the wall. |
| 3 shifts | 7 job categories | 40 men | 5 methods | 4 types | The common background of "underground" skill is more important than the task differences. | |

other face workers is most easily expressed by leaving in some of the gummings, which is particularly likely under conditions of fatigue and difficulty.

There are, of course, instances where effective leadership is exercised over the gummers by the front cutting man. But it was stressed at the same time that management could hold the cutters responsible only for the cut, and that to exercise detailed supervision was an impossible task for a deputy, especially on "back shifts" where his territory of responsibility is apt to be more extensive than on day shift. In shift groups where a good spirit of cooperation obtains, the belt breakers are often willing to help out the gummers. It was suggested that fewer lapses occurred when these interchanges took place. But the pattern of the cutting shift works against such cooperation, as it consists of four different categories of workers, who successively traverse the face at their own separately institutionalized tasks, without a common goal or functionally defined responsibilities to each other.

The borers are off by themselves, and, as the belt breakers and builders are on different shifts, neither can feel the satisfaction of accepting responsibility for the conveyor system as a whole.

By contrast, the ripping team is a well-organized primary work group of seven or eight with an intelligible total task for which it carries complete responsibility. Rippers are frequently referred to by others as a "good crowd" who seldom "go absent on each other." Pride of craft is considerable. A main ripper and, usually, individuals of very varying experience compose the group, but it appears to manage its internal relationships without status difficulties. Here, responsible autonomy persists; however, like the other face-work groups, the ripping team is a group by itself and there is as a result no transfer of its more stable morale to other groups in the system. Working, as it does, in the main and side gates, it is felt to be a closed group very much apart from the main interaction between the preparation and filling operations carried out in the face itself.

In all essential respects the ripping team represents a survival of the hand-got past in the mechanical present, for the gates in which ripping parties of varying sizes operate are, as it were, their own "stalls," continuously and autonomously worked. All relevant operations are carried out within the group which completes them within the compass of one shift. Rippers have retained intact their total task, their multiple skills, their artisan independence, and their small group organization.

The filler is the modern version of the second collier of the older hand-got systems, whose hewer has departed to the cutting shift. While his former mate has acquired a new partner in the back man on the coal cutter, and is serviced by a new group of laborers (gummers), the filler is alone in his stint, the dimensions of which are those of the short face formerly worked in common. The advent of mechanization has changed little of the character of the filling process, except that the filler has, in his air pick, the assistance of one power-driven tool and, instead of a hand-pushed tub, a mechanically driven conveyor onto which to load his coal. However, the introduction of mechanized methods of face preparation and conveying, along with the retention of manual filling, has resulted not only in isolating the filler from those with whom he formerly shared the coal-getting task as a whole, but also in making him one of a large aggregate serviced by the same small group of preparation workers.

In place of an actually present partner, who belonged to him solely as the second member of an interdependent pair, he has acquired an "absent group," whom he must share with nineteen others.

The filler is unusually dependent upon the quality of the work done in previous shifts. If a borer fails to drill to the proper depth, the shot firer's task is no more difficult, but the filler must contend with sticky tops. If gummings are left in, the work of the cutter is not affected, but the mass is left solid for the filler. If the belt builders don't sight the conveyor in a straight line, the work of the belt breakers is not changed, but the fillers must contend with frequent stoppages. Difficulties are increased still further by the fact that the concern of this succession of pairs is with the entire 180–200 yards of the face. For them the face is a single continuous region, whereas for the fillers it is differentiated into a series of short adjacent sections—the eight to ten yards of the individual filler's own length. In the corner of this length he usually chalks up his name, but these chalk marks mean little more than just the name to traversing pairs, to whom individual fillers are personally little known. The pattern of these relationships is shown in Figure 3.

### FIGURE 3

Position and Locomotion of Successive Groups of Face Workers on the Longwall

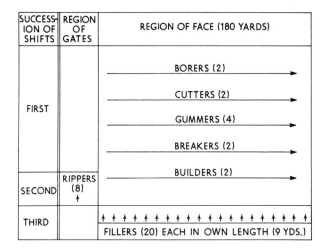

| SUCCESSION OF SHIFTS | REGION OF GATES | REGION OF FACE (180 YARDS) |
|---|---|---|
| FIRST | | BORERS (2) ——————▶ |
| | | CUTTERS (2) ——————▶ |
| | | GUMMERS (4) ——————▶ |
| | | BREAKERS (2) ——————▶ |
| | | BUILDERS (2) ——————▶ |
| SECOND | RIPPERS (8) ↑ | |
| THIRD | | ↟↟↟↟↟↟↟↟↟↟↟↟↟↟↟↟↟↟↟↟ FILLERS (20) EACH IN OWN LENGTH (9 YDS.) |

Most of the troubles seem to accumulate on the filling shift. It may be noted that the face is not "filled off" until each and every length has been cleared, and that until this has been done, the new cycle cannot begin. Disorganization on the filling shift disorganizes the subsequent shifts, and its own disorganization is often produced by the bad preparation left by these teams. Every time the cycle is stopped, some 200 tons of coal are lost. The closeness of the interdependence of the tasks tends to rebound upon itself. Mistakes and difficulties made or encountered at one stage are carried forward, producing yet other difficulties in the next, as the inflexible character of the succession gives no scope for proceeding with later tasks when hold ups have occurred earlier.

The main burden of keeping down the number of cycle stoppages falls on the deputy, who is the only person in the face area with cycle, as distinct from task, responsibility. In view of the darkness and spread-out character of the work there is no possibility of close supervision. Responsibility for seeing to it that bad work is not done, however adverse the working conditions, rests with the face workers themselves. Management complains of lack of support from their men, accusing them of being concerned only with their fractional tasks and being unwilling to take broader cycle responsibility. Workers complain of being tricked by management who are resented as outsiders. On occasions, the deputy is reduced to bargaining with the men as to whether they will agree to carry out essential "bye-work" (special tasks of any kind, over and above the specific production operation for which a given category of face worker receives his basic pay).

## THE PHYSICAL CONDITIONS

The environment in which the face workers perform their tasks makes the work even more difficult and uncertain. Some of the most dreaded conditions, such as wet, heat, or dust, are permanent features of the working environment of certain faces. But others, less known outside the industry, may also make the production tasks of the face worker both difficult and dangerous, even when the seam in which he is working is well ventilated, cool, and dry without being dusty. Rolls or faults may appear in the seam. Control may be lost over the roof for considerable periods; especially in the middle of a long face, certain types of roof are apt to sag down. Changes may occur in the floor; the condition known as "rising floor" is not uncommon. Since some of these conditions, described in Table 2 and Figure 4, reduce working heights, their appearance is particularly troublesome in thin seams. If the difference between working in 5 feet 6 inches and 5 feet may be of small account, that between working in 3 feet and 2 feet 6 inches may often produce intolerable conditions. Loss of roof control is serious whatever the working height. In general, bad conditions mean not only additional danger but attitional labor, such as the need to insert packs to support a loose roof.

A large amount of bye-work is usually necessary when unfavorable physical conditions are encountered. Though many bye-work tasks have gained the status of specially remunerated activities, the rates are such that the overall wage received at the end of a week during which a good

## TABLE 2

### Cumulative and Differential Incidence of Bad Condition and Bad Work in the Filling Shift

| Types of Adverse Factor | Positions Across the Face of 20 Fillers | | | | | | | | | | | | | | | | | | | |
|---|---|---|---|---|---|---|---|---|---|---|---|---|---|---|---|---|---|---|---|---|
| | 1 | 2 | 3 | 4 | 5 | 6 | 7 | 8 | 9 | 10 | 11 | 12 | 13 | 14 | 15 | 16 | 17 | 18 | 19 | 20 |
| Loose roof – roof broken up by weight or natural "slips" (cracks) making it difficult to support; extra time required for timbering reduces that for filling. | | | | x | x | x | | | | x | | | | x | x | x | | | | |
| Faults – sudden changes in slope of seam either up or down, producing bad conditions capable of anticipation, possibly lasting over a considerable period. | x | x | | | | | | | | | | | | | | | | | | x |
| Rolls – temporary unevenness in floor or roof reducing working height and producing severely cramped conditions in thin seams. As above for anticipation and duration. | x | | | | x | | | | | | | | | x | | | | | | |
| Roof weight – roof sagging down – especially in middle positions along the face where weight is greatest; not dissimilar to above in effect. | | | | | x | x | x | | | | | | | | x | x | x | | | |
| Rising floor – from natural bad stone floor, or from the cut having been made into the coal so that the gas in the coal lifts up the floor, or from naturally inferior coal which is left down but which lifts (gas). | | | | | x | | x | | | | | | | x | x | | | | | |
| Bad boring – holes bored short so that coal at the back of the undercut is unaffected by shot (hard backs); heavy extraction task with air pick at end of shift, when tired; or holes too low, so that shot leaves coal clinging to roof (sticky tops). Both these conditions tend to occur through naturally hard coal and certain types of roof. | | | | | | x | | | | | | x | | | | | x | | | |
| Uneven cut – from the coal cutter having gone up into the coal. This reduces the filler's working height, of rolls, and the tonnage on which his wages depend. Also, as with rolls, faults, etc., it means that 3-ft. props have to be inserted in 2-ft. 6-in. height, which means sinking them in floor (dirting props) as an additional unrenumerated task. | x | | | | x | | | | | x | x | | | | | x | | | | x |
| Gummings left in – failure on the part of the gummers to clear coal from undercut so that coal cannot drop and shot is wasted. The result is a solid mass of hard coal, requiring constant use of air pick and back-breaking effort. The amount left in varies. | | | | x | x | x | | | | x | x | | | x | | | x | | | x |
| Belt trouble – the belt may not have been set in a straight line, or bad joints may have been made, or it may not have been made tight enough. On top-delivery belts coal going back on the bottom belt very soon stops it. Belt stoppages may produce exceedingly awkward delays, especially if conditions are otherwise bad. | | | | | | x | x | x | x | | | | | | | | | | | |
| Total* | 3 | 1 | – | 3 | 7 | 5 | 2 | 1 | – | 3 | 2 | 1 | – | 3 | 4 | 2 | 2 | 2 | – | 3 |
| Skill† | + | | | + | | | | | | | | | – | + | | – | | – | | + |
| Stamina† | | | | + | | | – | | | | | | | – | | | | – | + | |
| Conscientiousness† | | | | – | | | | | | | | | | | + | | | – | | |
| Subgroup membership‡ | a | a | a | I | b | b | I | c | c | c | d | d | I | e | e | e | e | I | f | f |

This table has been built up as a "model" of the situation from the experience of a group of face workers who acted as informants. It relates the effect of bad conditions and bad work, traversing the face unevenly, to the unequal personal and group qualities of the fillers.

x indicates local distribution of difficulty in typical examples of different kinds of bad conditions and bad work.

* These numbers simply indicate the fact that several different kinds of things often go wrong in the same length. Severity varies. At one extreme there may be a series of minor nuisances, at the other one major interference. When conditions seriously deteriorate the interaction of factors and effects is such that some degree of disturbance is apt to be felt from most quarters at one or other point along the face.

† Plus or minus ratings have been given for supra- or infra-norm group status on the three attributes of skill, stamina, and conscientiousness on the job, which represent the type of judgments of each other that men need to make, and do in fact make.

‡ Members of the same informal subgroup are indicated by the same letter; I = Isolate.

## FIGURE 4

### The Course of a Roll, or Fault, Across a Longwall Face

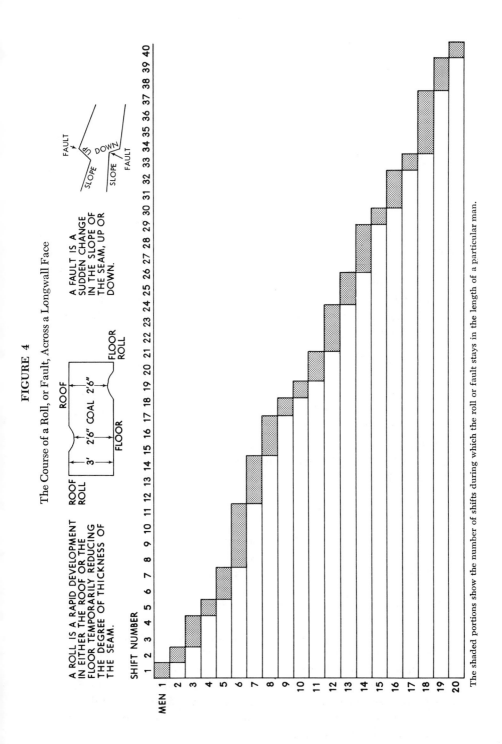

The shaded portions show the number of shifts during which the roll or fault stays in the length of a particular man.

deal of bye-work has been necessary is less than that which would have been received had the whole of the five shifts been available for production work. From the face worker's point of view, bad conditions mean not only more danger and harder work but less pay; they may also compel overtime. Staying behind an hour or sometimes three hours longer under bad conditions may involve a degree of hardship beyond the capacity that many face workers can endure, especially if they are older, and if overtime demands are repeated in close succession.

Bad conditions tend to induce bad work. Bad work can, and does arise when conditions are good, from personal shortcomings and social tensions, but difficulties arising from human failings are more readily—and conveniently—expressed when the additional hindrance and excuse of bad conditions is also present. The result is a tendency for circular causal processes of a disruptive character to be touched off. Unless rapidly checked by special measures, often of an emergency character, these processes, once started, threaten to culminate in the fillers' not filling off, and the cycle's being stopped. The system creates tension and anxiety in the workers as it is always to some extent working against the threat of its own breakdown.

The local arrival of certain types of bad conditions, such as rolls that move across the face, can be anticipated, so that anxiety piles up. The passage across the face of a roll that continues for different periods of time in various lengths is shown in Figure 4. As regards bad work left by the other shifts, the filler is in the situation of never knowing what he may find, so that anxiety of a second kind arises that tends to produce chronic uncertainty and irritation. There is little doubt that these two circumstances contribute to the widespread incidence of psychosomatic and kindred neurotic disorders among those concerned.

## REACTIONS OF THE MEN

The men who face these unequal conditions are themselves unequal, but the length of face they clear is the same. The detailed implications of this situation are set out in Table 2; there the differential incidence of some of the most common types of bad conditions and of bad work, in the different lengths of a typical face is shown in relation to the variations in skill, conscientiousness, and stamina in a typical group of fillers, fractionated into informal subgroups interspersed with isolates.

That the fillers experience a great deal of stress is indicated by widespread instances of neurotic episodes occurring on shift—of men sitting in their lengths in stony silence, attacking their coal in towering rage, or leaving the face in panic. To protect themselves against their dependent isolation, some of the men have formed protective defenses. These might be categorized into four types:

1. Some informal small groups have formed in which private arrange-

ments to help each other out are made among neighbors in twos, threes, or fours. However, these arrangements are often undependable and open to manipulation for antisocial and competitive ends. A number of isolates are left over. There is no loyalty felt beyond this small informal group and even these groups are highly susceptible to breakup through internal "rows."

Where the groups do become stable and work well together for long periods of time, they are envied but also criticized for being too close. Isolates, it appears, are either individualists who "won't even share timber," or men with bad reputations, with whom others refuse to work. Among these are the unconscientious who "won't help out at the end of a shift" and who are frequently absent, and the helpless who "cannot learn to look after themselves under bad conditions." Others, whose stamina is deficient (whether through age, illness, or neurosis) and whose lengths are often uncleared in consequence, are dropped from the informal groups.

2. To protect themselves, the fillers have developed a strong individualism involving a great deal of personal secrecy. Among his own shift mates there is competitive intrigue for the better places—middle positions are avoided, for from these "it is a long way to creep"—and for jobs in workings where conditions are good. However, nowhere is the mistrust that shift mates have of each other more in evidence than in controversies over bye-work "slipping off the note." On what is referred to as the "big note" is entered all the contract and bye-work done during the week by the shift aggregate. This note is issued to one man called "the number man" since he is identified by his check number. In no sense is this individual a representative appointed by his mates, and only rarely is he an informal leader. Customarily he is a "corner man," whose length adjoins the main gate, i.e., the man most conveniently within reach of the deputy. When asked about bye-work he does not always know what has been done at the far ends of the face and he is under no obligation to stop his own work to find out. But though a number of men will grouse about their pay being short, mentioning this or that item as having "slipped off the note," very few ever bother to check up. There are men who have worked on a face for three or four years and never once seen their own big note. Yet these are among the more ready to accuse the corner man or the deputy. The corner man is suspected at least of never forgetting to make the most of his own assignments. To the deputy is ascribed the intention of keeping the costs of his district down. Conspiracy between the two is often alleged. Only when a major rumpus occurs are such suspicions put to the test, but showdowns of this kind rarely result, as they are apt to peter out in squabbles proving nothing.

On some faces, fear of victimization is rife, particularly in the form of being sent to work in a "bad place." Against the deputy, workers take advantage of the scope afforded in the underground situation for petty deception over such matters as time of leaving the pit, or the "measure that is sent up" (amount of coal filled onto the conveyor). With the deputy, however, men are also prepared to enter into alliance against each other, often for very good reasons, such as to stop mates from going absent and by so doing throwing more work on to the others.

There are also instances of bribing members of the other shifts in the hope of getting a "good deal" in one's own length. Tobacco is taken to the cutter; gummers are stood a pint on Sunday.

3. The third protective device might be called mutual scapegoating. Fillers almost never see those who work on the "back shifts," and this absence of contact gives full rein to mutual and irresponsible scapegoating. When there is a crisis, and the filling shift is unable to fill off, the "buck" is passed to the other shifts—or vice versa if disorganization has occurred elsewhere. It is frequently also passed to the deputy, who is blamed for not finding substitutes, and to repair men brought in who are too old to stand the pace.

It is fruitless for these men to pass the buck back to the fillers, as the individual filler can always exempt himself. Since bad conditions and bad work interact so closely, it is usually difficult to pin blame specifically. Mutual scapegoating is a self-perpetuating system, in which nothing is resolved and no one feels guilty.

4. Absenteeism is the fourth form of defense. For example, one filler, returning from his week's holiday with pay, complained that the first two shifts had "knocked it all out of him." The gummings had been left in. His coal was solid. He had to have an air pick on all day. "I've tried cursing them, but it's no use, and pleading with them, but it's no use. I'll take a day off for this."

When conditions on a face deteriorate, especially in ways that are predictable, absenteeism among fillers sometimes piles up to a point where the remainder have to stay down an extra two or three hours in order to clear the face. Should this situation repeat itself more than a day or two, those coming on shift often meet at the pit-head baths before presenting themselves for work. If less than a certain number arrive, all go home.

## CONCLUSIONS AND SUGGESTIONS

Since the introduction of the longwall techniques into the pits, production has not met expectations. Despite improved equipment, productivity has remained low. Evidence suggests that a norm of low productivity has developed well below the potential of the men. It has been suggested by some that this norm is an adaptive method of handling the contingencies of the underground situation and the demands of a complicated and rigid work program. Those in authority have been likewise disturbed by the drift of the face workers from the pits, despite higher wages and better amenities.

# Lewis Equipment Company

When William Conrad, a case writer from the Harvard Business School, approached Samuel Coates, the plant manager at Lewis Equipment, about case possibilities, he found that Coates did have a number of concerns that sounded like good case leads. Coates explained that, even though he had been promoted to his present assignment several months earlier, he did not feel that he had as yet made nearly as many improvements in the plant's operations as he believed were possible. In particular, Coates expressed concern about his general foremen (see Exhibit 1 for a partial organization chart of the company).

Sam went on to explain that he personally was under considerable pressure from his superiors to improve factory performance. He did not

**EXHIBIT 1**

Partial Organization Chart

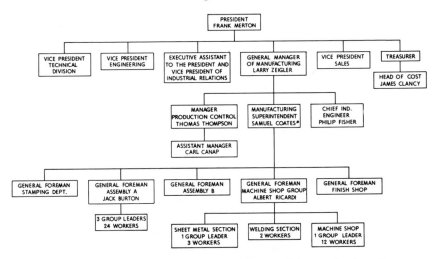

* Mr. Coates had left his former position as general foreman of the stamping dept. about a year earlier.

believe these demands were entirely reasonable, but he believed he could make progress in meeting these demands if only he could find a way to get better coordination between his foremen. Sam also wanted his foremen to spend more of their time and interest on helping their own people overcome the daily problems on the factory floor. He believed his foremen were often too distracted to attend to the practical issues of training and encouraging their employees in getting their work done properly and on time. He wanted his foremen to feel responsible for all aspects of their unit and to fight for the things they felt were necessary to make their unit effective. Sam reported that he was having difficulty in getting his foremen thinking and working along these lines. Starting with this lead, William Conrad decided to spend some time with two of the foremen involved to learn more about the situation.

## COMPANY BACKGROUND

The Lewis Equipment Company had been started some fifteen years earlier as a science based company producing an increasing line of equipment and instruments that were used primarily in the oil industry. After a period of early financial success and rapid growth the company had, in recent years, experienced severe competition and had been operating at a loss for about two years. At this time the company employed approximately 900 people, of whom a considerable number were engineers and scientists. The factory operated on a job order basis, and most of the products were produced to customer specifications.

## ASSEMBLY DEPARTMENT A

The first department that Conrad chose to study was Assembly Department A under the general foremanship of Jack Burton. During their first conversation Jack explained about the nature of his work and his problems:

BURTON:    I have one main final assembly line that makes up twelve different types of equipment that are each produced two to six times a year. There are ten people in this production line along with a group leader. I also have a subassembly line that makes small quantities of a variety of components, and also finishes some assemblies that are produced only once or twice a year. Then I have the wire and harness line—these are the harnesses and cables used in the finished assemblies.

We're having a lot of trouble with the specifications. The trouble is that we are not given enough time to work out the problems in specifications when they come to us. I have to accept what the engineers give me as the bible, even though there are plenty of errors from the engineers. All the control around here is really in the engineering department. The final test is also done by the engineers, but there is a logic in this because we could develop our own slipshod technique if we did not have the engineers for final tests.

I get a monthly schedule in rough draft form from production control that tells me what to do and when to do it. It keeps the material flowing. I usually get the report on the first of each month which I don't like, because if I knew in advance what the work would be like for the ensuing months I could go around to the paint foreman, etc., and put pressure on him to get the specific materials that I need for a crash program, so I would be better off.

I get a weekly direct labor utilization report made out by accounting. The accounting department makes this report up from the time cards and tells me what percentage of productivity resulted from our past weekly efforts. My yearly percentage of productivity to date is 62 percent, officially, but this note on the side of the sheet shows that actually I should be at 64 percent productivity. Only a small amount of the jobs are actually timed. The standards on about 90 percent of the jobs are estimated. Management is interested in improving the percent of productivity over last year's productivity. For instance, we are now at 62 percent while last year this department was at a 45 percent productivity. But that improvement isn't much help, because the selling price and the budget are based on the standard times so that no matter how high the productivity is, if it is anything lower than 100 percent, they always complain.

We would show an even better precentage productivity figure if the rework hours were counted in the proper place. For example, last January we had 21 percent rework. On rework we have to eat it. If a late engineering spec change causes rework, we have to eat it, as far as the productivity figures go.

I think they are hiding their heads in the sand. They don't want to know the true cost picture. If they cross-charged rework costs to the department that caused the trouble it would be waving a red flag in their faces and showing where the real problem lies.

## THE DIRECT LABOR UTILIZATION REPORT

Burton's frequent references to the direct labor utilization report prompted Conrad to look into this subject. He learned that this particular control system had been initiated by Mr. Merton, the company president, shortly after he had arrived at the company some three years previously. This system, designed to alert management to possible problem areas and to assist in product and inventory control, encompassed all of the company's manufacturing and assembly activities and a somewhat smaller proportion of the remaining hourly-paid labor force. Mr. Merton had made every attempt to have all of the manufacturing jobs and assembly operations rated, but with frequent design modifications requested by customers and the frequent introduction of new products, this goal had never quite been achieved. Currently, some 70 percent of the direct labor force in the manufacturing division were working on rated jobs.

Generally the control system was not unlike progressive cost accounting procedures found in other medium-sized firms working on a job order basis. It was primarily aimed at controlling manufacturing labor costs by comparing the total actual time expended in manufacturing work to the accumulated standard times for each part or assembly produced. These standard times for manufacturing the necessary individual parts and for their assembly were determined by industrial engineering.

The cost accounting department distributed weekly on Friday afternoon a direct labor utilization report for each department covered by the system along with a summary for the total factory organization and the total company. (See Exhibit 2 for a guide to the method of calculation of the various items.) The two most significant measures upon which subordinate organizations were evaluated were known as the productivity and efficiency ratings. Of these two ratings, the productivity figure was the more frequently quoted and discussed rating. Conrad asked James Clancy,

**EXHIBIT 2**

Sample Direct Labor Utilization Report with Guide to Method of Calculation

1. Total hours available = the total hours recorded on the time cards of the employees in the department concerned during the reporting period

2. Hours used on indirect labor = % of group leader's × 8 $\frac{hrs.}{day}$ × number of working time spent on supr. days in reporting plus inspector's and period clerical help's time

3. Hours available for direct labor = #1 minus #2

4. Hours direct labor on nonrated jobs = total hours expended on jobs that industrial engineering hasn't rated and/or on special jobs requested by other departments.

5. Hours variance = hours expended due to "acts of God" ( e.g., machine breakdowns, power failures, snow storms ) plus total rework hours.*

6. Hours direct labor on rated jobs = #3 minus ( #4 plus #5 )

7. Standard hours produced = standard hours allowed for × jobs completed in reeach job. porting period

8. % efficiency on rated jobs = #7 divided by #6

9. % total productivity = #7 plus #4 divided by #1

10. Rework*
    a. Responsible
    b. Not responsible

* Work hours expended on rework were broken down into two classifications:
a. The unacceptable workmanship of the particular organization being measured.
b. The rework occasioned by subsequent faulty work in other departments or by revisions in product design made by engineering, necessitating a rework of the job.
   Mention was usually made at the bottom of the Utilization Report of the absolute amounts of rework completed during the reporting period.

the head of cost accounting, what the significance was of these weekly reports. The latter commented as follows:

CLANCY:    The reports are of some significance since the president looks at the figures every week. He usually gets the productivity and efficiency for total company and total manufacturing and plots them on a big chart in his office, which goes back several years. Sometimes he asks for reports on individual departments but he never looks at them for more than ten minutes. I would say Mr. Zeigler[1] better be interested in them, since he knows Merton is going to talk to him every week manufacturing's performance doesn't look good. . . . A lot of the managers say that the system is a bunch of rubbish—Mr. Zeigler always says that he doesn't believe in the system. But I know they're concerned because Merton believes in it. You watch them on Friday pacing up and down, waiting to see what the results are. Their actions show that they are interested in it.

The total factory productivity and efficiency percentages were currently averaging approximately 69 percent and 79 percent respectively, which were slight increases over the previous two years. Exhibit 3 charts the

**EXHIBIT 3**

Total Factory Labor "Efficiency" and "Productivity"

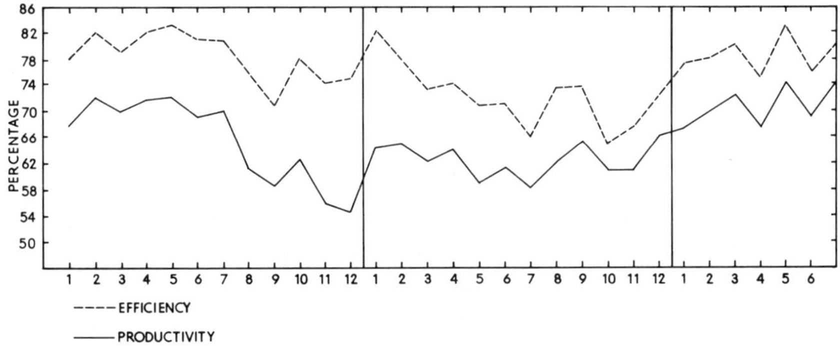

```
----EFFICIENCY
——— PRODUCTIVITY
```

productivity and efficiency percentages for the factory by months for the two preceding years. The company percentages followed closely the total factory figures, owing to the fact that of the total company hours available, 75 percent were made up of hours contributed by the factory. Exhibit 4 is a sample of the actual reports that were distributed on a weekly basis to the managers and foremen concerned.

Conrad also secured direct evidence of Mr. Zeigler's concern with the productivity records. At the end of the first quarter of the current year,

[1] Mr. Zeigler was the general manager of manufacturing.

**EXHIBIT 4**

Direct Labor Utilization Report
Total Machine Shop Group
(including the sheet metal and welding shops)

| | | Week Ending | | | | Total Month Ending |
|---|---|---|---|---|---|---|
| | 6/4 | 6/11 | 6/12 | 6/25 | 7/2 | 7/2 |
| 1. Total hrs. available............565 | 565 | 892 | 946 | 800 | 812 | 4015 |
| 2. Hrs. used on indirect labor....... 59 | 59 | 86 | 85 | 90 | 89 | 409 |
| 3. Hrs. available for direct labor.....506 | 506 | 806 | 861 | 710 | 723 | 3606 |
| 4. Hrs. direct labor on nonrated jobs.. 8 | 8 | 26 | 37 | 44 | 17 | 132 |
| 5. Hrs. variance................... 18 | 18 | 19 | 13 | 16 | 5 | 71 |
| 6. Hrs. direct labor on rated jobs.....480 | 480 | 761 | 811 | 650 | 701 | 3403 |
| 7. Std. hrs. produced...............303 | 303 | 388 | 508 | 484 | 266 | 1949 |
| 8. % efficiency on rated jobs (std. hrs. produced/hrs. on rated jobs, 7/6).. 63 | 63 | 51 | 63 | 74 | 38 | 57 |
| 9. % total productivity (std. hrs. + non std. hrs./hrs. available 7+4/1). 55 | 55 | 46 | 58 | 66 | 35 | 52 |
| Rework | | | | | | |
| a. Responsible ............. 0 | 0 | 0 | 0 | 0 | 0 | 0 |
| b. Not responsible .......... 18 | 18 | 19 | 13 | 16 | 5 | 71 |

when labor utilization percentages were dropping in successive weeks, Mr. Zeigler sent the following note to his subordinates:

Please write up your suggestions on how we are to salvage this situation. Remember, last month's productivity was only 69 percent. By Tuesday I will expect concrete courses of action from each of you, if you are to meet or beat budget.

Conrad learned that Mr. Zeigler had sent similar notes on other occasions.

Fortified with this information, Conrad went back to observing activities in Assembly Department A.

## THE PUMP EPISODE

On one of his early trips to the assembly department Jack Burton started telling Conrad of a problem he was having:

BURTON:   A little while ago my group leader of the subassembly group brought to my attention a problem concerning this pump unit. He was asking me how we could put them together and be sure they would pass final test. I noticed that there might be a chance of having some brass filings get in the critical parts if we were not careful. My group leader dug up the assembly specs which the engineers had drawn up in order to put this critical subassembly together. It called for cleaning the parts twice so that there would be positive assurance of a positive test. Then the group leader saw that the industrial engineers had not allowed enough time for the double cleaning. My group leader actually timed how long it took him to make the double cleaning, and it was considerably over the allotted time. I had the group leader figure the correct amount it would take so that we could resubmit it and get the actual time that we were spending on this cleaning operation put down.

Later in the afternoon when the case writer was talking to Burton, Phil Fisher, the head of the industrial engineering department, came up and raised the topic of the standard allowed time on the cleaning operation.

FISHER:    What's wrong on this pump assembly operation?

BURTON:    Come over here and look at this. Our cleaning operation on the pump asembly is taking more time than you people have allowed. (Hands him the engineering assembly sheet which describes the dual cleaning operation.)

FISHER:    (After reading the sheet.) I can't understand why they have duplicate cleaning operations on this. I don't think it's needed. Look, they've got 16 operations for this part. Look, the three sections to this assembly procedure show that parts A and C are almost the same thing. They're exactly alike.

BURTON:    I've got to have those chips out of there to get these pumps past final assembly test. We go by the engineering specifications. Look, this is the engineering assembly S. O. P.[2] It says that we should have two cleaning operations.

FISHER:    There's not such a thing as an engineering S. O. P. concerning assembly. I'm going up and see about this. I'm going to see if we can't get one of the duplicate operations for cleaning taken out of the specifications. We've got an ultrasonic cleaner that will do this job perfectly and eliminate one of these operations. That's what we've got the cleaner for anyway, to do jobs like this. This is ridiculous having so many operations. We'll be spending more time cleaning it than it takes to make it. How are we going to make any money doing this? (Fisher leaves the room.)

BURTON:    (To case writer.) He's worried about the cost of this—claiming that we will never be able to make a profit on the product if we have to have so many operations. Look at him worried about something like this. That's the chief engineer's job. The chief engineer is the one to worry about whether or not we can make a profit using so many operations with such designs. It's up to the chief engineer to determine whether we can sell a product and make a profit. It's not up to Phil Fisher.

Jack Burton leaves the room and and the case writer talks to Phil Fisher, who is coming into Burton's office as the latter leaves.

FISHER:    Boy, I just can't understand it. If I were to have seen that specification sheet with that many operations on it, I would have blown my top. Some

---

2 Standard Operating Procedure.

engineer started on this and because he didn't know what he was doing, he just kept applying more operations on operations. I know that if I were a foreman, I wouldn't allow that specification to come into my department without saying anything about it. How is the company going to make any money anyway? (Jack Burton comes back into his office.)

FISHER:    I want to try and clean a couple of pumps, using just one operation. I've got an idea how we can cut this down.

BURTON:    Oh no you're not. I want to first check and see what final test has to say about the ones we've already done using two cleaning operations. I'm not going to have you trying to clean them with only one operation when maybe they aren't getting a positive test with two. (Burton goes out and talks to the final test engineer and returns.)

BURTON:    (To Fisher.) The test engineer said that the one we cleaned using the double operation didn't test positively. I'm not going to have you try to make a single operation out of it when we can't even get it with a double. I'm way behind on rework anyway and I can't afford the time messing around with it.

A little later on in the afternoon the case writer had a chance to talk to Jack Burton further about the pump-cleaning incident.

BURTON:    You know what Phil Fisher tried to do? He got my group leader behind my back and asked him to make up two complete units so he could try to test them, using only one cleaning operation. My group leader said definitely no. I'd already warned the group leader of what Phil might do and I told him not to play his game. It's this kind of thing that he does behind my back that really makes me mad. This is no isolated incident. This happens every day around here with him. He's always going off on a different set of directions. He tells me every once in a while that I'm not cooperating with him. I don't know why I have to keep shuffling my people around to try out his ideas when I am so far behind on my work. If they want to test some parts and make a better operation, they can do it themselves. They can set it up. I'm not going to have them disrupting my operation.

A little while later Fisher approached Burton.

FISHER:    Hey, Jack. Come on in the test room. I want to show you what we're doing. (The group moves to the test room.) Look, we have a valve on the pump in the ultrasonic cleaner. Using this device, we could eliminate the operation "C" (pointing to the engineering specifications).

BURTON:    I don't care what you do. I just want a final result!

FISHER:    I just wanted to show you what we were doing to keep you up to date. This way we can be sure that the top isn't scarred when we put it in the tester.

BURTON:    (Caustically.) I don't care if there's any scars on the top!

FISHER:    I thought you said it had to pass final test with a good visual inspection?

BURTON:    It's the fingerprints and the filings inside the pump that cause the trouble. I'm not interested in the outward appearance. It goes in a shield anyway.

FISHER:    Oh. It goes in a shield? I didn't know that.

In a later interview with the case writer, Fisher had a chance to explain some of his motives and methods in running the industrial engineering department.

FISHER:   This pump-cleaning operation is the type of thing that Jack Burton should be doing and working on. That's the foreman's job. Jack's a good man but he doesn't have enough work to do. When Burton and I get together, it's rather rough between us. He's firm in his opinion and I'm firm in mine.

I guess some people consider me the most hated man in the firm, but I'm rather proud of that position if we can get out of our present rut. I just don't have enough men in the industrial engineering department to do any real big work so I have to rely on the foremen doing the job. What I have to do is create a big stink or something so that we get some reaction from these people. We raise the commotion in the department and let the foremen take over and do the improvements from there. I think we're on the verge of a breakthrough here if we can get these foremen up using a stop watch and watching these people and seeing if they're using the correct procedures. Why, on this pump-cleaning operation—sure, we're spending. We've got two of our men spending two hours of their time this afternoon in order that we can save a half hour when we finally go to assembly. But if this works out we'll save the company a lot of money. You've got to spend a dollar in order to make three.

Later, Jack Burton told the case writer some of his views on Philip Fisher.

BURTON:   Phil Fisher isn't held in very high esteem because when he came in to the company a little less than a year ago he had too much initiative and tried to do too many things. He got so many projects going that he hasn't had time to finish them up.

I really don't know what the industrial engineers do. It's all I can do to compose myself when I have to talk about them. I get so mad when I think about all their activities. Fisher has them doing so many projects that they don't have time to do the things that they're really supposed to be doing. Take, for instance, the harness board that I showed you earlier this morning. They're supposed to be making those up for us. The boards take about four hours to make up so that we can begin assembly. We're having to make up our own boards, eight hours of nonproductive time that we get charged with. The last run-through, we had to clear the boards that we already made several weeks before. It took one hour to clear them and then four hours of nonproductive time to build new ones. This is the type of job that they should be doing. They should be working on giving us better standards, too. The standards are way off because they are based on methods that haven't been worked out yet. That makes the productivity report an unfair basis for measuring our work. That's my big gripe with industrial engineering.

## FINAL ASSEMBLY SHUTDOWN

When William Conrad arrived at the plant on the following day, he found that the main final assembly line had been temporarily shut down.

This was necessary because production scheduling was unable to supply some front plates that were essential. The required plates had just been started into the paint shop that morning.

Burton commented

This shutdown is not unusual because we always have this. It's typical. Tom Thompson[3] works his production schedule from a predicted percentage of productivity figure that Zeigler gives him. I don't know where they get the figure. I know that recently they were talking about an 85 percent productivity. I don't know where they got that. I think it was something about fixing up the line so it would be more efficient, but it certainly has never reached that level of productivity. That 85 percent figure means Purchasing has to hurry up and buy some more parts and materials. Then someone gets blamed for high inventories and it swings way over the other way.

## THE MACHINE SHOP

Knowing that Sam Coates was also particularly concerned about the machine shop, Conrad decided to spend a few days observing this department and it's foreman, Albert Ricardi.

In one of their early conversations Ricardi explained,

When I took over this shop last year it was rapidly moving backwards. I took over and started instituting some changes. We've made some real progress, but it doesn't show in the figures. Accounting has been cutting us into bits. The standards being used are not real standards. They're guesses—pulled out of the air. Then we get hit with the productivity report and we're bums. All they're interested in is making us look bad. I have to spend about 97 percent of my time just coddling all the people who come down here from other departments.

The case writer came in early the following Monday morning and was present when Tom Thompson, the production control supervisor for the manufacturing division, came into Ricardi's office.

THOMPSON:    Al, we really need this job. There's only one operation left on it and it has to be done. Al, I know you're in a bind, but we need this by today. Is there anything you can do?

RICARDI:    We're really shorthanded today. Well, I could see what we could do about putting it in the process.

THOMPSON:    I've talked to Brown over in the model shop and he said he could do it for me, that is, if it's all right with you.

RICARDI:    No. We don't get any credit on it that way. We've started the job and I want to finish it.

THOMPSON:    Well, Al, I understand how you feel about it and I know it will disrupt your operation.

RICARDI:    Well, we'll see what we can do about it, but I'm not guaranteeing anything. Maybe we can get it out this afternoon. (Thompson leaves.)

---

[3] Production control manager.

CONRAD:    Well, Al, how do you feel on this blue Monday?

RICARDI:    Not so good. All my good workers and good machinists are out and I don't know what I'm going to do. My inspector is out and I'm really going to be running around like a chicken with his head cut off. I guess when your luck runs out, it really goes all at once. Saturday we were running around and found that the drill press operator had drilled the counterbore shallow on those plates we were doing. We had to run 84 of those pieces over again. You don't have to be a machinist to see that the men around here leave a lot to be desired. And then there's Tom Thompson coming down here. If they would leave us alone we would get ahead and get something running and we wouldn't have all these rush jobs. Every time they send in and ask us to do something of a rush nature, that cuts out our general efficiency and we just can't get ahead. That's why I ignored Thompson. When the men quit a job in the middle of it, they get confused or forget and make mistakes. It takes them time to get started again. Here's Thompson asking me to do a rush job. I just can't afford to do it.

## SCHEDULING PROBLEMS

Several days later Conrad was walking through the shop with Ricardi when he commented on a pile of finished parts.

CONRAD:    These castings really look nice, Al. I think Archie did a pretty good job on them.

RICARDI:    Yes, they look nice all right, there is no doubt about that. But we have another lot of 50 more coming along right now. I just got the order in today.

CONRAD:    What? I thought Archie just finished up this lot.

RICARDI:    Yes, I know. They should all have been done at the same time. If we had had the order of 50 that we got today, it would have been a complete gift. As it is now we will have to set up the machines again and run the whole batch through. They really don't know how much it is costing them. That's what's wrong with this company. They are afraid to ask how much something costs. When someone asks them or they try to price a product they use the standard hours, but the standards hours aren't near what we actually spend on making the product. They don't allow us any time for setups or making fixtures or for any unforeseen events. Those are the main times that are involved. I asked the accounting department one day how much it really cost to make a product and they gave me the computations from the standard hours; I told them that they were no good. They were left without any answer.

## MACHINE SHOP AND PRODUCTION CONTROL

In the course of a number of conversations with Sam Coates, Conrad learned that Coates was well aware of the same signs of trouble in the Assembly Department and the Machine Shop that Conrad had seen. For instance, Coates told Conrad of a recent talk he had had with Ricardi.

COATES:    Just today I happened to mention the production control group to Ricardi and he about exploded. He started pacing up and down. He said that

Carl Canap, the assistant production control manager, was personally out for him. I was shocked by the vehemence. When he calmed down I asked him, "Al, what have I been saying to you!" He stopped. "You are running the shop, not Sam Coates or Larry Zeigler or Production Control. Now why do you feel threatened? Don't you realize that you have forgotten more machine shop operations and the scheduling of machine shop work than Carl Canap will ever learn?" I told him that he had to assert himself in a positive way. I told him that he was running the shop and no one else.

Mr. Coates told the case writer that since this conversation he was attempting to remedy the conflict between Ricardi and Carl Canap by having the latter's boss, Tom Thompson, temporarily work with Ricardi instead of Mr. Canap. Sam continued, "If Tom can charm Al so that they work well together, then, later, when Al deals with Canap, he'll let all the little things that have been bothering him go by. Just for Al to be with Thompson will help out a lot in smoothing over the relationship between Al and Carl."

In the morning of the day following the Ricardi-Coates conversation Conrad observed Tom Thompson talking to Ricardi about scheduling problems and procedures. Carl Canap had not made an appearance. Later in the day Coates and Ricardi were sitting in the former's office, when Ricardi's assistant came in and stated that Carl Canap had just requested that the machine shop stop production of an item that was only partially completed and substitute a "rush job" which used the same machine. Ricardi immediately commented to Coates.

RICARDI:    See, Sam, this is the type of thing that I have been talking about. We lose all our efficiency by breaking down in the middle of an operation.

COATES:    Al, what have I been telling you for the last week and a half? You don't stop an order in the middle of production. You clear out the job before you start another.

RICARDI:    (After a long pause.) What do I do?

COATES:    Al, you're the foreman, not Carl Canap. You're the foreman of this shop, not anyone else.

RICARDI:    (Turning to face the assistant.) Don't do anything.

Approximately 15 minutes later Coates and Ricardi were interrupted in their conversation by Carl Canap, who burst through the doorway and with an angered tone of voice questioned Mr. Coates.

CANAP:    Sam, I understand you and Al won't allow that rush job to be substituted. Is that true?

COATES:    Don't look at me, Carl. Al is the foreman of this outfit, you talk to him.

CANAP:    What about that, Al?

RICARDI:    (Pause.) That's right.

CANAP:    Do you realize you are hurting the company, losing sales, losing money? What is this company coming to if we can't rearrange the schedule a little just because somebody wants to get a little extra credit on the weekly report. Do you realize what this means?

COATES:    (Angrily.) Listen here, Carl, Al is right. We're not going to switch and henceforth you'll not be stopping production in the middle of any operation. This is my decision and I want you to stick by it.

CANAP:    (Walking out of the office.) If that's the way you want it, that's the way it will be.

## SAM COATES' VIEWS

Some few days later Sam Coates was talking to the case writer about the general situation:

COATES:    Higher management has become so concerned with the figures that they forget about what we're actually producing, what's finished and what's good quality. The figures get divorced from what they stand for. But if you're going to have the system, you have to play along with it. I'm sure there are a lot of details about the figures that my foremen and particularly Al are overlooking. In fact, I think he's making himself look poor. His desk is in such a disarray and things come so fast that he just gives up and says, "Oh, to hell with it!" Al has got to learn that he can't work on a bunch of long and hard jobs at the same time and expect to get a good productivity rating. He's got to get his work finished up by Saturday so he can get credit for it. He's not making the most of what he's got down there.

# Empire Glass Company (A)

IN THE FALL of 1963, Peter Small of the Harvard Business School undertook to write case material dealing with the budgetary control system of the Empire Glass Company, a Canadian manufacturing company with a number of plants located throughout Canada. In particular, Peter Small was interested in how Mr. James Walker, the corporate controller, perceived the company's budgetary control system. So as to reduce his case research to manageable proportions, Mr. Small focused his research on the budgetary control system as it related to the company's Glass Products division. This division was responsible for manufacturing and selling glass food and beverage bottles.

## ORGANIZATION

Empire Glass Company was a diversified company organized into several major product divisions, one of which was the Glass Products Division. Each division was headed by a divisional vice president who reported directly to the company's executive vice president, Mr. Landon McGregor. Exhibit 1 shows an organization chart of the company's top management group.

Mr. McGregor's corporate staff included three men in the financial area: the controller, the chief accountant, and the treasurer. The controller's department consisted of only two men—Mr. Walker and the assistant controller, Mr. Allen Newell. The market research and labor relations departments also reported in a staff capacity to Mr. McGregor.

All of the product divisions were organized along similar lines. Reporting to each product division vice president were several staff members in the customer service and product research areas. Reporting in a line capacity to each divisional vice president were also a general manager of manufacturing and a general manager of marketing. The general manager of manufacturing was responsible for all of the division's manufacturing activities. Similarly, the general manager of marketing was responsible

**EXHIBIT 1**

Top Management Group

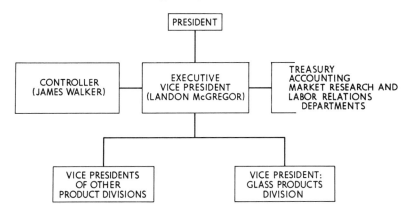

for all of the division's marketing activities. Both of these executives were assisted by a small staff of specialists. Exhibit 2 presents an organization chart of the Glass Products Division's top management group.

All of the corporate and divisional management group were located in British City, Canada.

**EXHIBIT 2**

Glass Products Division Top Management and Staff

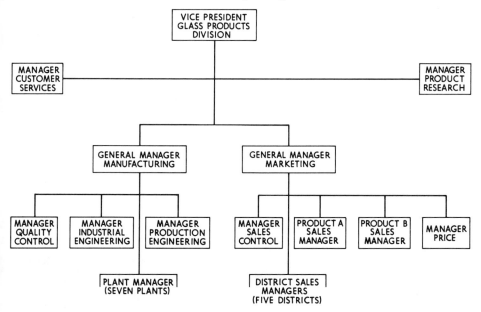

Exhibit 3 shows the typical organization structure of a plant within the Glass Products Division.

**EXHIBIT 3**

Typical Plant Organization—Glass Products Division

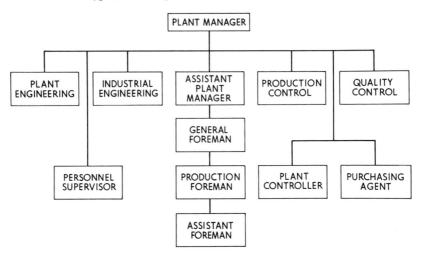

## PRODUCTS AND TECHNOLOGY

The Glass Products Division operated a number of plants in Canada producing glass food and beverage bottles. Of these products, food jars constituted the largest group, including jars for products like tomato catsup, mayonnaise, jams and jellies, honey, and soluble coffee. Milk bottles, beer, and soft drink bottles were also produced in large quantities. A great variety of shapes and sizes of containers for wines, liquors, drugs, cosmetics, and chemicals were produced in smaller quantities.

Most of the thousands of different products, varying in size, shape, color, and decoration were produced to order. According to British City executives the typical lead time between the customer's order and shipment from the plant was between two and three weeks during 1963.

The principal raw materials for container glass were sand, soda ash, and lime. The first step in the manufacturing process was to melt batches of these materials in furnaces or "tanks." The molten mass was then passed into automatic or semiautomatic machines which filled molds with the molten glass and blew the glass into the desired shape. The "ware" then went through an automatic annealing oven or lehr where it was cooled slowly under carefully controlled conditions. If the glass was to be coated on the exterior to increase its resistance to abrasion and scratches, this coating—often a silicone film—was applied in the lehr. Any decorating (such as a trademark or other design) was then added; the product in-inspected again; and the finished goods packed in corrugated containers (or wooden cases for some bottles).

Quality inspection was critical in the manufacturing process. If the "melt" in the furnace was not completely free from bubbles and "stones" (unmelted ingredients or pieces of refractory material), or if the fabricating machinery was slightly out of adjustment, or molds were worn, the rejection rate was very high. Although a number of machines were used in the inspection process, including electric eyes, much of the inspection was still visual.

Although glass making was one of the oldest arts and bottles and jars had been machine-molded at relatively high speeds for over half a century, the Glass Products Division had spent substantial sums each year modernizing its equipment. These improvements had greatly increased the speed of operations and had reduced substantially the visual inspection and manual handling of glassware.

No hand blowing was done in the division's plants and, contrary to the early days of the industry, most of the jobs were relatively unskilled, highly repetitive and gave the worker little control over work methods or pace. The mold makers, who made and repaired the molds, the machine repairmen, and those who made the equipment setup changes between different products were considered to be the highest skilled classes of workers.

Wages were relatively high in the glass industry. However, the rumble of the machinery, the hiss of compressed air in the molding operation, plus the roar of fuel in the furnaces made the plants extremely noisy. Also, the great amount of heat given off by the furnaces and molten glass made working conditions difficult. Production employees belonged to two national unions, and for many years bargaining had been conducted on a national basis. Output standards were established for all jobs, but no bonus was paid to hourly plant workers for exceeding standard.

## MARKETING

Over the years, the sales of the Glass Products divisions had grown at a slightly faster rate than had the total market for glass jars. Until the late 1950's, the division had charged a premium for most of its products, primarily because they were of better quality than competitive products. In recent years, however, the quality of the competitive products had improved to the point where they now matched the division's quality level. In the meantime, the division's competitors had retained their former price structure. Consequently, the Glass Products Division had been forced to lower its prices to meet its competitors' lower market prices. According to one division executive:

Currently, price competition is not severe, particularly among the two or three larger companies that dominate the glass bottle industry. Most of our competition is with respect to product quality and customer service. . . . In fact, our biggest competitive threat is from packages other than glass. . . .

Each of the division's various plants to some extent shipped their products throughout Canada, although transportation costs limited each plant's market primarily to its immediate vicinity. While some of the customers were large and bought in huge quantities, many were relatively small.

## BUDGETARY CONTROL SYSTEM

In the fall of 1963, Peter Small of the Harvard Business School interviewed James Walker, controller, Empire Glass Company. Mr. Walker had been controller for some fifteen years. Excerpts from that interview are reproduced below.

SMALL:    Mr. Walker, what is the overall function of your budgetary control system?

WALKER:    Well, Peter, to understand the role of the budgetary control systems you must first understand our management philosophy. Fundamentally, we have a divisional organization based on broad product categories. These divisional activities are coordinated by the company's executive vice president, with the head office group providing a policy and review function for the company's executive vice president.

Within the broad policy limits we operate on a decentralized basis, with each of the decentralized divisions performing the full management job which normally would be inherent in any independent company. The only exception to this philosophy is that the head office group is solely responsible for the sources of funds and the labor relations with those bargaining units which cross division lines.

Given this form of organization, the budget is the principal management tool used by the head office to coordinate the efforts of the various segments of the company toward a common goal. Certainly, in our case, the budget is much more than a narrow statistical accounting device.

### Sales Budget

Mr. Walker and Mr. Small discussed the preparation of the sales budget. This was the first step in the budget preparation procedure. Excerpts from their discussions follow.

WALKER:    . . . As early as May 15 of the year preceding the budget year, the top management of the company asks the various product division vice presidents to submit preliminary reports stating what they think their division's capital requirements and outlook in terms of sales and income will be during the next budget year. In addition, corporate top management also wants an expression of the division vice presidents' general feelings toward the trends in these particular items over the two years following the upcoming budget year. At this stage head office is not interested in too much detail.

SMALL:    Does the market research group get involved in these forecasts?

WALKER:    No. What we want is an interpretive statement about sales and income based on the operating executives' practical feel for the market.

Since all divisions plan their capital requirements five years in advance and have made predictions of the forthcoming budget year's market when the budget estimates were prepared last year, these rough estimates of next year's conditions and requirements are far from wild guesses.

SMALL:    What happens next?

WALKER:    After the opinions of the divisional vice presidents are in, the market research staff goes to work. They develop a formal statement of the marketing climate in detail for the forthcoming budget year and in general terms for the subsequent two years.

SMALL:    Putting together the sales forecast then is the first step in developing the budget?

WALKER:    Yes. This is an important first step since practically all of the forecasts or estimates used in planning either start with or depend in some way on a sales forecast.

The market research group begins by projecting such factors as: the general economic condition; growth of our various markets; weather conditions related to the end uses of our products; competitive effort; and labor disturbances. Once these general factors have been assessed, a sales forecast for the company and each division is developed. Consideration is given to the relationship of the general economic climate to our customer's needs and Empire's share of each market. Also, basic assumptions as to price, weather conditions, etc., are developed and stated explicitly.

In sales forecasting consideration is given also to the introduction of new products, gains or losses in particular accounts, forward buying, new manufacturing plants, and any changes in our definition of, say, gross sales. The probable impact of such information as the following is also taken into account: industry growth trends; packaging trends; inventory carry-overs; and the development of alternative packages to or from glass. . . .

This review of all the relevant factors is followed for each of our product lines, regardless of its size and importance. . . . The completed forecasts of the market research group are then forwarded to the appropriate divisions for review, criticism and adjustments.

SMALL:    How would you summarize the role of the head office group in developing these sales forecasts?

WALKER:    Well, I suppose our primary goal is to assure uniformity between the divisions with respect to the basic assumptions on business conditions, pricing, and the treatment of possible emergencies. Also, we provide a yardstick so as to assure us that the company's overall sales forecast will be reasonable and attainable.

SMALL:    What happens next?

WALKER:    Next, the product division top management goes back to its district sales managers. Each district sales manager is asked to tell his top management what he expects to do in the way of sales during the budget year. Head office and the divisional staffs will give the district sales managers as much guidance as they request, but it is the sole responsibility of each district sales manager to come up with his particular forecast.

After the district sales managers forecasts are received by the divisional top management, the forecasts are consolidated and reviewed by the division's general manager of marketing. At this time the general manager of marketing may go back to the district sales managers and suggest they revise their budgets. For instance, a situation such as this might arise: We enjoy a very large share of the liquor market. In one year, however, it may be predicted on the basis of the consolidated district sales manager's estimates that we can look forward to a twenty to twenty-five percent increase in sales.

Obviously, this is unreasonable. What has happened is this: Each district sales manager has been told by each of his liquor customers that they expect an increase in sales. When all these anticipated individual sales increases are summed, it looks like the market is going to grow considerably. However, this is not going to happen. What is going to occur is that company A will take sales from company B and company C will take sales from company D, etc. Individually, the district sales managers know little of what's happening outside their territory. However, from the headquarter's point of view, we can ascertain the size of the whole market and the customer's probable relative market share. That's where the market research group's studies come in handy.

Let me emphasize, however, even in this case nothing is changed in the district sales manager's budget, unless the district manager agrees. Then, once the budget is approved, nobody is relieved of his responsibility without top mangement approval. Also, no arbitrary changes are made in the approved budgets without the concurrence of all the people responsible for the budget.

SMALL:    At this point have the plant managers—or the divisional general managers of manufacturing—been involved in the preparation of the sales budget?

WALKER:    Not in a formal way. Informally, of course, the plant managers know what's going on. For example, when a plant manager prepares his capital equipment investment program he is sure to talk to the district sales manager closest to his plant about the district's sales plans.

SMALL:    Sorry I interrupted you. What happens next?

WALKER:    That's all right.

Next, we go through the same process at the division and headquarters levels. We keep on repeating the process until everyone agrees the sales budgets are sound. Then, each level of management takes responsibility for its particular portion of the budget. These sales budgets then become fixed objectives.

SMALL:    Besides coming up with a realistic sales budget, what other objectives do the divisions have in mind when they review the sales forecasts?

WALKER:    I would say they have four general objectives in mind: First, a review of the division's competitive position, including plans for improving that position. Second, an evaluation of its efforts to gain either a larger share of the market or offset competitors' activities. Third, a consideration of the need to expand facilities to improve the division's products or introduce new products. Finally, a review and development of plans to improve product quality, delivery methods, and service.

## Manufacturing Budgets

Next, Walker and Small turned their conversation to the preparation of the manufacturing budgets. According to Mr. Walker, each plant had a fixed profit responsibility.

SMALL:    When are the plant budgets prepared?

WALKER:    Once the vice presidents, executive vice president, and company president have given final approval to the sales budgets, we make a sales budget for each plant by breaking the division sales budgets down according to the plants from which the finished goods will be shipped. These plant sales budgets are then further broken down on a monthly basis by price, volume, and end use. With this information available, the plants then budget their gross profit, fixed expenses, and income before taxes.

SMALL:    How do you define gross profit and income?

WALKER:    Gross profit is the difference between gross sales, less discounts, and variable manufacturing costs—such as direct labor, direct material, and variable manufacturing overheads. Income is the difference between the gross profit and the fixed costs.

SMALL:    Is the principal constraint within which the plants work the sales budget?

WALKER:    That's right. Given his sales budget, it is up to the plant manager to determine the fixed overhead and variable costs—at standard—that he will need to incur so as to meet the demands of the sales budget. . . .

In some companies I know of, the head office gives each plant manager sales and income figures that the plant has to meet. We don't operate that way, however. We believe that type of directive misses the benefit of all the field experience of those at the district sales and plant levels. If we gave a profit figure to our plant managers to meet, how could we say it was their responsibility to meet it?

What we say to the plant manager is this: Assuming that you have to produce this much sales valoume, how much do you expect to spend producing this volume? And what do you expect to spend for your programs allied to obtaining these current and future sales?

SMALL:    Then the plant managers make their own plans?

WALKER:    Yes. In my opinion requiring the plant managers to make their own plans is one of the most valuable things associated with the budget system. . . . Each plant manager divides the preparation of the overall plant budget among his plant's various departments. First, the departments spell out the programs in terms of the physical requirements—such as tons of raw material—and then the plans are priced at standard cost.

SMALL:    What items might some of these departmental budgets include?

WALKER:    Let me tell you about the phase of the budget preparation our industrial engineering people are responsible for. The Plant Industrial Engineering Department is assigned the responsibility for developing engineered cost standards and reduced costs. Consequently, the phase of budget preparation covered by the industrial engineers includes budget standards of performance for each operation, cost center, and department within the plant. This phase of the budget also includes budgeted cost reductions, budgeted unfavorable variances from standards, and certain budgeted programmed fixed costs in the manufacturing area such as service labor. The industrial engineer prepares this phase of the budget in conjunction with departmental line supervision.

SMALL:    Once the plant budgets are completed, are they sent directly to the divisional top management?

WALKER:    No. Before each plant sends its budget into British City, a group of us from head office goes out and visits each plant. For example, in the case of the Glass Products Division, Allen [Newell, assistant controller] and I, along with representatives of the Glass Products Division manufacturing staffs visit each of the division's plants.

Let me stress this point: We do not go on these trips to pass judgment on the plant's proposed budget. Rather, we go with two purposes in mind. First, we wish to acquaint ourselves with the thinking behind the figures that each plant manager will send in to British City. This is helpful because when we come to review these budgets with the top management, that is, the management above our level, we will have to answer questions about the budgets, and we will know the answers. Second, the review is a way of giving guidance to the plant managers as to whether or not they are in line with what the company needs to make in the way of profits.

Of course, when we make our field reviews we do not know what each of the other plants are doing. Therefore, we explain to the plant managers that, while their budget may look good now, when we put all the plants together in a consolidated budget, the plant managers may have to make some changes because the projected profit is not high enough. When this happens we have to tell the plant managers that it is not their programs that are unsound. The problem is that the company cannot afford the programs. . . .

I think it is very important that each plant manager has a chance to tell his story. Also, it gives them the feeling that we at headquarters are not living in an ivory tower.

SMALL:    How long do these plant visits take?

WALKER:    They are spread over a three-week period and we spend an average of half a day at each plant.

SMALL:    I gather the role of the head office and divisional staff is to recommend, not decide. That's the plant manager's right.

WALKER:    Correct.

SMALL:    Who on the plant staff attends these meetings?

WALKER:    The plant manager is free to bring in any of his supervisors he wishes. We asked him not to bring in anybody below the supervisory level. Then, of course, you get into organized labor.

SMALL:    What do you do on these plant visits?

WALKER:    During the half day we spend at each plant we discuss the budget primarily. However, if I have time, I like to wander through the plant and see how things are going. Also, I go over in great detail the property replacement and maintenance budget with the plant engineer.

SMALL:    After you have completed the plant tours, do the plant budgets go to the respective division top management?

WALKER:    That's right. About September 1, the plant budgets come into

British City and the accounting department consolidates them. Then the product division vice presidents review their respective divisional budgets to see if the division budget is reasonable in terms of what the vice president thinks the corporate top management wants. If he is not satisfied with the consolidated plant budgets, he will ask the various plants within the division to trim their budget figures.

When the division vice presidents and the executive vice president are happy, they will send their budgets to the company president. He may accept the division budgets at this point. If he doesn't, he will specify the areas to be reexamined by division; and, if necessary, plant management. . . .

The final budget is approved at our December Board of Directors meeting.

SMALL:    As I understand it, the district sales managers have a responsibility for sales. . . .

WALKER:    Specifically volume, price, and sales mix. . . .

SMALL:    And the plant manager is responsible for manufacturing costs?

WALKER:    His primary responsibility extends to profits. The budget plant profit is the difference between the fixed sales dollar budget and the budgeted variable costs at standard and the fixed overhead budget. It is the plant manager's responsibility to meet this budgeted profit figure. . . .

SMALL:    Even if actual dollar sales drop below the budgeted level?

WALKER:    Yes.


## Comparison of Actual and Standard Performance

The discussion turned next to the procedures and management philosophy related to the periodic comparison by the head office group of the actual and standard performance of the field organization. In particular, the two men discussed the manufacturing area.

SMALL:    . . . What do you do with the actual results that come into the head office?

WALKER:    We go over them on the basis of exception: that is, we only look at those figures that are in excess of the budgeted amounts. We believe this has a good effect on morale. The plant managers don't have to explain everything they do. They only have to explain where they go off base.

SMALL:    What cost and revenue items are of greatest interest to you?

WALKER:    In particular, we pay close attention to the net sales, gross margin, and the plant's ability to meet its standard manufacturing cost. Incidentally, when analyzing the gross sales, we look closely at the price and mix changes.

All this information is summarized on a form known as the Profit Planning and Control Report #1 (see Exhibit 4). This document is backed up by a number of supporting documents (see Exhibit 5).

SMALL:    When you look at the fixed costs, what are you interested in?

WALKER:    We want to know whether or not the plants carried out the programs that they said they would carry out. If they have not, we want to know why they have not. Here we are looking for sound reasons. Also, we want to know if they have carried out their projected programs at the cost they said they would.

SMALL:    Do you have to wait until you receive the monthly PPCR #1 [Profit

## EXHIBIT 4

### Profit Planning and Control Report #1

| MONTH | | | | | | YEAR TO DATE | | |
|---|---|---|---|---|---|---|---|---|
| Income Gain(+) or Loss(−) From | | ACTUAL | REF. | | | ACTUAL | Income Gain(+) or Loss(−) From | |
| PREV. YEAR | BUDGET | | | | | | BUDGET | PREV. YEAR |
| | | | 1 | GROSS SALES TO CUSTOMERS | | | | |
| | | | 2 | DISCOUNTS & ALLOWANCES | | | | |
| | | | 3 | NET SALES TO CUSTOMERS | | | | |
| % | % | | 4 | % GAIN (+)/LOSS (−) | | | % | % |
| | | | | DOLLAR VOLUME GAIN (+)/LOSS (−) DUE TO: | | | | |
| | | | 5 | SALES PRICE | | | | |
| | | | 6 | SALES VOLUME | | | | |
| | | | 6(a) | TRADE MIX | | | | |
| | | | 7 | VARIABLE COST OF SALES | | | | |
| | | | 8 | PROFIT MARGIN | | | | |
| | | | | PROFIT MARGIN GAIN (+)/LOSS (−) DUE TO: | | | | |
| | | | 9 | PROFIT VOLUME RATIO (P/V) | | | | |
| | | | 10 | DOLLAR VOLUME | | | | |
| % | % | % | 11 | PROFIT VOLUME RATIO (P/V) | | % | % | % |
| | Income Addition (+) | | | | | Income Addition (+) | | |
| | | | 12 | TOTAL FIXED MANUFACTURING COST | | | | |
| | | | 13 | FIXED MANUFACTURING COST − TRANSFERS | | | | |
| | | | 14 | PLANT INCOME (STANDARD) | | | | |
| % | % | % | 15 | % OF NET SALES | | % | % | % |
| | Income Addition (+) Income Reduction (−) | | | | | Income Addition (+) Income Reduction (−) | | |
| % | % | % | 16 | % PERFORMANCE | | % | % | % |
| | | | 17 | MANUFACTURING EFFICIENCY | | | | |
| | Income Addition (+) | | | | | Income Addition (+) | | |
| | | | 18 | METHODS IMPROVEMENTS | | | | |
| | | | 19 | OTHER REVISIONS OF STANDARDS | | | | |
| | | | 20 | MATERIAL PRICE CHANGES | | | | |
| | | | 21 | DIVISION SPECIAL PROJECTS | | | | |
| | | | 22 | COMPANY SPECIAL PROJECTS | | | | |
| | | | 23 | NEW PLANT EXPENSE | | | | |
| | | | 24 | OTHER PLANT EXPENSES | | | | |
| | | | 25 | INCOME ON SECONDS | | | | |
| | | | 26 | | | | | |
| | | | 27 | | | | | |
| | | | 28 | PLANT INCOME (ACTUAL) | | | | |
| % | % | % | 29 | % GAIN (+)/LOSS (−) | | | % | % |
| % | % | % | 30 | % OF NET SALES | | % | % | % |
| | | | 36a | | | | | |
| Increase (+) or Decrease (−) | | | | EMPLOYED CAPITAL | | Increase (+) or Decrease (−) | | |
| | | | 37 | TOTAL EMPLOYED CAPITAL | | | | |
| % | % | % | 38 | % RETURN | | % | % | % |
| | | | 39 | TURNOVER RATE | | | | |

_____     _____     _____ 19____
PLANT                       DIVISION                  MONTH

Exhibit 4 *(continued)*

During his conversation with Mr. James Walker, controller, Empire Glass Company, Mr. Small asked Mr. Walker to describe the various items listed on PPCR #1. Here is an excerpt from their conversation concerning this document:

SMALL:    Would you explain a few of the items listed on PPCR #1?

WALKER:    Certainly. Let's start with Reference 3: "Net Sales to Customers." This is the difference between the gross sales to customers [Ref. 1] and any discounts or allowances [Ref. 2].

The next line "% gain (+)/loss (−)" [Ref. 4], is the increase or decrease in net sales dollars expressed as a percentage of the budget and previous year's actual figures.

Next, we break the cause of the dollar volume gain or loss into its component parts: namely, changes due to sales price, volume, and mix. . . .

"Variable cost of sales" [Ref. 7] includes such items as direct materials, operating labor, and that part of indirect labor that varies in monthly dollar amounts directly with changes in unit production volume. These costs are constant per unit of production. The amount listed in the budget column is the standard cost of the actual production.

Reference 8, "profit margin," is the difference between the total net dollar sales and the total variable manufacturing costs of products sold.

Next, we identify further the causes of the change in profit margin. . . .

The item, Reference 9, "profit margin gain (+)/loss (−) due to: profit volume ratio (P/V)," is that portion of the profit margin gain or loss resulting from changes in the relationship between the net selling price and the standard variable manufacturing costs of the products sold to customers. This relationship, expressed as a percentage, is known as the "P/V ratio" (see Ref. 11).

The "profit margin gain (+)/loss (−) due to: dollar volume" [Ref. 10] is that portion of the profit margin or loss resulting from the changes in dollar volume of net sales to customers, exclusive of changes in P/V. It is the algebraic difference between the profit margin and Reference 9. . . .

We keep a close check on the P/V ratio because it shows us how much we are making over our variable costs. . . . Of course, volume changes alone never affect the P/V ratio.

"Total fixed manufacturing costs," [Ref. 12], are the costs that should remain unchanged irrespective of fluctuation in volume during the year. Included in this category are depreciation, rent, general insurance, general taxes, and most supervision costs. Fixed costs are calculated on an annual basis, and each monthly figure is shown as one-twelfth of the annual total.

The next item, "fixed manufacturing cost-transfers" [Ref. 13], doesn't apply to the Glass Products Division as they have very little intra or interdivision transfers.

Therefore, in the case of the Glass Products Division, Reference 14, "plant income (standard)" is the difference between profit margin dollars [Ref. 8] and total fixed manufacturing costs [Ref. 12].

In the "actual" column of Reference 16, "% performance," we enter the difference between the standard and actual manufacturing cost expressed as a percentage of standard.

In the "gain/loss" columns for this same item, we enter the difference in percentage points between current performance and budget, and between the current performance and previous year.

In the "actual" column of Reference 17, "manufacturing efficiency," we put the difference between standard and actual manufacturing dollar costs.

In the "gain/loss" columns of Reference 17, we enter the increase or decrease in income resulting from changes in manufacturing efficiency dollar savings or excesses.

References 18 through 25 are self-explanatory. In addition to cost savings or excesses resulting from efficiency, special conditions may arise to cause other departures from standard cost. These additional differences are classified according to cause and the more significant ones are shown individually on separate lines in this portion of PPCR #1.

Reference 28, "plant income (actual)" is the income remaining after adjusting Ref-

## Exhibit 4 *(continued)*

erence 14 for all the departures from standard manufacturing listed on References 18 through 25, inclusive.

"Total employed capital" [Ref. 37] is the value of employed capital at the end of the month, and average for the year to date. At the plant level employed capital consists of inventories [mostly work-in-process and finished goods] valued at their standard direct costs plus the replacement value of fixed assets. At the division level accounts receivable are included in employed capital.

SMALL:    How do you calculate the replacement value of fixed assets?

WALKER:    We have formulas that give us the current cost of equipment capable of doing the same job as the installed equipment.

SMALL:    Why do you use replacement costs?

WALKER:    We have two basic reasons. First, within a single division it places all plants on an equal footing from the standpoint of measuring return, since it eliminates distortions arising from the use of widely disparate acquistion costs for similar equipment.

Second, it eliminates distortions arising from the use of unrecovered costs which, even though based on comparable replacement values, are heavily influenced by cumulative depreciation charges that vary widely depending upon the length of time a given facility has been in use.

SMALL:    What about the rest of the items on PPCR #1?

WALKER:    Reference 38 is "plant income (actual)" dollars expressed as a percentage of "employed capital."

Reference 39 is the net sales dollars divided by employed capital and expressed as a multiple of employed capital.

SMALL:    What are the three most important items on PPCR #1?

WALKER:    The P/V ratio, "plant income (actual)" and "% return (employed capital)."

SMALL:    Are the budgets prepared on forms similar to the PPCR series?

WALKER:    Yes. The only major difference is that the budget forms include columns for recording the current year's budget figures, and previous years' actual figures. In addition, variances are shown between the proposed budget figures and the current year's estimated actuals* and the previous years' actual figures. . . .

---

* Actual-to-date plus estimated costs for the remainder of the year.

## EXHIBIT 5

Brief Description of PPCR #2—PPCR #11

(individual plant reports)

| Report | Description |
|---|---|
| PPCR #2 | *Manufacturing Expense:* Plant materials, labor and variable overhead consumed. Detail of actual figures compared with budget and previous years' figures for year-to-date and current month. |
| PPCR #3 | *Plant Expense:* Plant fixed expenses incurred. Details of actual figures compared with budget and previous years' figures for year-to-date and current month. |
| PPCR #4 | *Analysis of Sales and Income:* Plant operating gains and losses due to changes in sales revenue, profit margins, and other sources of income. Details of actual figures compared with budget and previous years' figures for year-to-date and current month. |

**Exhibit 5** *(continued)*

| Report | Description |
|---|---|
| PPCR #5 | *Plant Control Statement:* Analysis of plant raw material gains and losses, spoilage costs, and cost reductions programs. Actual figures compared with budget figures for current month and year-to-date. |
| PPCR #6 | *Comparison of Sales by Plant and Product Groups:* Plant sales dollars, profit margin, and P/V ratios broken down by end product use (i.e., soft drinks, beer, etc.). Compares actual figures with budgeted figures for year-to-date and current month. |

(division summary reports)

| Report | Description |
|---|---|
| PPCR #7 | *Comparative Plant Performance, Sales and Income:* Gross sales and income figures by plants. Actual figures compared with budget figures for year-to-date and current month. |
| PPCR #8 | *Comparative Plant Performance, Total Plant Expenses:* Profit margin, total fixed costs, manufacturing efficiency, other plant expenses, and P/V ratios by plants. Actual figures compared with budgeted and previous year figures for current month and year-to-date. |
| PPCR #9 | *Manufacturing Efficiency:* Analysis of gains and losses by plant in areas of materials, spoilage, supplies, and labor. Current month and year-to-date actuals reported in total dollars and as a percentage of budget. |
| PPCR #10 | *Inventory:* Comparison of actual and budget inventory figures by major inventory accounts and plants. |
| PPCR #11 | *Status of Capital Expenditures:* Analysis of the status of capital expenditures by plants, months, and relative to budget. |

Planning and Control Report #1] before you know how well the various plants performed during the month?

WALKER: No. At the end of the sixth business day after the close of the month, each plant wires to the head office certain operating variances, which we put together on what we call the variance analysis sheet (see Exhibit 6). Within a half hour after the last plant report comes through, variance analysis sheets for the divisions and plants are compiled. On the morning of the seventh business day after the end of the month, these reports are usually on the desks of the interested top management.

The variance analysis sheet highlights the variances in what we consider to be critical areas. . . . Receiving this report as soon as we do helps us at head office to take timely action. Let me emphasize, however, we do not accept the excuse that the plant manager has to go to the end of the month to know what happened during the month. He has to be on top of these particular items daily.

SMALL: Is there any way head office can detect an adverse trend in operations before you receive the monthly variance analysis sheet?

# EXHIBIT 6

Variances from Budget Sheet

| LINE NO. | ADJUSTED INCOME BY VOLUME | ACTUAL INCOME | DIVISION EXPENSES | PRICE CHANGES | WAGE CHGS | INCOME FROM SECONDS | OTHER OPERATING GAINS & LOSSES | COST REDUCTION | MFG. EFFICIENCY | OTHER FIXED COST | CONTROL-LABLE PLANT FIXED COST | DEPRECIA-TION-RENT INSURANCE & TAXES | OVERHAUL & REPAIR | UTILITIES | OUTSIDE WAREHOUSE | EMPLOYEE BENEFITS | OVERTIME | LABOR | MFG. COST | SALES PRICE | GROSS SALES | BUDGET INCOME | | LINE NO. |
|---|---|---|---|---|---|---|---|---|---|---|---|---|---|---|---|---|---|---|---|---|---|---|---|---|
| 1 | | | | | | | | | | | | | | | | | | | | | | | | 1 |
| 2 | | | | | | | | | | | | | | | | | | | | | | | | 2 |
| 3 | | | | | | | | | | | | | | | | | | | | | | | | 3 |
| 4 | | | | | | | | | | | | | | | | | | | | | | | | 4 |
| 5 | | | | | | | | | | | | | | | | | | | | | | | | 5 |
| 6 | | | | | | | | | | | | | | | | | | | | | | | | 6 |
| 7 | | | | | | | | | | | | | | | | | | | | | | | | 7 |
| 8 | | | | | | | | | | | | | | | | | | | | | | | | 8 |
| 9 | | | | | | | | | | | | | | | | | | | | | | | | 9 |
| 10 | | | | | | | | | | | | | | | | | | | | | | | | 10 |
| 11 | | | | | | | | | | | | | | | | | | | | | | | | 11 |
| 12 | | | | | | | | | | | | | | | | | | | | | | | | 12 |
| 13 | | | | | | | | | | | | | | | | | | | | | | | | 13 |
| 14 | | | | | | | | | | | | | | | | | | | | | | | | 14 |
| 15 | | | | | | | | | | | | | | | | | | | | | | | | 15 |
| 16 | | | | | | | | | | | | | | | | | | | | | | | | 16 |
| 17 | | | | | | | | | | | | | | | | | | | | | | | | 17 |
| 18 | | | | | | | | | | | | | | | | | | | | | | | | 18 |
| 19 | | | | | | | | | | | | | | | | | | | | | | | | 19 |
| 20 | | | | | | | | | | | | | | | | | | | | | | | | 20 |
| 21 | | | | | | | | | | | | | | | | | | | | | | | | 21 |
| 22 | | | | | | | | | | | | | | | | | | | | | | | | 22 |
| 23 | | | | | | | | | | | | | | | | | | | | | | | | 23 |
| 24 | | | | | | | | | | | | | | | | | | | | | | | | 24 |
| 25 | | | | | | | | | | | | | | | | | | | | | | | | 25 |
| 26 | | | | | | | | | | | | | | | | | | | | | | | | 26 |
| 27 | | | | | | | | | | | | | | | | | | | | | | | | 27 |
| 28 | | | | | | | | | | | | | | | | | | | | | | | | 28 |
| 29 | | | | | | | | | | | | | | | | | | | | | | | | 29 |
| 30 | | | | | | | | | | | | | | | | | | | | | | | | 30 |
| 31 | | | | | | | | | | | | | | | | | | | | | | | | 31 |
| 32 | | | | | | | | | | | | | | | | | | | | | | | | 32 |
| 33 | | | | | | | | | | | | | | | | | | | | | | | | 33 |
| 34 | | | | | | | | | | | | | | | | | | | | | | | | 34 |
| 35 | | | | | | | | | | | | | | | | | | | | | | | | 35 |

◄——————— VARIOUS DIVISIONS AND PLANTS LISTED ———————►

WALKER:    Yes. At the beginning of each month, the plant managers prepare current estimates for the upcoming month and quarter on forms similar to the variance analysis sheets. Since our budget is based on known programs, the value of this current estimate is that it gets the plant people to look at their programs. Hopefully, they will realize that they can not run their plants on a day-to-day basis.

If we see a sore spot coming up, or if the plant manager draws our attention to a potential trouble area, we may ask for daily reports concerning this item to be sent to the particular division top management involved. In addition, the division top management may send a division staff specialist—say, a quality control expert if it is a quality problem—to the plant concerned. The division staff members can make recommendations, but it is up to the plant manager to accept or reject these recommendations. Of course, it is well known throughout the company that we expect the plant managers to accept gracefully the help of the head office and division staffs.

SMALL:    I think I forgot to ask you this question. When is the monthly PPCR #1 received at British City?

WALKER:    The plant PPCR #1 and the month-end trial balance showing both actual and budget figures are received in British City at the close of the eighth business day after the end of the month. These two very important reports, along with the supporting reports [PPCR #2—PPCR #11] are then consolidated by the accounting department on PPCR type forms to show the results of operations by division and company. The consolidated reports are distributed the next day.

## Sales–Manufacturing Relations

Mr. Small was curious about the relationship between the sales and manufacturing groups, particularly at the plant level. Also, he wished to know what changes were made in plant budgets when actual sales fell below budgeted sales. The following conversation concerns these two topics:

SMALL:    If, during the year, the actual sales volume is less than the budgeted sales volume, what changes do you make in the plant budgets?

WALKER:    This is one of the biggest risks we run with our budget system. If the sales decline occurs during the early part of the year, and if the plant managers can convince us that the change is permanent, we may revise the plant budgets to reflect these new circumstances.

However, if toward the end of the year the actual sales volume suddenly drops below the predicted sales volume, we don't have much time to change the budget plans. What we do is ask the plant managers to go back over their budget with their staffs and see where reduction of expense programs will do the least harm. Specifically, we ask them to consider what they may be able to eliminate this year or delay until next year. . . .

I believe it was Confucius who said: "We make plans so we have plans to discard." Nevertheless, I believe it is wise to make plans, even if you have to discard them. Having plans makes it a lot easier to figure out what to do when sales fall off from the budgeted level. The understanding of operations that comes from preparing the budget takes a lot of the potential chaos and confusion that might arise if we were under pressure to meet a stated profit goal and sales decline quickly and unexpectedly at year-end; just as they did this year.

Under these circumstances, we don't try to ram anything down the plant managers' throats. We ask them to tell us where they can reasonably expect to cut costs below the budgeted level. . . .

SMALL:    What happens when a plant manager's costs are adversely affected by the sales group's insisting that a production schedule be changed so as to get out an unexpected rush order?

WALKER:    As far as we are concerned, the customer's wants are primary— our company is a case where sales wags the rest of the dog.

Whenever a problem arises at a plant between sales and production, the local people are supposed to solve the problem themselves. Let's take your example, a customer's purchasing agent insists he wants an immediate delivery and this delivery will disrupt the production department's plans. The production group can make recommendations as to alternative ways to take care of the problem, but it's the sales manager's responsibility to get the product to the customer. The salesmen are supposed to know their customers well enough to judge whether or not the customer really needs the product. If the sales manager says the customer needs the product, that ends the matter.

Of course, if the change in the sales program involves a major expense at the plant which is out of line with the budget, then the matter is passed up to division for decision.

As I said earlier, the sales department has the sole responsibility for the product price, sales mix, and delivery schedules. They do not have direct responsibility for plant operations or profit. That's the plant management's responsibility. However, it is understood that sales group will cooperate with the plant people whenever possible.

SMALL:    I guess cooperation is very important to the success of your system.

WALKER:    Definitely. We believe the whole budgetary control system works best if we can get cooperation. But within the framework of cooperation the sales and production groups have very clear responsibilities.

## Motivation

Walker and Small also discussed how the plant personnel were motivated to achieve the plant's budgeted profit objective.

SMALL:    How do you motivate the plant managers to meet their profits goals?

WALKER:    Well, first of all, we only promote capable people. Also, a monetary incentive program has been established that stimulates their efforts to achieve their profit goal.

SMALL:    What other incentive devices do you use?

WALKER:    Each month we put together a bar chart which shows, by division and plant, the ranking of the various manufacturing units with respect to manufacturing efficiency.[1]

---

[1] Manufacturing efficiency $= \dfrac{\text{total standard variable manufacturing costs}}{\text{total actual variable manufacturing costs}} \times 100\%.$

We feel the plant managers are one hundred percent responsible for variable manufacturing costs. . . . I believe this is true since all manufacturing standards have to be approved by plant managers.

Most of the plant managers give wide publicity to these bar charts. . . . The efficiency bar chart and efficiency measure itself is perhaps a little unfair in some respects when you are comparing one plant with another. Different kinds of products are run through different plants. These require different setups, etc., which have an important impact on a position of the plant. However, in general, the efficiency rating is a good indication of the quality of the plant manager and his supervisory staff. Also, a number of plants run competitions within their plants which reward department heads, or foremen, based on their relative standing with respect to a certain cost item (see Exhibit 7). The plant managers, their staffs and employees, have great pride in their plants. . . .

### EXHIBIT 7

Plant Display Reporting Winners of "Housekeeping Contest"

SMALL:    While I waited to see you this morning, I read some of the company publications for employees. They all seemed to stress profits and product quality (see Exhibit 8).

WALKER:    That's true. In my opinion, the number one item now stressed at the plant level is *quality*. The market situation is such that in order to make sales you have to meet the market price and exceed the market quality. By "quality" I mean not only the physical characteristics of the product but also such things as delivery schedules.

## EXHIBIT 8

Excerpt from Employee Magazine

As I read the company employee publications, their message is that if the company is to be profitable it must produce high quality items at a reasonable cost. This is necessary so that the plants can meet their obligation to produce the maximum profits for the company under the circumstances prevailing. . . .

SMALL:   . . . Do you analyze the sales reports?

WALKER:   No. It is the sales group's responsibility to comment on the sales activity. They prepare their own reports. They also control their selling costs against budgets prepared by the sales managers.

Initial sales statistics are developed from plant billings summarized by end use and are available on the third business day after month end. Detailed sales statistics by end use and customer indicating actual and variance to both budget and prior year are prepared by Data Processing at British City and available on the eighth business day after month end. . . . Sales and price and mix variances by plant and end use can be obtained from PPCR #1, PPCR #4, and PPCR #6.

## The Future:

SMALL:   . . . Mr. Walker, do you intend to make any changes in your budgetary control system?

WALKER:   An essential part of the budgetary control system is planning. We have developed a philosophy that we must begin our plans where the work is done—in the line organization and out in the field. Perhaps, in the future, we can avoid or cut back some of the budget preparation steps and start putting our sales budget together later on in the year than May 15. However, I doubt if we will change the basic philosophy.

Frankly, I doubt if the line operators would want any major change in the system—they are very jealous of the management prerogatives the system gives to them. . . .

It is very important that we manage the budget. We have to be continually on guard against its managing us. Sometimes, the plants lose sight of this fact. They have to be made conscious daily of the necessity of having the sales volume to make a profit. And, when sales fall off and their plant programs are reduced they do not always appear to see the justification for budget cuts. Although I do suspect that they see more of the justification for these cuts than they will admit. . . . It is this human side of the budget to which we will have to pay more attention in the future.

# Empire Glass Company (B)

IN THE FALL of 1963 a Harvard Business School case researcher visited the glass container plant of Empire Glass Company in French City, Canada. He was interested in studying the way a control system is perceived and used by plant personnel in a multiplant company and how it related to the other parts of the plant conceived as a sociotechnical system. Empire Glass Company had developed, in the years following World War II, a control system for use by its plants which was considered by some accountants to be quite sophisticated. Within its division of Empire, the French City plant was a preferred site for production management trainees because, according to a division training executive:

The French City chaps look at the controls as tools. They show trainees that they really work. The French-Canadian atmosphere is good too. In a French-Canadian family everything is open and aboveboard. There are no secrets. The trainees can ask anyone anything and the friendliness and company parties give him a feel for good employee relations.

Empire Glass Company, in 1963, operated a number of plants in Canada. The principal products of the French City plant were glass jars and bottles.

The French City plant to some extent shipped its products throughout Canada, although transportation costs limited its market primarily to Eastern Canada. While some of the customers were large and bought in huge quantities, many were relatively small.

## THE PLANT ORGANIZATION

### Plant Manager, James Hunt

James Hunt had been manager of the French City plant since January 1961. Prior to that he had been assistant plant manager. He had risen from hourly worker through foreman up to plant manufacturing engineer in the maintenance end of the business. He presented to the researcher the appearance of self-assurance and intimate, firsthand knowledge of operations and events within the plant. He was seldom without a cigar clutched in his teeth, commonly at a rakish upward tilt.

As plant manager, Hunt had no responsibility for sales or research and development activities. In fact, both Hunt and the district sales manager in his area had separate executives to whom they reported in the division headquarters and it was in the superior of these executives that responsibility for both sales and production first came together.

At the case researcher's first meeting with Hunt, he welcomed him to the plant with the comment: "Everything here is open to you. We think we have a pretty good plant here, but we want you to see for yourself."

In response to the researcher's indication of interest in the interrelationships of the people in plant management, Hunt went to a cabinet in his office and from a number of manuals prepared by corporate staff in British City pulled out a large loose-leaf volume labelled "Position Analysis Manual" and handed it to the researcher. There, for each person from assistant foreman to plant manager, he found six to ten pages reproduced from typewritten sheets which described the individuals' responsibilities and duties. Hunt said:

You will see that frequently two managers with different job titles are assigned responsibility for the same task. (He implied that it was up to them to work out their own pattern of mutual support and cooperation.) However, I don't have to adhere strictly to the description. I may end up asking a lot more of the man at certain times and under certain conditions than is ever put down on paper.

In effect, the staff[1] runs the plant. We delegate to the various staff depart-

## EXHIBIT 1

French City Plant
(March 1, 1963)

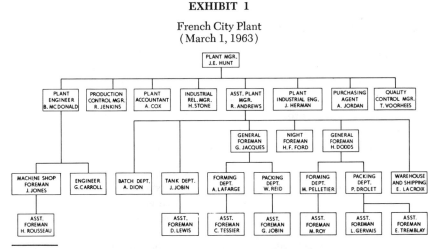

[1] The personnel reporting directly to Hunt. The organization chart (Exhibit 1), which included a photograph of each individual, was widely distributed. An enlarged version, under glass, was mounted on a wall of the lobby at the main entrance where it could be seen by all plant personnel and visitors.

ment heads the authority to implement decisions within the framework of our budget planning. This method of handling responsibility means that staff members have to be prepared to substantiate their decisions. At the same time, it gives them a greater sense of participation in and responsibility for plant income. We endeavor to carry this principle into the operating and service departments. The foreman is given responsibility and encouraged to act as though he were operating a business of his own. He is held responsible for all results generated in his department and is fully aware of how any decisions of his affect plant income.

As our division personnel counsel and assist the plant staff, so do the plant staff counsel and assist the department foreman. Regular visits are made to the plant by our division manager and members of his staff. The principal contact is through the division manager of manufacturing and his staff; the manager of industrial engineering, the manager of production engineering, and the manager of quality control. (There was no division staff officer in production control.)

However, the onus is on the plant to request help or assistance of any kind. We can contact the many resources of Empire Glass Company, usually on an informal basis. That is, we deal with other plant managers directly for information when manufacturing problems exist without going through the division office.

Each member of the staff understands that we, as a plant, have committed ourselves through the budget to provide a stated amount of income, and regardless of conditions which develop, this income figure must be maintained. If sales are off and a continuing trend is anticipated, we will reduce expenses wherever possible to retain income. Conversely, if we have a gain in sales volume we look for the complete conversion of the extra sales at the profit margin rate. However, this is not always possible, especially if the increase in sales comes at a peak time when facilities are already strained.

### Assistant Plant Manager, Robert Andrews

Andrews was something of a contrast to Hunt. He was tall and slender, while Hunt was relatively short with a tendency toward overweight. Andrews talked intently but with a reserve which contrasted with Hunt's ebullience. However Andrews, too, had a ready smile. He thought and moved quickly but without giving off as much visible nervous energy as Hunt. He had been promoted from quality control manager to his present position in January 1961. In talking about his job, Andrews said:

I am responsible for all manufacturing operations within the plant. The operating group reports directly to me and I also stay in constant contact with the staff departments to assume good communication and expedient handling of some items. During the summer months, which is our busiest period, the plant employs about 500 hourly persons. Approximately 250 work on the day shift, 150 on second, and 100 on the third shift. They are supervised by 15 salaried members of the supervisory staff plus a number of working supervisors who are appointed as activity increases. They usually supervise second- and third-shift operations.

Our foremen have full responsibility for running their departments: quality, conditions of equipment, employee relations, production according to schedule, control of inventory through accurate reporting of spoilage and production, and cost control. They are just as accountable for these in their departments as the plant manager is for the entire plant.

We have given the supervisory personnel status. Such things as "the white shirt,"[2] a personal parking spot, an office—these all assist in maintaining his position of authority in the eyes of his employees. He is no longer the best man with the wrench—he is the man with the best overall supervisory qualifications.

## Production Control Manager, Ray Jenkins

Ray Jenkins was slight of build, moved fast and talked fast. Like James Hunt, he was practically a chain smoker, only he smoked cigarettes and a pipe instead of cigars. Jenkins described his job as follows:

The production control manager is basically responsible to plan and control plant inventories and production schedules to meet sales requirements consistent with effective and efficient utilization of facilities, materials, and manpower. Our aim is to attain maximum length of run without affecting service and exceeding inventory budgets.

I have a scheduler for each of the major operating departments, plus clerks to service the schedulers and a schedule coordinator reporting directly to me. The scheduler works very closely with his department foreman. Although their desks are just outside my office, the schedulers spend a good deal of time in the plant.

---

[2] Andrews was referring to a norm that the researcher had already observed while circulating in the plant. The plant manager, the management staff, the foreman, the clerks in the office departments, all wore white shirts with ties but no coat. The union president, who worked at his production job except while handling union affairs, also wore a white shirt but without a tie. The vice president and other production workers wore colored shirts, usually sport shirts.

The force of this practice was observed by the researcher in an exchange between Ray Jenkins, Production Control Manager, and Tom Voorhees, Quality Control Manager, which took place in the main office area of the plant.

JENKINS:    Hey Tom, where are you going? Knocking off for the day? Why are you so dressed up? (Voorhees had on a suit, white shirt, and tie.)

VOORHEES:    No, I've just been in the office all morning. I usually don't stay there so long, but my assistant is kind of a fat fellow and likes the window open so I put my coat on because it was cool. I just kept it on when I ran down here.

JENKINS:    Well, we'll let it pass this time.

RESEARCHER:    I take it this is a coats-off organization?

JENKINS:    Oh, very definitely. I would never think, for example, of wearing my coat out on the floor of the factory. That would be absolutely out of bounds.

RESEARCHER:    Is it just accidental that everyone wears a white shirt, too?

JENKINS:    Oh, no, it's a French City plant practice. You wouldn't last five minutes in here with that shirt (pointing to researcher's striped shirt) if you worked for Empire. You'd probably get a comment before you even got to your desk in the morning.

RESEARCHER:    Is this requirement written down somewhere?

JENKINS:    No, it's just sort of in the air. A new man comes to work here and he gets the message right away—no coat but a white shirt.

They are also in frequent telephone contact with the sales offices at least once a week.

Our high volume food and beverage lines are, generally speaking, manufactured to estimate. We make a monthly manufacturing program which then is converted to a daily schedule. The lower volume lines are scheduled formally on a weekly basis with job priority listing made several times a week by the foreman and the scheduler.

### Plant Accountant, Andrew Cox

This man appeared to be the oldest of the management staff, and rather more serene. Cox talked of his job:

I am responsible directly to the plant manager, but functionally to the division controller. My basic function is to develop and supervise an organization for the maintenance of accounting records and the preparation of reports therefrom in accordance with company policies and procedures. My organization is divided into three groups—general accounting, cost accounting, and office services. A few years ago we developed a stenographic pool in office services and now only the plant manager has a private secretary. Because of the diversity of products, many thousands of individual product costs must be developed and applied by the cost section. The annual proposed sales and income budget, because of its essentially financial nature, is coordinated by the plant controller. However, complete responsibilities for the development of departmental budgets are assigned by the plant manager to the responsible operating and staff groups concerned.

We are the auditors who see that every other department is obeying rules and procedures. It is our responsibility to know all that is in the instruction manuals. There are 12 volumes of general instructions and lots of special manuals.

### Plant Industrial Engineer, Joe Herman

The researcher was impressed with the mobility of Herman's face and the high level of activity which he, as well as most of the other members of the management staff, exhibited. Herman stated:

Industrial engineering in Empire Glass Company is active in the fields of time study, budgetary control, job evaluation, and methods improvement. Our Company is on a standard cost system—that is, all our product costs are based on engineered standards, accurately measuring all labor, direct and indirect, and material that is expended in the manufacture of each and every item we make in our plants. All the jobs in the French City plant, up to and including the foreman, have been measured and standards set. Actually, there are company-wide benchmarks for most jobs, including the foreman's. For foremen the standard is used as a guide in increasing or reducing the supervisory force. If measurement shows that the quantity of supervisory work is less than 75 percent of standard, a foreman is taken off. If the workload is heavy and we find 75 percent of a supervisory job is there, we add a supervisor.

Most of the machinery is just like that in other Empire Glass Company plants. Standards are established wherever the equipment is first used—which may be in the development engineering department in British City. We, of course, may make adjustment for local conditions. However, all our standards are forwarded to division which checks them against standards in use at other plants.

Industrial engineering spearheads the cost reduction program within the organization. In fact, we should spend three-quarters of our time on cost reduction. We have recently made an arrangement with the cost accounting group which is going to eliminate a lot of time this department has been spending in checking to see which standards applied to particular products being manufactured. Now cost accounting will do this work, which is essentially clerical and took time we could otherwise spend on cost reduction work. The budgeted savings this year from methods improvement is in six figures, and we now expect to exceed that by a substantial amount.

### Industrial Relations Manager, Harold Stone

Stone was a large, slow-speaking man who wore a small mustache. He had been with Empire Glass Company a long time and had been assistant plant manager of one of its smaller plants before coming to French City. He was proud of the fact that the French City plant had never experienced a strike and that formal written grievances were almost unheard of.

In discussing company training programs which he conducted at the plant, Stone said that all management personnel, including foremen and assistant foremen, had taken the four-day "Communications Course," designed by the Empire corporate staff but conducted at the plant level, often with personnel from other Empire plants participating. The emphasis was on learning how to listen more effectively to unblock the flow of information up and down in the organization. A four-day course, "Conference Leadership," had been given to some of the management people and others were scheduled for its next repetition. Emphasis in this course was on role playing as a conference participant as well as conference leader.

Stone then commented on some of his other responsibilities. Several of them were represented by an impressive display in the manufacturing area near the main entrance, occupying a space about 50 by 20 feet. During the time the researcher was in the plant, the backdrop contained several panels about 12 or 14 feet high on safety, a housekeeping contest then underway, and on job security and industrial competition. All slogans and other comments were in both French and English. In the open area in front of the backdrop there were smaller displays, including a five-foot chart on an easel which showed the manufacturing efficiency rating (actual production cost vs. standard cost) of the previous month for each of the Empire Glass Company plants, and their standings within their divisions.

Contests between departments were conducted frequently. Prior to the 13-week housekeeping contest, there had been a safety contest. Stone declared that in two of the last five years there had been only one lost time accident. Absenteeism was so low that statistics were no longer kept on it. Turnover was exceptionally low, which he attributed in part to the high wages and fringe benefits of the plant.

Turning to another aspect of Empire's personnel policy, Stone stated:

We believe that it is important that the supervisor and the employee understand each other, that they know what the other person thinks about business, profit, importance of satisfying the customer, and any other aspect of business. While a great deal can be and is done within the regular business framework, we also believe that rapport between the supervisor and the employee can be improved in the social contacts which exist or can be organized. For this reason we sponsor dances, bowling leagues, golf days, fishing derbies, picnics, baseball leagues, supervision parties, management weekends, and many unofficial get-togethers. Over many years we have been convinced that these activities really improve management-labor relations. They also provide a means for union and management to work closely together in organizing and planning these events. These opportunities help provide a mutual respect for the other fellow's point of view.

Some of these events were held in the plant cafeteria, which was another of Stone's responsibilities. The researcher was able to see the elaborate decorations prepared for an employees' children's Christmas party and for a supervisors' party. In addition, all employees, including the plant management, ate their lunches in the plant cafeteria, which was plain and functional except when decorated for a party.

It was Stone's responsibility to maintain the confidential file in connection with Empire's performance appraisal program for salaried employees. Procedures for handling the program were spelled out in one of the corporate manuals. Two forms were completed annually. One called for a rating of the employee by his supervisor, first on his performance of each of his responsibilities outlined in the Position Analysis Manual and then on each of 12 general characteristics such as cooperation, initiative, job knowledge, and delegation. In another section the supervisor and the appraised employee were jointly required to indicate what experience, training, or self-development would improve performance or prepare for advancement by the employee prior to the next appraisal. The appraisal was to be discussed between the supervisor and the employee, the latter was required to sign the form, and space was given for any comments he might want to make. The second form was not shown to the employee. It called for a rating on overall performance, an indication of promotability, and a listing of potential replacements. It was used for manpower planning, and after comments by the supervisor or the appraiser, it was forwarded to the division office.

## MANAGERIAL PRACTICES AND RELATIONSHIPS

After becoming acquainted with most of the key executives at the French City plant and with their major responsibilities, the researcher turned his attention to some of their activities and how they related to each other in performing their duties.

He observed that Hunt and the four staff managers whose offices were closest to his[3] seldom worked alone at their desks. They were either in

### EXHIBIT 2

Information About Certain Personnel

| Name | Position | Approx. Age | Approx. Length of Service | | College Education |
|------|----------|-------------|---------|---------|-------------------|
| | | | French City | EGC | |
| James Hunt | Plant Manager | 40–45 | 8 | 18 | None |
| Robert Andrews | Assistant Plant Manager | 35 | 3 | 8 | Agricultural Engineering |
| Andrew Cox | Plant Accountant | 50 | 15 | 23 | None |
| Ray Jenkins | Production Control Supervisor | 45 | 18 | 18 | None |
| Harold Stone | Personnel Supervisor | 45–50 | 5 | 29 | None |
| Joe Herman | Plant Industrial Engineer | 30–35 | 1 | 10 | Engineering |
| Tom Voorhees | Quality Control Supervisor | 30 | 5 | 5 | Engineering in Netherlands |
| G. E. Jacques | General Foreman | 45–50 | 25 | 25 | None |
| Henry Dodds | General Foreman | 50 | 18 | 18 | None |
| L. G. Adams | District Sales, Gr. | 45–50 | 18 | 18 | None |

the manufacturing area or in each other's offices having impromptu meetings of twos, threes, or fours much of the time. Often a production supervisor or an office staff person would be in the group. The offices of Andrews, Jenkins, Herman, and Cox were identical to each other and similar to Hunt's except they lacked the carpet, drapes, and polished wood furniture he was provided, and the upper part of their partitions were entirely of glass. They all contained a conference table and extra chairs.

In addition to these frequent informal meetings there were a number of regular meetings involving plant management personnel. Most of these were held in a large, well-appointed conference room with a highly polished wooden table seating 20 or more people. The plant manager met monthly with the management staff and also with the production super-

---

[3] See Exhibit 2.

visors to discuss performance against the budget. The plant manager, assistant plant manager, and the industrial relations manager also held a monthly meeting with key union representatives. This was informal and the discussion centered on problems of one of the parties or mutual problems which were not current grievances.

**EXHIBIT 3**

French City Plant
(diagram of office areas)

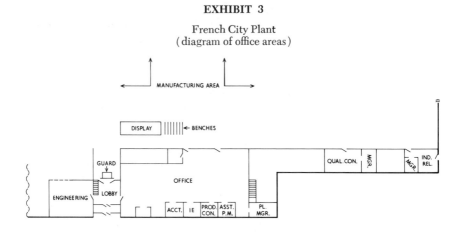

The production control manager chaired a meeting held every Tuesday and Friday morning attended by the assistant plant manager and both general foremen. Each department foreman and his scheduler appeared briefly to discuss scheduling problems. A plant cost reduction committee was chaired by the plant industrial engineer; the plant manager, assistant manager, the plant engineer, the production control manager, and the general foremen were members. There were other committees involving fewer different interests or meeting less frequently.

Later interviews added to the researcher's understanding not only of the management practices but of the attitudes of the key executives toward their jobs and the requirements of the organization.

### James Hunt, Plant Manager

During a discussion of the budget Hunt told the researcher that plant income was the actual sales realization, not a transfer price. Therefore income was adversely affected when either sales failed to come up to the forecast on which the budget was based or sales prices were reduced to meet competition. Hunt also informed the researcher that sales managers too have their incentives based on making or exceeding the budget and that their forecasts had tended to be quite accurate. Over-optimism of one group of products had usually been offset by underestimation of sales on other products. However, because no adjustment was permitted in budgeted profit when sales income was below forecast, the fact that sales were running 3 percent below the level budgeted for 1963 was forcing the plant to reduce expenses substantially in order to equal or exceed the profit budgeted for the year.

RESEARCHER:    The budget rather puts you in a straitjacket then.

HUNT:    No, the budget is a guide—a kind of signpost—not a straitjacket.

The researcher then suggested to Hunt that there were probably some accounts in the budget which left some slack for reducing expenses if sales fell below forecast.

HUNT:    No, we never put anything in the budget that is unknown or guessed at. We have to be able to back up every single figure in the budget. We have to budget our costs at standard assuming that we can operate at standard. We know we won't all the time. There will be errors and failures, but we are never allowed to budget for them.

RESEARCHER:    It seems to me that there must be some give somewhere.

HUNT:    Well, I suppose there are some contentious accounts like overtime and outside storage. We do have arguments with division on those. For example, I might ask for $140,000 in the budget for overtime. The division manager will probably say $130,000—so we compromise at $130,000.

RESEARCHER:    How about cost reduction? You budget a certain amount there, I understand. Do you have the specific projects planned when you prepare the budget?

HUNT:    We budget for more than the savings expected from specific projects. We might have $100,000 in specific projects and budget $150,000.

RESEARCHER:    I would think this is one place where you might really push for extra cost savings in order to offset an income loss like you've had this year.

HUNT:    Yes, this is one of the areas we're pushing hard this year.

RESEARCHER:    Can you delay repairs and overhauls to reduce expenses?

HUNT:    At the time we make the budget we prepare an overhaul schedule in detail. It establishes the amount of labor and material that we expect to go into the overhaul as well as setting the time—which is cleared with production control so it will be the least inconvenient. Then any change from this schedule must be approved at the division level.

RESEARCHER:    I understand you have an incentive for managers based on performance of the plant compared to budget.

HUNT:    The bonus is paid on the year's results. It is paid as a percentage of salary to all who are eligible—they are the ones on the organization chart I gave you. There are three parts to it—one part is based on plant income, one on standards improvement or cost cutting, and the third on operating performance. We can make up to 20 percent by beating our plant income target and 25 percent on cost reduction and operating efficiency together. But we have to make 90 percent of our budgeted income figure to participate in any bonus at all.

I think we have the 25 percent on efficiency and cost reduction pretty well sewn up this year. If we go over our budgeted income, we can get almost 35 percent bonus.

RESEARCHER:    Has the French City plant made a bonus in recent years?

HUNT:    We have always made a certain amount—about 10 percent. In the past the bonus was based more on efficiency than anything else. We're one of the larger plants, and it made it harder for us. The larger plants just don't have the control. We don't know as well what the individual men are doing as in the smaller plants.

While Hunt and the researcher were at lunch early in December the conversation drifted back to the maintenance operation.

HUNT:    We have been holding off work on molds (for shaping the jars and bottles) until next year. Jones (machine shop foreman) had been planning to wait until the new year to fix up the molds. They were laid aside after the production runs ended in which they were used. The only trouble is he started his program too early. Now we are going to have to run some more of some of those bottles this year and he'll have to repair the molds.

I told Jones he knew what had to be done, that I expected him to keep the savings he planned and I didn't want to hear about his troubles. However, I know I will have to go along if he can back up his reasons why he can't save all the money he projected for December.

At another time Hunt discussed with the researcher some of his practices as plant manager:

HUNT:    I never look for answers to problems in these (pointing to manuals in a cabinet in his office). If I get a memo that refers specifically to an instruction in a manual, then I look it up. Otherwise I never touch them. I count on my accountant to keep me straight on rules and procedures. He has several shelves full of manuals and he's supposed to know what is in them. I don't look at this (loose-leaf book containing accounting reports) either. I don't look backward, I look forward. When I get information, I act on it right away. Once it goes in the book, I don't look at it except when I'm trying to spread a new budget over the year. Then I use past history.

Nor do I write many memos. When I have something to say I go tell the person or persons right away. I think people read into letters what they want. I guess you could say I follow the head-on approach. Unfortunately, I use the same approach with my superiors and once in a while I get called down for it.

RESEARCHER:    I am interested in knowing which of the things you do you believe could not be delegated to someone else.

HUNT:    For one thing, I can't delegate relations with sales. Production control handles individual scheduling problems with sales people, but the manager has to look at the overall relationship. There are a lot of things production control can't do. The manager has to make the final decisions. Then there is capital budgeting. Third, the manager must be close to the people. For example, one of our foremen was having some trouble with his men. I suggested that he take them out and I allotted him some money to do it. He took them bowling and bought them some drinks. He got closer to them and his relationship with them improved a lot. He still has a lot of parties. At the foreman level I believe you can't get too close to your men. I think maybe a manager can get too close.[4]

## Robert Andrews, Assistant Plant Manager

ANDREWS:    Well, a budget system like this certainly doesn't leave much for the imagination. Your job is pretty well laid out for you. I suppose we could run a plant this size if this were the whole company without such an elaborate system. But with a big company, if you don't have a budget system that is pretty explicit, you can lose an awful lot of ground.

RESEARCHER:    How important to you are the sales estimates?

ANDREWS:    They affect everybody in the operation. Sales people can put a lot of blue sky into their estimates because they can't afford to send a pessimistic estimate up to division. But it ends up hurting us. It simply causes inefficiency around here when things don't turn out the way sales predicted. I think we'd almost rather they would hand in pessimistic reports so we could be a little bit more sure where we stand on the production line.

RESEARCHER:    When you talk of your duties, I don't hear you say anything about increasing production volume.

ANDREWS:    We have standards. So long as we are meeting the standards we are meeting our costs and we do not worry about increasing production. We don't tell the foreman that he needs to get more goods out the door. We tell him to get rid of the red in his budget. I'm content with a 100 percent performance. I'd like 105 percent, but if we want more production it is up to IE to develop methods change.

RESEARCHER:    What then are the principal skills you expect of a foreman?

ANDREWS:    Communications and use of available control procedures. The foreman is expected to communicate effectively with all plant personnel, including staff heads. He must be able to convince his employees of the importance of certain aspects of their job, discipline or praise them when it is deserved. In all cases he must get his point across as "boss" and yet maintain the spirit of cooperation and teamwork that has marked our operation. Our control procedures are easy to apply. In each department there is an engineered standard for each operation covering labor, materials, and spoilage. Without waiting for a formal statement from accounting, a foreman can analyze his performance in any area and take corrective action if necessary. Then he receives reports from accounting to assist him in maintaining tight cost control. One is a daily report which records labor and spoilage performance against standard. The monthly report provides a more detailed breakdown of labor costs, materials and supplies used, and spoilage. It also establishes the efficiency figure for the month. This report is discussed at a monthly meeting of all of my supervisors. Generally the plant industrial engineer and a member of the accounting staff are present. Each foreman explains his variances from standard and submits a forecast of his next month's performance.

---

[4] Hunt took a daily tour of the plant and was observed by the researcher to call by name and speak in a folksy manner with many production workers and foremen.

RESEARCHER:   You mentioned communication between the foreman and staff managers. Does the foreman go directly to a staff manager with a problem or through you?

ANDREWS:   A foreman may go directly to a staff manager, or more usually one of his assistants, or he may go to his general foreman or myself. And a staff manager may go direct to a foreman. I'm usually brought in on the more important ones.

RESEARCHER:   How does the foreman know which ones to bring to you?

ANDREWS:   I really don't know how, but they seem to know.

RESEARCHER:   Do they keep you sufficiently informed, or bring too much to you?

ANDREWS:   Oh, they do pretty well, on the whole. I don't think I ever get too much information, but I do have to get after a foreman occasionally for failing to tell me something he should have.

## Production Control

The biweekly production control meetings observed by the researcher lasted about an hour. Jenkins and Andrews sat at the head of the conference table. The two general foremen were also present throughout the meeting while Hunt frequently dropped in for a time. Each production foreman and the production control scheduler working for his department came into the meeting at a prearranged time and when their turn came they reported on what products they were currently running and any problems they were having or which they anticipated. Most of the questions as well as instructions given in the meeting came from Andrews. It was also he who usually dismissed one foreman-scheduler pair and called on the next. Questions from Andrews or Jenkins were seldom clearly addressed to either the foreman or scheduler. They were answered more frequently by the scheduler than the foreman and often a scheduler would supplement comments made by the foreman. Generally the schedulers were younger but spoke with more self-assurance than the foremen.

There were frequent references to specific customers, their needs, complaints, and present attitude toward Empire Glass. Both Jenkins and Andrews tended to put instructions and decisions in terms of what was required to satisfy some particular customer or French City plant customers in general.

The researcher was especially interested in a part of a Tuesday production control meeting involving a foreman, "Mo" Pelletier, and the scheduler for his department, Dan Brown. While Dan was making the status report, the researcher observed that Mo was shaking his head in disagreement with Dan, but without saying anything. Dan was telling of his plan to discontinue on Friday the order being processed on a certain line, to shift to another order on Friday and then return on Tuesday to the product currently being produced.

ANDREWS:    I don't think your plan makes much sense. You go off on Friday and then on again Tuesday.

MO:    (To Dan) Is this all required before the end of the year? (This was asked with obvious negative emotional feeling and then followed by comments by both Andrews and Jenkins.)

DAN:    Mind you, I could call sales again.

JENKINS:    I can see the point, Dan. It is sort of nonsensical to change back after so short a run.

MO:    This would mean our production would be reduced all week to around 300 instead of 350. You know it takes four hours to make the changeover.

DAN:    But the order has been backed up.

ANDREWS:    It is backed up only because their (sales) demands are unreasonable.

DAN:    They only asked us to do the best we can.

ANDREWS:    They always do this. We should never have put this order on in the first place.

MO:    If you want to we could. . . . (Makes a suggestion about how to handle the problem.)

ANDREWS:    Production-wise, this is the best deal. (Agreeing with Mo's plan.)

DAN:    Let me look at it again.

ANDREWS:    Production-wise, this is best; make the changeover on the weekend.

JENKINS:    (Summarizes; then to Dan.) The whole argument is the lost production you would have.

MO:    It'll mean backing up the order only one day.

ANDREWS:    (After another matter in Mo's department has been discussed and there is apparently nothing further, Andrews turns to Dan and smiles.) It's been a pleasure, Dan.

Dan then returned the smile weakly and got up to go somewhat nervously. As Jenkins and the researcher were leaving the conference room after the meeting Jenkins commented to the researcher.

Danny got clobbered, as you could see. I used to stand up for him but he just doesn't come up here prepared. He should have the plans worked out with his foreman before they come up.

After another one of the production control meetings, Jenkins again discussed an incident which had occurred in the meeting.

We in production control are the buffer between sales and operating people. That discussion about the Smith bottle you heard is an example. Andrews is basically concerned with efficiency. He doesn't want to make anything that can't be made to standard. Now those little cracks we're getting means that if we continue running, our spoilage rate will skyrocket—maybe double or triple what it normally would be. Andrews hates this because it drives his efficiency down. But what he didn't know upstairs was that Jim Hunt had made a personal commitment to the customer to get those 50,000 bottles out today and he was going to do it come hell or high water. Andrews just never had a chance when he started making noises about shutting the line down. So I won and Bob lost this time, but he's able to be big about it and see the real issue. Where it really gets tough for him, though, is that by the end of the month this particular problem will have become lost in the figures. People will have forgotten that today, November 8, a decision went against Bob Andrews. All they will notice is that according to the accounting reports, Andrews had bad efficiency for the month of November. To avoid looking bad he has to find another operation where there is some slack and produce more efficiently. That's the only way he can protect himself, but it puts a lot of pressure on him. Bob and I are usually able to work these things out fairly well. We know that the problem is more or less built into our jobs.

In discussing his job Jenkins frequently commented on how he thought a decision or problem would affect someone else in the plant.

If all you had to do was manage the nuts and bolts of production scheduling and not worry about the customer or how people were going to react, this would be the easiest job in the whole plant. You could just sit down with a paper and pencil and lay it out the best way. But because the customer is so important and because you've got to look ahead to how people are going to react to a given kind of schedule, it makes the whole job tremendously complicated. It isn't easy!

### Andrew Cox, Plant Accountant

Cox:   We want the budget to be realistic; but we also want it to be something of a target for our management and operating personnel. At the French City plant our goal over the years has been to present budgets which reflect improvement in the percent return of gross plant income to gross plant sales as well as return on employed capital. We have been reasonably successful in this despite constantly rising labor and material costs.

The budget is a plan to insure the success of the company. We put a lot of stress on competition within the company and against other companies in our field. We here at French City want to do as well as any other plant in Empire Glass. . . . The essence of the present control system was developed fifteen years ago. There were a lot of gripes and criticism when it was introduced. The big difference between then and now is that now the people on the floor use the reports as a tool. . . . We've done a lot of training since then. It took maybe ten years to get the job done.

RESEARCHER:   Have there been changes in the bonus plan over the years?

Cox:   Yes, at one time the bonus plan was based on departmental results on department efficiency. Under this there was a tendency for the departments to work at cross purposes, to compete rather than cooperate with each other. For the last seven or eight years, the emphasis has been on the plant, not the department. The latest plan is geared not only to the attainment of budgeted cost goals, but also the attainment of budgeted income. This is consistent with the attention we are placing on sales. I think the company was disturbed by what they sensed was a belief that those at the plant level can't do much about sales. Now we are trying to get the idea across that if we make better cans and give better service, we will sell more.

RESEARCHER:    I assume there must be some accounts in the budget where you leave yourself some room to maneuver.

COX:    Well, in this company there is very little opportunity to play footsy with the figures.

### Guillaume Jacques, General Foreman

Jacques was completely bilingual, and he felt his French background was an advantage in dealing with the workers, an estimated 90 percent of whom were French-Canadians. In describing his job he stated that he worked closely with both the assistant plant manager and the production control manager, but more with the latter. He said the job of general foreman was to regulate the troubles of the department and compared it to the relationship of a father and his children.

RESEARCHER:    Are the standards and the budget important in your work?

JACQUES:    Yes, very important. Most of the time they ask you not only to meet your budget but to do better, saving such and such amount of money. The assistant foreman has to check constantly, each production line each hour, to be sure they are close to standard.

RESEARCHER:    Can you keep the employee satisfied as well as meet the budget requirements?

JACQUES:    Yes, you've got to make the worker understand the importance of keeping the budget. I get them in the office and explain that if we don't meet the budget we'll have to cut down somewhere else. It is mathematical. I explain all this to them, they have given me a budget to meet, I need them for this, they need me to give them work. We work like a team. I try to understand them.

RESEARCHER.    Do you feel under tension in your work?

JACQUES:    Sure I work under tension, but don't all supervisors? You try to go along with the temperament of the men as much as possible. Myself, I ask the men to go out to have a beer with me, to go to a party. It relaxes them from our preoccupations. Right now, for example, there is this party with the foremen coming up. At these gatherings it is strictly against the rules to talk about work. These things are necessary.

Jacques commented on the advances in technology and reduction in the number of employees needed. He said that he felt management had done a good job with the union in persuading the workers that cost cutting, although it meant reducing the number of people on the floor, actually increases job security in the long run.

### Henry Dodds, General Foreman

RESEARCHER:    Do you and the foremen participate in establishing the budget?

DODDS:    I'm responsible for preparing the budgets for my department, and the foreman participates in my area because I ask him for his thoughts. We have to make budget for each production department.

RESEARCHER:    Does the foreman get a copy of the budget?

DODDS:    Yes, they have a copy of the budget for their department. It's prepared by the industrial engineers and the accounting department from our work sheets.

RESEARCHER:    Does the production worker see the budget?

DODDS:    He doesn't see the budget. He has the machine operating standard; if he meets this he is doing his share. The standard is set so that if he works the machine at full capacity he achieves 110 percent of standard.

RESEARCHER:    Since you don't have wage incentives, is there any problem in getting the employees to produce up to standard?

DODDS:    Well, there is usually some needling when a man is down below standard. He's told, "Why don't you get to be part of the crew?" It doesn't hurt anything. . . . You only get a good day's work out of people if they are happy. We strive to keep our people happy so they'll produce the standard and make the budget. We try to familiarize them with what is expected of them. We have targets set for us. The budget is reasonable, but it is not simple to attain. By explaining our problems to the workers we find it easier to reach the budget.

Dodds emphasized that an understanding of plant problems and objectives on the part of the foremen was also important. He told of a current program to try to fill the need for a certain type of cutting machine in one plant area by releasing several similar machines from another area for conversion to accomplish the new purpose.

DODDS:    Beceause the foremen understood the program they will cooperate to clear the machines of work and make them available.

RESEARCHER:    Do you have situations where a foreman thinks a standard is too high and the worker cannot make it?

DODDS:    We haven't run into an instance of that in eight years. The industrial engineer goes over the standard with the foreman and he has an opportunity to question it before it is approved by management. Usually they explain the standard to the operator, and they always tell the operator what the industrial engineer is doing.

### Foremen and Production Workers

Foremen and production workers who were interviewed were all very much aware of the budget, and workers often explained behavior of foremen in terms of the requirements of the budget. Most of the foremen and many of the workers accepted the necessity of keying their activities to the work standards and the budget. One notable exception was a foreman of many years' service who said:

We have a meeting once a month upstairs. They talk to us about budgets, quality, etc. That's all on the surface; that's b——— s———. It looks good. It has to look good but it is all bull. For example, the other day (a foreman) had a meeting with the workers to talk about quality. After that an employee brought to his attention a defect in some products. He answered, "Send it out anyway." And they had just finished talking to us about quality.

Although they accepted the necessity of standards and budgets, many foremen and workers expressed feelings of pressure from superiors and from the control system. In contrast were the comments of one of the younger and more ambitious foremen—a French-Canadian.

What I like about this department is that I am in charge. I can do anything I like as long as I meet up with the budget. I can have that machine moved— send it over there—as long as I have good reasons to justify it. The department, that's me. I do all the planning and I'm responsible for results. I'm perfectly free in the use of my time (gives examples of his different arrival times during the past week and the fact that he came in twice on Saturday and once on Sunday for short periods). . . . One thing I like here is that we don't get swelled heads about the positions we hold. Each man here—foreman, manager, etc.,—is an employee of the company. We each have a job to do. You can talk freely with any of the staff heads.

Most of the foremen were bilingual French-Canadians. Some expressed dislike of the troublesome problems they felt were inherent in a job direct- ing the work of others. One declared he would not want the manager's job for this reason, "although he is well paid for it."

No negative statements by foremen about the plant manager or the management staff were heard by the researcher. However, one expressed a desire to return to hourly work. Another felt that the foremen needed a union.

Foremen tended to view the production worker as irresponsible and in- terested, insofar as his job is concerned, only in his pay check and quitting time. One foreman expressed himself as follows: "We do all the work; they do nothing." Even an officer of the union commented:

They don't give a damn about the standards. They work nonchalantly and they are very happy when their work slows up. If the foreman is obliged to stop the line for two minutes every one goes to the toilet. There are some workers who do their work conscientiously, but this is not the case with the majority.

When speaking of their work, several of the production workers ex- pressed feelings of pressure, although others declared they were accus- tomed to their work and it did not bother them. One said:

Everyone is obsessed with meeting the standards—the machine adjuster, the foreman, the assistant foreman. They all get on my nerves.

One old-timer clearly differentiated the company, which he considered benevolent, from his foreman:

I'm not talking about the company. I'm talking about the foreman. I can understand that these men are under tension as well as we are. They have meetings every week. I don't know what they talk about up there. . . . The foremen have their standards to live up to. They're nervous. They don't even have a union like us. So if things go bad, well, that's all. . . . They make us nervous with all this. But there's a way with people. We don't say to a man, "Do this, do that." If we said, "Would you do this?" it is not the same thing. You know a guy like myself who has been here for 35 years knows a few tricks. If I am mad at the foreman I could do a few little things to the machine to prevent it from keeping up with the standards and no one would know.

Another said:

I'd prefer working for a dollar an hour less and have a job that is less tiring. It is not really hard but you have to work fast. . . . Our nerves are on edge here. . . . The worst ones aren't the foremen but the schedulers. It is never the fault of the machines but always the operator. . . . They are always on us. But they are good people here just the same. They replace us when we are tired or want to go to the toilet. The foremen could be much worse.

Those who complained about their foremen, however, tended to contrast the manager and the management staff, as did one worker, who said, "They're people—polite people. They speak to you properly."

Although a number of workers expressed sentiments similar to those quoted above, most workers conveyed to the researcher a feeling of overall satisfaction with their jobs. Typical was the comment of the worker who said, "Truly, it is a good company, and it pays well." In a recent Harvard research study of a number of jobs in twelve plants in several different industries in the United States and Canada, the French City plant workers who were included ranked highest of the twelve plants in job satisfaction.

## IN PURSUIT OF BUDGETED GOALS

The researcher was particularly interested in a series of events he observed which related to a special meeting of the entire French City plant management held in November. On his first visit to the plant, James Hunt and several of the staff managers had mentioned to him the fact that sales for the year had fallen below expectations and that their bonus was in jeopardy as a result.

One day in early November the researcher noticed an unusual amount of activity in the accounting section. Hunt came into the area frequently and he and Cox from time to time would huddle with one of the accountants over some figures. In the afternoon the researcher observed several management staff members saunter by the plant accountant's office, one of them two or three times, without the purposeful air they usually had when walking in the office. The researcher learned from Cox that the extra activity was due to the fact that the report on the October results was to be issued that day.

At one point in the afternoon, while the researcher was in Cox's office for a prearranged interview, Hunt walked in and sat down but said nothing. After a few minutes he started out the door.

Cox:    Jim, did you want to see me about something?

Hunt:    I'm waiting for your story (referring to the report of October results.)

Hunt then strolled about the accounting area for a time and then left.

A week later Hunt scheduled a joint meeting of the management staff and the line organization to go over the October results. This was a departure from the usual practice of having the groups in separate meetings. Prior to the meeting Hunt discussed with the researcher what he hoped to accomplish in the meeting.

The meeting this afternoon is simply to get things straightened out. Those figures we got last week showed that some of the accounts did what they were expected to do, some did more, and some did a good deal less. The thing we have to do now is kick those accounts in the pants that are not making the savings they planned to make. What we've been doing is raising the expected savings as the time gets shorter. It may be easy to save 10 percent on your budget when you've got six months; but with only six weeks, it is an entirely different matter. The thing to do now is to get everybody together and excited about the possibility of doing it. We know how it can be done. Those decisions have already been made. It's not unattainable even though I realize we are asking an awful lot from these men. You see we are in a position now where just a few thousand dollars one way or the other can make as much as 10 percent difference in the amount of bonus the men get. There is some real money on the line. It can come either from a sales increase or an expense decrease, but the big chunk has to come out of an expense decrease.

Researcher:    Do you expect some wrangles this afternoon about who is right and who is wrong?

Hunt:    No, we never fight about the budget. It is simply a tool. All we want to know is what is going on. Then we can get to work and fix it. There are never any disagreements about the budget itself. Our purpose this afternoon is to pinpoint those areas where savings can be made, where there is a little bit of slack, and then get to work and pick up the slack.

Researcher:    Am I right that any time there is a departure from budgeted expense or budgeted sales, you and the other managers immediately begin to look for other plant accounts where the losses can be made up?

Hunt:    Yes, that is an automatic decision, or else we'll give the department that has been losing money a certain period of time to make it up. Also, any time anybody has a gain, I tell them I expect them to maintain that gain.

The researcher also talked to Bob Andrews concerning the methods used to pick up the projected savings.

ANDREWS:   When you have lost money in one sector you have to look around for something else that you can "milk" to make up the difference.

RESEARCHER:   Do you ever ask for volunteers?

ANDREWS:   No, we do the "milking." Those guys just have to do what we say. How much we can save pretty much depends on how hard the man in the corner office wants to push on the thing. I mean if we really wanted to save money we probably could do it, but it would take a tremendous effort on everybody's part and Jim would really have to crack the whip.

## Special Line and Staff Meeting

The meeting was held in the conference room at 4:00 p.m. To accommodate everyone two extra tables were brought in from the cafeteria and placed at the end of the polished table toward the door. Hunt and Cox sat at the far end of the table, facing the door, with an easel bearing a flip chart near them. The chart listed the projected savings in budgeted expense for November and December, account by account. The group of about thirty arranged themselves at the table so that, with only a couple of exceptions, the management staff personnel and general foremen sat closest to Hunt and Cox and the foremen and assistant foremen sat toward the foot of the table.

Hunt opened the meeting one or two minutes after four and declared that performance against budget for October would first be reviewed, followed by discussion of the November and December projections. He stated rather emphatically that he was "disappointed" in the October performance. Although money had been saved, it represented good performance in some areas but rather poor performance in others. The gains made in the areas where performance had been good must be maintained and the weak areas brought up, Hunt declared.

He then turned the meeting over to Cox, who reviewed the October results, reading from the report which everyone had in front of him. Where performance was not good, he called on the individual responsible for that area to explain. The essence of the typical explanation was that the original budgeted figure was unrealistic and that the actual amount expended was as low as it could possibly be under the circumstances. Hunt frequently broke into the explanation with a comment like, "Well, that is not good enough," or "Can you possibly do better for the rest of the year?" or "I hope we have that straightened out now." When he sat down, the person giving the explanation was invariably thanked by Cox.

Following this part of the meeting, Cox, followed by Jenkins, commented on the sales outlook for the remainder of the year. They indicated that for the two months as a whole sales were expected to be about on budget. After asking for questions and getting one from a foreman, Hunt said:

Well now, are there any more questions? Ask them now if you have them. Everybody sees where we stand on the bonus, I assume. Right?

Hunt then referred to the chart on plant expense savings and began to discuss it, saying:

The problem now is time. We keep compressing the time and raising the gain (the projected savings for the year had been raised $32,000 above what had been projected in October). You can only do that so long. Time is running out, fellows. We've got to get on the stick.

Several times Hunt demanded better upward communication on problems as they came up. He gave an example from the previous month and declared:

This sort of thing is absolutely inexcusable. We simply cannot have such a thing happen again. We've got to know ahead of time when these mix-ups are going to occur so that we can allow for and correct them.

As Cox was covering projections for November, account by account, the following exchange took place when he came to manufacturing efficiency:

Cox:    Now we have come to you, Bob. I see you're getting a little bit more optimistic on what you think you can do.
Andrews:    Yes, the boss keeps telling me I'm just an old pessimist and I don't have any faith in my people. I'm still a pessimist, but we are doing tremendously. I think it's terrific, fellows (pointing to a line graph); I don't know whether we can get off the top of this chart or not, but at the rate this actual performance line is climbing, we might make it. All I can say is, keep up the good work. . . . I guess I'm an optimistic pessimist.

The following comments were made during the discussion of projected savings for December in the equipment maintenance account.

Cox:    Where in the world are you fellows going to save $8,000 more than you originally said you would save?
McDonald:    (A noncommittal response.)
Jones:    I'd just like to say at this point to the group that it would be a big help if you guys would take it easy on your machines. That's where we are going to save an extra $8,000—simply by only coming down to fix the stuff that won't run. You're really going to have to make it go as best you can. That's the only way we can possibly save the kind of money we have to save. You have been going along pretty well, but all I've got to say is I hope you can keep it up and not push those machines too hard.

Although Jones spoke with sincerity, the researcher noted that a number of sly smiles and pokes in the ribs were exchanged by foremen at the end of the table nearest the door.

Hunt concluded the meeting at about 5:30, still chewing on his cigar.

There are just a couple of things I want to say before we break up. First, we've got to stop making stupid errors in shipping. Joe, (foreman of shipping) you've absolutely *got* to get after those people to straighten them out. Second, I think it should be clear, fellows, that we can't break any more promises. Sales is our bread and butter. If we don't get those orders out in time we'll have no one but ourselves to blame for missing our budget. So I just hope it is clear that production control is running the show for the rest of the year. Third, the big push is on *now!* We sit around here expecting these problems to solve themselves, but they don't! It ought to be clear to all of you that no problem gets solved until it's spotted. Damn it, I just don't want any more dewy-eyed estimates about performance for the rest of the year. If something is going sour we want to hear about it. And there's no reason for not hearing about it! (Pounds the table, then voice falls and a smile begins to form.) It can mean a nice penny in your pocket if you can keep up the good work.

That's all I've got to say. Thank you very much.

### Interview with Ray Jenkins

The room cleared immediately but the researcher engaged Ray Jenkins in further conversation in his office:

RESEARCHER:    You got a nice little boost there at the end of the meeting.

JENKINS:    No, I'm afraid that little bit of advice there at the end won't make a great deal of difference in the way things work out. I mean that; not that I don't appreciate that sort of thing. It's just that it won't make any difference. As I was telling you before, you have to play off sales against production. It's built into the job. When I attend a meeting like that one upstairs and I see all those production people with their assistants and see the other staff managers with their assistants, and I hear fellows refer to corporate policy that dictates and supports their action at the plant level, I suddenly realize that I'm all alone up there. I can't sit down and fire off a letter to my boss at the division level like the rest of these guys can do. I haven't got any authority at all. It is all based strictly on my own guts and strength. Now Bob is a wonderful guy, I like him and I have a lot of respect for him, but it just so happens that 80 percent of the time he and I disagree. He knows it and I know it; I mean it's nothing we run away from, we just find ourselves on opposite sides of the question and I'm dependent upon his tact and good judgment to keep from starting a war.

Boy, it can get you down, it really can after awhile, and I've been at it for —God—twenty years. But in production control you've just got to accept it— you're an outcast. They tell you you're cold, that you're inhuman, that you're a bastard, that you don't care about anything except your schedule. And what are you going to say? You're just going to have to swallow it because basically you haven't got the authority to back up the things you know need to be done. Four nights out of five I am like this at the end of the day—just completely drained out—and it comes from having to fight my way through to try to get the plant running as smoothly as I can.

And Andrews up there in that meeting. He stands up with his chart and he compliments everybody about how well they are doing on efficiency. You know, he says, "Keep up the good work," and all that sort of stuff. I just sat there, shaking my head. I was so dazed you know, I mean I kept saying to my-self, "What's he doing? What's he saying? What's so great about this?" You know, if I could have, I'd have stood up and I'd have said, "Somebody go down to my files in production control and pick out any five customer orders at random—and letters—and bring them back up here and read them—at random, pick any five." You know what they would show? Do you know how many broken promises and how many missed delivery dates and how many slightly off-standard items we've been pushing out the door here? I mean, what is an efficient operation? Why the stress on operating efficiency? That's why I just couldn't figure out why in the world Andrews was getting as much mileage out of his efficiency performance as he was. Look at all the things we sacrifice to get that efficiency. But what could I do?

### Interview with District Sales Manager

Having heard how Jenkins felt about the pressures of the budget on sales, the researcher visited the district sales manager, L. G. Adams, and discussed the impact of the plant budget on the sales department with him.

ADAMS:    That's probably my biggest problem on this job, getting the boys here to see that if they really want to serve the customer, they can't hold their own budget up as a shining standard all the time. The budget comes to domi-nate people's thinking and influence all their actions. I'm afraid even my sales-men have swallowed the production line whole. They can understand the budget so well they can't understand their customers. And the French City plant boys are getting more and more local in their thinking with this budget. They're not thinking about what the customer needs today or may need tomorrow, they just think about their god damned budget.

If the customer will not take account of your shortcomings, and if you can't take account of the customer's shortcomings, the two of you will eventually end up at each other's throats. That's what this budget system has built into it. Suppose, for example, you want to give a customer a break. Say he has originally planned for a two-week delivery date, but he phones you and says he really has problems and if you possibly could he would like about four days knocked off that delivery date. So I go trotting over to the plant, and I say, "Can we get it four days sooner?" Those guys go out of their minds, and they start holler-ing about the budget and how everything is planned just right and how I'm stirring them up.

RESEARCHER:    It is probably hard to do this very frequently.

ADAMS:    That's for sure! You can't go running to them all the time, but only when you really need something in the worst way. You can't let those plant guys see your strategy, you know. I want to tell you, it is taking an awful lot out of a guy's life around here when he has to do everything by the numbers.

The researcher learned after the first of the year that the report being sent by Hunt to division would show, despite the fact that sales had fallen about 3 percent below budget, that profits for 1963 had exceeded the amount budgeted and that operating efficiency and cost reduction had both exceeded the budget by a comfortable margin. This enabled the managers and supervisors at the French City plant to obtain the salary bonuses for which they had been striving.

# Olympic Foods Inc.

In April 1969, Mr. David Brown, President of Olympic Foods, Inc., a chain of ice cream and sandwich stores in San Francisco, California, was reviewing his organization and considering several alternatives to his present manner of operating. He was particularly concerned about the long-term implications of any changes he might institute. Mr. Brown, in his mid-thirties and a graduate of the Stanford Business School, had been president of the company since March 1967.

Employees of the company described the conditions prevailing in Olympic when Mr. Brown took over as president as "terrible." The whole organization was demoralized and was lacking in direction. Most of the people were poorly paid.

Under his leadership, the chain showed considerable progress. Over the two-year period, the total number of stores went up to 50 from 40 in 1967, and the sales increased by 20 percent. Mr. Brown attributed most of his success to the informal relationships and the conducive psychological climate that had come to prevail in the company. "I spend a lot of time with my people. Periodically I also write personal letters to the staff," he explained.

## THE COMPANY

Olympic owned and operated a chain of ice cream, soda fountain, and sandwich shops serving nearly 300,000 customers a week. Olympic had established a reputation for high product quality, good customer service, and attractive store appearance. In 1968, the company reported sales of $10.6 million. In 1969, it planned to add 10 units including 5 ice cream shops and 5 sandwich shops.

The ice cream division had 17 stores and the sandwich division had 27 shops. A third division, called the Olympia division, managed six small stores. Each division was managed by a divisional manager assisted by district managers, normally at the ratio of one district manager for 10 stores. The organizational chart is presented in Exhibit 1.

**EXHIBIT 1**

Organization Chart

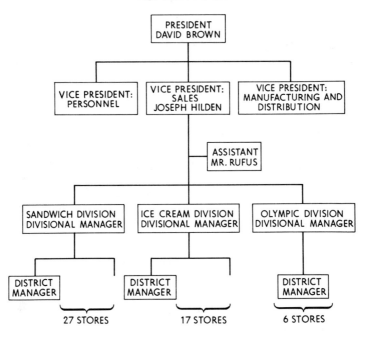

## THE BUSINESS

Many executives of the company described food service as a very difficult type of business. One executive commented:

Room for error is great in this business. We are serving thousands of people every day. Twenty-five thousand people use our Telegraph Hill stores each week. Our is basically a "nickel and dime" business and we deal in perishable products. You know how things should go, but to do it that way is difficult. The greatest problem in this business is to get the right kind of people and keep them motivated, stimulated, and interested. As this is a seven-day operation with no holidays it is found difficult to fill positions like store managers, grillmen, sandwichmen, etc.

In the case of store managers, with the kind of people we want, it is necessary to find and keep service-oriented individuals. The people who serve in our stores are servants of the customers. A store manager has to know his people. This, surprisingly enough, is not obvious to many of the store managers. Many young people fail in our business because they are not people oriented.

The following comments about the business were made by Olympic store managers:

Most employees work part time. These are mostly high school girls and housewives, who resent working late and on weekends.

Lack of intelligent ordering can also adversely affect the operations of the store. The store should never run out of products. If we disappoint somebody, he will try our competitor.

This is a seasonal business. Some days the volume is very heavy. On a warm day, customers come rushing in. The place is deluged with people. Our reputation is at stake. We have a good product line, but service is the most important thing. Proper scheduling of product requirements and awareness of customer needs are important factors in the success of our stores.

A manager of any one of these stores has to be in charge of a number of things. Most of the products are perishable and a little carelessness could cost a lot of money. The store would sustain serious losses if supplies are not used soon enough.

Customers have to be cared for. You have got to be solicitous. You have got to be a bit of a psychologist on a real busy day. The problem is not one of getting customers, but to ensure that the customers are kept satisfied.

The stores were located in different localities and attracted a variety of customers. One store manager said: "Each store has its own personality. Mine is a store where a lot of juveniles hang out at night."

Security of the store property was another pressing problem for the store manager. "The back door should not be left open. If you are not careful, there could be a lot of thievery and pilferage. Even some of our customers are thieves."

## SUPERVISION

A district manager supervised 8 to 12 stores. He was expected to visit each store once in 2 days. He spent anywhere from 20 minutes to 2 hours at each store.

When asked to comment about their leadership style, one executive said that district managers normally acted as policemen. "Sometimes they are very tough on store managers. Some raise hell."

Olympic management felt that close supervision was necessary to ensure the office bulletins were followed, and that stores were kept clean and attractive. Close supervision was also necessary to ensure that "products unfit for sale" were not used in the store. A divisional manager declared: "While you may call it close supervision, this is in no way oversupervision."

A manager of one of Olympic's newer stores explained his attitude about district managers and supervision:

I am in favor of close supervision because it helps you to learn the business. The more I can draw on someone's experience the more it is to my advantage.

They have different styles. One man yells, another persuades. Supervision is not geared to sales but to keeping the place clean and hairnets on the girls. The philosophy is that if you keep the store clean and hairnets on the girls, then sales will increase—this may be true.

The district managers reported to the divisional managers. The divisional managers were "on their back" to ensure that the district managers carried out their duties effectively.

## MANAGEMENT DEVELOPMENT IN OLYMPIC FOODS

According to Mr. Brown, most of the Olympic store managers were high school graduates who came from lower middle class families. Normally the store manager had some debt. One manager, Mr. Joseph Corbin, had been in theater management with Paramount Pictures before joining Olympic as a management trainee. The manager of the San Mateo store described his background:

I have a middle class background. My father was very industrious and I always admired him. I had a hard time at college—I guess I'm not much of a thinker. I worked in a bank and didn't enjoy it. I was supposed to be a book-keeper in International Banking, which sounded very glamorous, but I ended up punching cards. I got bored and joined a company working in food services.

It is a people business—I have always enjoyed working with people. Sometimes you get thoroughly demoralized, because people are so unpredictable. I am here to learn and I have to learn a lot from this company. It is far more lucrative than I thought.

The candidates selected for the position of store managers were under the supervision of the training manager of the company, who operated two stores for training purposes. The candidates spent three weeks in ice cream stores and another three weeks in a sandwich shop. During this period of training, the trainee was taught various operations in the store. "At this level we want to make him more of a mechanic rather than a manager." He was trained by working with customers. He was taught how to take spot checks, open a store, and set it up. He was taught the "booth concept"—that certain girls were assigned to booths—and how the booth girls worked. The trainee was also taught "Olympic standards."

Asked to comment on "Olympic standards," the training manager said,

The Olympic standard is cleanliness. If you keep a store clean, everything else seems to go with it. If you run a dirty store, everything goes wrong—customers complain; even the trainees don't want to stay. Olympic has had that standard always.

After six weeks of initial training, the trainee was assigned to a store to function as an assistant manager. Here he was trained in personnel relations, customer services, housekeeping, and merchandising. Then he was rotated from one store to another, and this took at least another six months.

## Incentive Plans

The great need to find and retain competent store managers required that the managers be adequately motivated and rewarded. The company had been trying various incentive schemes. Commenting on the need for an incentive system for the company, Mr. Rufus, Personal Assistant to the Vice President of Sales, commented,

There has to be an incentive for doing a good job. This persuades the manager to give his best and control his best. So we thought an incentive plan was required. I am all for an incentive plan; otherwise, everyone will be deadwood.

## OLYMPICS PLAN

For years, the company had been paying straight weekly wages to the store managers. An incentive plan for store managers was first initiated in the company in 1964 by Edward Ralston, then the sales manager of the company. Known as the "Olympic Plan for Store Managers," this plan was developed with the following objectives:

1. To make store managers feel that they were an integral part of management and in operating their stores they were, in effect, operating a business of their own.
2. To provide managers with an incentive for greater interest and effort to improve their operations and develop greater profits.
3. To enable those who produced to earn substantial incomes by sharing in the extra profits they created.

Essentially this plan provided that the income of the store be divided into two parts. The part initially retained by the company was intended to cover all overhead expenses, certain operating expenses the manager could not control, and a normal profit developed by a good average store. (For details of the plan, see Exhibit 2.) The part allocated to the manager

### EXHIBIT 2

The Olympic Plan

This Plan is available only to STORE MANAGERS.

As a Store Manager you have proven your ability and ambition.

As a partner, you will now share in the profits of your store.

You then will have every reason and opportunity to demonstrate your full business ability to increase sales and reduce costs and *share in the results!*

In the past you have been held accountable for sales. Now, as a "partner" you will be expected to assume full responsibility for sales. . . .

Perhaps more importantly, as a "partner" you will have gained the greater opportunity to maximize your personal income through increased sales—through reduced costs—

Exhibit 2 *(continued)*

And the ultimate attainment of these goals can only mean more dollars in your pocket as "partnership profits" become available for sharing!

And Olympic supplies to you, and absorbs the cost of, many specialized functions including:

* Accounting
* Legal service
* Payroll calculation, distribution, and reports
* Personnel services
* Insurance program administration
* Industrial engineering & work simplification
* Construction & maintenance facilities
* Sanitation & bacterial controls
* Quality control & new product development

Plus Olympic will provide and absorb the cost of staff services designed to maximize the profits of your store:

* Supervision
* Training
* Sales promotion & merchandising aids
* Advertising
* Shopping service
* Administrative knowledge & experience

plus

* Dozens of specialists stand ready to serve you at all times

In addition, Olympic will absorb for you and your employees the full company share of:

* Federal & state payroll taxes
* Holiday & vacation pay
* Blue Cross & Blue Shield coverage
* Group insurance & death benefits

And beyond all this, Olympic continues to guarantee *you* a drawing account in the amount of your basic weekly wage!

However, as a partner, *you* . . .

1. Will be responsible for the operation of your store as though it were your own.
2. Will strive to make your store a source of pride and profit both to you and to Olympic.
3. Since one poor store could damage Olympic's reputation, thereby hurting all stores and other partnerships, any deviation from company standards and policies could result in the termination of our partnership agreement.

How are profits to be made—thereafter to be shared? First, through *sales.* Sales is the measure of your success with customers. *Increased sales—increased profits.* A typical store enjoys annual sales of $100,000 total. You and Olympic working together can build increased sales for your store!

From these total sales is derived a *gross profit figure.* To cover the controllable costs *you* must absorb, and to provide for the profit you expect to develop, Olympic allows *you* a gross profit of 70 percent of every fountain sale. The calculation of gross profit in a typical store would show

$$100 \times 70\% = 70,000.$$

From these gross profit dollars ($70,000)

1. You will be charged for merchandise at regular transfer prices, or $42,000.

In this typical illustration elimination of carelessness and waste can make dramatic reductions in your merchandise used percentages. Lower merchandise used percentages—higher profits.

Also from these gross profit dollars ($70,000)

2. You will be charged for payroll costs generated by your store.
   a. Your personal drawing account.
   b. The direct wages of all your employees.

## Exhibit 2 *(continued)*

Again in this typical illustration:

$$\begin{aligned}
\text{store sales} &= \$100,000 \\
\text{actual payroll} &= \$\ 19,000 \\
\text{payroll \% to sales} &= 19\%
\end{aligned}$$

Speed, efficiency, and flexibility of personnel affect payroll costs. These costs can be reduced through planned coaching and training by the store manager.
Intelligent scheduling is the most important factor in payroll control!!
Also from these gross profit dollars ( $70,000 )

3. You will be charged for your containers at regular prices.

And in this typical illustration:

$$\begin{aligned}
\text{store sales} &= \$100,000 \\
\text{container costs} &= \$\ \ \ 4,000 \\
\text{container \% to sales} &= 4\%
\end{aligned}$$

Elimination of carelessness in storing, rotating, and packaging can substantially reduce your cost of containers.
Finally, from these gross profit dollars ( $70,000 )

4. You will be charged for other controllable expenses:

| *Other Expenses* | *Typical Store* |
|---|---|
| Cash discounts | $     400 |
| Cash shortages | 100 |
| Floor and window cleaning | 1,000 |
| General expense | 200 |
| Laundry | 1,100 |
| Loss on returns | 100 |
| Utensils | 100 |
| | $   3,000 |
| | $100,000 |

On typical sales of $100,000, the "other expense" percentage to sales is 3%. Tighter controls mean greater profits.
. . . . . . . . . . . . . . . . . . . . . . . . . . . . . . . . . . . . . . . . . . . . . . . . . . . . . . . . . . . . . . .

Your gross profit dollars minus your controllable expenses equal profit before adjustment. In our typical illustration ( sales $100,000 )

| | | |
|---|---|---|
| Gross profits | | $70,000 |
| Less: expenses | | |
|    merchandise | $42,000 | |
|    payroll | 19,000 | |
|    containers | 4,000 | |
|    other expenses | 3,000 | |
|     TOTAL EXPENSES | $68,000 | 68,000 |
| Profit before development | | |
|    fund adjustment | | $  2,000 |

*Why a development fund?*

This Development Fund is designed to provide an equal opportunity for *you* and all store managers to produce partnership profits.

*How does it work?*

Stores in choice, high volume locations will contribute to the Fund. Those in less active locations receive help from it. Most stores, however, including the "typical store" used in the illustrations are not affected one way or the other. Sales standards in a store, upon which the development fund is based:

Exhibit 2 *(continued)*

over $150,000—will contribute
$100,000—not affected
under $75,000—will receive

*Development fund contributors*

If you are one of the fortunate few assigned to a high volume store, you are already receiving an above average opportunity to increase your income through Partnership Profits. Therefore, to assist in the development of low volume stores, you will contribute 10% of your store sales in excess of $150,000. This contribution goes into the Development Fund.

*Development fund recipients*

If your store is a low volume location, you need help during your development period to enable you to enjoy a reasonable drawing account and to give you a fair chance to show a profit. Therefore, your gross profit will be increased by 10% of the amount by which your sales are below minimum standards. This would be 10% of the difference between actual sales and $75,000. This money comes out of the Development Fund.

*How are profits shared?*

The profits shown after the Development Fund adjustment will be divided equally between the partners.

| | |
|---|---:|
| Sales | $100,000 |
| Gross profit | 70,000 |
| Expenses | 68,000 |
| Profit before adjustment | 2,000 |
| Development fund | —— |
| Partnership profit | 2,000 |
| *Your share, 50%* | $   1,000 |

was intended to cover the cost of merchandise, containers, payroll, and all other operating expenses which were under his direct control. If the manager maintained a good average operation, he should share in a modest "partnership profit." A substandard operation would result in a deficit, while a superior performance could produce a very substantial partnership profit, to be equally divided between the manager and the company.

The plan recognized that on the basis of straight book figures, all stores would not offer equal opportunity to the store managers. Stores varied in product mix, volume, location, number of days in the week the store was open, etc. For example, the managers of low volume stores would be severely penalized while managers of high volume stores could receive large benefits even on substandard operations.

The development fund was intended to correct these inequalities. It subsidized the low volume stores to the extent of 10 percent of the volume by which their sales were less than the specified minimum. The funds required to subsidize were provided by assessing high volume stores to the extent of 10 percent of the amount by which their sales exceeded a specified maximum.

During the three years the plan was in force, the operations of Olympic had changed considerably due to management thinking and decisions. Food service had been added to many of the old stores, many low volume stores which included food service had been opened; a number of large stores which were expensive to operate had been built; and low-volume high-cost departments had been added to other stores. As a result, a constantly declining percentage of managers had been able to earn profits and this was having a detrimental effect on the morale of the organization. Though the store managers' earnings had ranged from $5,200 to $13,500, only one-third of the managers made any partnership profit.

In a report to the senior executives of the company, Ed Ralston commented,

The Olympics Plan can be a very effective tool, but it is a very sensitive device. Whenever any decision is made, such as types and locations of the new stores, manager transfers, changes in retail prices, changes in transfer prices, changes in servings, or changes in wage scales, the impact must be considered and adjustments made to protect managers' incomes and maintain management's reputation for integrity.

In practice, management often found it difficult to get store managers to accept transfers, to maintain equitable earnings, and to hold down turnover. Moreover, some store managers seemed to show little interest in increasing volume. On occasion, a store manager would complain that higher volume "hurt him."

Some of the store managers who had operated stores under this plan felt that the plan was complicated and most of them did not understand how incentives were figured. One of the managers who had benefited from the plan expressed surprise: "I did not do a thing, other than what I was ordinarily expected to do." Another one said, "The big guy could make money; the little one could make money; but the middle guy got nothing."

## THE INCENTIVE PLAN

By early 1967, Edward Ralston, the originator of the "Olympics Plan," had left Olympic and was replaced by Mr. Joseph Hilden. In October 1967, the plan was revised and replaced by the Incentive Plan.

"The Incentive Plan" was devised to rectify the above problems. It was to be simple and easy to understand and was designed to involve the store manager in day-to-day operations. Basically the plan rewarded the store managers for (1) increasing sales, and (2) reducing costs in operation. For details of the plan and how to figure out the incentive remuneration, see Exhibit 3.

Each store manager, with the assistance of his district manager, was required under the plan to submit a sales budget and a controllable cost budget for each quarter. These budgets were reviewed by the Salary and

## EXHIBIT 3

### The Incentive Plan

1. All store operators, with the assistance of their District Managers, will budget the sales and controllable expenses of their stores by period.
2. These budgets will be reviewed by a Salary and Budget Committee composed of David Brown, Robert Jacobson, Joseph Hilden, your Division Manager, and your District Manager. The budget will be accepted or modified and returned.
3. All operators' salaries will be reviewed when his or her initial budget is submitted and at least annually thereafter.
4. Operators whose sales exceed budget and whose contributions to fixed expense and overhead exceed budget will receive 10% of the increase. For example, if a store is budgeted at:

| | |
|---|---|
| Sales | $300,000 |
| Controllable expenses | $209,000 |
| Contribution to fixed expense and overhead | $ 91,000 |

and the Salary and Budget Committee accepts the budget, and then the year end actual figures are:

| | |
|---|---|
| Sales | $310,000 |
| Controllable expense | $214,000 |
| Contribution to fixed expense and overhead | $ 96,000 |

the operator would receive $1,500.

| | Budget | Actual | Incentive |
|---|---|---|---|
| Sales | $300,000 | $310,000 | $1,000 (10% of $10,000) |
| Contribution to fixed expense and overhead | $ 91,000 | $ 96,000 | $ 500 (10% of $ 5,000) |

Each period "P&L" sheet will show performance in relation to the budgeted figures so that each four weeks you will know your standing exactly. One-half of the incentive profit due will be distributed quarterly, with any remaining balance paid following the year end; however, the partner must be associated with Olympic at that time.

Poor performance in one area can offset good performance in another. Using our example:

| | Budget | Actual | Incentive |
|---|---|---|---|
| Sales | $300,000 | $295,000 | −$500 (10% of $5,000) |
| Contribution to fixed expense and overhead | $ 91,000 | $ 92,000 | +$100 (10% of $1,000) |
| | | | −$400 |

In this illustration, there would not be a profit payment to the manager, however the new business year would start fresh with no loss carry-forward.

The purpose of this modification is to reward Managers more accurately for their performance in their stores. In essence, *each manager and his or her store have their own individual plan.* Please do not hesitate to ask questions that you may have now or in the future. Excellence is a result of our combined effort, and we must all, as members of Olympic's management, seek constantly to improve whatever we do.

### Questions and Answers

The following may help to give you a better understanding of this plan:

1. Question: What does the manager budget?
   Answer: Every item of the "P&L" except training and contribution of fixed expenses and overhead.
2. Question: When and how will managers receive their incentive?
   Answer: Managers will be paid as soon as possible after close of quarterly period. 50% of earned incentive paid quarterly. Balance to be paid at end of fiscal year providing Manager is still in our employ.

Exhibit 3 *(continued)*

3. Question: Will manager losses be carried forward from one year to the next?
   Answer: No.
4. Question: Who is eligible?
   Answer: Any manager permanently assigned.
5. Question: How are quarterly periods divided?
   Answer: First quarter, 12 weeks; second quarter 16 weeks; third and fourth quarters, 12 weeks.
6. Question: What is the starting date for newly assigned partners?
   Answer: Beginning of period nearest to the date of assignment as permanent manager.
7. Question: What is the "cutoff" date for a manager who is transferred?
   Answer: Beginning of period nearest to the effective date of transfer.
8. Question: Will profit sharing continue for partners?
   Answer: Yes.
9. Question: Will my salary be affected if operating figures are poor?
   Answer: No.
10. Question: How will price increases be handled?
    Answer: All price increases will be made quarterly. Budgets will be reviewed and adjusted accordingly.
11. Question: Is a robbery a controllable charge if the manager was not negligent?
    Answer: No.
12. Question: What allowance is made for a *new* store?
    Answer: New stores will not be budgeted until the first three full periods have been completed. Budget goals and objectives will begin with the fourth period.
13. Question: Will managers receive incentive during extended absences?
    Answer: They will receive their share up to the period when a permanent manager is assigned.
14. Question: When will managers get figures?
    Answer: Approximately two weeks after the close of each period.
15. Question: How soon after budget projections have been submitted will managers be notified of acceptance or modification.
    Answer: Within four weeks.
16. Question: What happens to incentive profits or losses if transferred to another store?
    Answer: Incentive profits or losses are carried to his new assignment. For example, if a manager is transferred at the end of four weeks, he would carry forward his incentive profit or loss for *his* four weeks.

Budget Committee of the company. For sales above the approved sales budget and savings in cost below the approved cost budget, the store manager would get 10 percent as his reward in addition to his monthly salary. As feedback to the manager, "P&L sheets" were used.

Referring to the controllable cost budget, Mr. Rufus, Personal Assistant to the Vice President of Sales, said "savings could be made in the payroll, containers, utensils, window and floor washings, and merchandise." Employment of personnel (part-time help) should be made daily, taking into account the weather conditions. Savings could be made in the use of containers—"paper cups could be saved, if regular cups are used in serving customers." A manager by being watchful could avoid pilferage. Savings could be effected in weekly washing of windows and stores by using the store personnel instead of professional help—if necessary, "a manager should do his own store." Similarly, by avoiding "over orders" and by ensuring that customers were not given more than what they pay for, merchandise could be saved.

### Results of the New Plan

Dave Brown reported that the Incentive Plan resulted in a dramatic improvement:

Turnover among store managers, which had been as high as 50 percent a year, was sharply reduced. We were able to make sure that the people who were making the greatest contributions received the most money. The reduced turnover came not so much because of the Incentive Plan, as such, but because we bought a lot of flexibility when we went into it. We obtained the flexibility to do what had to be done, i.e., make transfers, raise and lower income selectively. When I came into the company, some of the store managers were making more than they deserved and others were not making enough. We were able to correct that through the budgets. Under the Olympics Plan there was just no way to make adjustments.

The store managers who were doing well were very enthusiastic about the new plan when is was put into effect. Mr. Robbins, manager of a store in San Mateo, talked about how the Incentive Plan had worked for him.

This a way to make extra money. Every manager makes out a sales projection for a period and an expense budget. If he increases it a good deal, 10 percent of the increase in sales and 10 percent of the savings in expenses go to him as his reward. I have been able to make money under this program. Length of service is helpful in knowing the things that will help you make money—experience in knowing where to concentrate to make money. During warm weather, concentrate on ice cream. Control your expenses on payroll and merchandise.

For payroll, you should decide the number of people required as situations come out—find out whether anyone else would like to take a day off. If it is a hot day, call some more people to work. If you are having a storm, persuade people not to come to work. Also avoid waste and spoilage.

I don't know how many make money under this program. But some don't —these people have not tried. They don't keep their shops clean.

I am happy with the present incentive scheme. It is fair to the company and pretty good to the manager. However, I would look around for some other kind of incentive, maybe something where every manager could participate, some guaranteed payment—say half of 1 percent of sales. That way every manager would like it. I would design a program whereby everyone would get something. If they are good enough to become a manager, they should be able to get some incentive at least. Under the present program, we have only had one or two disbursements. Some do not make it.

The store manager makes the budget and sends it to the district manager. If the district manager does not approve it, he "suggests" changes. The budget then goes to the central committee. They either approve it or send it back. In my case, my first budget was approved. The second one was increased. On the third budget I sent, I have not yet heard anything from the company.

The manager of a store on Mission Hill described his reactions to the new program.

Originally each profit dollar was divided equally between the stores and the company. This plan has now been revised. The old plan was more lucrative, but this plan is also good. We have a salary which is predetermined by the company. You have no say in this. Your enthusiasm and past performance are all taken into account. Then you have a chance at the "incentive."

The present improvement in the plan was made by Mr. Hilden. He gave us a voice in determining what the budget should be. I have never gone without payment under this plan. It has been very good to me. I don't understand why others cannot also be benefited under this plan. The Olympic name is helpful in getting business. The supervision has been good—you are being constantly helped.

However, the plan also resulted in a number of problems for the company. The Salary and Budget Committee's revision of budgets (usually upwards) was resented by a number of managers. One manager ruefully remarked, "For the last budget, the committee revised it upwards by 15 percent. I have been increasing my sales by 20 percent each period. I worked hard, but there was no increase in business this time. The sales just did not come."

The greater problem arose out of the cost budget. The move to the Incentive Program had reduced many of the problems in this area, but in order to lower costs, many of the managers were still tempted to try short cuts. Some managers served stale foods, such as "over-ordered" bread. Cream would be diluted with milk. Drinking straws and napkins were not supplied to customers. Managers also skimped on servings. Often the floors and windows were not washed.

In order to ensure that Olympic standards were maintained and customers were not cheated, the district managers felt they had to do a "real police job" and the close supervision kept the supervisory cost high.

Another limitation of the plan was the time it consumed in the process of preparing and getting budgets approved.

## Dave Brown's Concerns

These problems concerned Dave Brown, but he saw them as manageable.

The thing that really concerns me is their effect on growth, both in terms of R.O.I. and volume. At present, our supervisory costs are high. I'd like to cut that down, but just reducing the number of supervisors without changing anything else won't work. I have been thinking about some training for our supervisors. I have given each a copy of McGregor's book, *The Human Side of Enterprise*, and I've asked them to read it and be ready to come and discuss it. I have also thought about bringing in someone to give them management training. If they could learn to help the store managers manage themselves better, we could begin to do something about those supervisory costs after a while.

Perhaps more importantly, we're missing opportunities to grow because we can't recruit, motivate, and retain enough good store managers to fill the needs we see. There is growth potential here in the Bay Area, but there is also plenty of potentially profitable business beyond San Francisco, into Sacramento, Stockton, and Oregon. To grow along either of those dimensions, I think we might have to change our setup in some way.

## Alternatives

In early 1969 Mr. Brown was considering several possible courses of action. First, he could continue to operate as at present. Profits were good, the company had a good reputation, and they had grown using their existing set up. It was his opinion, however, that both profits and growth could be enhanced if he could reduce the need for close supervision and thereby reduce supervisory costs. While he saw real advantages forthcoming if the store managers were allowed more freedom and initiative, he felt that any change should adequately motivate the store managers to maintain Olympic standards in the stores with respect to cleanliness, quality of food served, and customer service.

Mr. Brown felt that the above objectives of reducing supervisory costs, expanding operations of Olympic, and acquiring competent personnel could be achieved, either by (1) franchising Olympic Stores or by (2) a revised incentive plan that would involve the store manager in the day-to-day operations of the store and would adequately reward him for the efforts involved.

*Franchising Olympic Stores.*  Under this plan, Olympic would sell the right to operate Olympic ice cream stores to carefully selected operators. The operators selected would be required to make an investment towards the equipment provided in their stores by Olympic. This initial investment would vary depending on the size of the store and volume of sales desired. For a store with an annual sales volume of $60,000, the initial investment required from the operator would be $10,000.

The operators selected would be given training in all aspects of running an Olympic food store. The company would actively assist the operator in planning the layout of the stores, sales strategies, marketing techniques. Where required, the company would also help the operator to buy dairy and paper products at lower costs.

The operator would be required to carry the product lines of Olympic exclusively and no other products would be sold in the franchised stores. In addition, the operator would agree to maintain Olympic standards with respect to cleanliness and customer service. In order to ensure that only Olympic products were served in the stores and that Olympic standards were maintained, the store owners would agree to permit weekly inspection by an Olympic official and would also agree to comply with the recommendations made by this official.

In turn Olympic would agree to supply quality products at competitive prices and provide assistance in promoting the sale of its products. In addition, the store would be permitted to use the Olympic name.

According to information put out by firms who had gone into the franchising business, an efficiently operated store could provide from good to excellent returns for the franchisee. On annual sales of only $60,000.00 an operator could earn over $12,000.00 after meeting all expenses (see Exhibit 4), and Olympic's experience demonstrated that in a reasonably

### EXHIBIT 4

#### A Note on Franchising

The following note on franchising was prepared on the basis of an interview with the San Francisco district manager of a leading food store franchiser, Carsons Ice Cream Stores:

The profits in franchising come from sale of goods to the operators of the stores. As the store increases it's sales volume, the franchiser is directly benefited. The rationale of franchising is to increase the sale of your products without incurring any additional overhead. Through franchising, it is possible to extend the operations nationwide, through carefully selected operators. The operator has great motivation to ensure the success of his store as he has invested his money—most often his entire life savings. "The more the guy sells, the happier and wealthier he should be." This way the franchiser ensures increased sales without increase in overheads and managerial responsibility. "The advantage lies in that both the parties could make money without hurting each other."

To own a store under this plan, the operator is expected to invest around $10,000. The operator is then trained in all aspects of running a store. The company will actively assist the operator with planning of sales strategy, marketing techniques, and window display. The company would also assist the operator to buy dairy and paper products at lowest possible rates, if such assistance is required.

The franchiser's representative visits the shops once a week to ensure that the operator is not violating franchise regulations (see Appendix 1 to this exhibit). He would particularly ensure that the shop is kept clean, is attractive, and that only franchised goods are sold in the shop. The representative would help the operator in window display, accounting, etc., if need be. "We like to call our representatives 'business consultants' and they are not to 'bother' the operators."

The success of franchising lies in being honest with the operators. There should be no "kick back" to the franchiser in the purchase of dairy products, paper products, etc. "If you try to take a bigger piece of the pie, they will get disenchanted."

For the individual who becomes an operator, it is mainly an "emotional" experience. Normally these are individuals who have worked for large corporations, "who want action on their own. They want to make decisions themselves. Yet they are not entrepreneurs. A typical operator is in his mid-forties and he is willing to take only limited risks."

An efficient operator should make over 20 percent of the sales as his profits. Increased sales should yield higher returns to the operator. For a breakdown of expenses, see Appendix 2.

well-selected location, a volume of several times that figure could be attained.

A franchising arrangement would allow Olympic to greatly increase the sales without extensive additional overhead and supervisory costs. It would facilitate extension of the operations of Olympic in California and nearby states within a short period and with a minimum investment by Olympic. An advantage of franchising, of course, is that the franchisees invest their own money, often their entire life savings, and they frequently exert great personal effort to insure the success of the venture. Moreover, they tend to remain with the store. When franchising works well, both the franchisee and the franchiser benefit from this effort. Mr. Brown could see some real benefits for Olympic if they moved into franchising, but he had reservations about the accompanying loss of control.

A friend of his in the franchising business had found himself negotiating with a strong association formed by the franchisees he had helped set up in business: "In franchising," said Brown, "if you go in and tell an operator to clean up his parking lot, he'll take you in and show you how the tiles are coming loose from the building you had built for him."

**Own Your Own Store Plan.**    The other alternative he was considering was a revised incentive plan for the store managers. This plan, which was called the "Own Your Own Store Plan," was conceived by the company as an improvement over the existing Incentive Plan. Mr. Brown believed that the plan as conceived would serve the following purposes:

1.  It would reduce operating costs.
2.  It would reduce the need for close supervision and thereby result in reduced supervisory costs.
3.  It would help in getting and retaining capable managers.
4.  It would provide psychic income to the store managers (in addition to monetary benefits) and thereby greatly motivate them.

Under this plan, the store in a sense would "belong" to the store manager. The store manager would be supplied with a fully equipped and furnished store by Olympic. He would be required to buy all the inventory from Olympic.

Of the sales receipts of each store, the company would charge for the following: equipment, insurance, advertising, accounting, store rent, and royalty.

From the balance of the sales receipts the store manager would pay for the cost of merchandise, wages, and other expenses, if any. Whatever remained after meeting these expenses would be his. One of the managers believed that his profits on this basis would be around 6 percent of the gross sales receipts. On anticipated annual sales of $400,000 for his store, he hoped to get $24,000, twice his present salary. The income range to the store managers under the Incentive Plan had been $8,500 to $16,000, with an average of $11,000.

Mr. Brown had some concerns about the plan.

This year the store manager will be happy that he is doubling his income. But next year he may find it difficult to increase his earnings any further. Then he may be inclined to tinker with his shop maintenance expenses. His relations with supervisors might also get strained.

Mr. Brown was also concerned about the impact of the new plan on the supervisors.

Under this plan, the supervisor's role will be changed—his task will be to represent the customer more than the management. He should be concerned with cleanliness, maintenance of stores, quality of the food served, and *not with the costs*. He should talk like an outspoken customer. He should help the store manager only when he is asked. Under this plan, he is more a consultant than a supervisor. I expect the ratio of supervisors to stores to go down, and hence our supervisory expenses. The supervisor should realize that he is on a different career path from the store managers and he should not compare his income with that of store managers under the Plan. The company plans to increase his salary and would also constantly evaluate him with a view to rewarding him.

The plan would also help the company in retaining competent store managers.

With his educational and social background, the store manager will find it difficult to find another job paying over $20,000. Even if he is willing to take a cut, his wife would not permit him to do so. In addition, the plan offers intrinsic benefits to the manager. After all, he is running his own store.

Mr. Brown believed that the sense of "ownership" of the stores would motivate the store managers to give their best and they would do this under minimum supervision. In fact, he believed that reduced supervision by itself would be another positive factor to motivate the managers. This would help Olympic to extend the operation throughout the Bay Area. While this plan would require greater capital investment than franchising, it would retain greater managerial and organizational control of all the stores. It would also bring higher profits per unit.

## Other Considerations

From the study he had made, Brown was convinced that different kinds of men would be needed, depending on the alternative he chose:

In franchising, you need a stronger, more self-sustaining guy. Our present setup attracts and utilizes someone best who likes and can use some supervision —someone who likes working on a team, who functions better with the support, the security, and the advancement opportunity that comes from being a part of a big organization.

In franchising, you also have to deal with different motivations and take a closer look at the family. In franchising you get an older man, maybe 45, who's taking maybe his last chance to get out from under and to get on his own. He might work like the devil, and stick with it, but he may be harder to handle. In franchising you also have to look hard at the wife. She has to give the O.K. on investing the savings and she will probably work in the store. (In fact, it can help if he has two or three teenagers.)

In fact, one of the biggest issues is how you move from one plan to the other. The guys who work out well and are satisfied under one plan may not be the ones you need under a new setup. When I was at Stanford, we used to talk a lot about what to do, which alternative to choose. That's the easiest part; the tough issues concern how you get there from where you are.

## APPENDIX 1

### Rules for Operation of Carsons Ice Cream Stores

1. Store shall be kept open for business for twelve months of each year and on each and every day, including holidays, during the hours of 10:00 a.m. to 11:00 p.m. during the months of May through September, and during the hours of 11:00 a.m. to 10:00 p.m. during the months of October through April, excepting only on Christmas Day and as required by public law. The premises may be kept open in excess of the hours indicated above at the option of the store owner.
2. Inside fluorescent ceiling lights will be kept on during business hours. Soffit fluorescent lights over back bar will be kept on 24 hours per day.
3. The outside electrically illuminated sign will be lighted for not less than the period of time between dusk and 30 minutes after closing.
4. There will be no change in original store layout or equipment without prior permission in writing from Carsons Ice Cream.
5. Store owner will maintain in stock at all times a complete assortment and sufficient quantity of every Carsons Ice Cream flavor available for delivery to store. The only ice cream, sherbets, ices, or other frozen confections which may be sold, served, or used in the store are those made or distributed by Carsons, or its authorized territorial franchise holder, and marked on the container or package in which they are delivered to the store "Carsons," or with other trademark or authorized marking of Carsons. Only such syrups, toppings, flavorings, or similar products for mixing with, covering of, or serving with Carsons ice cream sundaes, servings of Carsons ice cream, sherbet, or ice may be served, used, or sold in or from the store as bear a label indicating approval of Carsons, or are the type and quality which has been otherwise approved in writing by Carsons.
6. Birthday sign-up cards and sign-up poster sign will be displayed, and mailed postals will be redeemed for free ice cream cone.
7. Store owner and all employees will wear approved, clean uniforms with "Carsons" emblem, and wear head covering.
8. The store, sidewalk, and parking area will always be kept clean and neat.
9. There will be no smoking or gum chewing within store area by store owner or his employees, except in rest room or storage area.
10. Store owner and his employees will participate in approved method of using sample spoon merchandising of the various ice cream flavors.
11. The only window, interior and exterior signs, trade name, or advertising permitted will be those furnished by, or approved in writing by, Carsons or its authorized territorial franchise holder.

## Appendix 1 *(continued)*

12. No grocery items, food items, or beverages such as: sandwiches, pie, cake, hamburgers, soup, coffee, hot chocolate, bottled or fountain drinks (except approved root beer), etc. will be sold or distributed in or from this store. No products of any kind or nature other than Carsons' authorized products will be sold or distributed in or from this store.

13. No additional kinds of goods shall be added to the store's inventory or offered for sale after opening of store without prior permission first obtained in writing from Carsons Ice Cream.

14. Portions and formulas on all fountain and carry out items will be as per attached list.

15. All cartons, cups, boxes, bags, and other containers or paper goods used in the store to package or dispense or wrap Carsons Ice Cream products must bear the trademarked imprint, and only approved type of dishes, tableware, spoons, scoops, cones, and utensils and other items used in serving ice cream products will be used.

16. Dry ice will be maintained in stock at all times.

17. No cigarettes or other smoking items shall be sold, and no coin operated machine of any type will be permitted on premises.

18. Customers will not be allowed in back room or behind counter at any time.

19. Store owner agrees to contract for yellow pages trademark advertising where made available, and will subscribe to white pages listing in local telephone directory as "Carsons Ice Cream Stores."

20. Store will be repainted inside at least once every twenty-four months, following designated color scheme.

21. Store owner is responsible for cutting down and emptying cans, and rearranging ice cream, so as to have adequate spaces available in freezer cabinets for ice cream which store owner has ordered.

22. All advertising copy placed by or for store owners must have prior written approval of Carsons Ice Cream.

23. Store owner shall comply with all federal, state, county, and city laws and ordinances affecting or respecting the use or occupancy of the premises.

24. Store owner agrees to receive inspection relative to cleanliness and operation in accordance with "Store Visit Report Form" and agrees to comply with recommendations regarding these matters.

25. Store owner shall at all times maintain the store premises, including all exterior signs, and the interior of the store, including all fixtures and equipment, in good and neat condition.

26. Store owner will review above "Rules For Operation" with all store employees.

## APPENDIX 2

Typical Operating Statement for a
Carson's Store Doing a Volume of
under $60,000

| Sales | 100% |
|---|---|
| Cost of ice cream | 42 |
| Gross profit | 58 |
| Expenses | |
|   Insurance | |
|   Rent | |
|   Accounting | |
|   Paper goods | |
|   Fountain supplies | |
|   Dry ice | |
|   Milk | |

**Appendix 2** *(continued)*

Laundry
Telephone
Utilities
Licenses
Maintenance
Advertising

|                      |         |
|----------------------|---------|
|                      | 23      |
| Profit before payroll | 35      |
| Payroll              | 12–14   |
| Operating profit     | 21–23%  |

# Pennsylvania Metals Corporation*

PENNSYLVANIA METALS CORPORATION was founded in the 1890's to mine, refine, and sell iron bauxite. The foundry was built next to the mine in the small Quaker town of Newton and the organization of PMC was set up on strict functional lines with mining, refining, production, and sales reporting to the president. The concern prospered and rapidly grew, and slowly diversified into other metals, acquiring mines all over the North American continent. As the company grew and diversified, communications between functional groups became more difficult. The small town atmosphere of friendliness helped resolve these communications blocks by providing an adaptive device of informal communications across functional boundaries. The president approved of these informal arrangements, and there soon grew up within the company the expressed norm of openness, friendliness, and persuasion as the PMC modus operandi.

By 1964 PMC was one of the largest producers of metals and related products in the world. Headquarters for the worldwide operations was still in Newton, where all employees above a certain rank were required to spend a year's acclimatization period to learn their way about the organizational maze. PMC was proud that it published no organization chart, and most business was conducted across organizational lines by means of friendly persuasion. Because of the "formalized" informal procedure, it was not uncommon for a man to have two or even three persons above him, sometimes in different geographical locations, to whom he was equally responsible.

Exhibit 1 shows the case writer's impression of the sales department organization at PMC. The sales product groups, sales service groups, and the sales offices all reported directly to top sales management. In keeping with the PMC philosophy, however, all groups communicated directly with

---

* This case study originated directly from a sales management situation in The Dow Chemical Company in the early sixties. The systems analysis, planning implementation, and follow-up were conducted by M. H. P. Morand and G. T. Westbrook over a three-year period.

## EXHIBIT 1

Sales Department Organization

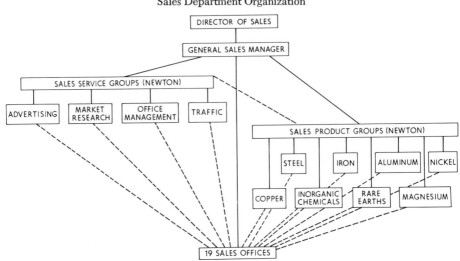

each other. In day-to-day activities, the managers of product and service groups operated much as line executives. The Newton sales groups were constantly in touch with the field sales offices.

Exhibit 2 shows the sales organization as seen by an aluminum district sales manager (DSM). The DSM reported to two bosses: to his office manager on administrative issues, and to the aluminum sales manager at Newton on issues dealing with aluminum. The aluminum sales force was divided into three groups: sheeting, building materials (BM), and extrusion sales (ES), all reporting to the DSM, but with an informal relationship to their respective departments at Newton.

While the DSM's were responsible for all aluminum sales in their territories, the department managers, such as Bob Kapp, the ES manager, were responsible for coordinating the efforts of all salesmen in their departments and for long-range market strategy. Bob Kapp explained his relationship with the DSM as follows:

I don't have a direct autocratic control over them. I have a high degree of influence, but there is a certain amount of persuasion that has to be used with some of them who are more concerned with their prerogatives at times than in getting the job done.

Field salesmen were recruited centrally by the personnel department at Newton, which was also responsible for the training of all salesmen. Lectures, role-play, case discussions, and plant tours were used to train salesmen in an intensive program which lasted five to ten months and

## EXHIBIT 2

District Sales Office Organization as Seen by NY DSM, Aluminum

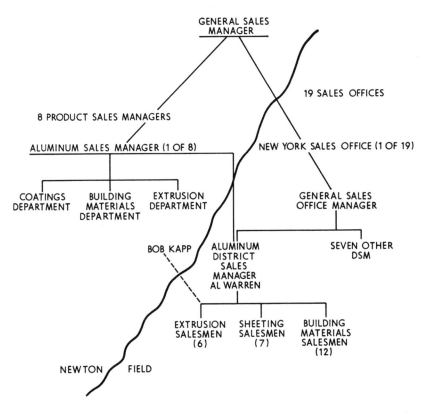

consisted of a company orientation program, sales techniques clinics, and product technology training. Salesmen were paid a straight salary, and increase in pay was related to promotion to higher categories and finally to administrative positions. This was consistent with the general policy of paying for the job and moving the more experienced men up to more central positions.

The sales offices were located in major industrial centers. Salesmen were allocated on the basis of volume sold and assigned geographical territories within the districts. The geographical division of labor was used to minimize the salesmen's travel time. Salesmen usually spent four days a week on the road, often not returning home at night. One day a week was usually spent in the office touching base and doing clerical work.

The PMC philosophy of openness and friendliness extended to the sales offices and gave the company a reputation for helpfulness and service to its customers. District managers were loath to be "autocratic" with their salesmen, preferring influence and expecting the salesmen to make many of their own decisions. The DSM's saw themselves more in the role of helpers than bosses. Al Warren, the New York DSM, explained:

I wouldn't say that it was a 100 percent permissive management, but it leans a great deal in that direction. We search for salesmen who are self-starters, who supply their own motivation. Because we are organized so loosely, the salesmen have no authority over staff functions, technical groups, or the research departments at Newton. Our solution to problems that require the services of various groups depends on the salesman's skill in motivating the proper people at the proper level in the other departments to bring resources to bear against his customers' problems.

It takes three sides of a triangle to make a good salesman—knowledge of the customer, the product, and the company. The younger salesmen have the knowledge of the product and the technology, but they don't know the customer and they don't know the company. It is easier for them to get to know the small account than the larger one, because the small fellow needs his help.

I regard at least a major part of my job as motivating men to handle themselves properly in their relationships with other departments so as to get maximum efforts from those departments on our customers' problems. This is the reason that our product sales managers insisted that no one should be a DSM unless he had extensive Newton experience sufficient to understand all the departments and all the services we have as resources.

Salesmen were assigned territories and were responsible for all accounts within that area. A young salesman in the New York office told the case writer:

You go where the business is, but you often get mouse-trapped into spending several hours with a very small account. Small accounts depend on us to give them help, and most of the time it is things we can solve for them ourselves. When you're in the area and you have an hour left in the day you drop in to see a small account and before you know it 'you've spent a couple of hours. But it is hard for me to refuse to help an account that has been buying 50,000 pounds from me for the last five years. Big accounts are much harder to crack; you need an appointment and you have to see many people; unless you can get a fast answer back to them from Newton they lose interest.

The salesmen in the New York office considered their highest motivator the experience of a successful sale, and all rated monetary rewards lower on the scale. The New York DSM explained to the case writer that a modest cash bonus existed, but that he did not use it as he felt that none of his salesmen really deserved it.

Early in 1962 Robert Kapp was faced with statistics that showed a decline in 1961 total extrusion sales. In analyzing the sales figures he became aware that a great deal of the salesmen's effort was allocated to small accounts and that only 35 percent of the field sales effort was planned on customers who produced 85 percent of the dollar volume. Starting with the conviction that the distribution of sales effort was unbalanced, he initiated a computer simulation to optimize sales effort. Exhibit 3 shows the result of the study.

## EXHIBIT 3

### Computer Simulation of Sales Effort, June 1962
Summary

A. *An Outline of the Project*

This report summarizes the *results* of a study on the allocation of sales effort in the extrusion sales area. The objective of the allocation problem was to distribute the available field sales time to six customer groupings, defined by peak annual sales for accounts over: $1,000,000; $500,000; $250,000; $100,000; $50,000; and finally, below $50,000. Accounts were placed in these classes based on their peak sales in the past five years.

A computer model was built to solve an optimization problem in six variables, e.g., the time spent in each class. The basis for this model was a set of six estimated sales response–sales effort curves. It was assumed a unique S-shaped response curve would exist for each class. However, only limited data were available upon which to base these curves. As a result, several different S curves were used for each class. These passed through the current sales-time position and asymptotically approached the estimated sales maximum. This sales maximum was based on the sums of the peak sales years for accounts in Classes 1 to 5. For Class 6, a value of double the current sales was used.

Based on such curves, several computer and other studies were made on the optimal time allocation and sales force size.

B. *Observations*

1. For all different S curves combinations used, the computer model could never justify investing any time in Class 6 (below $50,000 accounts).
2. The allocation of time to the six classes was relatively insensitive to the set of S curves used. The maximum sales, on the other hand, varied considerably from an indicated increase of 18 MM $/yr. for a pessimistic case up to almost 47 MM $/yr. for an optimistic case.
3. A reduction as small as 20 percent in the time spent in Class 6 resulted in an indicated return of from 45 to 58 percent of the total indicated potential, of approximately 14 to 18 MM $/yr.
4. The computer model was used to estimate a curve of optimum sales force size as a function of the cost of salesmen in M $ sales/year. If the unit cost of salesmen was placed at 500 M $ sales/year, an optimum sales force size of 39 to 41 men would be predicted.
5. A probability study was made on a random sample of Class 6 accounts. Two probabilities were estimated:
   a. Probability an account would move up to Class 4 or 5 was 1 out of 18.
   b. Probability an account would move down to zero sales was 1 out of 3. Thus out of 18 accounts, one would be expected to move up, six go out of business, and 11 remain in the same class.

C. *Recommendations*

1. No changes appear needed, for the present, in the existing sales force size.
2. The time spent in Class 6 should be reduced by at least 20 to 30 percent and redistributed to the other classes.
3. In order to evaluate the influence of the above change, provision should be made to carefully monitor the sales responses, sales calls, and any other significant variables from the time any change is initiated.

Exhibit 3 *(continued)*

### INTRODUCTION

This report summarizes the basis, and results obtained, from a quantitative study into the sales time allocation problem for extrusion sales. The objective of this study was to establish quantitative guides which, *on the average,* and *in the absence of additional data,* would allocate the available sales time to distinct customer classes. Six classes were used in this study, composed of accounts with sales in *any* of the past five years

Above $1,000,000———Class 1
"     500,000———Class 2
"     250,000———Class 3
"     100,000———Class 4
"      50,000———Class 5
Below   50,000———Class 6

If quantitative guides could be developed, a means to establish a time budget for each *class* would be at hand. It is important to note it would still be up to the individual salesmen to allocate this class time to *individual accounts.* However, this budget would highlight the penalty of excessive effort on the more numerous and accessible smaller accounts at the expense of the larger, more productive accounts.

The question was posed—"What could the techniques of operations research contribute toward an evaluation of this distribution? Further, what methods or criteria could be used to estimate the optimum allocation?" As an approach to this problem, a computer model was built, simulating, as best as possible, the sales-time structure in each class. All other factors that affect sales were assumed constant. The *hypothesis* was made that an S-shaped relationship would exist between sales response and sales time invested in a specific class. With such a curve, no sales effort would lead to very small, if any, sales. As more effort was invested, some sales would result, slowly at first, but gradually accelerating. This response would eventually level off as a point of saturation was approached. Let:

$S_i$    = Sales response in class $i$ MM $/year
$t_i$    = Time invested in class $i$ man days/year
$S_i(t_i)$ = S-shaped $S - t$ relationship in class $i$
$L_i$   = Least time allowed in class $i$ man days/year
$M_i$  = Most time allowed in class $i$ man days/year
$S$    = Total sales from all classes MM $/year
$T$    = Total sales force size man days/year
$N$   = Number of classes

The allocation problem can now be stated mathematically: *Find* the set of times, $(t_1, t_2, \ldots t_N)$, that *maximizes*

$$S = S_1 \neq S_2 \neq \ldots S_N \qquad (1)$$

*subject to*

$$T = t_1 \neq t_2 \neq \ldots t_N$$

and

$$L_i \leq t_i \leq M_i \qquad i = 1, 2, \ldots N^*$$

It is possible to visualize this optimization problem if only two or three classes are involved. A *hypothetical* case is shown in Figure 1 for three classes. Here the times spent in Class 1 and Class 2 are plotted on two of the axes. The third time can always be found from:

$$t_3 = T - t_1 - t_2 \qquad (2)$$

Given the individual S curves $S_1(t_1)$, $S_2(t_2)$, $S_3(t_3)$, the total sales resulting from any combination of the three times can be calculated and plotted on the vertical axis. Figure 1 illustrates a typical sales response surface or "mountain."

If more than three classes exist, recourse must be made to mathematics and computers to obtain the optimum allocation.

The real sales world is an extremely complex place with many intangible and dynamic factors that could influence the purchase of a product. Thus the actual

---

\* The symbol $\leq$ may be read as "less than or equal to."

**Exhibit 3** *(continued)*

## FIGURE 1

Sales Time Allocation Three Customer Classes
( $ response surface )

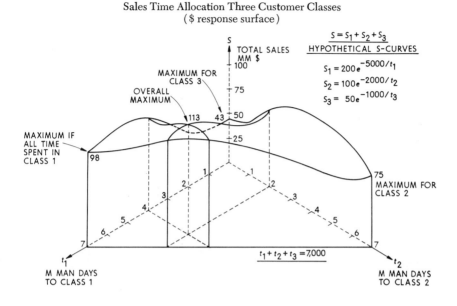

$$S = S_1 + S_2 + S_3$$
HYPOTHETICAL S-CURVES

$$S_1 = 200e^{-5000/t_1}$$
$$S_2 = 100e^{-2000/t_2}$$
$$S_3 = 50e^{-1000/t_3}$$

TOTAL SALES MM $

MAXIMUM FOR CLASS 3

OVERALL MAXIMUM

MAXIMUM IF ALL TIME SPENT IN CLASS 1

113    43

98

MAXIMUM FOR CLASS 2

$$t_1 + t_2 + t_3 = 7{,}000$$

$t_1$
M MAN DAYS TO CLASS 1

$t_2$
M MAN DAYS TO CLASS 2

## FIGURE 2

Effort Required per Million Dollars of Sales in 1963

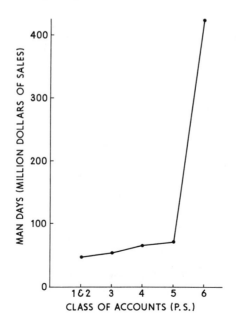

Exhibit 3 *(continued)*

## FIGURE 3

Sales Allocation as a Multistage Decision Process
(Maximize $S = S_1(t_1) + S_2(t_2) \ldots S_N(t_N)$
subject to $T = t_1 + t_2 + \ldots t_N$)

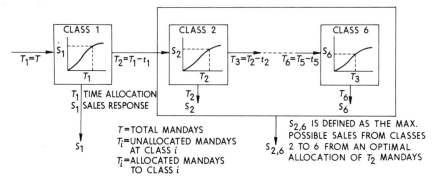

METHOD

1. If $S_{2,6}$ were known for any value of $T_2$, the 6 stage process could be divided into 2 as shown. For any decision at Class 1, $t_1$ and hence $t_2$ would be known. $S_1$ and $S_{2,6}$ would follow.
2. If $S_{1,6}$ is defined analogously to $S_{2,6}$, one could write:
$$S_{1,6} = \text{maximum } [S_1(t_1) = S_{2,6}(T_2)]$$
3. The value of $t_1$ that gives this maximum would be the optimal policy for Class 1.
4. The relations $S_{6,6}(T_6)$; $S_{5,6}(T_5)$; $S_{4,6}(T_4)$, etc. must be generated initially by the above rule.

allocation of sales effort is a very difficult and critical management decision. The model used here is perhaps an idealized analog of the real world. Yet this is essential if any mathematical allocation of the available manpower is to be contemplated. Only one type of variable is considered: sales time. However this is one of the few control variables at the manager's disposal. It should be emphasized that this model does not presume that other factors will not influence sales, but rather that these could be considered separately and that no major interactions would exist between these and sales time. Because profits by account cannot be accurately determined, this model uses the premise that maximum sales equal maximum profits.

### ALLOCATION CASE STUDIES

*Computer Results for Cases 1 to 6*

Six basic case studies were run on the computer. Case 1 was a test run to insure the validity of the computer model. Results from the model are essentially identical to the results shown in Figure 1. Cases 2, 3, and 4 are parametric studies for three different sets of S curves. Case 5 was the special case where the MR was set equal to the AR. Case 6 was an identical study as Case 4, but with a linear S–t relationship in place of an S curve for Class 6. The rather startling results for Cases 2 to 6 are listed in Table 1. In all cases, the computer model could find no incentive for investing any time in Class 6. Thus *if the real world was similar to any of the five sets of S–t relationships used,* the results from the computer model would indicate a redistribution of Class 6 time to the other five classes was

Exhibit 3 *(continued)*

**TABLE 1**

Sales Allocation Model (in Man Days)
(output results)

| Case Number | Current Status | 1 Test Case | 2 $C = 3$ | 3 $C = 4$ | 4 $C = 1$ | 5 $AR = MR$ | 6 Linear $S_6 - t_6$ |
|---|---|---|---|---|---|---|---|
| $t_1$ | 780 | 3950 | 1690 | 1690 | 1690 | 1690 | 1690 |
| $t_2$ | 510 | 2054 | 1280 | 1280 | 1540 | 1400 | 1540 |
| $t_3$ | 880 | 996 | 2150 | 2150 | 2320 | 2230 | 2320 |
| $t_4$ | 1180 | — | 2600 | 2560 | 2570 | 2560 | 2570 |
| $t_5$ | 1120 | — | 2280 | 2320 | 1880 | 2120 | 1880 |
| $t_6$ | 5530 | — | 0 | 0 | 0 | 0 | 0 |
| Total sales MM $ | 86.0 | 112.4 | 128.0 | 133.0 | 104.0 | 117.0 | 104.0 |
| Indicated sales increase MM $ | — | — | 42.0 | 47.0 | 18.0 | 31.0 | 18.0 |

Note: Parameter $C$ equals different values of S curves.

desirable. In optimization studies such as this, the results or allocation policy ($t_1,$* $t_2$* ... $t_6$*) that yield the optimum are the most interesting and important features. Although rather drastic changes were made on the input data, the allocation policy proved relatively insensitive. On the other hand, the actual maximum resultant sales, estimated by the model, varied from 104 MM $ for a pessimistic case to 133 MM $ for the most optimistic case. For the pessimistic case, this still represented an increase of 18 MM $.

*The Allocation of Time to Class 6*

It is obvious that such a drastic change as reducing 5530 man days down to zero would be completely impractical and unrealistic. Some time must be allocated to Class 6. As noted in Equation 1, the computer model was designed with lower and upper restrictions on the time allocated to each class. This feature could now be used to study the influence of this restriction ($L_6$) on the optimal allocation. Case 7 was thus set up where $L_6$ was varied from 950 to 4750 man days. Results are tabulated in Table 2. These indicated that *a relatively small reduction in time spent in Class 6 would produce a significant percentage of the potential improvement.*

The resultant curves for Cases 3 and 4 again give strong indication of a significant response in sales from a small percentage change in time. Thus a 20 percent reduction of $t_6$ from 5530 to 4440 man days would lead to an indicated 45 to 58 percent of the total potential sales increase.

### PREREQUISITES TO IMPLEMENTATION

If it is found desirable to implement some portion of the findings of this study, several factors must be considered. The average value could be used as the time allocation to each class, at the desired level of implementation. This would provide a guide on the time allocation to each class. These budgets would now have to be converted into individual allotments to provide a guide for the 40 salesmen. Let:

$$B_i = \text{the man day budget for class } i$$
$$t_{ij} = \text{time spent in class } i \text{ by salesman } j$$

Exhibit 3 *(continued)*

## TABLE 2

Case 7—Sales Allocation Results with Time Restriction on Class 6
(input data for case 5)

| Man Day Restriction on Class 6 ($L_6$) | 0 (Case 5) | 950 | 1900 | 2850 | 3800 | 4750 | 5530 (Current) |
|---|---|---|---|---|---|---|---|
| $t_1$ | 1690 | 1530 | 1360 | 1330 | 1150 | 1150 | 780 |
| $t_2$ | 1400 | 1270 | 1130 | 1090 | 940 | 950 | 510 |
| $t_3$ | 2210 | 2050 | 1870 | 1600 | 1430 | 1470 | 880 |
| $t_4$ | 2540 | 2350 | 2070 | 1790 | 1520 | 1670 | 1180 |
| $t_5$ | 2160 | 1850 | 1670 | 1340 | 1160 | 0 | 1120 |
| $t_6$ | 0 | 950 | 1900 | 2850 | 3800 | 4750 | 5530 |
| Total sales MM $ | 117.0 | 114.0 | 111.0 | 108.0 | 104.0 | 89.0 | 86.0 |
| Indicated sales increase MM $ | 31.0 | 28.0 | 25.0 | 22.0 | 18.0 | 13.0 | 0 |
| % of total potential | 100.0 | 90.0 | 80.5 | 71.0 | 58.0 | 41.8 | 0 |

A total of 240 $t_{ij}$ values would have to be assigned. Several criteria could be used in this selection:

1. Forty salesman time balance equations of the form

$$t_{1,j} \neq t_{2,j} = \ldots t_{6,j} = 250; j = 1 \text{ to } 40 \tag{12}$$

2. Six class budget equations of the form

$$t_{i,1} \neq t_{i,2} \neq \ldots t_{i,35} = B_i; i = 1 \text{ to } 6 \tag{13}$$

These equations can be written very compactly in a 6-row by 40-column matrix as illustrated below. Here, the sum of the elements in each row and in each column must equal the indicated value.

| Class \ Man | 1 | 2 | 3 | | 40 | Class Budget |
|---|---|---|---|---|---|---|
| 1 | $t_{1,1}$ | $t_{1,2}$ | $t_{1,3}$ | ... | $t_{1,40}$ | $B_1$ |
| 2 | $t_{2,1}$ | $t_{2,2}$ | $t_{2,3}$ | ... | $t_{2,40}$ | $B_2$ |
| ⋮ | | | | | | ⋮ |
| 6 | $t_{6,1}$ | $t_{6,2}$ | $t_{6,3}$ | ... | $t_{6,40}$ | $B_6$ |
| Man days / Man/yr. | 250 | 250 | 250 | | 250 | 10,000 |

3. The individual values of $t_{ij}$ could be prorated by the number and size of accounts handled by each salesman in a given class. Some exceptions may occur where a given set of accounts could not possibly absorb the prorated time. In some sensitive cases they might require more. Some of the $t_{ij}$ will be zero. For example, all of the 40 salesmen could not call on the 11 Class 1 accounts. All of these factors would have to be accounted for and balanced out by trial and error so the above equations were met.

Finally, provision would have to be made to proceed with the implementation on a planned experiment basis where the results could be followed very closely and the influence of other variables could be factored out. This would permit the observation and measurement of any significant sales response, the individual marginal response, the response profile, and, finally, the time lag from initiation of the time change to the final steady state condition. From the strategic viewpoint, this analysis can be used to derive a salesman's time budgets for time allocation to each class of account.

Exhibit 3 *(continued)*

A PROBABILITY STUDY ON CLASS 6

One of the major reasons for investing time in Class 6 is the fact that there is some probability that an account in this class will eventually move up to a more valuable position. What are the odds for the transition of an account from Class 6 to Class 5, or better? In order to answer this question, a random selection of accounts from Class 6 was studied. Class 6 consists of hundreds of accounts, with a small number of these customers accounting for a large percentage of the sales. Hence, in order to avoid any possible bias, the sample was selected by "throwing the dice," e. g., via the selection of a random number from a random number table.

Six-year sales histories were available from 1956 to 1961. The first of these three years were used to define Class 6. The last three years could then be studied to determine the transition probabilities. The accounts were thus selected randomly from the 1958 list, but only those retained whose annual sales were below $50,000 in 1958, 1957, and 1956. The probability of moving up ($p_u$) to Class 5 or 4 was estimated at 0.0555, or 1 chance in 18. The probability of going out of business, ($P_d$), in terms of purchases from PMC, was estimated at 0.3385, or 1 chance in 3. Thus the odds were 6 to 1 that a Class 6 account would move down and not up.

Since these probabilities are statistical values, a confidence limit can be placed on the estimate. Thus one could be 95 percent certain that the true value of $p_u$ lay within the limits 0.0236 to 0.0874, with the most likely value equal to 0.0555. If one were in an optimistic frame, he could expect 1 account in 12 to move up. If one were pessimistically inclined, these odds would be 1 out of 42.

The computer simulation clearly showed that the salesmen should spend more time on the larger accounts. Mr. Kapp explained:

When we say that the time should be trebled on an account, that does not at all necessarily mean three times as many calls. The confrontation does not necessarily increase threefold, but the time spent on behalf of that account can be time spent back at Newton; it can be spent on visits by these people to our plants; it can be spent in libraries; it is time spent in noodling that account. It's like a football game—you prepare all week for 60 minutes of play on the field. You don't prepare nearly so much for a scrub game as you do for a professional game. The confrontation in most cases is identical except that you are selling in depth. The salesman becomes the focal point or the catalyst for the potential utilization of all types of resources with PMC.

Salesmen play this role with varying degrees of success depending upon the degree of respect that the groups here have for a salesman. One guy can call and he can get going like that! Another guy may have a much better reason, but because his posture may not be as healthy he may have to work twice or three times as hard to get the same resource employed—or he may have a record of having cried "wolf" a couple of times. There is nothing better than a good track record for getting resources used and there is nothing more retarding than a poor record.

Although the simulation showed that salesmen, as a whole, should spend very little time on the smaller accounts, Mr. Kapp felt that the individual salesmen themselves should determine which of their small accounts they should eliminate. Salesmen were therefore put on a time budget by class of account. To further test the validity of the model Mr. Kapp devised a controlled experiment to implement the desired change in salesmen's call patterns:

After this was run out on the computer, it indicated that we should shift time from class 6[1] accounts from the current 60 percent down to 0 percent. We felt that this would be going too far. We wanted to change this more gradually. We divided our 19 offices into two groups from a product and a market mix. We then expected that in one group we would have a controlled shift of class 6 by 20 percent and a concomitant increase in effort on classes 1 through 5. We expected the second group would reduce class 6 by 40 percent. We tried to break it down so that the two groups would be comparable.

The computer findings as well as the experimental plan were unveiled to the district sales managers at the yearly sales meeting in 1963.

We gave them a rough outline of what we wanted done and expected the DSM's to follow through as they saw fit. They all agreed to make these changes.

Although the DSM's had agreed in 1963 to the logic of the proposed shift in the ES salesmen's call patterns, the sales analyses conducted a year later showed:

1. The distribution of the effort today differs little from what it was in 1961. Thus, the recommended shifts in sales effort generally did not take place. The salesmen apparently did not accept the recommendations.
2. The great imbalance in effort still exists.
3. Since the experiment was not actually performed, no effect on sales can be determined.

As he reviewed the failure of his experiment, Bob Kapp pondered what steps he should take to implement a change in the salesmen's call patterns in the future.

---

[1] See Exhibit 3 for explanation of classes of accounts.

# Alcon Laboratories, Inc.

IN THE SUMMER of 1966, Mr. George Leone, National Sales Manager of Alcon Laboratories, initiated an appraisal of the organization and morale of his 70-man sales force. Mr. Leone expressed particular concern over the high turnover in the sales force (28 percent in the fiscal year 1965–1966). He had before him proposals for two changes: one proposed change was in the organization and management of the Alcon sales force; the other proposal was to increase salesmen's compensations as an inducement to their staying longer with the company. While he was willing to make any changes that might improve the situation, he felt that it would be better to do nothing than to attempt changes that were inappropriate to the needs of his organization.

## THE COMPANY HISTORY

In 1947 in Fort Worth, Texas, two pharmacists founded Alcon Laboratories upon the principle that more accurate, sterile, stable pharmaceutical compounds could be manufactured by Alcon on a large-scale basis than was possible in retail drug stores, where most prescribed drugs were being compounded at that time.

In early years Alcon management decided to achieve growth by concentrating their marketing efforts in specialty fields. The field in which Alcon first specialized was ophthalmological drugs (drugs used in the treatment of defects and diseases of the eye). In 1947, 85 percent of all eye-care drugs were being compounded in drug stores.

As doctors became familiar with the company's products and their quality, they prescribed them more and more, and Alcon prospered. By 1957 a sales force of 30 men was promoting the company's eye-care products nationally, and sales had grown to nearly $1 million.

Alcon Laboratories continued to grow both domestically and internationally. In fiscal 1966 total domestic and international sales of Alcon Laboratories were $9.1 million. The consolidated income statement is shown below.

Year Ended
April 30, 1966

| | |
|---|---:|
| Net sales ......................................... | $9,114 |
| Costs and expenses | |
|    Costs of goods sold .............................. | 3,129 |
|    Selling, general, and administrative expenses* ........ | 4,411 |
|      Total costs and expenses ...................... | $7,450 |
| Income before provision for federal taxes .............. | $1,574 |
| Provision for federal income taxes .................. | 753 |
|      Net income ................................. | $ 821 |

* Research and development represented a significant portion of general and administrative expenses.

Exhibit 1 shows selected historical operating and financial information for the period 1958 to 1966. Exhibit 2 shows the consolidated balance sheet for 1966.

**EXHIBIT 1**

Highlights of Operating and Financial Data

| | Net Sales | Net Income | Earnings Per Share | Net Working Capital | Current Ratio | Total Assets |
|---|---|---|---|---|---|---|
| 1966..... | $9,114,329 | $821,129 | $1.30 | $3,261,854 | $3.24 | $7,015,740 |
| 1965..... | 8,749,438 | 663,039 | 1.05 | 2,447,996 | 3.06 | 6,006,671 |
| 1964..... | 8,696,600 | 749,647 | 1.20 | 1,845,882 | 2.39 | 5,426,280 |
| 1963..... | 7,718,310 | 534,164 | 0.86 | 1,064,999 | 1.96 | 4,413,063 |
| 1962..... | 6,392,141 | 403,761 | 0.66 | 734,241 | 1.87 | 3,648,339 |
| 1961..... | 3,057,399 | 267,710 | 0.50 | 185,737 | 1.31 | 2,606,424 |
| 1960..... | 3,094,197 | 214,892 | 0.40 | 531,879 | 2.25 | 1,809,876 |
| 1959..... | 2,034,758 | 162,985 | 0.31 | 380,518 | 2.03 | 1,478,230 |
| 1958..... | 1,347,283 | 69,277 | 0.13 | 169,478 | 2.02 | 544,686 |

Domestically, a 70-man sales force was promoting 33 eye-care products, and annual sales of these products had grown to $6 million by 1966. In addition, by purchasing another small specialized pharmaceutical firm, Alcon had entered a second specialty field. Furthermore, Alcon had achieved some backward integration by purchasing a manufacturer of plastic containers for pharmaceutical products.

Internationally, Alcon manufactured and sold its product line through foreign subsidiaries and joint agreements.

## ALCON'S EYE-CARE PRODUCTS—THEIR USE AND DISTRIBUTION

Pharmaceuticals used and prescribed by ophthalmologists (medical doctors specializing in the treatment of eye diseases and defects) were gen-

## EXHIBIT 2

Consolidated Balance Sheets
(as of end of fiscal year)

*May 1, 1966*

Assets
  Current assets
    Cash ............................................. $  343
    Marketable securities ............................... 1,856
    Accounts receivable (less allowance-doubt. accts.) ....... 1,578
    Inventories ....................................... 940
    Total ........................................... $4,717
  Investment in unconsolidated subsidiaries ................. 237
  Other assets ...................................... 102
  Property, plant, and equipment ....................... 4,172
  Less accumulated depreciation ....................... 2,213
    Net fixed assets ................................. $1,959
    Total assets ................................... $7,015

Liabilities
  Current liabilities
    Current maturities of long-term debt ................. $   18
    Accounts payable ................................. 335
    Accrued federal income taxes ....................... 585
    Other accrued liabilities ........................... 517
    Total current liabilities ......................... $1,455
  Long-term debt
    First mortgage bond ............................... $   91
    Notes ........................................... —
    Total long term debt ............................. $   91
  Capital stock and surplus
    Common stock (50c par value) ..................... $  315
    Capital surplus ................................... 1,006
    Earned surplus ................................... 4,148
  Less treasury stock at cost ........................... —
    Net capital stock and surplus ..................... $5,469
    Total liabilities ................................. $7,015

erally classified into seven categories, depending on their use. These were:

1. Glaucoma products—for aid in the treatment of glaucoma, a disease where fluid pressure in the eye causes hardness of the eyeball and impairment or loss of vision.
2. Steroid products—for elimination of irritation and inflammation of the eye.
3. Antibiotic products—for anti-infective uses on the eye.
4. Surgical products—for use during eye surgery such as cataract operations.
5. Diagnostics/anesthetics—for use in identifying eye damage and anesthetizing for treatment.

6. Mydriadics/cycloplegics—for use when refraction or immobilization of the eye is needed.

7. Lubricants and astringents—for use in cleaning and lubricating the eye.

Alcon manufactured products in all seven of the above categories.

Although some of these products could be purchased over the counter (i.e., without a prescription), 90 percent of Alcon's total sales of ophthalmological drugs were prescription products. Most prescriptions were written by the 6,000 ophthalmologists and 2,000 eye-ear-nose-throat doctors who practiced in the United States and who were called on regularly by Alcon salesmen.

Alcon products were available either directly or through wholesalers both to hospitals and to retail drug stores.

## THE MARKET AND COMPETITION

In 1965, total retail sales of ophthalmological drugs in the United States were $30 million. Seventy-five percent of these sales were manufacturer-compounded products, and 25 percent were compounded from basic ingredients by pharmacists in drug stores.

Alcon Laboratories' share of the total domestic ophthalmological drug market was nearly 30 percent. Their competition came primarily from retail druggists, and from both small and large pharmaceutical firms. Retail druggists, when given a choice in how to fill a prescription, might prefer to compound the drug themselves and earn a gross margin of 80 to 90 percent instead of dispensing a precompounded brand name drug which typically offered a margin of only 40 to 50 percent. Other small, specialized manufacturers like Alcon which attempted to find a niche in the total market by catering specifically to the ophthalmic market competed directly with Alcon. Finally, Alcon competed with large, diversified drug manufacturers for whom certain segments of the ophthalmic market were large and lucrative enough to warrant attention. Alcon management stated that in 1966 two large drug manufacturing firms controlled about 30 percent of the domestic ophthalmic market.

The active chemical compounds used in various ophthalmological preparations were essentially the same, regardless of manufacturer. Competing products were differentiated primarily on the basis of their form[1] and vehicle.[2] Competing manufacturers were constantly looking for new preparations which would have performance superior to existing ones. While Alcon was interested in developing new compounds of active ingredients,

---

[1] Form referred to whether the compounds came in solution, ointment, cream, pill, etc.

[2] The vehicle was comprised of the inactive ingredients which were important in determining such product qualities as the stability of the product, how well the product stayed in the eyes (instead of "sweating out"), the irritation and/or side effects of the product, etc.

the major thrust of their research was to improve the performance of existing compounds by developing better or new forms and vehicles.

Doctors were not unaware of the prices of various prescriptions, but industry sources thought that they did not typically consider price to be an important factor in deciding what to prescribe unless there was a large price difference among similar products. The average price of an ophthalmic prescription in 1965 was $2.34.

Alcon management believed that the company had been highly successful in filling a specialized need in the market, but that changing environmental factors might make success more difficult to achieve in the future. Threatening changes came from competing firms and the government.

If large diversified pharmaceutical manufacturers became more interested in specialty areas and increased their activities in the ophthalmic market, they would be able to devote resources to product development and promotion which the smaller, specialized firms could not hope to match.

Within the government, the Food and Drug Administration had promulgated more stringent requirements for the testing and acceptance of drugs. Under these conditions, large and diversified companies had another advantage over small, specialized firms, because small firms were unable to spread the increased costs of development and testing over many end uses of the drug in question. For example, when a diversified drug company developed a new antibiotic it would be promoted not only in drugs for the treatment of eye diseases and defects, but also in drugs for treating diseases affecting all parts of the body. In its different forms the drug would be prescribed by virtually all kinds of doctors.

Also, political pressure was rising to encourage doctors to use generic names rather than brand names in writing prescriptions. A generic name specified only the active chemical compound in a drug preparation, but not necessarily the form or vehicle. Prescriptions written by generic name gave the druggist the choice of filling the prescription either by compounding the drug himself or by using one of several manufacturers' products which contained the prescribed chemical compound. The advocates of generically written prescriptions maintained that, if given a choice among several products, the retail druggist would be able to fill a prescription more cheaply than if he was limited to one product by a brand name prescription.

## THE MARKETING DEPARTMENT

### Organization

The marketing department of Alcon Laboratories was under the direction of the marketing director, who was also a vice president of Alcon and a member of the company's executive management group. Ed Schollmaier, who currently held this position, was 32 years old and had risen rapidly at Alcon. After receiving his MBA at the Harvard Business School in 1958 he had started as a salesman with Alcon and in a short time he had been promoted to district sales manager. After less than two years with Alcon he had been called into the home office to assist in directing the sales effort. In 1963 he had been appointed director of marketing.

The men under Mr. Schollmaier were grouped into three functional areas:

1. Sales: The sales group was comprised of the field sales force and the supervisory group which directed it.
2. Product management: The product management group was comprised of product managers, each of whom had total marketing responsibility (other than direct sales) for a particular group of products.
3. Market research: The director of market research was responsible for gathering and making available to others information on the ophthalmic drug market and on the competitive activities of other firms. In the summer of 1966 the duties of the director of market research were being performed by one of the product managers.

Shown below is an organization chart of the marketing department.

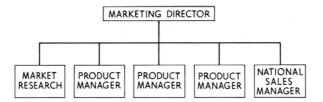

### Activity

The primary responsibility of the marketing department was to assure the success of the sales effort. The home office was responsible for the design of the sales program, while the field sales organization was responsible for the program's execution. Great time and effort were typically expended in both areas. According to a 1965 study, drug and pharmaceutical firms' selling costs were twice those of U. S. industry as a whole. The survey showed that in 1964 the cost of selling pharmaceuticals amounted to 30.5 percent of gross sales revenue. The study presented the following breakdown of total selling costs:[3]

---

[3] This study included as selling costs such items as seminars held for doctors to acquaint them with new drugs, and samples sent out as part of a product's introductory stage. Other industries did not have such expenses to the degree that the drug industry had, and some companies included similar costs in research and development for accounting purposes. Another factor to consider in comparing drug industry costs with

|                                                | Drug Industry | Average (All Industries) |
| ---------------------------------------------- | ------------- | ------------------------ |
| Salesmen's compensation                        | 37.3%         | 45.2%                    |
| Salesmen's travel and other expenses           | 13.6          | 12.8                     |
| Sales management costs                         | 14.0          | 16.2                     |
| Advertising, merchandising, and promotion      | 29.9          | 14.2                     |
| Servicing                                      | 3.0           | 7.4                      |
| All other costs                                | 2.2           | 4.2                      |
| Total                                          | 100.0%        | 100.0%                   |

Between 1961 and 1966, Alcon's total annual expenses for advertising, merchandising, and promotion increased from $90,000 to $750,000.

At Alcon the central activity was the planning of promotion programs, a joint responsibility of the product managers and the national sales manager. Prior to the beginning of each fiscal year, the product managers would meet with Mr. Leone, the national sales manager. On the basis of the size of the total promotion budget, the length of time since a product had been actively promoted, Mr. Leone's estimate of market potential, the current share of market held by the products involved, and competitive activity, this group would draw up a list of the particular products to be promoted in the coming year. Products on the list were then assigned specific dates for promotion. This promotion schedule was then approved by the marketing director.

In designing a promotional campaign, the product managers consulted with the national sales manager to obtain his ideas on what might go well in the market and his impressions on how the campaign would be received and handled by the sales force. Each product manager would design the entire promotional campaign for those of his products which were on the schedule. With the aid of an advertising agency, the product manager developed the direct mail literature, journal advertising, or visual aid material that was to be used. He would also write any technical, informational brochures that might be needed to reacquaint the sales force with aspects of the product. If the sales force was scheduled to promote an item to a customer on several individual calls, the product manager might even suggest which selling points should be made on the first and subsequent calls.

After the promotional campaign had been designed, it was turned over to the national sales manager who, with the help of his immediate subordinates, would teach the sales force how to carry out the promotion. Frequently, the product managers would attend meetings of the field sales organization to help present to the salesman the plans for the upcoming promotion.

---

those of other industries was that most consumer goods manufacturers shared costs of advertising with retailers; drug companies, on the other hand, bore most of these costs alone. In addition, allowances for returned merchandise were higher in the drug industry, since companies regularly took back unopened stock that was out of date.

A typical three-month promotional campaign for one product cost about $300,000 including salesmen's costs as well as advertising, direct mail, and other promotional materials. These costs were charged to the budget of the product manager responsible for that product. Each product manager was evaluated annually on the basis of the performance of his product(s) with respect to the achievement of sales goals and budgeted promotional spending.

To provide salesmen with the information that was desired by doctors, the marketing department needed the aid of the medical department and the research department.

The medical department was responsible for professional contact with members of the medical profession. Through a "Clinical Liaison Group" the medical department engaged physicians doing clinical research to conduct studies to test the uses or find new uses for Alcon's products. The findings were frequently used, in the form of professional articles or in technical bulletins, in promotional campaigns. It was not uncommon for a member of the marketing department to ask the medical department to help in developing some technical data to support particular claims for a product.

Alcon's R&D department was also important to the marketing effort. The development of new chemical compounds, new uses of existing compounds, and improvements in existing compounds were all considered to be of prime importance. Introducing new and improved drug preparations was considered to be one of the most effective ways to increase sales and enhance the company's reputation in the medical community. Sales of various ophthalmological preparations tended to be more stable than the sales of pharmaceutical preparations in general, which were characterized by extreme volatility due to the frequent introduction of new chemical compounds which made existing compounds, in all types of forms and vehicles, obsolete. Alcon management stated, however, that "the impact of new products (i.e. new formulations of existing ophthalmological compounds) since 1960 accounted for more than half of Alcon's growth, and half of that growth was attributable to innovations in the steroid product category in particular."

The mutual interests of the marketing, medical, and R&D departments were coordinated through meetings of the product committee, whose members included Mr. Ed Schollmaier, Marketing Vice President, Dr. Earl Maxwell, Medical Director and Director of R&D, Mr. Frank Buhler, Director of International Operations, and Mr. William Conner, who was Chairman of the Board and President. For example, through the product committee the time and resources of the R&D department might be allocated to fill gaps in the product line, as determined by sales management and product managers. The need for and provision of technical data by the medical department was also coordinated through the product committee.

## The National Sales Manager

Mr. George Leone headed the 70-man sales force in 1966. He had been with Alcon since 1950, when there were only six salesmen in the company. After doing an outstanding job as a salesman he was made a district sales manager in 1955, a regional sales manager in 1960, and national sales manager in 1963.

As national sales manager, Mr. Leone was responsible for the overall administration and performance of the sales force and for coordinating the activities of the sales force with other groups in the marketing department. In his administrative capacity, Mr. Leone was primarily concerned with the establishment of company programs in the areas of recruitment and selection, training and development, supervision, standards of performance appraisal, and compensation and benefits. He was also responsible for identifying and developing field sales managers.

Mr. Leone directed three groups of men: regional sales managers, district sales managers, and medical sales representatives. The latter were more commonly known within the industry as salesmen, and were frequently identified by physicians as "detail men." Exhibit 3 is an organization chart of the sales organization.

### EXHIBIT 3

Organization Chart of the Sales Group

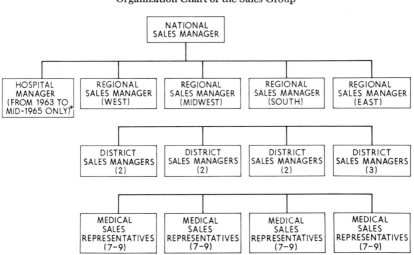

\* Dropped in 1965 because of the overlap between calls on doctors when they were at the hospital and when they were at their private offices.

## The Regional Sales Managers

Alcon divided the United States into four large sales regions, each supervised by a regional sales manager. The job description in the company's supervisory reference manual listed five major functions for the regional sales manager (RSM):

1. Recruitment and selection of candidates for field sales work (medical service representatives) with special emphasis on applicants with managerial potential.
2. Training and developing the district managers.
3. Supervising, directing, and controlling the activities of the district sales managers.
4. Maintaining communication with the home office through weekly reports and with the sales force through quarterly regional sales meetings.
5. Planning and organizing to help set the objectives for the region and to help the district sales managers set their goals.

The job description stated that the RSM should spend a minimum of 35 percent of his time in personal field visits with his district sales managers. He had no direct customer responsibilities.

Three of the four regional sales managers worked in the home office and spent a good deal of their time working with Mr. Leone in planning the national sales effort. They were involved in sales promotion, planning meetings, and in developing company policies and procedures for recruiting, selection, training, and supervision of the sales force. The fourth RSM was in the process of moving from Chicago to the home office.

## The District Sales Managers

Reporting to each of the four regional sales managers were two to three district sales managers (DSM's). An Alcon district was a subdivision of a region (for example, the New England states comprised one district of Alcon's eastern region). The district sales manager's job description listed five major duties.

1. Recruiting, selecting, and, with the approval from the RSM, hiring salesmen to become medical sales representatives.
2. Training and developing the field sales force.
3. Supervising, directing, and controlling the activities of the field sales force.
4. Maintaining communications with home office and with RSM, and conducting quarterly district sales meetings.
5. Planning and organizing operation of districts through setting objectives for field salesmen.

The job description further stated that the DSM should allocate his time as follows: A minimum of 75 percent of his time in personal field visits with the medical sales representatives, and the remainder (25 percent) at medical meetings, sales meetings, and visits with the regional sales manager. The DSM's, like the RSM's, had no direct customer responsibilities.

The job description stated that both the RSM's and the DSM's were evaluated on the following performance factors:

1. Growth in sales of products being promoted or "detailed" by the sales force.
2. Increase in overall sales of territory, including both the products which were being detailed and those which were not.
3. Change in the sales to cost of sales ratio. For example:

$$\frac{\text{Total sales}}{\text{Total cost of operation}} = \frac{900,000}{115,000} = 7.8 \text{ in } 1965$$

$$\frac{1,000,000}{120,000} = 8.3 \text{ in } 1966$$

4. Number of physician calls made in the territory.
5. Sales costs (all operating costs in the manager's territory).
6. Territory coverage (keeping territories fully manned).
7. Personnel turnover.
8. Distribution of product line, measured by the dollar volume of "turnover order" (orders which were written by an Alcon salesman in a retail drug store and turned over by him to a wholesaler to be filled).
9. Personnel development as measured by number and quality of projects completed by salesmen training for advancement in the Advanced Development Program (ADP).
10. Skill in making verbal and written reports.

The evaluation took the form of an annual performance appraisal of the manager by his superiors.

This list of performance factors and the annual performance appraisal had been instituted after Mr. Leone was made national sales manager in 1963. Mr. Leone believed that these steps had done much to improve performance and morale in the organization.

## The Salesmen

Reporting to each of the nine district sales managers were seven to nine medical sales representatives (MSR's), or salesmen. These 70 salesmen were responsible for Alcon's direct customer contacts. Each MSR covered one Alcon "territory." The medical sales representatives' job description listed six major duties:

1. Call on each of the following:
   a. All eye physicians within his territory.
   b. All pharmacies on his drug call list.
   c. All hospitals on his call list.
   d. All wholesalers on his call list.
2. Follow the sales program including using all sales tools outlined by the program.
3. All MSR's must fulfill their performance standards and objectives each month in the following areas:
   a. Doctor call standards (item a above).
   b. Retail call standards (item b above).
   c. Wholesale call standards (item d above).
   d. Increase sales objective (the DSM and MSR together set a specific objective as to how much sales will increase in the current year over the previous year).
   e. Ratio of increase sales to sales cost. For example:

|  | 1965 |  | 1966 |  |
|---|---|---|---|---|
| Total territory sales | $100,000 | 8 | $120,000 | 6 |
| Total territory costs | $ 12,000 | 1 | $ 20,000 | 1 |

$$\frac{\$100,000}{\$12,000} = \frac{8}{1} \qquad \frac{\$120,000}{\$20,000} = \frac{6}{1}$$

   f. Featured product (the one being promoted or detailed) objective.
   g. Turnover order[4] objective.
4. Planning and organizing territory coverage by maintaining territory coverage plan and territory records.
5. Maintaining communications with supervisor and the home office by submitting the required daily, weekly, and monthly reports.
6. Meeting standards of self-development by attaining an adequate product knowledge, and knowing and complying with company policies on appearance, conduct, and maintaining company property.

Top management described the salesmen's activities as falling into two distinct categories: *creating demand* (when the MSR is in the doctor's office, trying to get him to prescribe Alcon's products) and *distribution* (supporting demand by getting the product to the wholesaler and retailer).

## THE SALESMEN'S JOB

Salesmen in the drug industry as a whole made an average of 48 calls per week. Industry statistics indicated that the cost of making a sales call in the pharmaceutical field averaged $9, and ranged from $1.50 to $20. The average drug sale was $192. Alcon's medical service representatives, or salesmen, made three major types of calls: doctor calls, retailer calls, and wholesaler calls.

---

[4] Turnover orders were those which the drug salesman wrote for the drug retailer and carried or mailed to the drug wholesaler to be filled.

Each Alcon salesman used his home as the base of operations, and traveled by car to see clients within his territory. The size of Alcon's territories typically required salesmen to spend three to four days each month in overnight travel. Each salesman carried at all times a case full of drug samples and other promotional materials.

The casewriter accompanied several salesmen on the daily rounds of calls. On one day he accompanied a salesman who called on nine doctors, one drug wholesaler, and three drug retailers. The casewriter believed, on the basis of the salesman's statements and from his own observations of other salesmen's activities, that this was a typical day.

The salesman began his day by driving 50 miles from his home to the city where he had planned calls for that day. Once in the designated city, the salesman spent a considerable part of his day simply getting from one client to another. Once in a client's office, he had to wait until he could be seen. One doctor kept him waiting as long as 30 minutes. While waiting to see the doctor, the salesman talked with the receptionist and gave away such small favors as notepads and other secretarial aids. (A kindly disposed receptionist could substantially aid a salesman in gaining prompt access, or access at all, to a doctor.)

The salesman the casewriter accompanied was able to see only five of the nine doctors he called on. With each of these five doctors he spent approximately five minutes. One doctor saw the salesman while having a sandwich between patients' appointments.

With the drug wholesaler and with each drug retailer, the salesman spent about fifteen minutes.

At the end of the day the salesman returned the 50 miles to his home.

An Alcon salesman typically saw his DSM only once a month, but maintained contact with him weekly by telephone. Alcon salesmen generally saw each other only at the bimonthly sales meetings. Although he had infrequent contact with other Alcon salesmen, the typical MSR had opportunity to have more frequent contact with other companies' salesmen who were detailing the same area as himself.

### The Doctor Call

Alcon, as well as other drug companies, considered that "detailing" the doctor was one of the best ways to create demand for both new and existing products. It was for this reason that Alcon salesmen concentrated their attention on calls on eye doctors.

Large diversified drug firms did not detail eye specialists as much as they detailed general practitioners, obstetricians, and pediatricians, because eye specialists did not use as wide a range of drugs. Most drug companies that detailed eye doctors called only once every three to six months, while they called on less specialized doctors every month. Alcon, however, as well as two other companies which specialized in ophthalmological drugs, called on eye doctors once a month.

Most eye doctors were ophthalmologists, typically located in large and medium-sized cities. A few older eye-ear-nose-and-throat doctors were still practicing in smaller communities, but their number was dwindling.

On a typical visit to an eye specialist, the Alcon salesman was expected to detail one primary product, one secondary product, and one "door-handle" product (one which was just mentioned on the way out). Any one product was usually detailed for three consecutive months. Some were detailed for only one month, while others were detailed as long as seven consecutive months.

While visiting the doctor the MSR was expected by management to show the doctor a "detail piece" (a visual aid that showed when to use the product and the advantages of Alcon's product). Exhibit 4 is a representative detail piece. In addition he often left a journal reprint discussing the product, or a pamphlet (printed in a professional manner), along with some samples of the product. The MSR was supposed to discuss with the doctor whether he used the product being detailed and, if possible, to get a commitment that he would use it if he was not doing so already.

It was necessary for the salesmen to do this in a very brief period, however, as most doctors were extremely busy. One doctor commented to the casewriter that "[the detail men] have to see you at your office. I am very busy there so it is hard to find time to see them. I can only give them five to ten minutes and that is time away from seeing my patients." It was hoped that the salesman's brief presentation would make a lasting impression on the doctor. Journal advertising and direct mail promotions from Alcon were timed to support the salesmen's message to the doctor. Exhibit 5 contains samples of a journal advertisement and a direct mail piece.

### The Retailer Call

The Alcon salesman also called on the retail druggist. There were 55,000 drug stores in the United States, but, according to Alcon management, the Alcon sales force called only on the 10 percent which did the most business in ophthalmological drugs.

In the course of his call on the retail druggist the salesman would make it known which product(s) were being detailed in the area and thus which drug(s) doctors would probably be prescribing. It was anticipated that the retail druggist would consequently increase his stock of the product(s) in question. If Alcon had any promotional deals on over-the-counter items (usually an offer of free goods with each purchase, e.g., one free item with each 12 purchased) the MSR would bring these to the druggist's

## EXHIBIT 4

Detail Piece—Actual Size, 8¾″ x 12¾″

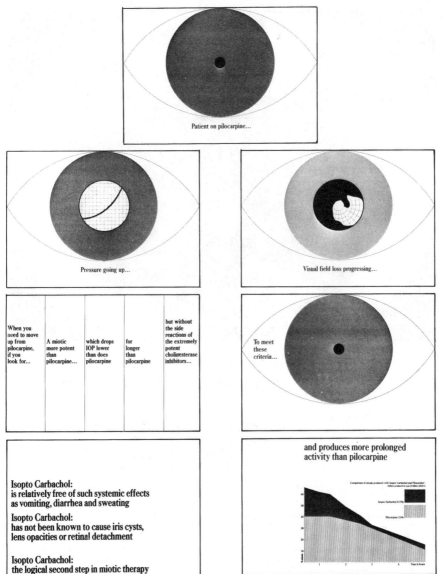

attention. During the call, the MSR checked the druggist's stock of Alcon products and indicated those areas which the druggist should replenish. The MSR attempted to pursuade the druggist to stock at least one bottle of all Alcon products and several bottles of the fast moving items. The

## EXHIBIT 5

Journal Advertisement

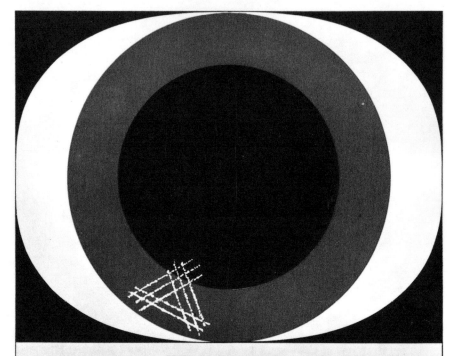

## Exhibit 5 *(continued)*

### Direct Mail Piece—Actual Size, 8½″ x 11″

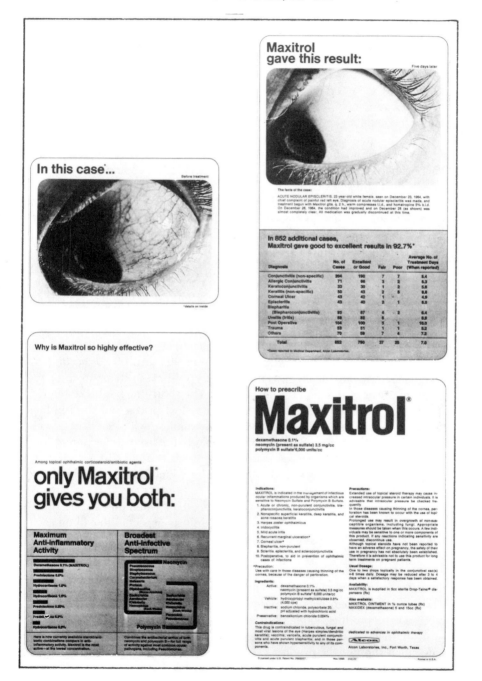

MSR would write up the order and mail it or take it to the wholesaler of the druggist's choosing.

### The Wholesaler Call

To obtain adequate distribution of a product it was also important to call on drug wholesalers. The average Alcon territory contained six drug wholesalers who served as intermediaries between drug manufacturers and drug retailers. Wholesalers maintained sales staffs of their own by which they contacted many more retail druggists than Alcon was able to do. A wholesaler's salesmen would call on each retail druggist once a week, and would have daily contact with each druggist by telephone. Thus wholesalers, once sold on Alcon products, could shoulder a considerable part of the sales effort.

In 1964 U.S. drug wholesalers had annual sales of $3.7 billion. Two types of wholesale houses controlled this business: the full-line, full-service wholesalers, and the short-line or specialty houses.

The average sized full-line house typically carried 20,000 to 25,000 different items (each size of each brand of a product being considered a separate item) which had been purchased from some 1200 to 1500 manufacturers. Full-line houses sold about 90 percent of their dollar volume to retail drug outlets, and the remainder to hospitals, nursing homes, and clinics. The full-line houses' 1964 dollar volume of $1.76 billion represented almost 48 percent of total wholesale drug sales.

Short-line or specialty houses carried from 900 to 2500 of the highest margin, fastest moving items, and typically sold these items to drug retailers at lower prices than full-line houses. The short-line houses competed by offering little more than selected items at low prices, but the full-line houses depended on their ability to offer the retailer several services as well as a wide product line. These services included assistance in finding and evaluating sites for new stores, store layout and fixturing assistance, instore merchandising techniques, and anything else which might help the druggist in his retailing efforts.

When a new product was being introduced, or when an existing product was being promoted, the Alcon salesman was expected to call on each wholesaler to gain his support of the product(s) in question. He was instructed to contact the wholesaler's sales manager initially and try to sell him on the product. The purpose of this effort was to persuade the sales manager to use his sales force to give special attention to Alcon's product. The Alcon salesman was supposed to show the sales manager the detail piece on the product, along with any literature he had.

After making this presentation to the sales manager and finding out how much support the product would get, the Alcon salesman would then go to the wholesaler's buyer. The salesman tried to persuade the buyer to order a large enough supply of the product (six to eight weeks' supply) to avoid the danger of running out.

During the months when Alcon did not introduce a new product or begin a new promotion on existing products, the MSR would simply call on the buyer and ask to go over the inventory record. If, on the basis of current or expected rates of movement, the wholesaler did not have the six to eight weeks of supply, the MSR would attempt to sell enough additional units of the product to raise the supply to the desired level.

It appeared to the casewriter, after observing several wholesale calls and talking to several salesmen, that most of the wholesale calls made by Alcon salesmen, whether or not there was a promotion involved, were of the latter, simpler type. The buyer and the sales manager of the wholesaler were likely to be pressed for time in which to listen to the presentation of the salesman in as much as they saw about 100 drug salesmen per week.

## The Call Mix

Alcon's management explained that one salesman called on the doctor, the retailer, and the wholesaler because the calls were highly related and needed careful coordination. For instance, since no order was written in the doctor's office, the salesman would not know if the doctor would actually prescribe the detailed product or not. One of the best ways to find out was to call on the pharmacist a few days after detailing the doctor and inquire whether Dr. X was writing the product in question. If the salesman had established a good relationship with the pharmacist, the pharmacist would, in all likelihood, tell him. In fact the pharmacist often went so far as to let the salesmen check through the pharmacy's prescription file to see what all of the doctors were prescribing. With this type of information, the salesman knew which products were selling well and which products he should discuss with a doctor on his next visit.

In addition, Alcon managers emphasized that distribution and demand creation had to be closely coordinated. By handling all three types of calls, the salesman could assure the doctor that the pharmacist had in stock the drug he prescribed, and he could assure the pharmacist that the doctor would prescribe the drugs he stocked.

Alcon managers observed that the retailer calls and the wholesaler calls were directly related. First, they were both distribution calls. Second, the turnover order took the salesman back to the wholesaler with a definite order from the retailer, thus giving the salesman an opportunity to urge further purchases of Alcon's products.

While Alcon's management had agreed that one salesman should handle both demand creation (doctor calls) and distribution (wholesaler and retailer calls), in the past there had been a difference of opinion in the marketing department as to which of the two areas should receive the greatest emphasis. As a result emphasis had shifted from time to time.

In the past, when a new product was introduced, Alcon management had emphasized demand creation. Historically, this had resulted in a sales increase which was consistent with top management's commitment to rapid growth. As sales began to level off, however, an easy way to boost sales was to emphasize distribution by loading up the wholesaler and retailer with inventory. The distribution campaigns had included deals, the use of promotion money to the wholesaler's salesmen, and sales contests for Alcon's salesmen. In addition, "automatic" shipments (i.e., shipments of goods which Alcon estimated could be sold, but which had not been ordered by the wholesaler) would often be made to wholesalers during these periods.

There had been a number of "distribution campaigns" during periods of slow sales growth. The most recent one had been in May 1964, when a six months distribution campaign was launched and a sales contest was initiated, in which the winner from each of the four regions won a trip to Mexico. When the contest was over, however, some wholesalers shipped goods back to Alcon (all of Alcon's sales were guaranteed, i.e., Alcon agreed to take back products which were unsold after a specific time). In one winter's territory, returns exceeded sales for a month or two. During the nine months following the contest, three of the four winners left Alcon.

Such distribution campaigns caused wide fluctuations in sales, and strained relations with wholesalers and retailers. Management recognized the undesirable consequences of such actions and concluded that enduring sales growth came only from demand creation. In October 1964, with this in mind, Mr. Leone shifted the emphasis of the sales effort to demand creation. He instructed salesmen to spend 75 percent of their time calling on doctors (compared to 40 percent during the distribution campaign). The salesmen told the casewriter they welcomed this shift in their call mix because they preferred doctor calls to distribution calls. Management believed that men who preferred distribution calls, such as the four contest winners, left the company when the shift in emphasis took place.

Alcon maintained this emphasis on demand creation and managers stated that they did not intend to return to the practice of using distribution campaigns to boost sales in periods of slow growth.

## ADMINISTRATION OF SALESMEN

Alcon, like the rest of the industry, had found that it was difficult to find and keep a man who could perform all of the required functions of the medical service representative. In the past six years the annual turnover of Alcon's sales force had averaged approximately 33 percent.

## Recruiting and Selection

The district sales manager was responsible for recruiting and selection of salesmen for his territory. He had an instruction manual to help him. One page was entitled "The Man You Want" and listed the following characteristics:

25 to 35 years of age.
Preferably married—stable domestic life.
College degree.
Scientific and business courses.
Above average grades in school.
Good work history, preferably in sales/marketing.
Good grooming and physical appearance.
Good health, past and present.
Sound financial position.
Good diction and use of grammar—articulate.
Able to understand and project emotions and ideas.
Has self-confidence and poise.
Self-started.
Doesn't object to travel.
Enjoys working with people.
Ambitious with maturity.
Honesty and integrity.
Enthusiasm and capacity for work.

The district managers used several techniques to find men with these qualifications. When a vacancy occurred in an area, the district manager typically first contacted schools if the opening occurred around commencement time.

Mr. Leone said that Alcon recruited at business schools in particular because Alcon liked to hire MBA's. He felt that the training and ambition of MBA's made them compatible with Alcon's objectives and organization.[5]

---

[5] Mr. Leone believed that Alcon had hired approximately 20 MBA's within the last 10 years. Four to eight had left the company. Mr. Leone identified those still with Alcon as listed below. He believed that there were two others whom he had not included on the list.

| Salesman | School and Date MBA Received | Present Position |
|---|---|---|
| A | HBS '57 | Financial Vice President |
| B* | HBS '58 | Marketing Vice President |
| C | HBS '60 | Controller's Department |
| D | HBS '59 | Product Manager |
| E* | HBS '62 | Product Manager |
| F* | HBS '64 | Assistant Product Manager |
| G | Chicago | International Controller |
| H* | N. Texas | Salesman |
| I* | Northwestern | District Manager |
| J | Wharton '65 | — |

* Began by working as an MSR.

A brochure in the Harvard Business School Placement Office contained the following statement:

The company is small by usual standards, but it offers the opportunity for easy recognition of contribution and rapid promotion to greater management responsibilities. Initial assignments are in field sales. MBA's are expected to reach district manager level within 18 to 24 months.

If qualified applicants were unavailable at schools, the district sales manager next contacted an employment agency, where he would typically interview about 40 people. After the first round of interviews he would narrow his interests to 10 to 12 applicants, with whom he would have second interviews.

If he was unable to fill positions on his sales force using these sources, a district sales manager would then use a classified advertisement to recruit applicants. One district sales manager had used the following ad several times under such circumstances:

### CAREERS IN SALES

Leading to sales management for qualified men based on performance. Young dynamic pharmaceutical company, growth rate of 47 percent per year. Leader in its field has openings local and away. Creative ambitious men with drive and determination, college degree. Science background helpful. Unusual remuneration and incentive plan tops in the industry. Excellent training program, liberal benefits, insurance, pension, stock options, profit sharing. Rare opportunity for growth for self-motivators. Men with an outstanding record of success in selling considered. Call OL 3-4818, Sunday, 1 to 5 P.M. Resumes to: Box X (City, State).

This sales manager reported to the casewriter that the ad had brought him an average of 75 resumes each time he had used it in a large east coast city. Forty to forty-five of the resumes he could discard immediately on the basis of age or educational background. After a telephone interview with the remaining 30 to 35 applicants, the sales manager would discard 10 to 15 more. He would then personally interview the remaining 10 to 15 applicants.

One district manager was quoted as saying,

My selection is generally made during the second interview as to my first, second, and third choices for a man to fill a vacancy. Then I have two or three more interviews with these men and their wives. The average interview time for a man who is hired is a total of approximately ten hours. By the time he is hired we really know one another and what we expect from one another. In rare instances, where there is competition for manpower from other industries in a given area, I may make a tentative offer on the spot during the first interview. In a case like this the first interview would run 1½ to 2 hours.

Selection was based primarily on the characteristics listed previously under "The Man You Want." The extent to which applicants fulfilled these characteristics was determined on the basis of information gathered through interviews, on application forms, and by testing.

The district sales manager was required to spend a good deal of his time recruiting because of the high turnover in the sales force. In 1965–1966, the region with the highest turnover had 6 men leave out of 19. It had the equivalent of 4 sales territories vacant for the year.

## Training

After a new salesman was hired he entered a four-week training program. The program was under the direction of the DSM and took place in the field. In the first week the DSM worked with the new salesman and showed him how to call on the doctor, the wholesaler, and the retailer. In the evening the new MSR was expected to learn company policies and procedures, and to gain an adequate product knowledge, including (a) basic anatomy, physiology, and pathology of the eye; (b) basic ocular therapy and medical concepts; (c) basic pharmacology; (d) Alcon product advantages; and (e) competitive products.

During the second and third weeks the new MSR went into the territory of a senior salesman in the district and made as many field calls with the senior salesmen as possible, to perfect the first week's training. In addition he was expected to spend his evenings expanding his product knowledge.

In the fourth week the new MSR was to work in his own area under the supervision of the DSM. At this point the MSR was to be making most of the calls while the DSM was observing. The DSM made sure that the new MSR was prepared to handle his own territory.

This concluded the formal training of the new MSR. After his initial training the DSM worked with the salesmen only periodically to give him any additional training that was necessary. The new salesmen reported to the casewriter that while an effort was made to do this, the DSM was often too busy to carry out the training as planned.

In order to develop field sales managers, at the end of 1964, Alcon introduced a program for training managers called the Advanced Development Program (ADP). Outstanding salesmen who were interested in advancement were included in this program (there were nine ADP's in the summer of 1966). The program consisted of each ADP's doing a number of individual projects which were usually activities performed by field managers; for example, the ADP would recruit and train new salesmen. Mr. Leone said, "Four of our best field managers today came from this program."

### Control and Evaluation

In order to keep track of what each salesman was doing, Alcon required that two reports be submitted by each salesman to the DSM and the home office, including the following:

1. A daily report of all calls made, by type of call, and the number and amount of turnover orders. (Sample is shown in Exhibit 6.) This report is cumulative on a monthly basis.

**EXHIBIT 6**

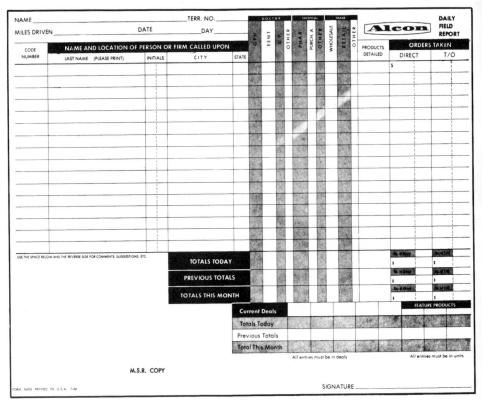

2. An expense voucher to be filled in daily and mailed to Fort Worth on Saturday morning.

In addition the MSR was required to keep territory records including a doctor call book with information such as the doctor's day off, the best time to see him, his specialty, etc.

Once a year the district sales manager conducted a performance appraisal of the MSR. Exhibit 7 contains sample forms for reports made by the DSM regarding the MSR. The DSM then made a recommendation for a salary increase for the salesman, based upon this performance appraisal and the MSR's commission for the past year. Management maintained that the introduction of regular performance appraisals greatly improved the compensation of the sales force at Alcon, making it more equitable by

## EXHIBIT 7

### District Manager Visit with MSR

Beginning Visit: Date_____Time_____MSR Visited: Name_____No.__
End Visit:          Date_____Time_____Reg. Mgr:_____Date Received_____
District Mgr.'s Name_____No.__

| I. PERFORMANCE DATE | CHECK LIST |
|---|---|
| | Feature product |
| | Inc. sales |
| | Sales cost |
| | Standards call-mix |
| | Ratio inc. sales to exp. |
| | No. T.O.'s and $ value |
| II. PERSONAL FACTORS | Appearance |
| | Attitude |
| | Confidence |
| | Initiative |
| | Persuasiveness |
| | Cooperation |
| III. PLANNING & ORGANIZING FACTORS | Daily planning |
| | Use of reports |
| | Following plans |
| IV. PHYSICIAN ACTIVITIES | Sales presentation |
| | Use of sales tools |
| | Product knowledge |
| | Handling objections |
| | Creativity |
| | Doctor response |
| | Stimulating questions |
| | Precall planning |
| | Receiptionists & nurse |
| | How did he project himself? |
| |     1. Enthusiasm |
| |     2. Aggressiveness |
| |     3. Persuasiveness |
| |     4. Confidence |
| |     5. Conviction |
| |     6. Alertness |
| |     7. Determination |
| V. PHARMACY ACTIVITIES | Use of tools |
| | Presentation |
| | Pharmacist |
| | Sales clerks |
| | No. of T.O.'s |
| | $ value of T.O. |
| | Precall plans |
| | Promotions O-T-C products |

Exhibit 7 *(continued)*

| VI. WHOLESALE ACTIVITIES | Use of sales tools |
| --- | --- |
| | Presentation |
| | Personnel contacted |
| | Buyer |
| | Sales manager |
| | Merchandise manager |
| | Phone sales personnel |
| | Cooperation |
| | Inventory level |
| | Precall planning |
| | Promotions O-T-C |
| VII. CONCLUSIONS & COURSES OF ACTION | Problems identified |
| | Areas helped |
| | What's to be done |
| | How to be done |
| | When to be accomplished |
| | Problem recognition |

relating salary increases more closely to performance. In addition the company made it a practice to terminate salesmen who did not meet the high standards set for salesmen.

## Compensation

Compensation for salesmen was in the form of salary plus commission. Alcon's starting salaries ranged from $400 to $700 per month, depending on the training and experience of the new man. In 1966 Alcon's salesmen's salaries ranged from $500 to $916 per month, and averaged $580 per month. Each salesman was eligible for a salary increase each year and the annual increase could be up to one half of the commission he received the preceeding year. Exhibit 8 presents salesmen's salaries from 1962 to 1966.

### EXHIBIT 8

Salesmen's Salaries at Alcon, Inc.*

| Year Ending | Average Annual Salary of All Salesmen |
| --- | --- |
| April 30, 1962 | $5760 |
| April 30, 1963 | 6168 |
| April 30, 1964 | 6744 |
| April 30, 1965 | 6900 |
| April 30, 1966 | $6960 |

\* Excludes commission.

Management expressed the opinion that although Alcon had been behind the industry in compensation a few years before, their significant salary increase in the past three years had made Alcon quite competitive with the drug industry. Exhibit 9 presents data on the drug industry's compensation of salesmen in 1964.

**EXHIBIT 9**

Data for the Pharmaceutical Industry's
Salesmen's Total Compensation
*(Salary and Commission, 1964)*

| | |
|---|---|
| 100th percentile | $25,000 |
| 75th percentile | 9,000 |
| 50th percentile | 8,000 |
| 25th percentile | 7,000 |
| 1st percentile | 5,000 |

A group of 28 companies manufacturing drugs, chemicals, and cosmetics reported the following data concerning the compensation (salary and commission) of their salesmen:

| | Midpoint | Range |
|---|---|---|
| Highest man | $12,000 | $8,000–$25,000 |
| Top half of sales force | 9,000 | 8,000– 10,000 |
| Lowest man | 6,000 | 5,000– 7,000 |
| Lower half of sales force | 7,000 | 6,000– 8,000 |

Source: *Sales Management,* January 21, 1966.

Commissions were handled in the following manner. A new salesman was placed on commission after three months of employment with Alcon and following a performance review and approval by all levels of field supervision. Commissions were paid twice each fiscal year and were based on 10 percent of increased sales after total MSR expenses (including car expenses, motel, telephone, meals) had been deducted. The following is an illustration of the commission plan:

| | |
|---|---|
| MSR's sales in 1965 | $ 75,000 |
| MSR's sales in 1964 | 50,000 |
| Sales increase | $ 25,000 |
| Salesman's expenses | −12,000 |
| | $13,000 |
| | 10% |
| Commission | $ 1,300 |

The current commission plan had been introduced in 1960 when the company was having trouble controlling salesmen's expenses. Recently some Alcon managers had expressed the feeling that the current plan was not equitable because it penalized the salesmen with a large territory requiring overnight travel. Total commissions paid to the 50 salesmen in 1965–1966 were $26,000, ranging from $0 to $1500 individually, but Mr. Leone observed that 80 percent of the commission payments went to 20 percent of the salesmen.

### Profile of Current Salesmen

A profile of salesmen who had been hired since January 1964, and who were still with the company in June 1966, is shown in Exhibit 10.

**EXHIBIT 10**

Profile of Alcon Salesmen Hired and Retained Since January 1964

| Salesman | Age | Marital Status | College Degree | Grade Average | Sales Experience | Other Experience |
|---|---|---|---|---|---|---|
| 1 | 34 | Married | B.S.—Parmacy | Top ½ | 2*—Drugs | 2*—Manager, Drug Store |
| 2 | ? | Married | Pharmacy | C | None | 4—Technician, Pharmacy |
| 3 | ? | Married | Bus. Adm. | C | 2 | 2—Office Merchandise |
| 4 | ? | Married | Sociology | C+ | None | Social Worker |
| 5 | ? | Married | Lib. Arts, Bus., So. Sci. | B | 2—Office Equip. Clothing | 2—Acct. Clerk, Cashier |
| 6 | 29 | Single | Lib. Arts, Bus. Adm. | C+ | 2—Encyclopedia, Med. Equip. | 3—Truck Checker, Freight Handler, Adjuster |
| 7 | ? | Married | B.A.—Psychology | C+ | 1—Sales & Service | 2—Clerk, Adm. Asst. |
| 8 | ? | Married | Pre-optometry | Top 5% | None | 4—Asst. Research, Pub. Rel., Clerk |
| 9 | ? | Married | B.A.—Pol. Sci. | C | 1—Am. Credit Bureau | 1—Tax Search |
| 10 | ? | Married | Marketing | — | None | 3—Stock Clerk, Timekeeper, Assembly |
| 11 | 25 | Single | B.S.—Zoology | Top ½ | None | Camera Assistant |
| 12 | 28 | Married | B.S.—Math Ed. | B | 1—Food | Math Teacher |
| 13 | 40 | Married | Pre-Med—3 yrs. | C | 1—Drugs | 1—Police Officer |
| 14 | 27 | Married | Gen. Ed., Bus. Adm. | C | | 1—Lifeguard |
| 15 | 26 | Single | No degree—Law | B+ | Shoes, Elec. | 1—Teacher |
| 16 | 26 | Married | B.S.—P.E. & Pol. Sci. | C | None | 2—Examiner, Janitor |
| 17 | 25 | Single | Pol. Sci. | Top 25% | 1—Shoes | 1—Administrative |
| 18 | 33 | Married | B.A.—Eng. & Psy. | Top 10% | 2 | 2—Clerk, Claims, Supervisor |
| 19 | 32 | Single | B.A.—Bus. Adm. | Top 40% | 1—Retail & Wholesale | 1—Int'l Trading Corp. |
| 20 | 25 | Married | Spec. Ed. | Top 50% | — | 5—Teacher |
| 21 | 28 | Single | B.A.—Gen. Bus., Marketing | 1.50 | 2 | 3—Repairman, Drugstore, Mailman |
| 22 | 30 | Married | No degree—Eco. & Marketing | — | 2—Drugs, Printing | 8—Insurance |
| 23 | 29 | Married | B.S.—Finance | C | 2—Insurance, Drugs | — |
| 24 | 26 | Married | B.S.—Pub. Adm. | B | None | — |
| 25 | 28 | Married | No degree—Marketing | C+ | 1—Shoes | Pub. Rel., Gen. Motors |

**Exhibit 10** (*continued*)

| Salesman | Age | Marital Status | College Degree | Grade Average | Sales Experience | Other Experience |
|---|---|---|---|---|---|---|
| 26 | 26 | Single | Economics | 80–85 | None | — |
| 27 | 24 | Married | B.S.—Bio, Bus. | Top ⅓ | None | — |
| 28 | 36 | Single | B.S.—Biology | Middle | None | 2 —Chemist |
| 29 | 27 | Married | Sci.—Chiropr. | 80's | 2 —Med. Equip. | — |
| 30 | 32 | Married | Mkt. and Sales | C | 1 — | Cashier, Foods Mgr. |
| 31 | 32 | Engaged | Police Science | C | 2 — | Post Office |
| 32 | 29 | Married | Industrial Tech. | C+ | None | 2 —Insurance Inspector |
| 33 | 28 | Married | Education & Psy. | B | None | School Guidance Counselor |
| 34 | 24 | Married | History | B | None | Drug Store, Book Store, Service Station |
| 35 | 26 | Single | History | C+ | 2 — | Gimbel's Toy Mgr. |
| 36 | 25 | Married | Marketing | 2.6 | None | Teacher |
| 37 | 26 | Married | B.S.—Biology | 78 | 1 — | Lab Technician |
| 38 | 28 | Married | B.A.—Philsopohy | 2.4 (A) | None | U.S.A.F. Recruiting |

\* Years.

## MANAGEMENT, SALESMEN, AND CUSTOMER ATTITUDES

In the course of gathering material for the case, the casewriter interviewed individuals at different organizational levels within Alcon. In addition he interviewed a number of eye doctors, drug retailers, and drug wholesalers concerning their attitudes toward drug salesmen.

### Sales Management's Point of View

The following statements are from an interview with Howard Clemens, one of the regional sales managers based in the home office with Mr. Leone. In the interview he described his relationship to the district sales managers.

I have three DSM's reporting to me. My job is to see that they follow company policies and procedures. I am concerned about recruiting and selection. That's delegated to the DSM, but I play an active part.

I also work on training the salesmen. I don't do all of it—it's delegated too —but I am concerned about whether our techniques for training are adequate. I also make presentations at sales meetings. I try to get the DSM to run his own meeting, but sometimes there is no time for me to present the program to the DSM beforehand so I have to run the district sales meeting myself.

I also spend some time with individual physicians talking about products— ours and competitors—and I feed that information to George Leone.

I am also concerned about trade (retailer and wholesaler) relations.

The two DSM's interviewed by the casewriter reported that other activities prevented them from spending 75 percent of their time with the MSR as their job description required. With a high turnover in the sales force it was necessary for them to spend a great deal of time on recruiting and selection of new salesmen. One DSM had three vacancies to fill in a four-month period, and it was necessary for him to spend nearly all his time trying to fill those vacancies during that period.

Another DSM found that it took a lot of time to do the paperwork required of him by the company. In addition, the MSR's liked him to give them comparative figures on their sales in the current month compared to those of the previous month and other similar kinds of information. As a result, a lot of this DSM's time was occupied in sales analysis and filling out reports. In addition, the DSM reported that, "the job has changed a lot in the past two to three years. Before, I just worked with the men, but now I am running an organization. I hire, fire, train, and evaluate men. I also run a good bit of the sales meetings. We have one about every two months."

## The Medical Sales Representatives' View

The following interview with Don Wade, who had been with Alcon over eight years, indicates what the casewriter believes to be a fairly typical attitude toward customers of Alcon's older salesmen.

CASEWRITER:    What is your job as medical service representative?

WADE:    The most important thing is to sell the doctor and create demand for your product. If you just get into the retailer and then the doctor doesn't write it you have problems because the retailer will send it back. I provide information to the doctor. The doctors ask me about drugs, ours and our competition's; they ask me what they are and what they do, etc. If I don't know about a product I don't try to bluff it, so they trust me. If a competitor's product is good I tell the doctor it is. I've been with Alcon a long time so I know the doctors and they write my products. When I come around with a new drug the doctors trust me so they'll start right in and use it.

The doctor call is indirect selling; you don't write up an order and you don't know if you have sold him. But a distribution call is direct selling. The pharmacist trusts me so I just check his inventory, decide what he needs, and write up the turnover order. Usually he doesn't even see it. I just send it to the wholesaler. It's the same way with the wholesalers. I have a good relationship with them and they just let me write up the orders.

With the doctors it's different. You have to use more finesse—it's a soft sell. You have to know your doctor, where he went to school, his likes and dislikes. If you know your doctor, you can sell him. Everybody likes to be sold. The more you can get him to talk the better you can sell him. The doctor is more professional and ethical. But the pharmacist is more interested in money so you have to show how your product will make him a profit. I just call on the key pharmacies in my area, which is only probably 1 to 2 percent of all the pharmacies.

CASEWRITER:    Do you prefer to make a doctor call or a distribution call?

WADE:    I'd rather make a doctor call any time because it's more of a challenge. I enjoy trying to match wits with him, and I can tell about 80 percent of the time whether I have sold him or not. But you have to know what they are saying. A doctor will promise you anything. They want to be nice to you like they are to their patients, so they will say they will use your drug and then they won't follow up and do it. However, when we have a good retail promotion I enjoy selling the druggist, because then it's a challenge.

CASEWRITER:    What is your call mix?

WADE:    I spend about 80 percent of my time calling on doctors and the other 20 percent on distribution calls. A couple of years ago we went on a retail kick and we were spending about 65 percent of our time on distribution. The boys in the home office get on a retail kick every once in a while. They like to use distribution campaigns. It's a quick way to get sales increases but it doesn't last. George Leone is for the doctor; he knows you've got to create demand and you can't do it with just distribution.

CASEWRITER:   Do you keep up with the others during the distribution campaign?

WADE:   Oh yes, you've got to. But it strains your relationship with the wholesalers and retailers. They especially dislike automatic shipments. But things are better now—25 percent of the wholesalers let me check the stock record and write up the order. They trust me and I only have to sell them when we are doing a promotion.

An interview with John Cook revealed the attitude of the younger, more ambitious salesmen. Cook had been with Alcon just one year, and was described by the DSM as a good management prospect.

CASEWRITER:   What is your job as a medical service representative?

COOK:   It's a hard sell with the doctor. You're in there as a salesman to sell your product. You really have to know your doctors because you can really pin some of them down and get a commitment to write your product, but with others you can't do much. So you have to know which ones to push. You have to get to know the receptionist too because she guards the doctor and can prevent you from seeing him. The eye doctors like Alcon. I tell them "we're eye specialists, and if you don't write our products nobody will."

CASEWRITER:   Do you prefer to make a doctor call or a distribution call?

COOK:   I would rather call on the doctor because he treats me like a professional man. It's just a chore to make retail calls. I spend 85 percent of my time calling on doctors because I'd rather call on them. Some of our wholesalers are upset because they say Alcon is high pressure as a result of the distribution campaign two years ago.

Bob Jensen, another salesman the casewriter interviewed, had been with Alcon for three years.

CASEWRITER:   Why did you take this job?

JENSEN:   I studied pre-med in college but I didn't have good enough grades to get into medical school. However, I still wanted some dealings with the medical profession so after I got some sales experience I came with Alcon. The eye doctors know that Alcon only calls on eye doctors so they like to see the Alcon man. So I am accepted more by doctors than the detail men from other companies are.

CASEWRITER:   Which would you rather make, a doctor call or a distribution call?

JENSEN:   I enjoy calling on the doctor because he is more professional—ethical. The only problem is that you don't know when you've sold the doctor. You get better feedback from the pharmacist because you write up an order there. But a pharmacist is like the average businessman and is interested in making money. Ninety-nine percent of the doctors accept me very well; about 50 percent of them call me by my first name, but it's taken two years to get on a first name basis. The doctor would rather discuss products with a friend so if you have been calling on him a while and he knows you, he'll listen.

Jack Green had only been with Alcon for four months, but he had these comments about the customers:

It used to bother me to call on the doctor because he has all the degrees. But I soon realized that he puts his pants on one leg at a time just like the rest of us, so why worry. Now I enjoy calling on the doctor because he appreciates what I do for him. The doctor treats me okay; his opening statement is "What's new"— he's glad to see me. The pharmacist is just a businessman and I can come and go and he doesn't appreciate what I do for him.

## Doctors' Views of the Salesmen

Doctor Jones was about 45, had a large practice, and also did some work with a well-respected eye clinic in the large eastern city where he practiced. The casewriter believed that his views were typical of the busy, successful ophthalmologist.

CASEWRITER:   What is the job of the detail man?

DOCTOR:   He keeps the doctor informed. He makes the information available before it comes out in the journals (the journals are always months behind) and you can ask questions of him directly. The most important thing is that he keeps the doctor informed.

CASEWRITER:   What kind of detail man do you like or dislike?

DOCTOR:   I like one that is pleasant and sincere, and one who has a knowledge of his product or at least is honest enough to let you know when he doesn't. Also I prefer one that makes no demands. Some of them will say, "I'll be back in ten days to see how you've gotten along with my product," and it puts you on the spot.

CASEWRITER:   Which companies are doing the best job of promoting their products?

DOCTOR:   The question really should be which ones see you most frequently. The answer is Alcon, Smith Miller Patch, and Upjohn, I guess.

CASEWRITER:   In what way do they do a better job?

DOCTOR:   Frequency of call. I tend to write more of their products when they call frequently and I have more knowledge of their products. The detail man is very important to me. It's hard to keep up with all of the information coming out, and they are a big help. When I am at conventions I spend a lot of time at the booths. But I depend on the detail man to get information on things like products, sizes, availability, etc. They keep me up to date on new developments.

Dr. Barron was about 50 years old. He did not seem to be as busy as some of the other eye doctors and he spent 20 minutes with the casewriter while the others would only spend 5 to 10 minutes.

CASEWRITER:   What is the role of the detail man?

BARRON:   I am influenced by the detail man. I have an emotional affinity for him and he leaves a lot of samples. I feel an obligation to him and I'll write his drugs.

CASEWRITER:   What kind of detail man do you like or dislike?

BARRON:   I don't like the overpowering salesman. I like a neat, well dressed, polite man who just gives me information. I think all detail men are frustrated doctors—you wouldn't really want to be a detail man. Generally the salesmen are very nice people and very cooperative. They all say that if there is ever anything that they can do, I shouldn't hesitate to call them. I could call them at three o'clock in the morning if I needed a drug and the pharmacy was closed. They are selling me good will.

Let me give you an example, I like neat polite guys but I didn't like one who called on me. He was an Italian. Now, I've got nothing against Italians, but he didn't speak correct English and his fingernails were dirty. I had an emotional antipathy to this fellow. A doctor has two degrees and he likes to meet and talk to intelligent people who are somewhat on his level.

CASEWRITER:    How many detail men call on you?

BARRON:    Quite a few—probably eight or nine. I probably see three or four detail men every week. They'll try to sell you a bill of goods. They try to tell you their products are better than someone else's. One says its better in suspension and another says its better in solution. I don't know which is the best vehicle.

CASEWRITER:    Which companies do the best job of detailing?

BARRON:    Oh, Alcon's the big one. They've been in the field the longest. They were the first ones to specialize in ophthalmic drugs and they were the first ones to use the plastic bottles which are more sanitary.

## Pharmacists' View of the Salesman

The attitude of the pharmacist toward the salesman was evident in this interview:

CASEWRITER:    What is the job of the ethical drug salesman?

PHARMACIST:    He tells us about new products, price changes, and what's being detailed, because that's what sells. He comes in and writes up the order. Then we check it over and cut back if he's put in too much of any product.

CASEWRITER:    Which companies do the best job in calling on you?

PHARMACIST:    All the major companies do a good job. Upjohn, Merck, etc. But the small companies have high turnover. They'll have a new man in here about every month. We sometimes have problems with them.

CASEWRITER:    What does the salesman expect you to do for him?

PHARMACIST:    He expects us to keep his products in stock; he sells the products to the doctor. He also asks for information on what the doctors are writing. We have a prescription file and he's welcome to look through it.

CASEWRITER:    We are studying Alcon Laboratories. What kind of a job do they do?

PHARMACIST:    Alcon! They're excellent. See all the drugs on that shelf there? They are Alcon's. They're the number one company in the eye market. Their salesman does a good job in keeping us stocked and replacing outdated merchandise.

In making calls with Alcon salesmen the casewriter noted that Alcon seemed to have an excellent reputation with the pharmacist. In the eye section of the pharmacist's drugs Alcon usually had by far the most shelf space, and the Alcon drugs were usually the most accessible to the pharmacist.

## Wholesalers' View of the Salesmen

The following interview with a buyer at a busy wholesaler's gives an indication of his attitude toward salesmen:

CASEWRITER:    What kind of salesmen do you like or dislike?

BUYER:    I like one that takes care of the details on his products, such as price changes, returns, checking inventory, and giving us information on new items.

Also, I don't like pressure. We are trying to sell merchandise and in order to sell we have to buy. We don't need anyone to pressure us. It's just the new man or the fly-by-night guy who gets this pitch from the home office and tries to shove it down our throat. But by and large they tend to be quite professional in their approach.

CASEWRITER:    We're currently writing a case on Alcon. Do they do a good job?

BUYER:    Yes and no . . . they're a little pushy, a little bang-bang.

CASEWRITER:    Is this more so now than in the past?

BUYER:    No, if anything it's less so now than in the past. They tended to put up these deals at the home office and then put them off on us.

## Sales Force's View of the Marketing Effort

A number of managers and salesmen pointed out that the quality of the promotion developed by the product managers could greatly influence a salesman's success. With a high-quality program and the support of direct mail and journal advertising a salesman could significantly increase sales of a featured product. The salesmen appeared to agree that the work of the product managers had improved a great deal in the past two to three years and that they were doing an excellent job.

Many of the salesmen expressed concern, however, about the infrequency with which Alcon had introduced new products. One salesman said that in the past six years Alcon had introduced only "two big new products," and that it was only in those periods that the company had experienced rapid sales growth. One manager pointed out that Alcon had significantly expanded its R&D effort in the past two years and that "we now have in R&D more PhD's per sales dollar than anyone in the industry, and we are currently spending 10 percent of sales for that purpose."

## Salesmen's Views of the Company, Compensation, and Opportunity for Advancement

The following is another part of the interview with Don Wade who had been with Alcon over eight years.

CASEWRITER:    How does Alcon compare with the industry on compensation?

WADE:    You can't make big money in the drug business, and if you compare Alcon with the others in the industry their salary is not the best, but they hit a happy medium. I've been offered more money by other drug companies, but Alcon has a great future and they have a good relationship with the doctors.

On the commission, no man is happy when you deduct his expenses before you start paying commission. I can't help it if my territory is large and I have to travel a lot. In addition, its hard to get a sales increase every year, especially when you don't have any new products. I've built my area up considerably and I'll sell $160,000 this year. To get an increase I have to hold what the doctor is already writing for Alcon, plus getting him to try more of our products. The easiest way to get a sales increase is with new products but you can get it with a good promotion on an old product. Doctors work from habit, so if you can get him to write it for three months he'll continue to write it.

CASEWRITER:    How does Alcon compare on opportunities for advancement?

WADE:    Alcon has the best opportunity for advancement in the industry, if you're looking for that. I'm not. I just want to be a salesman. The DSM has to travel too much and I don't want to be away from my family any more than I am now.

CASEWRITER:    How does Alcon's first line supervision compare with other companies?

WADE:    Our company has been weak in supervision compared with other drug companies. At least we've been weak in the past. But now they're doing a better job of training a man before they make him a DSM. Nobody can learn the drug business in two years so our managers just haven't had enough field experience.

CASEWRITER:    Why have so many salesmen left Alcon?

WADE:    Alcon promises you the sky in terms of advancement and then they just don't come through. So, when the boys have been here a while and they don't get a promotion as soon as they were told  they would, they leave.

The following is an interview with George Bell, who had been with Alcon two years. The casewriter believed that his comments were typical of the new salesman.

CASEWRITER:    How does Alcon compare with the industry on compensation?

BELL:    I really don't know, but salaries are low in the drug industry. However, I've seen what management salaries are and I've seen the company's net profit, and I don't think I'm getting my share.

CASEWRITER:    Are there opportunities for advancement with Alcon?

BELL:    Yes, there are very good opportunities, and they're getting better because Alcon's continuing to grow.

CASEWRITER:    How do you like Alcon's field supervisors?

BELL:    They're very good, much better here than in the rest of the industry. There's not a lot of pressure—you get the guidance and help that you need but they respect you. They leave it up to me to manage my own territory.

CASEWRITER:    Why have so many salesmen left Alcon?

BELL:    I only know three men that have left and two of them left because of lack of compensation. I could do better elsewhere financially right now but

I'm looking to the future with Alcon. They will treat me all right in the future.

George Jackson had been with Alcon three and one-half years. His comments follow:

CASEWRITER:    How do you feel about compensation at Alcon?
JACKSON:    It's not too good. I got a lot less commission in 1966 than I did in 1965 and I'm not alone in that.
CASEWRITER:    Are there advancement opportunities here?
JACKSON:    Yes, they are here. I'm an ADP and I expect to advance.
CASEWRITER:    Why has Alcon had such high turnover?
JACKSON:    Alcon expects more from its salesmen than other companies do so some guys leave because they can't live up to what Alcon expects. If a guy only wants to work 40 hours a week this is not the company to be with. If a guy wants to be a salesman all his life with little hope for advancement but only working 40 hours a week then he better go with one of the large companies that are institutionalized.

Jack Green, who had only been with Alcon four months, had these comments about compensation:

I'm really motivated by money. If I can sell the doctor I'll get ahead, i.e., I'll get more money and advancement. Alcon pays all right. It ranks with the bigger drug companies.
CASEWRITER:    How about supervision at Alcon?
GREEN:    My DSM is a real sharp guy, he's business all the way. He is kind of aloof and doesn't want to get to close to the men. If you don't do your job he'll fire you. I think that is the way it should be.
CASEWRITER:    Are there opportunities for advancement here?
GREEN:    Yes. I think advancement opportunities are excellent and that is why I came with Alcon. That wasn't the case with the other drug company I worked for. I give myself two years to make a lot of money—like $10,000 per year—or be promoted. If I don't make either, I'll quit.

Nearly everyone the casewriter interviewed said that they believed there were excellent opportunities for advancement with Alcon. Management indicated, however, that there were no plans to expand the sales force or the number of field managers in the immediate future. When the casewriter presented this apparent contradiction to Dave Colton, a salesman who had been with Alcon for five months, Colton had replied that he expected to advance with Alcon because he believed that there would be an opportunity for him to be promoted into a management position in one of the companies that had been acquired or that would be acquired by Alcon.

## SUMMARY

Management was aware that turnover was high among sales personnel throughout the drug industry (12.1 percent in 1964), but Alcon turnover was a great deal higher than other drug companies. In fact, it had been as high as 42 percent in 1964. (Exhibit 11 shows the turnover in Alcon's sales force from 1961 and 1966, and the length of service of the men leaving.)

**EXHIBIT 11**

Turnover of Alcon's Sales Force

| Year Ending April 30 | % Turnover |
|---|---|
| 1961 | 35 |
| 1962 | 27 |
| 1963 | 35 |
| 1964 | 42 |
| 1965 | 34 |
| 1966 | 28 |

Length of Service of Salesmen Terminating

| Number of Months Employment | Number of Personnel | Cumulative Number of Personnel |
|---|---|---|
| 6 months or less | 4—13.8% | 4— 13.8% |
| 12 months or less | 8—27.6 | 12— 41.4 |
| 18 months or less | 4—13.8 | 16— 55.0 |
| 24 months or less | 2— 6.9 | 18— 62.0 |
| 30 months or less | 5—17.2 | 23— 79.5 |
| 36 months or less | 1— 3.5 | 24— 82.7 |
| 42 months or less | 1— 3.5 | 25— 86.6 |
| 48 months or less | 1— 3.5 | 26— 89.6 |
| 60 months or less | 3—10.3% | 29—100.0% |

Management was concerned about the high turnover for several reasons. First of all, it was costly. Although Alcon's figures were not available, one survey reported, "The cost of selecting, training, and supervising a new drug salesman averages $7,612, excluding salary."[6] Just as important as cost was the fact that it took one to two years for a salesman to establish a satisfactory relationship with the doctor, the wholesaler, and the retailer. Most of the men who left had been with Alcon less than two and one-half years. These salesmen just barely got to know the customers before leaving.

Mr. Leone was uncertain about why so many men had left Alcon. He indicated that almost all of them said they were leaving because they were not earning enough money, but he was not sure that was the whole reason. Alcon had raised salaries considerably in the past three years, but men were still leaving. Mr. Leone felt that part of the problem may have been the shift in emphasis from "demand" to "distribution" and then back to "demand." Mr. Leone noted that Alcon's highest turnover had occurred in the years when they had distribution campaigns.

---

[6] *Sales Management*, January 21, 1966, pp. 45–52.

## Two Proposed Changes

In reviewing the organization and administration of the company's sales efforts, Mr. Leone was considering two changes in the operation. Under the present organization, Mr. Leone believed that there was too much duplication of work and responsibility. Specifically, he was not happy with the overlapping of the activities of the RSM's and the DSM's. Until recently the DSM's had been primarily concerned with training men and making calls with them. The RSM's had been presenting programs to them, recruiting, and selecting new salesmen.

The DSM's activities were changing, however. They were becoming more involved with the recruiting, selection, and training of new men. Simultaneously, Mr. Leone noted the RSM's, eager to obtain good performance from the salesmen, had bypassed the DSM's and developed a direct relationship with salesmen.

One effort to overcome this problem was to move the RSM's to the home office. Mr. Leone was eager to have the responsibility for motivating and directing the salesmen belong solely to the DSM's. He wanted the RSM's to rely on the DSM's for management of the field sales force. Mr. Leone also believed that more productive use of the regional sales managers' time could be made if their duties were expanded to include direct work with the product managers in planning promotional campaigns and with himself in formulating sales policies.

Exhibit 12 is an organization chart which depicted Mr. Leone's ideas on how the new organization should look. Mr. Leone wanted to reduce

**EXHIBIT 12**

Proposed Organization Chart of the Sales Group

the number of RSM's to two, and have them located in the home office. He also wanted to establish two new sections in the sales group: (1) sales training and development, which would be responsible for designing standard company training programs and other devices for helping to improve the performance of the sales force; and (2) sales services which would be responsible for maintaining master records or sales force activities and aiding the salesmen in obtaining any information or supplies they needed. For the time being, at least, Mr. Leone did not plan to change the defined duties of the DSM's and MSR's.

The other change which Mr. Leone was considering was a new compensation system for the salesmen. Mr. Leone believed that the current compensation system was unsuitable because the commission was paid on sales increases *after* deduction of total selling expenses, and the commission was not necessarily related to a man's efforts or performance but rather to whether the company was emphasizing demand or distribution effort at the time. Mr. Leone had been hearing increasing criticism of the company's compensation plan.

In an effort to correct this situation, Mr. Leone drew up a proposal which laid out the terms of a new compensation system for the MSR's. Exhibit 13 contains a description of the major items in the proposal. If such a compensation system were inaugurated, Mr. Leone believed it would prove to be more directly related to performance, regardless of the products or type of sales activity that the company was currently promoting. He also hoped the plan would provide major motivation for improved salesman performance.

### EXHIBIT 13

Proposed Compensation System

    I. Starting salary range for a new Field Representative is $500 to $600 per month and requires DSM's, RSM's, national sales manager's and marketing director's approval.

   II. Salary Increases.

     1. Salary increases will be given once each year after a performance review beginning June 1 and ending August 31. This applies to all salaries over $600/month.

     2. Salaries under $600 per month can be raised every six months after a performance review.

     3. All salary increases must be approved by all levels of supervision above the recipient before he is informed of the recommendation.

     4. Increases in salary are not to be retroactive.

     5. Total income concept will be used in all salary increases.

     6. All salary increases must be based on performance and contribution.

     7. All salary increases outside company policies require extensive study and analysis of all levels of management above recipient.

  III. Commission.

     1. New field representatives, after a performance review and approval of all levels of field supervision above the recipient, may be placed on commission (in addition to salary) after six months.

     2. Commissions are not to be retroactive.

## Exhibit 13 *(continued)*

3. Commissions will be based on increased sales as follows:

| | Sales Increase | Cumulative Sales Increase | Percent Commission | Commission Earned | Cumulative Commission Earned |
|---|---|---|---|---|---|
| 1st | $5000 | $ 5,000 | 2 | $100 | $ 100 |
| 2nd | 5000 | 10,000 | 4 | 200 | 300 |
| 3rd | 5000 | 15,000 | 6 | 300 | 600 |
| 4th | 5000 | 20,000 | 8 | 400 | 1000 |
| 5th | 5000 | 25,000 | 10 | 500 | 1500 |
| 6th | 5000 | 30,000 | 12 | 600 | 2100 |
| 7th | $5000 | $35,000 | 14 | $700 | $2800 |

4. Commissions are based on a fiscal year, which is the beginning of the first fiscal month (May) to the end of the last fiscal month.
5. Overpayment of commissions will be carried as a charge against future commissions and/or salary until balanced.
6. Commissions are not paid to any field representative who is terminated before the end of the commission period (and of the fiscal month of April).

IV. Salary deductions can be made to all field personnel for the following reasons:
   1. Overpayment of commissions—refer to III, #5.
   2. Overpayment of salary or expenses.
   3. Personal damages to company property—auto, supplies, etc.
   4. Legal liability is determined to be the individual's.
   5. Federal and state income tax.
   6. Profit sharing trust, hospitalization, savings bonds, etc., where employee requests participation.
   7. Social security.

Note: 14% commission paid on all increase sales over $30,000.

There was still a question in Mr. Leone's mind as to whether his analysis of the organization and administration of the sales group had led him to identify the most urgent problems and the proper solutions. He believed that if it was necessary to reorganize the sales organization and compensation system, these changes would be easier to carry out now than they would be several years hence, when Alcon's rapid growth would have magnified the problem.

# Baines Electronics Corporation

PAUL JEFFERSON, project manager on Baines' air defense missile contract with the U.S. Air Force, returned from a corporate level meeting late one afternoon in November 1961. The meeting had concerned the corporation's newly announced policy governing salary increases for all employees for the forthcoming year. After reviewing some notes and collecting his thoughts on what had transpired in the meeting, which had been chaired by the president of Baines, Jefferson called his secretary over the intercom and asked her to assemble the project's key leaders for a 4:00 p.m. meeting. The purpose of the meeting was to pass on details of the president's message.

## GENERAL COMPANY BACKGROUND

Baines Electronics Corporation, a medium-sized company with annual sales of about $280 million, had its principal plants in a small town located 40 miles outside of Boston. A majority of Baines' 13,000 employees worked at that location. Founded in the late 1930's by Carlton Baines and several other talented engineers from National Electronics, Baines Electronics grew rapidly in the early days of World War II due to heavy involvement in the production of aircraft instruments. The company successfully weathered the postwar transition period, and by the late 1950's Baines had rapidly rising sales and prospects for continued good growth.

An important element of the Baines corporate policy was the fair treatment of employees. The company had pioneered in granting real and fringe benefits and had a record of stable employment second to none in the industry. Carlton Baines, up until his death in 1957, had always maintained an "open door" policy for all his employees. Anyone could enter the president's office and "talk to the boss." Baines had also encouraged the formation of numerous company-sponsored activities, such as bowling and softball, and the founders' overall regard for the workers was an important factor in keeping the company nonunionized. When asked why

232

they worked at Baines, many employees would remark that it was an enjoyable place to work, where friendliness and unanimity of purpose were main motivating factors.

All of Carlton Baines' policies were continued when a new president was selected from within the company to carry on after his death in 1957.

## THE NEW PLAN

About ten people sat around Jefferson's conference table later that day. None of the men wore suit jackets, and it was apparent from the informal conversation that the missile project was a tightly knit organization, with relatively high morale. Most of the engineers on Jefferson's project and in other engineering groups at Baines had a B.S. or M.S. degree; about 5 percent of the engineers had a Ph.D. Jefferson had always prided himself on the fact that the men in his groups felt free to talk to him about both technical and personal problems. When all were present he began.

He explained that there had been a growing tendency, according to the president, for salary increases to be handed out annually without appropriate emphasis on the meaning behind the raise. Lately, or as it seemed to upper management, there was not much awareness on the part of either superior or subordinate that such raises were granted because of the specific contribution of the employee and because of a generally favorable overall corporate outlook. It was felt that the merit plan had acquired certain superficial aspects of a cost-of-living increase. Many employees, therefore, expected yearly increases, whether or not their work for the past period truly warranted special recognition and whether or not the company profit picture was favorable.

At this point Jefferson stopped and asked for comments, and in the ensuing discussion it was agreed by all those present that the situation had been accurately described by the president. Some changes certainly seemed in order. Jefferson returned to his notes.

In order to correct the problem and restore proper balance to the merit raise program, the president had requested that several measures be adopted immediately for the next year:

1. Over and above any plans now in progress, an immediate review was to be made of the salary status of all employees.
2. Those men who "really put out" were to be given raises in January or as soon thereafter as practicable.
3. Whenever a raise was granted, the supervisor was to make a special point—almost an ostentatious gesture of commendation—to highlight the relationship between salary increases and outstanding performance.
4. All raises intended for the next year were to be awarded before August (rather than spread throughout the entire year) with the general expectation that the better the man the earlier he was to receive his raise.

To further enhance the plan, the president announced that the dollar package set aside for raises for 1962 was to be nearly double the amount allotted in previous years. The president had ended his talk by reemphasizing that it was important to let people know where they stood so that they might be encouraged to improve both themselves and their value to the company.

As he summarized the president's remarks, Jefferson added his personal emphasis to the points listed above. He then requested that all his leaders forward their individual raise recommendations to him within one week.

## THE OLD MERIT INCREASE SYSTEM

Although certain areas within the plants used special practices, all engineering groups used the basic system which is shown in Figure 1. This

**FIGURE 1**

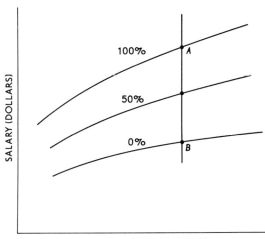

YEARS OF EXPERIENCE

curve plots salary against years of experience and was intended to show that for any given number of years of experience a man's salary range was between points A and B. These points were the outer limits of a band of possible salaries shown as "100 percent and 0 percent" lines. Everyone fell somewhere between these extremes, the idea being that everyone had a hypothetical evaluation factor between 100 percent and 0 percent. If one were a 90 percent man it meant that in the company's estimation only 10 percent of the people with similar experience were rated ahead of him. Similarly, if one were a 25 percent man, 75 percent of the men with identical experience were rated superior. The rating factor was accomplished in somewhat subjective terms at the project level and reviewed three times before final corporate approval.

A key point was that the individual ratings and the salary curves (the 100 percent and 0 percent limits) were known only to the evaluator (the immediate superior) and the salary administration group. These facts were not available to the individual employee and no one had any knowledge of his own or his fellow employees' standing, particularly since good and average raises were awarded at random times throughout the year. An engineer who was to be awarded a raise was asked to come to his superior's office for a discussion, and at this meeting he was informed of his increase in salary.

This system had been used for nearly twenty years and had produced little or no griping at any level. Jefferson could recall few instances when he had received complaints about salaries.

## WORKING OUT THE NEW PLAN

Jefferson spent many hours working over the recommendations of his subordinates and trying to fit these into a workable time-phased series of raises to be granted in 1962. When he finally submitted his project plan in December, both he and his project leaders were enthusiastic about the prospects for the coming year. More money was to be given out, and he felt that that facet of the plan certainly ought to be appreciated, since even the low-rated people would receive a bigger raise than usual.

# Seneca Steel Corporation

In November of 1967 Mr. Ted Cunningham, the production superintendent of the Charlestown Works of Seneca Steel, met with the plant manager. The plant manager had asked Cunningham to come to his office to discuss training and personnel development for the Production Department, and at the end of the meeting he told Cunningham that he had been selected to attend the PMD course at the Harvard Business School. Later the conversation turned to the most logical replacement for Cunningham during his sixteen-week absence. Cunningham suggested that he assemble some performance measurement data on the likely candidates before a final decision was made.

The candidates to be considered were all in the Production Department reporting to Cunningham (see Exhibit 1 for the department organization chart).

Since the plant manager was relatively new in his job and was not too familiar with the various superintendents in the Production Department, Cunningham first prepared a table which contained some personal background on each man, as well as pertinent comments on their individual strengths and weaknesses (see Exhibit 2). Previously prepared quarterly reports contained information on performance measurement results for the previous two years for the men being considered. In order to understand these ratings, however, it is necessary to describe the present performance measurement system, as well as the previously used system.

Cunningham used a "management by objectives" system with the people reporting to him. The performance of each of the line superintendents was measured in four categories; in their department they had relatively complete responsibility and authority in these four areas.

Table 1 shows the four areas of responsibility and the results or measurement methods used for performance appraisal.

The "management by objectives" system generally consisted of the setting of specific goals by each section superintendent for his department for the coming year. These goals were reviewed with the production super-

236

## EXHIBIT 1

Production Department Organization
( Charlestown works )

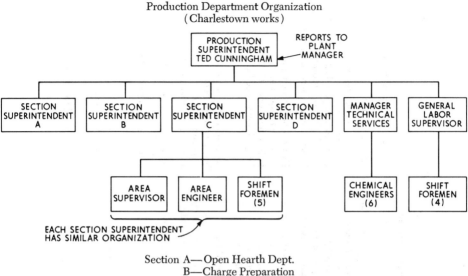

Section A—Open Hearth Dept.
B—Charge Preparation
C—Metallurgical Evaluation
D—Soaking Pits

## TABLE 1

Section Superintendent Responsibilities

| Performance Item | Methods of Measurements |
|---|---|
| 1. Safety | Monthly reports—safety experience and department report on program implementation |
| 2. Production losses | Monthly operating factor report |
| 3. Costs | Monthly cost reports<br>Superintendents' monthly budget cost analysis report |
| 4. Employee relations | Subjective measurement—jointly by Section, production, and industrial relations superintendents |

intendent, and if they were acceptable to him they became the "published" goals and objectives for that department for the next year. Goals, and wherever possible specific programs for achieving them, were developed on all items in Table 1. The production superintendent stressed the "contribution" theme wherever possible, pointing out that these goals belonged to the individual section superintendent and his men and not to the production superintendent. The implication was that achievement of these goals would at least represent "good" (or above average) performance. It was also understood that salary administration would be tied to this performance. Each item in Table 1 would generally result in four or five pro-

**EXHIBIT 2**

Section Superintendent—Personnel Background

| Sup't. | Total Yrs. Exper. | Yrs. with Seneca | Yrs. Present Job | Education | General Summary Comments | |
|---|---|---|---|---|---|---|
| | | | | | Strong Points | Weak Points |
| A | 5 | 3 | 2 | B.S. Chem. Engr. | High potential<br>Poised, personable<br>Technically very good | Performance poor last year<br>Interdep't cooperation poor<br>Worries about wrong things |
| B | 10 | 3 | 2 | B.S. Chem. Engr. | Excellent performance<br>Good managerial techniques<br>Well liked by subordinates | Expression, speech, poise need strengthening<br>Left Seneca once (?????)<br>Only "knows" Sec't B |
| C | 8 | 8 | 5 | B.S. Chem. Engr. | Experienced all sections<br>Performance improving<br>Technically adequate | No respect for peers<br>Some years of poor performance<br>Lacks long-range potential |
| D | 10 | 4 | 1 | B.S. Mech. Engr. | Strong Mech. Engr. | Serious mgmt. technique problems<br>Long-range potential low |
| Tech Services | 10 | 10 | 2 | M.S. Chem. Engr. | Strong technically | Poor Manager<br>Definitely a technical man only |
| Gen. Labor | 10 | 10 | 3 | B.S. Bus. Adm. | Excellent performance present job | No potential for prod. sup't. job |

grams for improved performance, and in the case of costs, some five to ten programs were usually developed for each department. A typical budget sheet and cost reduction program summary are shown in Exhibits 3 and 4.

### EXHIBIT 3

Typical Cost Summary Sheet, 1968 Budget
( 104—open hearth spending—1968 forward plan )

|  | 1968 Plan* | Average Month 1967 | 1967 Standard† | 1968 Standard (Predicted)‡ |
|---|---|---|---|---|
| Services labor .........$ | 200 | $    290 | $      0 | $    290 |
| Operating labor ....... | 15,700 | 21,890 | 21,100 | 15,000 |
| General labor ......... | 3,000 | 5,274 | 3,350 | 2,500 |
| Operating supplies ..... | 2,200 | 2,818 | 2,350 | 2,000 |
| Power .............. | 2,800 | 3,706 | 3,600 | 3,600 |
| Steam .............. | 126,600 | 132,344 | 129,574 | 116,000 |
| Air ................. | 500 | 554 | 546 | 550 |
| Total R & M.......... | 30,700 | 38,263 | 39,716 | 35,700 |
| Subtotal ...........$181,750 | | $205,246 | $200,236 | $175,640 |
| Major repair ......... | 4,500 | 9,000 | 14,800 | 14,800 |
| Total ..............$186,250 | | $214,246 | $215,036 | $190,440 |

* The "1968 Plan" was the superintendent's plan (goal for the coming year), subject to the approval of the production superintendent.

† The "1967 Standard" represents the year's engineered standard costs. Seneca Steel plants used industrial engineering standards as well as the forward plan system.

‡ The standards were prepared at year end. The plan was prepared in October. Therefore, the next year's standard could only be estimated at the time the plan was done.

Comparison of the 1968 plan to 1967 average "actual" performance gave some indication of the degree of difficulty in achieving the plan on a historical basis.

Comparison to standard costs showed the effect of capital improvements. The distinction looked for in this comparison was how much of the improvement was the result of the department management.

## THE PREVIOUS SYSTEM

Three years before, Cunningham had read several articles discussing the merits of management by objectives management systems. Seneca had recently instituted a forward planning program on a corporate-wide basis, and it seemed to Cunningham that these two programs could easily be combined into a single system that could accomplish the planning purpose and simultaneously set up a system of management by objectives.

Up to this point the leadership style at Charlestown had been rather authoritarian, with close control by the production superintendent over the section superintendent in as many variables in the total "process-cost-safety-technical" system as his personal ability and drive allowed. Cost control revolved around a standard cost system. Monthly cost meetings were held for the production department in which each section superintendent discussed the reasons for his variations from standard. The general atmosphere was one of pressure from the production superintendent to the sec-

## EXHIBIT 4

Cost Reduction Program Summary
( inter-office memorandum )

To:  T.E. Cunningham      DATE:   January 23, 1968
AT:  Charlestown          FROM:   F.O. Berger
                          AT:   Charlestown
                          SUBJECT:   1968 Forward Plan Program

---

There are seven cost reduction programs in the open hearth department which should yield definite savings.

1. Coke operator elimination: $3600/month—reduction made 10/1/67.
2. OP* facilities: $4750/month—savings are as promised in the RFI† except for steam, which is the actual expected. (The RFI did not include provision for steam pump steam.)
3. General labor reduction: $1600/month—savings are generally OP-related, but are above those promised in the RFI.
4. Operating supplies reduction: $400/month—savings are generally OP-related, but are above those promised in the RFI.
5. Power reduction: $1050/month—savings are generally OP-related, but are above those promised in the RFI. The power usage will have to be redivided after OP startup.
6. Maintenance reduction: $400/month—savings are as follows:

    Reduced production . . . . . . . . . . . . . . . . . . . . .$ 600
    OP-solved problems (above RFI) . . . . . . . . . .  850
    Problems already solved . . . . . . . . . . . . . . . . 2550
                                                       $4000

There is also a program for optimization of steam usage. Actual savings are unknown because OP operating conditions are not definite. A reduction in steam cost of 2 percent, however, would yield an annual saving of $2500 per month.

* Ore processing facilities.
† Request for improvement.

tion superintendent. Since the meeting revolved around the variances, the general tone of the meeting was negative. Cunningham was never very comfortable with this system and welcomed the opportunity to try the new system. (The production superintendent was free to use whatever management control system he felt best.) The plant manager only intervened when there was a deviation from generally expected normal performance (which always implied improvement over previous performance) in the areas of cost, safety, or production.

## DEVELOPING THE NEW SYSTEM

At first there was general reluctance by the section superintendents to follow (or believe) the spirit of the new system. Goals for the first year were hammered out by the production superintendent after several meetings with each section superintendent. In most cases the production superintendent actually set the goals, since the section superintendents were reluctant to set a goal that represented a really significant improvement.

Changes were also made in the monthly reporting. The cost meeting was eliminated and a written monthly report of progress towards goals on items in Table 1 was substituted. This report was reviewed in a meeting between the individual section superintendent and the production superintendent. Emphasis was on problems that were preventing the superintendent from reaching his goal. Cunningham attempted to remove as much pressure as possible from these meetings.

In the second year the original goals as set by the section superintendents were more nearly in line with Cunningham's estimate of feasible progress. On only two or three items did he feel it necessary to pressure the superintendent to raise the goal. By the third year, Cunningham actually found it necessary to scale down some of the goals submitted because he felt they were too optimistic. The new system seemed to be beginning to function as it was intended to function; throughout the past two years the overall performance of the production department was generally considered to be good.

### Narrowing Down the List of Candidates

After looking over the data in Exhibit 2, Cunningham concluded that the technical services superintendent was really not a valid candidate. In his opinion he did not have the right type of personality to be a line manager. He seemed to prefer the slower pace of technical work and did not appear to like working under pressure, which he would encounter in line work. Cunningham had discussed this point with him before. The technical services superintendent did not believe that he should be ruled out in being considered for line work. In past years, the men who had chosen line management work had generally moved ahead faster than those in technical management. Despite this lack of agreement, Cunningham decided to omit this man from the final list.

The general labor superintendent likewise was eliminated from consideration due to his lack of a technical background and a general feeling that he was approaching his maximum potential in his present job. (His present job did not require any great degree of technical ability, and his performance had been very good.) Cunningham was reasonably sure that this man did not expect to be considered for this particular job. Cunningham also eliminated the Section D superintendent because of a lack of managerial experience; he also had serious doubts about the ability of this man to succeed even in his present position.

### The Final Three Candidates

This narrowed the choice down to Superintendents A, B, and C. Cunningham assembled performance data for the previous two years on these

**EXHIBIT 5**

Performance Rating*
(production superintendent's opinion of long-range potential)

| Superintendent | Safety | Cost Reduction | Production | Employee Relations | Range of Potential† |
|---|---|---|---|---|---|
| A | Below average | Below average | Average | Average | 2–3 |
| B | Average | Average | Average | Above average | 1–2 |
| C | Above average | Average | Above average | Above average | 0–1 |

* Performance ratings: Outstanding, above average, average, below average.
† Number of levels to which he has potential to advance (above present level).

three men as shown in Exhibit 5. Performance was rated in two ways: (1) against budget, and (2) versus the prior year. The "general" rankings (average, above average, etc.) were used, as Cunningham did not feel the performance appraisal system could be quantified beyond this point at this time. The rankings were established jointly by the production and section superintendents at the conclusion of their individual monthly meeting on the prior month's goal results.

Analysis of the performance data showed that Superintendent C had turned in the best performance, followed by B and A, in that order. In developing and implementing the management by objectives system, Cunningham had often stressed to his men that "performance was the only thing that really counts." This had been rather rigidly followed by Cunningham in determining the amount of salary increase each man would get.

Cunningham began to be very concerned. If he really believed his statements that "results count," Superintendent C was the most logical candidate. He was also the most experienced man. At the same time, Cunningham was very reluctant to recommend "C" for a promotion: The comments in Exhibit 2 and the "potential" ranking given to him by Cunningham in Exhibit 5 were not consistent with his very good performance in recent years.

Superintendent B was also a good performer, but also had some personality traits which did not seem to warrant promotion. For example, it still worried Cunningham that he had quit Seneca several years before, only to return one year later.

Superintendent A was regarded as the man with the highest long-range potential by Cunningham. However, his performance to date definitely did not justify his high ranking.

It became obvious to Cunningham that his performance appraisal system just wasn't sufficient to evaluate his men for promotion.

Later he reviewed the above data with the plant manager and recommended that they look for a replacement at one of the other Seneca plants. Since he was not familiar with the men involved, the plant manager agreed to follow Cunningham's recommendation. Cunningham left the meeting wondering how he would tell Superintendent C that he would not get a chance at the new job.

# Marshall Company (A)

## INTRODUCTION

THE MARSHALL COMPANY, one of the oldest paper-making companies in the United States, was producing a greater tonnage of paper in the summer of 1947 than ever before in its history. During the war years the demand had risen sharply for paper of the high quality for which this company was noted. To meet this increased demand, the management after the war had doubled the capacity of two of its paper-making machines and was in the process of rebuilding another. At the same time, in anticipation of increased competition, it was rebuilding its steam plant and power house for more economical operations. Because of undiscriminating demand, coupled with a shortage of materials during the war, the quality of the products had necessarily suffered; the company was now retraining its personnel to the higher paper standards that the management considered customers would soon demand. Sales, production, and quality control personnel were working closely together on the problems involved in making paper in large volume of a quality satisfactory to the customers.

Mr. Austin Brewster, the vice president in charge of production, was dealing largely with the stresses and strains created by these conditions. In certain lines material shortages had become more acute; personnel problems took a large amount of his thought; he was considering certain revisions of the employees' pay system; supervisory problems were particularly important; and he was spending substantial time on the selection and training of management personnel to fill certain positions, including his own, that would ultimately open up as members of the company retired.

The Marshall Company enjoyed a high reputation for quality and reliability. It produced a wide variety of standard grades of paper used in high-quality book publishing and special grades requiring a specialized knowledge of paper chemistry as well as of manufacturing techniques. In 1947, the special grades comprised about a quarter of total output but accounted for a higher proportion of net profits. These grades had originally been developed to make use of equipment too old to turn out the standard grades in the large quantities that were necessary to make them profitable.

There were about 15 mills in the United States producing varying grades of book paper. The Marshall Company employed about one-half as many people as the largest mills and about twice as many as the smallest mills. There were, of course, many mills producing low-grade magazine and newsprint paper, but they did not compete with the Marshall Company.

The mill had provided the town in which it was located with a long history of economic security. Heavy investment in plant machinery and considerable know-how were necessary to operate a paper mill; profits depended in part on steady customer acceptance; customer contacts tended to become well established. For these reasons, it was not easy for a newcomer to enter the paper industry and threaten the positions of established companies. By observing progressive inventory and marketing policies, and by spreading the work among its employees, the Marshall Company had done much to protect its employees from even such sharp economic downswings as that of 1932. During this depression period, the mill operated at a loss but remained open five days a week.

In the summer of 1947, shortages of paper-making materials and limitations on productive capacity throughout the paper industry were still serious enough to make the volume fall short of customers' requirements. According to Mr. Brewster, customers seldom rejected a shipment, and in general were not inclined to be too particular about quality requirements. The Marshall Company, however, anticipated that within a year their customers' expectations regarding service and quality would tighten up considerably.

## Mill Location and Employee Relations

The mill had been located for more than 90 years in a small New England town with a population of 13,500. Although the town was only a few minutes from a nearby city, it was distinctly rural in atmosphere. The people were largely French Canadian and Yankee stock. Although some of the townspeople worked in a small shoe factory, the supervisors at the Marshall Company said that they had the pick of the town's labor supply. The mill provided the town's chief payroll and paid about half its taxes. About 2,600 people worked in the mill; of these, about 95 percent lived in the town. The yearly labor turnover at the mill amounted to about 1 percent. A large number of the employees had lived in the town for more than 25 years. Many families had members in the mill for two or three generations.

The employees were paid on an hourly basis. In some departments there was a bonus system based on output with a deduction for waste. Supervisory personnel were paid according to a salary schedule determined by Mr. Brewster. For many years it had been Mr. Brewster's policy to keep the mill "out in front" of other New England paper mills in wages paid the employees. Over the last 15 years, general pay raises at the Marshall Company had regularly preceded pay raises at other mills.

The company management often said that "What helps the town, helps us." Many of the employees were able to buy their homes when the company guaranteed their loans at the bank and deducted the payments from the weekly wages. Workers often sought Mr. Brewster's advice on whether the house in which they were interested was a "good buy."

Mr. Brewster was interested in keeping personal contact with his employees. It was well known among the workers that any one of them could talk to Mr. Brewster whenever he wished. The problems which the "help" brought to him were frequently financial; they needed loans to pay for a new home, for a new baby, or a divorce. Often an employee raised questions relating to his position, his desire for transfer or promotion, or dissatisfaction with the way a supervisor had handled him. One of the employees remarked about Mr. Brewster, "He's a great guy. He ain't no different from us."

The mill was originally a family concern and, within the memory of many of the employees still at the mill, headed by a member of the Marshall family. Mr. Mower, the president in 1947, whose office was located in a large eastern city at some distance from the mill, was known personally to many employees. Some years earlier he had spent a period of time in the mill, working in each of the departments. It was not uncommon for workers to reminisce about "when Bob Mower had my job."

Members of the Marshall family had, until the present generation, maintained a home in the town where the mill was located. The close personal relationship which had grown up between mill and community was encouraged by Mr. Brewster. It was not uncommon for a local clergyman to ask Mr. Brewster to hire a needy member of his parish or to confer with him when some member of the church who worked at the mill was in trouble. The top-ranking teams from the mill's bowling league and softball league played other teams in the state. Other activities such as the mill clubs and band also attracted attention in the town. A few years ago several of the top management at the mill were instrumental in raising the mortgage on the American Legion building in the town. Mr. Brewster himself believed that the most critical event in the town involving him was maintaining the solvency of the local bank when it was seriously threatened by the depression in 1932. By intervening with financial and legal aid, he succeeded not only in protecting the townspeople's deposits in the bank; he also arranged to have its stock transferred over a period of years to ownership by the depositors, many of whom were employees of the Marshall Company. He believed that these activities had played a most important part in setting the tone of the mill's labor relations.

Various locals of the Congress of Industrial Organizations, the American Federation of Labor, and the United Mine Workers had made frequent efforts to organize the mill.

### The Mill

The mill straddled a narrow river from which it took a large volume of water for operations. It was located on the northern side of the town and covered 40 to 50 acres on both sides of the river. The "mill gate" through which one entered the plant was near the main office of the company and was on the westernmost edge of the property. To the north of the main office were the buildings that housed the largest paper-making machines. With one exception, the large "production" machines were located near the company offices. The men who worked on these machines habitually spoke of them being "on this side of the river" and of those to the east of the river as being "on the other side." The soda pulp mill which produced part of the wood pulp used in the process was also "on this side of the river," as was the wood yard where the cord wood was stored in a pile nearly 100 feet high until it was brought into the soda mill for processing. To the west of these buildings were the boiler house and the foundations for the new construction work being done on the boiler house. On the east side of the river which ran alongside these buildings was the coating department (where special finishes were added to the plain paper that was made on the paper machine), the machine shop and maintenance department, the power plant, and the finishing department (where the paper was cut into sheets or rolled, inspected, and packed according to the customers' specifications, and shipped). On the easternmost edge of the mill property was located a building housing the research department.

More than two-thirds of the personnel of the mill were employed in the paper machine department where the paper itself was made and in the finishing department where the final inspection of the paper took place. Joe Murray, a member of the Harvard Business School Faculty, making an extended visit to the mill late in 1947, was particularly interested in these two departments and in the ways in which they were supervised, from the foremen up to Mr. Brewster himself. The material in this and the following cases was developed out of more than five years of contacts between the Marshall Company and the Harvard Business School, which culminated in the visit by Joe Murray.

### The Operation of the Mill

The logs, brought to the mill by railroad, were carried to the soda mill by conveyor, chipped, mixed with chemicals, "digested" by steam heat to form a pulp, and bleached. Economical operation of this department depended on the many recovery processes whereby the chemicals used in the process were reclaimed for further use. This department normally maintained a 24-hour reserve of pulp supply for the paper machines.

Operations in the paper-making department proper began with the "beater rooms" where the pulp was prepared for the paper machines. The purchased pulp in sheet form, soda pulp from the company's mill, paper waste recovered from the later stages of the operations, filling materials, dyes, water, and other ingredients were mixed together in the beaters according to specifications for each order of paper. From the beaters the prepared "stock" was pumped to the paper machines in adjoining rooms and buildings. Several hours' supply of pulp prepared for use by the paper machines was maintained in the beaters. Each of the two groups of machines was served by a beater room, and each machine was served by one or more separate beaters.

The paper machines varied in size. The largest was approximately 70 yards long and cost about a million dollars. Following the end of the war, the company had rebuilt two of its largest paper machines to combine the coating and paper-making processes and at the same time to increase their speed and capacity. The use of these combined machines was a major recent development in the industry. Another machine was being rebuilt in June 1947 to enlarge its speed and capacity; it was not, however, to receive coating equipment. Furthermore, plans for rebuilding two more of the largest machines were in their final stages.

The operation of making the paper itself started in the beater rooms where the pulp was prepared for the paper machines and water was added to transport the pulp to the paper machines. The operation at the paper machine was largely one of matting the fibers to form a continuous paper sheet. The "stock" was pumped into a "headbox" at the beginning of the paper machine, from which it flowed onto an endless wire screen traveling rapidly. As it traveled, the "wire" moved from side to side with a vibrating motion which matted the fiber. Thus a wet, weak paper was formed. From this wire, much of the water which carried the fibers to the wire dropped through into a pit below. Most of the rest of the process on the paper machine was one of drying the paper. Near the end of the wire screen, the paper passed over suction boxes and a suction roll; then it went under press rolls which squeezed the water out, and finally it passed along a series of steam-heated drying rolls. At the end of these drying rolls, it was passed through a vertical series of steel rolls, called "calender rolls," where a smooth, hard finish was put on the paper.

As it left the calender stacks, the paper was wound on a "reel." When this reel was full, it was moved to the winding equipment (the final section of the paper machines), where it was rewound as it was trimmed and cut into rolls of the required widths. This entire process, from the time the stock left the beaters until the paper was wound into rolls at the end of the paper machine, was continuous and on some machines reached speeds up to 750 feet per minute. The paper machines maintained a one or two-day backlog of work for the coating and finishing departments.

From the paper machines, the rolls might be sent in any one of four directions for further processing in the remainder of the mill. They might be sent to the coating department if the order required a certain kind of surface on the paper. There a liquid coating would be applied, dried, and calendered to give a smooth surface. On the other hand, the paper might be sent to the "super calendering" department, if a coated grade was not ordered, but a "super calendered" finish was required. If the surface of the paper as it left the paper machines was as ordered, the rolls of paper might be sent directly to either the "cutters" or "rewinders," where the paper would either be cut into flat sheets of required size and inspected to remove defective sheets or rewound and inspected for shipping as rolls. Sheet paper from the cutters was sent to another part of the finishing department, where it was sorted by grades, inspected again, packed in boxes or on "skids" made in the box shop, and prepared for shipment. The rolls were wrapped and sent to the shipping room.

Beginning with the beaters, the paper was manufactured under individual production orders sent out from the scheduling office. Many of these orders contained specifications for one of a large variety of standard grades. In the great majority of cases the orders included variations to suit individual customers' requirements. The few orders that were sent to the mill for purposes of building up inventory followed standard specifications exactly. A smaller proportion of the orders were for specialty items; these also involved numerous variations to suit the individual customer.

In scheduling production the office had to take into account the wide variety of characteristics among the paper machines. The scheduling office, headed by Mr. Elcott, performed the complex job of assigning individual customers' orders, which were seldom exactly alike, to the machines that were best suited to handle them. Elcott was concerned with such matters as the width of the machine in relation to the order, the weight of paper the machine was designed to dry effectively, and the type and grades that he had been scheduling for the crews on particular machines in the past and with which they were therefore familiar. The orders were changed on nearly all machines at least once every two or three days, and frequently several times a day. The scheduling personnel arranged the orders so as to utilize the width of the machines most efficiently and to minimize the variations in the furnish and in the machine adjustments that would be necessary in the mill. This personnel was skilled in achieving the maximum economical utilization of the paper machines.

The "control room" was located on the western side of the river in a building that spanned the river and served as a bridge between the two sides of the plant. Here the first supervisory step was taken in the continuous inspection process of making high quality paper. Although the "hands" on the paper machines inspected their own work and their foremen kept a close eye on the quality of the paper as it was being made, it was in this control room that the inspectors looked over the samples sent in hourly from each machine. The paper received two types of testing: mechanical and visual. Test girls carried on continuous testing of certain physical and chemical characteristics of the paper which were important in terms of the use for which the paper was intended, including basic weight, bulk, bursting strength, tearing strength, opacity, ash content, acidity, porosity, and certain other characteristics. The inspectors themselves looked every hour for such things as surface characteristics, fiber formation, dirt, color, and similar matters. All the supervisory personnel visited the control room periodically to look over the samples and test results and to exchange information. It was here that decisions were often reached and instructions issued for the most efficient handling of the orders in the later stages of the production process. For example, the specifications of an order might call for no further processing after it left the paper machines. Samples in the control room, however, might indicate that an "inadequate" finish was currently being put on the paper at the paper machine. The rolls of paper, therefore, would be sent to the "super calendering" department to bring the finish up to standard.

These test results often indicated changes that could be made at the paper machine before the order was completed. The "runners" who brought the samples hourly from the machines also brought back to the machines the results of these control room tests. For this information, the machine hands were often able to make adjustments that brought the paper within specifications for the order.

A similar control room was operated in the coating department to maintain the efficiency of the coating and calendering work done there. The "super calendering" department also took regular samples of the paper being "super calendered" for visual checks on the quality of its work.

From river water and wood pulp to the finished product, the work of producing paper that was satisfactory to the customer was highly complex. The characteristics of each of the ingredients—water, pulp, filler, sizing, color and other materials—were never exactly predictable or controllable. The possible combinations of ingredients were numberless. From the pulp mill through the paper mill, an infinite number of combinations of mechanical adjustments were possible in order to get a limited range of desired results. The effects of some of these tended to conflict with each other or cancel out. Many of the adjustments to keep the paper within the tolerances specified by the established "standard grades" and by the customers had to be made while the paper was running through the machines. On the paper machines more than 100 of these adjustments were possible, and less than half a dozen automatic devices had been found useful in controlling them. The customers' specifications were exacting, since printing presses were often set to work to paper thicknesses controlled to the third decimal place, and the imprint of ink on paper had to be exactly controlled both physically and chemically.

## The Mill Organization

While the president, the treasurer, and the vice president in charge of sales had their offices in a large eastern city, Mr. Austin Brewster, the vice president in charge of production, had his office at the mill (see Organization Chart, Exhibit 1). Mr. Brewster carried on the internal administration of the mill without detailed supervision by the head office. He was responsible for deciding on capital expenditures, with the approval of the board of directors. He had full responsibility for labor relations. He was accountable to the president and board of directors for keeping costs down and production up. Mr. Brewster kept the amount of detail he handled at a minimum in order to have ample time to consider many external relationships of the mill, such as those with the state and federal government and the public, and many other long-range problems. Mr. Brewster was assisted by Mr. Graham, the production manager; Mr. Shaw, the chief engineer; a purchasing agent; a director of research; and a personnel manager.

Mr. Perrin, shown on the organization chart as reporting directly to the treasurer in the city office, spent all his time at the plant. He not only handled the accounting system and funds for the treasurer, but also prepared accounting and statistical reports for Mr. Brewster. Mr. Perrin was assisted by a staff group which handled the accounting, cost, time study, payroll, and bonus routines.

The production manager, Mr. Graham, was assisted by Mr. Blanchard, a younger man who was responsible for the quality control of plain papers (i.e., uncoated papers), and the production and quality of all specialty papers (some of which were uncoated and therefore regarded as "plain" papers in addition to being called "specialties"). Mr. Blanchard was assisted by a group known as the "specialty department" responsible for quality control of all specialty grades. Mr. Graham was assisted also by the staff groups in charge of scheduling, waste control, and testing. Mr. Fletcher, the chief inspector, who worked under Mr. Graham, was responsible for the quality of all plain papers produced, both those which were sold as plain paper and those which were later coated. He worked closely with Mr. Nichols, superintendent of the paper mill, whose chief concern was production. Mr. Phinney, superintendent of the pulp mill (including the wood yard); Mr. Prout, superintendent of the coating department; and Mr. Goodwin, superintendent of the finishing department, as well as Mr. Nichols, the superintendent of the paper mill, were men who

Production Organization Chart[1]

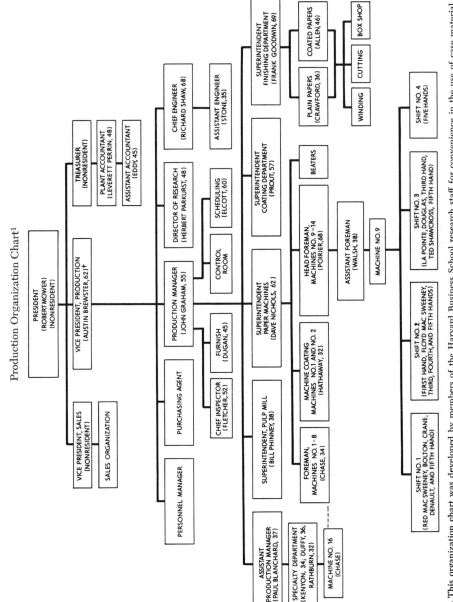

[1] This organization chart was developed by members of the Harvard Business School research staff for convenience in the use of case material. It is not an official or complete portrayal of the mill organization. The case material will show the actual relationships of the mill personnel, which the organization chart itself does not and cannot indicate.
[2] Figures represent approximate ages.

**Exhibit 1** (*continued*)

Papermaking Flowchart

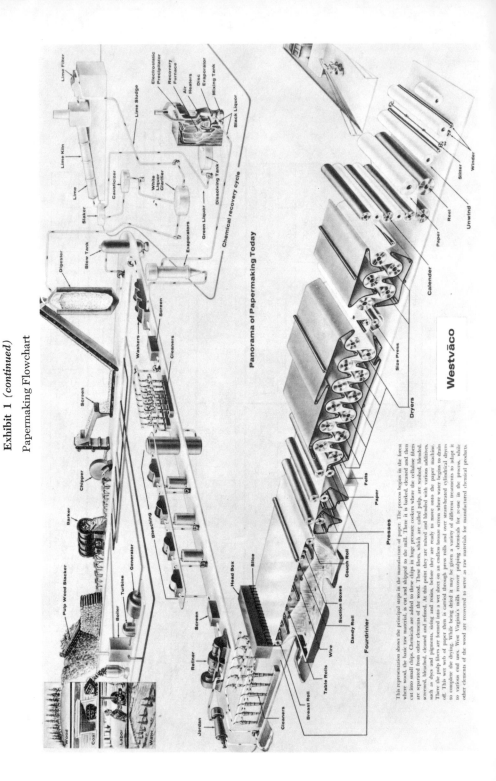

Panorama of Papermaking Today

This representation shows the principal steps in the manufacture of paper. The process begins in the forest where wood, the basic raw material, is cut and shipped to the mill. There it is barked, cleaned and then cut into small chips. Chemicals are added to these chips in huge pressure cookers where the cellulose fibers are separated from other elements of the wood. These fibers, which are called pulp, are washed, blended, screened, bleached, cleaned and refined. At this point they are mixed and blended with various additives, such as dyes and pigments, sizing and resins, before they are ready to move onto the paper machine. There the pulp fibers are formed into a wet sheet on an endless bronze screen where water begins to drain off. This wet web of paper then is carried through press rolls and over steam-heated cylindrical dryers to complete the drying. While being dried it may be given a variety of different treatments to adapt it to various end uses. West Virginia's mills recover pulping chemicals for re-use in the process, while other elements of the wood are recovered to serve as raw materials for manufactured chemical products.

Westvāco

had been with the company for many years and in whom the management felt a great deal of confidence. Each of the superintendents was assisted by one of more foremen directly supervising the machine hands.

Of particular significance in the Marshall Company were the close relationships between the sales office and the production group in the paper mill. All salesmen took a 52-week training course in the mill. Telephone calls between the mill and the sales office concerning specific customer problems were extremely frequent. Salesmen visited the mill often to discuss research and quality control problems. The quality control personnel visited the customers from time to time to help plan new uses for paper or to help solve technical difficulties. These activities played an informal but important part in the organization.

Mr. Shaw, the chief engineer, was in charge of the steam and power production, and the maintenance and construction work. He supervised a large and thoroughly trained staff. Mr. Brewster relied heavily on the ability of Mr. Shaw and his organization to keep the mill in running order and to make major changes from time to time in the production equipment.

The research staff, under the direction of Mr. Parkhurst, consisted of about 25 college-trained chemists who worked closely with the sales and production personnel in the development of new uses for paper in a wide variety of industrial and commercial fields and in the improvement of existing paper and processes. They also made a wide variety of chemical analyses of raw materials received.

The functions of the personnel department were limited mostly to employment and plant safety.

In the present case, it may be noted that the above comments regarding the mill organization and the organization chart in Exhibit 1 were drawn up by Joe Murray. For reasons that will become apparent, Murray found no organization charts in use at the mill.

# Marshall Company (B)

## PAPER MACHINE NUMBER 9

In 1946, when wartime restrictions had been relaxed, the management of the Marshall Company decided to rebuild some of its largest paper machines. The company had found this reconstruction necessary to keep up with the demands of customers which had been increasing since 1943. The rebuilding of machine number 9, the third to be undertaken, was completed in June 1947.

Number 9 had been rebuilt at a cost to the company of a quarter of a million dollars. In its present form it was expected to be one of the biggest and fastest machines in the mill. The process of rebuilding, carried out by the engineering department of the mill in close collaboration with the company which had originally designed the machine, had required six weeks. During that time the regularly assigned paper-making crews of number 9 had worked around the machine doing general cleanup and whatever other duties they could manage.

On the morning of Sunday, June 29, 1947, Joe Murray, a member of the Harvard Business School faculty, who had been studying the operations of the Marshall Paper Company for several weeks, went into the mill to watch the first starting up of number 9 machine following its rebuilding.

The day before, Dave Nichols, the mill superintendent, had remarked to Murray that the machine crews would be glad to resume their regular work as paper makers. He was aware, however, that the changes on the machine involved serious problems for the men, and he was concerned about making the transition as easy as possible for them. An upset on the paper machines was a serious matter, since both management and the men regarded the machines as the point around which the work of all the other departments focused.

It was because of these considerations, and because of general interest throughout the mill, that Murray wanted to be on hand when number 9 was started up. Synchronizing the various parts of the machine was expected to be a painstaking job, probably requiring several days. In addition, many parts of the machine were new; in particular, the drying rolls had been enlarged and considerable new automatic equipment had been added. Before the rebuilding, the machine had run at an average of 420 feet a minute; when first started up again, it would have to move at only about 200 feet, gradually working up to an expected average of 750 feet a minute as the bearings loosened up and the crew learned to handle it at that rate. These changes meant that the crews must not only learn to handle the new equipment, but also must make a double adjustment in their own movements, first working more slowly than they had before and then developing greater speed than ever before as the machine worked up to its maximum. Nichols had said that he expected maximum speed to be attained in about eight weeks.

Murray reviewed in his mind what he had learned about the process of paper making. The wood pulp and chemical ingredients constituting the furnish were prepared in the pulp mill and beater room and supplied to the paper machine either directly or through the jordan. From the jordan, stock flowed into the headbox of the machine. Water and certain chemicals could be added at the headbox as needed. From the headbox, pulp flowed out onto the "wire," a fine-meshed endless copper screen, which was agitated in a sidewise motion. During its travel on the wire most of the water in the stock fell out, and the fibers began to cohere. The sources of many potential defects in the paper had to be controlled on the wire. For instance, certain devices (e.g., slices, through which the pulp flowed from the headbox onto the wire) had to be controlled in such a way as to assure a spread of pulp at a given thickness equal at all points across the wire.

The entire crew assisted in starting a run of paper through a machine. When the pulp had built up on the wire so that the fiber cohered and the wet paper was sufficiently strong to support its own weight for a few inches, the first hand turned on a vertical jet of water which cut the moving stock into two streams. The wider stream was allowed to fall off the wire into a pit. The narrower stream formed a moving strip about a foot wide. The first hand turned on a flow of compressed air which lifted this strip and carried it to the "first felt." The felt was an endless conveyor, the same width as the wire, which carried the paper under the first press roll. The press roll squeezed much of the remaining water out of the paper.

These steps were repeated when the second hand fed the strip of paper from the first felt onto a second one, which also carried it under a press roll. From the second press roll, the second hand fed the paper into the driers, large steam-heated rolls which dried the paper as it passed over them. Next in line after the driers, and about six feet apart, were two "calender stacks," each a vertical series of rolls through which the paper was passed under pressure to give it a hard, smooth finish. From the calenders it passed to a "drum reel" on which it was wound into large rolls called "reels."

After the narrow strip was passing properly through the whole machine, the first hand got the signal from one of the crew at the dry end. He then moved the vertical jet of water slowly across the wire at a right angle to the flow of paper. As described above, this jet had cut the paper into two moving streams, one narrow and one wide. As the jet moved across the paper, the narrow strip gradually widened. By the time the jet had reached the far side of the paper, what had originally been a narrow strip was now the entire width of the paper passing from the wire on through the rest of the paper machine. Sometimes the first hand moved the jet across as soon as the paper was well started into the driers, but before it had reached the drum reel. Completed reels were moved to the winding equipment, located about ten feet behind the drum reel, where they were cut and rewound into rolls of specified widths.

Every point in the process at which the paper was handled manually was a potential trouble spot. One reason was that most of the hand operations occurred at points where there were gaps in the machinery over which the paper had to support its own weight. Another reason was that the speed at which the paper was fed into the appropriate roll had to be synchronized with the speed of the machinery or a break would occur. The crew members needed considerable skill, therefore, to handle the paper at these spots.

The crew had to be alert to control many adjustments at every stage in the operation. These adjustments were intended to control the texture of the paper, its thickness, finish, and to some extent its content; to prevent the paper from having cuts, wrinkles, holes, slime spots, and other defects; to regulate the speed, heat, and other factors in the operation of the machine, and in other ways to control the quality and speed of output.

To keep number 9 running 24 hours a day required four shifts of five-man crews; throughout the mill the standard shift was six hours. The smooth operation of the machine required close cooperation among the members of the machine crew. Although there was a commonly accepted division of labor among the men on the crews, Murray knew that it was not rigidly adhered to. Roughly, the first hand (who was also known as the machine tender, runner, or paper-maker) had overall responsibility for the operation of the machine and sole responsibility for the "wet end," that section of the machine extending from the headbox to the driers. He controlled the flow of stock into the headbox and onto the wire and made changes in composition of the stock. He frequently consulted the foreman or the chief inspector before making such changes. He made numerous adjustments affecting the quality of the paper, and tested samples regularly at the desk at the "dry end" to check these adjustments. These tests included weighing and examining the samples. More complicated tests were made in the control room on samples picked up once an hour. Results of all the tests were entered periodically in a "machine data sheet" kept at the desk of the machine, and the first and second hands examined these reports regularly. Many factors affecting quality which were controllable at the wet end showed up only when the paper was inspected at the dry end. The first hand relied on his second for this information. The first hand also watched at the wet end for trouble such as froth, dirt, lumps in the pulp, and holes in the wire. In addition to his work at the wet end, he handled much of the paper work at the desk. Although their duties were at the wet end except for the desk work, in practice many first hands spent a good deal of time at the dry end, relying on a mechanical signal (on number 9 this signal was a photoelectric cell) to warn them of breaks on the wet end.

The other four men on the crew worked at the dry end, that portion of the machine beginning with the drying rolls and extending through the winding equipment. The second hand was formally responsible for the dry end. He watched closely for defects in the paper coming off the driers. Many kinds of defects warned him that there was trouble in the machinery which required immediate action. In correcting certain kinds of defects, he worked very closely with the first hand. The second hand also took care of some of the tests and paper work. In addition to these duties, he supervised the work of the third, fourth, and fifth hands more closely than did the first hand, since their work was entirely at the dry end. For this reason he was often described as the man who was "really responsible for the crew." The primary work of the third hand was on the winding equipment, cutting and winding the reels off the paper machine into rolls of the sizes specified by the order. In this work he was assisted by the fourth and fifth hands, who also did the simple manual labor around the machine.

Nichols maintained close contact with the men on the machines. When they were having difficulty with a particular run of paper or with some part of the machine, they often sent for him. He habitually pitched in on such occasions and worked along with the men.

When Murray came into the mill on Sunday morning, he counted about 40 men already working on the machine. Besides the machine crew and the wire crew, which were under the direction of Dave Nichols, there were mechanics, carpenters, "pipers," and others from the engineering department. Mr. Stone, assistant to Mr. Shaw, the chief engineer, came in a little later and stayed several hours. During the day a number of workers also came into the room to watch operations. Men from machine number 14 next door, the next machine scheduled for rebuilding, stood in the doorway whenever matters on their own machine did not demand their attention. Several people from the control room came in to watch for a while. Mr. Fletcher, the chief inspector, who was in charge of the routine operations of the mill this Sunday, spent as much time by number 9 as his other work would permit. Mr. Graham, production manager of the company, was there all day. Nichols periodically reported to him about recent developments and his plans for taking care of them. Graham would characteristically nod his head when Nichols was finished, but make no comment. Nichols, in talking to Murray about this, later said, "Mr. Graham doesn't often say much to me when I am starting up a machine. Later on he will tell me some of the things he thought might have been improved—even some of the little things. But now he won't bother me." Most of the men from the production office spent at least a couple of hours around number 9. The three top men from the finishing department and some men from the pulp mill were also present for short visits. Machine number 9 occupied a room by itself, which was filled most of the day with men observing the starting up of the big new machine.

Murray particularly wanted to see the reactions of the men and the way those in charge handled the men. Soon after he arrived, he walked over and greeted Dave Nichols, who was making some adjustments on the automatic gauges at the wet end.

"We'll get her rolling this afternoon," Nichols said without preliminaries.

We're working on the gauges on the hydraulic rollers; the mechanics are working on them now. We can tell the pressure on the rolls from those gauges over on the wall panel. We've never had that before. If it works, we can tell how much pressure is being put on the paper. We'll try it before we start the run and see if it works. There are a lot of new things on this machine.

MURRAY:    There certainly are. Have you given the men any special instructions about the new equipment?

NICHOLS:    It's too early to give instructions yet. I have to see how it runs. It's new to me, too. Every machine is different, no matter if it is made by the same manufacturer to the same blueprint. You think when you've seen one machine you've seen them all, but that's not true. I learn as I go along. (Glances around.) Of course, the men are "on nerves," too. They don't know what to expect.

MURRAY:    They're all a little anxious.

NICHOLS:    Yes, indeed, as anxious as I am myself. I expect some accidents. We always have some when we start up a new machine; somebody gets hurt.

Nichols walked over and joined a group including both machine crewmen and mechanics, who were installing a roller. Several men raised the heavy bar with their shoulders, while one of their number adjusted its position with a wrench. The latter handed his wrench to Nichols when he came up, and Nichols worked with it until he was satisfied. The job took about fifteen minutes.

In the meantime Murray talked with Hunter, an engineer from the company which had originally built the machine. Murray had chatted with him occasionally during the rebuilding.

MURRAY:    What do you think of her now?

HUNTER:    Well, I'm pretty jittery. I'm always jittery when we start up a machine. There are so many parts that require nice adjustment. Each one has to be timed so that it will move a little faster than the one before."[1]

MURRAY:   That means a lot of points require careful judgment.

HUNTER:   It certainly does. It's almost impossible to calculate them. You have to find out by trying and sometimes you make mistakes.

Nichols had been working on number 9 constantly since 7 A.M. About 11 o'clock he gave instructions to start up the machine but to run no stock over it. After listening for a few minutes to the almost deafening noises from the hundreds of new bearings, Nichols went out to his own office for a smoke. Murray followed him.

MURRAY:   How's it going?

NICHOLS:   Pretty well.

MURRAY:   Sounds as if it were running pretty heavy.

NICHOLS:   Sure is. She tightened up on me. She'll sound better after a couple of weeks—like a car, you know. You have to break her in easy. Of course you know the engine broke down about an hour ago, but I think we got it fixed temporarily. Just didn't have enough power to turn her over. They'll change the pulley on the engine tonight, to give it more of a hold. I'll run stock over her for awhile this afternoon to see if she draws O.K.; then run her tonight to see if she will loosen up.

That afternoon Nichols ordered the first hand to start stock through the headbox. It ran freely for eight or ten minutes, building up on the wire. Gradually, as the load on the engine increased, the wire began to slow up and the stock thickened. The man nearest the switch stopped the machine, but the stock on the wire overflowed. In a moment pulp and water were running all over the floor. There were a number of hoses for wash-downs and other purposes around the base of the machine. The men standing nearest the hoses, both machine hands and mechanics, immediately picked up hoses and started washing down the wire. Hunter commented to Murray, "If it ever dries on them, they'll have an awful time." One of the men brought out a supply of hip boots, and most of the men put them on. Nichols did not take time to do so; he was working with the men all the time. All of the spectators retreated out of the way of the running stock. One of the men washing down the wire was splashed by a man handling the hose on the opposite side of the machine. He grinned and splashed back. The exchange lasted only a few seconds, and no one else paid any attention to it.

Nichols worked on the machine until about 4:30; by that time nothing more could be done until the engineers made some further adjustments. The men were allowed to go home. After talking with the engineers and the night supervisor, who had just come in, Nichols also left.

On Monday morning the 6 o'clock shift again was occupied with trying

---

[1] By maintaining a very slightly higher speed at each subsequent unit of the machine, it was possible to keep a certain degree of tension on the moving paper.

to get number 9 started. Murray noticed that several men from the night shifts, who had not worked the night before, since only the engineers had been needed, came in to see how the machine was working. During the morning Murray sat for a moment on the window sill beside two of the regular crewmen, Crane and Denault.

MURRAY:    So you're going to be making paper again.

CRANE:    Oh, yeah, we've had a five weeks' vacation.

MURRAY:    How do you feel about all this? (Nods toward the machine.)

CRANE:    Oh, fine, it needed to be done. It will take a while to get used to it, though.

MURRAY:    You mean all the new equipment?

DENAULT:    Yes, and then on the old machine we knew where to step and where to put our hands and where everything was. It was just like walking— you don't have to think about it. Now it's all different.

MURRAY:    It makes you kind of jittery.

CRANE:    A little nervous. You have to throw the paper on the pulleys at just the right speed so that it catches. There's quite a trick to it, but I'm not like some guys. They worry all the time, "Will this go wrong, can I do this?" When they feel like that, they have accidents. They get nervous and move a little faster than the machine. I used to be like that, but not any more.

DENAULT:    Oh, well, in five or six weeks we'll get used to this machine, too. It's a lot faster now. This will do 750 feet a minute.

MURRAY:    Does that mean it's harder work to keep up with it?

CRANE:    Oh no. The machine helps you. These gadgets were put on it to do things we had to do before. It's really easier to have them.

At that point the men moved over to the machine. On Sunday and so far on Monday the crew members had stood watching whenever they were not actually working on the machine or handling a trial run. Sometimes they approached the machine and appeared to be studying it. Other times they stood back by the windows. Occasionally they performed small mechanical tasks on the machine, such as helping to shift the rollers and adjust them. The first hand was in contact with Nichols or Walsh, the assistant foreman, continually; and no special message to him was necessary when Nichols was ready to start the stock over the wire. When the first hand mounted the headbox to start the trial run, the other crew members stood ready. As soon as the first hand moved over to the wire, the rest of the crew came running to help start the paper through the machine. Al Bolton, the second hand, climbed up on the machine by the press rolls and started to feed the pulp onto the felts. It went fairly smoothly, but when he tried to feed the strip from the second felt into the drying roll, he ran into difficulty.

At this spot, accurate timing was essential. To perform the operation the second hand stood balanced on foot rests placed several feet above the floor, straddling the walkway between the wet and dry ends. Facing the strip of paper coming off the press roll, he picked up the end of the strip, passed in into the air in hand-over-hand motion until his timing was synchronized with the speed of the paper coming off the roll, then twisted his body to follow the motion of the paper and tossed it onto ropes which were to pick it up and guide it through the driers. If he passed the paper only a little too fast or too slowly, it broke. As Al Bolton got up on the foot rests, most of the men in the room gathered to watch. Al tried a half dozen times, but each time the paper broke just as he got it into the ropes. After several minutes, Nichols, who was standing just behind him, put his hand on Al's leg without speaking. Al immediately got down, and the first hand, who had been standing in the walkway watching, climbed up. His second attempt was successful. Nichols said later, in referring to this incident, "Al's all right. He was just getting nervous."

The paper started several times, but each time it broke within a few minutes; adjustments had to be made on the machine, and the stock was started again. Nichols once fed the paper into the driers himself. Once Poirier, the elderly foreman, made two attempts to feed the paper into the ropes but did not succeed. That time the stock was so thin that the pulp was not strong enough to support its own weight. Each time the paper was passed from the wet to the dry end, Nichols stood beside or behind the man doing it. He frequently offered suggestions. When trouble developed with the paper winding on the drum reel, Nichols went over and worked with the men. Even when there was no specific problem, he stood near the men, occasionally talking to them. The men, too, were constantly moving around the machine or standing where they could watch certain key points. Only occasionally did they sit in the windows for a moment to catch the little breeze that was coming in.

At one such moment Bolton remarked to Murray, "I'll give you a tip on Dave Nichols. When he slaps that right foot down hard, that means he's nervous."

Murray noticed a number of times during the day that Nichols was "stomping," and it seemed to occur when something happened on the machine and he was not at the trouble spot. At the end of the day Nichols remarked to Murray, "I always get worried and excited when we start up a new machine. You could see I was nervous, but it went pretty well."

During the next week Nichols spent most of his time on number 9 working along with the men, helping to make the final adjustments on the machine and giving the men guidance in handling the problems that arose.

Murray also spent a good deal of time around number 9 during this week and the following weeks; thus he had opportunity to observe the crews in action and to talk to many of them. When the machine had been running about three weeks, Murray observed one day that the paper was breaking repeatedly after leaving the calender stacks. He had seen Mac-

Sweeney at the dry end talking with the crew and helping them make various adjustments, particularly in the amount of pressure on the calender stacks. The paper continued to break. The men finally agreed that to make an effective adjustment they would have to shut down the machine, and this they were reluctant to do. Consequently, they sent for Nichols. A few minutes later Nichols came into the room and went directly to the drum reel. He talked to Al for a moment, looked the situation over, and suggested that the difficulty might be handled by adjusting a spreader bar, which was designed to correct uneven tension in the moving paper. Nichols started to turn the adjusting screws at one end of the bar, calling directions to Al, who was working at the other end. After experimenting with various degrees of tension in several of the screws, they finally got the paper winding without a break. As soon as this was accomplished, Nichols walked away.

Murray had noticed that as the month advanced, Nichols took a less and less active part on the machine. When he was around he gradually moved back toward the wall so that he could observe the men. He came near the machine only to make a specific suggestion or to work on a definite problem. By the end of the month the machine was running at a speed of 500 feet.

Murray also noticed that a great many of the actions of the men were dictated by some occurrence on the machine that demanded immediate attention. This was particularly true of the third, fourth, and fifth hands, and decreasingly so for the second and first. These two men had more time to move back and forth on the machine and to sit and talk with any of the hands who were free for the moment. Frequently the men went behind the machine together for smokes. Asked about this latter practice, one hand told Murray that smoking around the machines was not allowed because of fire insurance regulation. "The company built a ten-thousand-dollar rest room for us," he said, "but we don't like to be away from the machines long enough to go down there. If you are around the machine, you might be able to avoid trouble—like lots of times you can catch wrinkles that would make bad paper if they went through."

On his way out, Murray passed one of the other machines scheduled for rebuilding in the near future. After some talk with the first hand about their interest in number 9, Murray mentioned the changes planned in Farmer's machine. "Yeah," Farmer said, "I'm glad I won't be running it when it's rebuilt. Too much trouble, with the coating machinery they're going to add on."

"What about the rest of the crew?" Murray inquired.

"The second hand won't be on," Farmer replied. "He's not fast enough. He's been on this machine 25 years and he's slowing down on some of the work. The third hand helps him with it. They wanted him to go on one of the slow machines two years ago but he wouldn't do it."

Several days later, Murray came into the mill about 9:30 in the morning. The men told him Nichols had scheduled number 9 for a wire change that morning and that the felts would be changed at the same time. They pointed out certain defects in the paper caused by the worn condition of the felts. Red MacSweeney, first hand, told Murray that a strip several inches wide had torn off the first felt during the night. The stretched felt remaining was so narrow that it travelled back and forth across the roller. Red kept a constant watch on it; every two or three minutes he had to go over and kick a bar which kept the felt in the proper position. Later in the day Nichols told Murray that they had run the felt as long as they could and then scheduled the wire change a day or so early, in order to stop the machine only once. He said this kind of compromise was a decision he frequently had to make.

About 10:50 a number of repair men from the engineering department came into the room one at a time and stood around waiting. The machine crew got out hip boots, shut down the machine, and entered the breakdown time on their job cards. Floyd MacSweeney, the second hand on this shift, told Murray, "The wire crew men are our bosses while the machine is down. We take orders from them. Well, we only get an hour of this, anyway. Glad we didn't start any sooner."

"You dislike it?" Murray asked.

"It's heavy work and you have to keep at it," Floyd explained. "And then there's a lot of hollering. It might be four to five months before we change the wire on our tour again, and we forget what to do between times."

At exactly 11 o'clock the wire crew came in. This crew consisted of five men who had all had some experience on the paper machines. Nichols had organized the crew for specialized maintenance work such as changing wires. When they started the job on number 9, both the wire crew and the machine crew hosed off the wire, cleaned out the headbox, and wound the wire by hand as it came off the machine. The third, fourth, and fifth hands, who had continued to work on the winders until the last reel was finished, joined the others at the wet end. The men began to lift off the small rollers which carried the wire, hose them, and pile them on a cart in a definite order. The fifth hand, a small fellow, managed one end of the rollers as they came off the machine. When they had to be lifted over the sides of the car, however, the first hand, a six-footer, took over. All removable parts of the wet end were taken off, cleaned, and repaired or replaced, if necessary, and the new wire and felts were put on. In the meantime some thirty men, electricians, engineers, carpenters, and "pipers," were overhauling the rest of the machine.

Murray commented to Red that it was surprising the men didn't get in one another's way. Red answered, "Oh, they've worked together for so long they know just when someone will be doing a particular job and they'd be in the way. It's second nature to them now." Around noon he commented, "The wire men are mad because they don't get any lunch hour once they start taking a machine down. That's what all the grousing is about right now. They didn't want to start at 11 without lunch first."

At the end of the shift, each machine man left as soon as his relief appeared. The reaction from most of the men on the afternoon shift as they saw what was happening was, "Well, looks like we'll be busy around here for a couple of hours." Dave Nichols worked through with the men until the job was done.

After the rebuilt machine had been in operation for four weeks, Murray decided to appraise his observations. He felt that, clearly understood, what he had seen would help him to grasp the problems of Mr. Graham and Mr. Nichols in administering this part of the mill. Although the changes on number 9 were less sweeping than those contemplated for some other parts of the mill, Murray believed that an understanding of the way the organization had adjusted to them would be helpful in following the development of the expansion program.

# Marshall Company (C)

FOR THE MONTH following the starting up of Number 9 paper machine, Joe Murray, a member of the Harvard Business School Faculty studying the Marshall Company paper mill, spent a good deal of time around it. During this month he found a number of things about the relations among the men that interested him.

Murray had already observed on machine Number 9, as on the other machines in the mill, that while the duties of the first hands were mainly at the wet end, most of them also spent much of their time at the dry end.[1] Since Number 9 had only a single calender stack prior to its rebuilding, the first hands on that machine were helping the second hands learn to manage the two stacks on the rebuilt machine. When there was a break, the first hands often jumped in with the other men; in case of a bad break, they even helped to pick up the waste paper, or "broke." When everything was going well, the first hand often sat on the edge of the table after he finished making his samples and chatted with any hands not occupied at the moment. The first hands discussed with their second and third hands the problems of handling the machine and of running the various orders on which they were working. Frequently they joined the other men at the back of the room for a smoke.

Aside from his contacts with the second hand, the first hand had comparatively little working contact with the rest of his crew. The second hand actually directed the others, trained them, answered their questions, and worked directly with them on many occasions such as changing the core on the drum reel or handling a break at the dry end. The third, fourth, and fifth hands worked more closely together since they handled the winding equipment. They worked elsewhere on the machine only in changing the core on which the paper was rolled or in case of a break at the dry end,

---

[1] See Marshall Company (B) for details about Machine Number 9.

although they usually gathered to watch when there was a break at the wet end. When they were not actually working, they wandered around the machine watching the others and asking questions.

Murray was interested in watching the crews when there was a break at the dry end. One day, for instance, he was near the machine while Red MacSweeney's crew was on. Suddenly he heard a shout, which he knew meant trouble. Ernie Crane, the third hand, had noticed a break between the drying rolls and the first calender stack. As he shouted to the rest of the crew, he stepped into the narrow walkway and starting stripping off the narrow shred of paper coming from the rolls. The rest of the crew, with the exception of the first hand, who was occupied at the wet end, arrived at a run. There was very little space for the waste to pile up between the drying rolls and the calender stack. The fourth hand, next to arrive at the trouble spot, picked up a spike with which to separate a narrow strip of paper from the broken sheet. By holding this spike against the paper as it passed over the last drying roll, he split the paper into two widths, one wide and one narrow. Al Bolton, the second hand, attempted without success to feed the narrow strip between the calender rolls in the first stack. The fourth and fifth hands attempted to tramp down the waste, but it quickly piled up a foot or more deep in spite of their efforts. Grasping a narrow bar only inches from the hot drying rolls, they stood on the heap of waste paper and kicked it under the machine to get it out of the way. Bolton, the second hand, finally succeeded in getting the narrow strip of paper moving properly between the calender rolls. While this strip went through the rolls, the remaining width of the sheet continued to pile up before the rolls as waste. The third hand then ran across the machine through the heaped-up waste, drawing his spike across the paper coming over the last drying roll and thus widening the strip that Bolton had fed through the calender rolls. The paper kept breaking, and the procedure was repeated six or seven times. The men worked quickly, keeping out of one another's way in the narrow space. When the paper was going through again, the process was repeated at the second calender stack and again at the drum reel to start the paper winding. In each case, the first man on the spot performed the first function necessary, no matter which hand he was.

Watching this operation, Murray was reminded of something Len Shawcross, one of the older first hands, had told him. Len's son, Teddy, worked in another crew on Number 9. Len said that Teddy had been on his shift when Teddy first began to work on a paper machine, but after he had made a good start, Shawcross said to him, "Son, it would be better for you if you were on someone else's crew. I'll jump on you quicker than anybody else on my crew. Besides, now you are working for the company and the crew, and for me, too. It would be more to your interest to be on a crew where you could work for the team without having to think about your father." Shawcross concluded, "Teddy thought it over and after a while he came around to my way of thinking. He is on the early shift now."

Talking with Al Bolton after the paper was again winding properly, Murray remarked,

I'm interested in the way you fellows jump to the breaks. You don't waste any time getting there, and the first fellow on the spot goes ahead.

BOLTON:    Oh, sure, you have to. The thing is, you all have to work together. You can't just do your own job; you have to pull with the crew.

MURRAY:    I wonder if that explains what I saw this morning? There was a break on the wet end, and I noticed your third hand feeding the paper into the drying rolls.

Bolton had let Ernie Crane, the third hand, manage the paper through the several steps between the wire and the driers. He had tried to show Crane how to use an air hose to get all the slack out of the paper and make it lie flat. Crane was unable to get the paper perfectly flat, and the result was that after a few minutes' run it would break. Several times Bolton let Crane manage all these steps, but it broke each time. Bolton then took care of the air hose while Crane fed the paper, and it went through without a break.

When Murray mentioned this incident to him, Al replied that he had been training Ernie in second hand's work. Murray inquired about this, and Al explained that each man was technically responsible for training the man under him. However, since the second hand was "really the active boss of the men on the machine," he carried the main responsibility for training the younger men. The first hand trained the second to be a first hand; the second trained all the men under him. Murray asked whether Bolton "put the men through a regular course of sprouts," but Al replied,

Oh, no. You really just learn by doing. You master your own job and then you watch the next fellow working and do as much as you can. Of course, some of the guys think if you do your own job and then stop, that's what you get paid for. But you don't learn anything that way.

MURRAY:    Isn't there any feeling that you cut in on someone else's job by learning it?

BOLTON:    Oh, no. You can do as much as you know how. A good man will keep you busy answering his questions, and when he does that, you bring him along. Of course, the thing is, you've gotta keep learning so you know more than the other guys.

Al paused and seemed for several seconds to be thinking intently. Then he said hesitantly,

There's one fellow—he's no good. He came over from the other side of the river during the war and worked up to be second hand. Now guys are coming back from the service who know more than he does. Men under him are better than he is, but he gives orders and pretends to know more than anyone else. No one likes him.

Murray had a good guess as to whom Bolton meant. He had long been aware that there was a difference between crews, and one stood out in his mind as the least effective of the four shifts. This crew was headed by LaPointe, a man of about 60. LaPointe stayed strictly at the wet end and didn't come near the dry end except to work at the desk or make his samples. Even these jobs he did quickly and hurried back to the wet end. Murray had seen him talk to the rest of his crew only once; on that occasion LaPointe came down to the dry end, issued an order, and immediately returned to his post near the wire. Murray had a clear impression that LaPointe was afraid of the rebuilt machine. It had struck him early that LaPointe set the few automatic controls and then showed great reluctance to change anything unless there was a break or a change in the kind of paper to be run.

Kenneth Douglas, the second hand on LaPointe's crew to whom Al referred, was a big man who looked younger than his 50 years. Murray had observed that Douglas yelled at the men a good deal but did not seem to get as quick results when trouble arose as did the other second hands. Although there seemed to be little small talk among the men on this crew, Murray found Douglas pleasant enough to talk with. He described one of his men as "a good Joe." "Everybody likes him," Douglas said. "He always has something to say that makes you laugh."

The third, fourth and fifth hands on LaPointe's crew spent most of their time working on the winding equipment. They handled their equipment with less skill than the men on the other shifts and they seemed to have a great many breaks in the winding. Murray knew that on all shifts the third, fourth, and fifth hands worked the most steadily, but on this crew alone they worked continuously, almost never taking time to talk with the others or to duck out for a smoke.

Because of what Al Bolton had told him, Murray became interested in LaPointe's crew. Several days after his conversation with Al, he noticed a new man working on the crew. He mentioned it to James, a young college graduate who was "going through the mill" as part of his training for an administrative position. Murray asked,

Isn't Teddy ordinarily on MacSweeney's crew?

JAMES: He used to be. This crew has just been changed. It was the poorest crew, so Teddy was brought in to help even it up.

Murray wondered whether the men knew why the transfer had been made, and James replied,

Oh, I think so. The output figures are kept posted at the desk. If one crew is always 10,000 pounds behind and hasn't had breakdowns, you know there's something wrong.

MURRAY:    You mean everyone knows there is a difference between crews?

JAMES:    Oh, sure. For instance, MacSweeney's crew is as good as we have. This one, LaPointe's crew, is so excitable. The second hand is the most excitable guy I have ever seen. The minute something goes wrong he's all up in the air, so the rest of them get excited and don't know what to do.

Murray wanted to know what had become of the man whom Teddy replaced. James did not know for sure but thought he had been sent to the beater room, where less skill was required.

That afternoon, Murray mentioned the change to Red MacSweeney, who was first hand on the crew from which Teddy had been taken, and whom Murray knew fairly well. MacSweeney replied that the fourth hand on LaPointe's crew had just been sent to work in the beater rooms because he had not done his job properly. "It wasn't really the boy's fault," Mac-Sweeney added. Murray thought he showed a trace of bitterness.

The kid is a little slow to catch on, but he could have been trained all right by a good second hand. Douglas just didn't teach the kid what to do, so of course it looked to the bosses as though the boy wasn't doing his job. It was really Douglas' fault, but he blamed it on the boy. That's what happens when a guy won't take responsibility for his own mistakes.

MURRAY:    Couldn't LaPointe do anything for him?

MACSWEENEY:    Well, Douglas and LaPointe are a pair. LaPointe has been a first hand for 20 years, and none of us can understand how he has gotten by. He's not too good a paper maker, and he certainly is poor with the men. It shows in the crew, too. The men get discouraged and don't care. Instead of working together, they all pull against each other.

MURRAY:    What do you mean?

MACSWEENEY:    For instance, when they see something wrong, if it is not their particular responsibility, they don't say anything about it. And when there's a break, they don't work together. They don't jump so fast to catch it, either.

Murray asked about Teddy, who had taken the fourth hand's place, and MacSweeney grinned.

It's not definite yet. He used to be our fifth hand. He's a nice kid and could handle the work, but he didn't really want the promotion because he didn't want to work under Douglas. Finally he took it when the personnel man promised him he could come back to this shift if he couldn't get along with Kenneth Douglas.

MacSweeney's comments caught Murray's interest, and he became alert for the opinions of the management group regarding this crew. Nichols, for instance, approached Murray a day or so later, while LaPointe's crew was operating Number 9 machine, and remarked that he had been having trouble with this crew. To locate the bottleneck, he said, he had spent his "loafing time" around Number 9 for a couple of weeks.

In this time it had become clear to him that the root of the difficulty was the fourth hand, who did not seem to Nichols to be doing his work. Consequently, Nichols had sent the man to work in the beater rooms, where there was a necessary minimum of work to do and he would not hold anyone up if he did no more than that.

Blanchard, in the course of a conversation with Murray, said there was some feeling that LaPointe was not good enough to take the higher speed on the new machine. Production records, however, indicated that he had held his own over a period of time. Blanchard said,

It is true that he doesn't like the speed and maybe he doesn't make as good quality as some of the others, but he always makes just about good enough paper to get by. When he gets the machine set, he is afraid to make any changes for fear he will get into difficulties. The others are always trying to do a little better, and they know more about their machines, but it doesn't show up in the records.

On another occasion Mr. Graham, the production manager, commented,

LaPointe should never have been put on Number 9 in the first place. The speed scares him. I know he ought to be moved, and I think Dave Nichols knows it. Some of the other foremen don't know it yet. They will find it out in a while and then we will be able to move him.

MURRAY:    You did move one of his hands, didn't you?

GRAHAM:    He was a big awkward boy who I don't think will ever make a hand. His father wanted him on the machines so we put him on. But he's an awkward boy, always getting in his own way. Sooner or later he'll get hurt.

# Marshall Company (D)

JACK WALSH

JOE MURRAY, a member of the Harvard Business School Faculty, who was studying the Marshall paper company mill, had been on hand when paper machine Number 9 started up for the first time since its rebuilding, and he had spent considerable time each day observing its operation.[1] In July 1947, four weeks after Number 9 had started up, Joe Murray heard from Mr. Blanchard, the assistant production manager, that the machine was running into trouble. Among other things, the new winding equipment ordered for the machine had not arrived, and the old equipment, which was obsolete, kept getting out of adjustment and lagging behind the output of the machine. The crew was having difficulties keeping proper tension on the new calender stacks. The gates, or "slices," which controlled the flow of pulp to the wire were giving them some kind of trouble.

After talking to Mr. Blanchard, Murray went out to the machine to see if he could learn more from Nichols and the men about the present outbreak of trouble.

Murray found Walsh, the foreman of Number 9 machine, sitting by himself by the dry end of the machine. Walsh appeared to be staring at the floor. A dial over Walsh's head registered the present machine speed: 600 feet per minute. Murray asked Walsh,

How well does she run at 600?

WALSH: Oh, the machine is running O.K., but we're having trouble with the winders. It's all we can do to keep up.

MURRAY: How about the slices—are they giving you any trouble?

WALSH: Yeah.

MURRAY: Any ideas what to do about it?

WALSH: I don't know. Maybe we won't be able to do anything about it.

---

[1] See Marshall Company (B) and Marshall Company (C).

You see the stock coming out from under the slices? It's supposed to flow out flat, but you see those places where it keeps bubbling up in spurts? That makes the paper thicker in some places than others and causes all kinds of trouble. I've never seen anything like it before. There's no way you can set the slices so the stock will flow like it should.

These slices are part of the new headbox. It's built for high-speed operation, and I don't know how it's going to work out. Maybe it'll work all right when we get the machine running about 750, but I don't know. We could try out some ideas now that might fix it, but every time we change anything at the headbox it changes the paper formation, and that throws the winders all off, so we haven't been able to do much. As far as I'm concerned, I wish we had the old machinery back again. Well, I guess I'll go have a look at Number 14.

After Walsh left, Murray wondered how this difficulty would work out. He knew that Walsh was one of the youngest foremen; he had been foreman for only about a year and had not been in charge of a rebuilt machine before, nor had he ever worked on one. On the other hand, Walsh's supervisor, Dave Nichols, had a great deal of experience and "know-how," and Walsh, like the men, had great respect for Nichols. Nichols had watched Walsh's progress from fifth to first hand on the paper machines and "brought him along" to be foreman.

Murray recalled what Walsh had told him about the way the men handled their own technical problems on the machines. If they ran into difficulties, Walsh said, they tried to fix things up themselves; if they failed, they called him in. Walsh believed that he helped the men sometimes because of his own "know-how," sometimes because he brought in a fresh point of view, and sometimes because he was in a position to take responsibility for the execution of an idea they had figured out by themselves.

From what some of the other "bosses" told Murray, he realized that the relationship between Walsh and his men was not accidental. A man did not get much specific training. The other hands and the bosses expected a new man to learn the job from working on it along with the rest of the crew. Once a new man learned his first job, he could stay in it as long as he wanted to. If he wanted to move ahead, it was up to him to "watch what was going on," to "take the initiative," and to keep asking questions. When the older hands and bosses saw that a new man was the kind that would "jump in there quick" and take hold of things, they would start keeping an eye on him and "bring him along." Nichols, for instance, said that he got a lot of fun out of working with the younger men and watching them grow. In five or six years, he said, you could see a great difference in a man, not just in his ability on the machine, but in his whole personality. During the past year, he had been bringing the young men along to replace first hands and foremen who were getting promotions or retiring, and more such vacancies were still opening up.

The reasons the bosses gave for not providing specific training were that each machine was different, that each crew did things in a different way, that they all "learned something new every day" about their jobs, and especially that they wanted the men to learn to do what they were most interested in doing.

Murray also recalled that on the day when machine Number 9 was starting up, Dave Nichols had explained how he planned to get up production on it. During the first day, the machine speed built up to 390 feet per minute. Nichols said,

It seems funny to me working on a machine that's running so slow. I've just finished starting up Number 1 and Number 2, and they're running twice as fast as this one—about 720 feet to 760 feet per minute. Working on this one throws you all off balance. We'll get the machine broken in after three or four weeks so she'll carry the load all right, but it'll take three or four months before we can get it up to top speed.

It'll take that long to train the men. It's too early to give them instructions yet. I have to see how it runs. I learn as I go along; then I teach the men. Up to 500 feet per minute, things will probably go pretty smooth. But around 500 feet, I expect we'll run into trouble. Well, I'll speed the machine up till the trouble starts, then slack off and figure out what to do about it—and then speed it up some more. At the same time that I'm putting new things on the machine to make it run better, I'll be explaining to the men what to do with them.

During the first month of operation, Murray had also observed that Nichols was active in training the men and the men were active in teaching each other. While Murray was thinking about some of these incidents that had occurred, Nichols appeared. After a few minutes' conversation, Murray asked, "How about the trouble on the slices?"

Nichols smiled. "Oh, I'm going to put something on to fix that!" He explained in detail how he was going to improve the flow of pulp after it left the slices by putting a "spreader bar" across the wire a few inches from the slices.

When he had finished, Murray asked,

Does Walsh know about your plans for the spreader bar?"

NICHOLS: (Grinning broadly.) No, I haven't told him yet. He's got enough to think about now, and there's no use in his trying to look too far ahead.

MURRAY: Does the crew ever get very discouraged when they speed up the machine and find themselves in trouble?

NICHOLS: Oh yes, the younger men get more discouraged than the older men do. The older men are more used to it.

Before leaving, Nichols remarked to Murray that he had told Mr. Graham about his plans for the spreader bar. "Mr. Graham just nodded, like he usually does, but he didn't say anything about it."

# Marshall Company (E)
## The Specialty Group

FOLLOWING ITS ENTRY into the field of specialty papers in the early 1930's, the Marshall Company accepted orders for various items in rapidly increasing numbers. The specialty items were those papers, either plain or coated, which the customers of the Marshall Company further processed to make a finished product. Stock for carbon paper and envelopes were typical of the items which the company produced. The company had entered this field to utilize certain of its paper machines which were too old to produce high-speed commercial printing paper efficiently. Although these machines were "not worth a nickel on the books," according to Mr. Brewster, the paper they produced brought a higher profit margin than did many of the standard commercial grades.

The mill made these specialty papers largely according to customers' individual specifications. The sales department, soon after the line was initiated, requested that someone be assigned to handle the production and quality problems that had developed around these specialized orders. Mr. Brewster selected for the job Paul Blanchard, who had come to the company upon graduation from a large engineering school and during his three years at the mill had acquired some experience with customers' problems. Mr. Brewster assigned Blanchard to work under Will Sawyer, who was responsible for making certain that all the plain paper sold by the company was up to the customers' specifications. Blanchard continued in this work for about ten years until Will Sawyer died suddenly in 1943. Blanchard then dropped the supervision of the specialty papers to take over Mr. Sawyer's work. Following the precedent set by Mr. Sawyer, he reported on his new work directly to Mr. Graham, the production manager, and had full responsibility for the quality standards of the plain paper shipped out of the mill. He could and did hold up any order that did not seem suitable.

Joe Murray, a member of the Harvard Business School Faculty who was studying the operation of the mill in the summer of 1947, held several discussions with Blanchard to learn more about the growth of the specialty

274

group. He had become particularly interested in its relations with the rest of the organization. According to Blanchard, at the time when he took over the plain papers (both standard grades and specialty items), the work he had been doing on specialty papers was largely absorbed by Ned Kenyon, George Duffy, and later Louis Rathbun, with help from Harry Chase in the paper machine department and Tom Sullivan in the coating department. These men constituted a loosely organized specialty department which worked closely with the research department and with each of the operating departments on these specialty grades. They knew more about the requirements on certain of these papers than anyone else in the mill.

When Murray asked Blanchard about the background of some of these men, he found that Ned Kenyon was a college graduate and senior member of this specialty group. He had been trained in the coating department and was well liked there. He remained much interested in the technical problems of coating papers. The coated specialty papers came under his supervision, and his work on them brought him into close contact with Tom Sullivan in the coating department.

George Duffy had been trained at Topsfield, a small branch mill of the Marshall Company, where he had gone to work when he graduated from high school. For some years the Topsfield mill had made a very thin tissue paper to be used as "body stock" by customers who manufactured carbon paper. About 1935, the company decided to make paper of this type at the Marshall mill and brought Duffy down to help with the change. Blanchard said that everyone had felt Duffy worked out so well that they "kept him on" to follow all orders for this type of paper.

Louis Rathbun was a comparatively new man in the department and acted largely as a handy man for Ned Kenyon, doing any sort of odd job that Kenyon might want done. Paul Blanchard, in talking to Joe Murray about Rathbun, said that "they found him working as a laborer mixing dyes in the coating department." Rathbun believed that this job gave him severe headaches, and he had to stay out of work for several days at a time. Blanchard explained,

Rathbun finally went to see the Baptist deacon about it a few months ago. The deacon spoke to Mr. Brewster, and Mr. Brewster said he would like to see Rathbun—you know his door is always open to the men. When Rathbun went in to see Mr. Brewster, he took his wife and child along with him. Mr. Brewster got quite a chuckle out of that. Rathbun just wanted to see if he could get some other kind of work. I don't think he had any idea that Austin would put him in the front office. However, Austin liked his looks. When he got out his record, he found that he was a college graduate. So he called me up at home—I had just gone home to lunch. He told me about him and asked me if I could come down and talk to him. I said, "Sure, I haven't started lunch yet. I'll be right down." Guess I talked to him for an hour or so and the upshot of it was that we put him to work here in the specialty department. He's been working in the coating department following runs we're interested in. Of course, the fumes are pretty bad around some of the runs and I asked him if he thought it would bother him. He said he didn't know but he would like to try. It doesn't seem to be doing him any harm. He hasn't been out since he has been up here.

Harry Chase originally came to work for the Marshall Company shortly after Paul Blanchard. He had worked with Blanchard on Number 16 paper machine which the company used at that time to treat papers with certain dyes. He continued to do this type of work, and eventually, when the company built up these orders sufficiently to justify Number 16 for this purpose, he was put in complete charge of it. Since there were never enough orders to keep this machine running full time, Chase also worked as an assistant foreman on paper machines numbered 5, 6, 7, and 8. He had worked closely for a long time on these machines and was thoroughly familiar with them.

Paul Blanchard continued in his talk with Murray.

During the war the specialty line grew so large that the sales department asked to have me assigned back to the specialty job, so sometime during 1945 I took it on in addition to my regular work with the plain papers. Mr. Brewster speaks of me as the assistant production manager, but my job really is in between manufacturing and sales. I get all the complaints. Whenever anything goes wrong with a product I hear about it—that is, on the specialty grades (both plain and coated) and all other plain papers. Perhaps I'm supposed to have something to do with the standard coated papers, but in actual practice I have nothing to do with them. The men who work on the plain papers come to me with their problems. On the other hand, Mr. Prout—he is superintendent of the coating department—talks directly to Mr. Graham. I have nothing to do with it.

As far as the specialty papers are concerned, Ned Kenyon does practically all of the detailed work. He talks directly with the salesmen and with the customers when it is necessary. Many of these papers involve the research department and Kenyon works closely with them. He works out all the details that he can handle and when he gets stuck, he comes to me. In dealing with the sales office I usually take only the situations where there is some policy decision involved. Once a month Dunn, the salesman for these specialty papers, comes to the mill. We get together with Kenyon and Pete Fraser of the research department for one or two evening sessions. I keep a record of our general conclusions in this little black book. In meetings of this sort we can keep the manufacturing problems and the customer requirements clearly in front of us.

Mr. Brewster was talking to me about this department the other day. We had hoped Kenyon would be able to take over the specialty department. In many ways he does. A great deal of the work deals with coated papers, which interest him, but he gets so interested in a problem that he drives it into the ground and tends to neglect other problems which are more important to the company but not so interesting to him. In many ways he has the attitude of a research worker.

Still, he is a hard worker; he has worked every night this week, for example, and all of his work is useful. He has an unusually good mind, one that I admire very much. We have been in many tough spots that we couldn't have gotten out of without his help.

At that point in the conversation the telephone rang, and Blanchard talked for a few minutes with Brad Dunn regarding the shipping date of a coated specialty paper scheduled to be delivered during that week. Since this paper was not on the schedule for the week, Dunn wanted to know when to expect it. Blanchard said he would look into the matter and call him back. As he hung up he said to Murray, "I guess he called me because he couldn't get hold of anyone else. He probably tried to reach Kenyon and couldn't find him." Blanchard then made several calls around the mill and found that the order was being held up because of a shortage of a particular dye that was necessary. This dye was expected during the week and the paper would probably be run the following week. He called Dunn and gave him this information.

He hardly finished this call when the director of research, Herb Parkhurst, called to discuss a coating problem in connection with a run of specialty paper which had gone through the mill a few days before. Blanchard and Kenyon had spent most of the previous afternoon working with the research department on this problem but had arrived at no conclusion. They had decided, after they left the research department, to make some experimental runs in the mill in order to find a solution for their problem. Now, however, Mr. Parkhurst apparently felt that some further discussion might be profitable. Blanchard finally agreed that he would find Kenyon, and they would both come over right away to see what could be worked out.

Several days later Murray came into Blanchard's office and said,

Paul, I was interested in the talk about the specialty department we had the other day. Would this be a good time to continue it?

BLANCHARD:   Sure.

MURRAY:   Mr. Brewster has told me several times that one of your most important needs at the moment is to find someone to "back up Paul." We've discussed Kenyon briefly. Now what about George Duffy? How does he fit in?

BLANCHARD:   Well, I think he's a good man. In fact, a very good man, although I don't think Austin Brewster agrees with me. We've had quite a few discussions about him first and last. Austin feels that his outlook is not right for a management position. I'm not so sure. He came down here from Topsfield, you know, when we started making tissue. He was on night inspection up there at the time. He is very good on the technical problems of Number 6, the machine we've used for tissues ever since he came. He's worked hard and built himself up to a position where the men now come to him with their problems. He works a lot with Mr. Fletcher, who, as you know, is the final authority on all plain papers, and he's getting a good knowledge of paper making. He works hard and gets along well with the men, but he has trouble getting things done—getting his ideas across.

MURRAY:    You mean he has difficulty expressing himself to the customers and the men above him? Does he have any experience in that sort of thing?

BLANCHARD:    No, I suppose he really hasn't much experience. He came up the hard way, after all. He didn't go to college and he has worked most of his time here in this mill. He drives so hard that he often upsets people. But he's doing a fine job in the mill. He's worked with me for a long while, several years longer than Kenyon. He reports directly to me on Number 6. He works only on plain papers, anyway, and Ned Kenyon isn't much interested in them. In theory Duffy has authority only over the quality of the thin paper made from Number 6, but because the men come to him with all types of problems on this machine, he is practically the foreman of it. The men ask him about mechanical or production matters on Number 6 and he tells them what to do. Then he tells Dave Nichols, the superintendent of the paper machines, what he has done. I've often heard Dave say that he doesn't have to worry about Number 6. "That's George's problem!"

MURRAY:    How does Harry Chase fit into the picture?

BLANCHARD:    He's been working on the dye papers ever since he came to the mill, just after he graduated from high school. As you know, he's in charge of Number 16 where all that kind of work is done. He knows more about those papers than anyone else in the mill. The problems on Number 16 are very different from those on the other paper machines. If we put one of the foremen in charge of it, say Jackie Walsh, it would keep him too busy. Although the machine is located in the basement on this side of the river right under the other machines that Walsh follows, it would still keep him out of the way too much. Chase is a good man. He's a top-grade mechanic and can tell at once when things are going wrong with the machine. He deals with the men well—you know, not rough handed—but he takes no nonsense from them. They always know where they stand with him. When we are running Number 16, we keep Harry Chase pretty busy, but he still manages to get some time to help out on the paper machines on the other side of the river. He has worked with the crews over there a long time and knows them well. He really has two jobs; we built them up to keep him busy where his skills are particularly useful. On the dye papers he reports directly to me and on his assistant foreman's work he reports to one of Dave Nichols's foremen.

MURRAY:    I see him around the front office more than any of the other foremen even when you're running dye papers.

BLANCHARD:    Yes, that's right. He gets up into the office whenever he can. He expected to have Ned Kenyon's job and was very disappointed when he did not get it. They still do not get along together at all well in the mill, although they see a lot of each other outside. Harry would like to have a desk somewhere up here near my office, but he really doesn't need one. We have given him drawer room here in one desk or another where he can keep some of his papers, but that doesn't seem to help. We have set up a perfectly good office for him down by Number 16 at the far end, but he doesn't like to use it any more than he can help. He likes to deal directly with the salesmen and the customers on the quality, production, and scheduling problems of the dye papers, and, on the whole, I'm glad to have him do it. We put in a telephone down in his office so that he can take care of this without leaving his machine. Still, he doesn't seem to like it very much.

We've often thought that it would be a good idea to organize a specialty division with the necessary production equipment all in one place. Number 16 is more like a coating machine than a paper machine and in some ways it ought to be in the coating department. On the other hand, if we put it in the coating department it will be like the buffing machine that's there now, an orphan, and it will not get the supervision that is necessary. We've thought of having a dye machine, a calender, a coating machine, and winder all in the same place to be used only on specialty orders. We don't want to build a new building; that would cost too much. The only place we have now big enough is in the old wood room in the pulp mill. We could fix that up so that it'll hold the equipment and it has a railroad siding that'll be handy for bringing in supplies and shipping paper. On the other hand, it's too far away from everything else. All the body stock will have to be trucked outside; that'll be difficult, particularly in winter, and will be sure to damage some paper. Perhaps the most serious problem is that it will be too far away from the coating and calendering and we won't be able to use the experience of that department.

Later that day Joe Murray discussed with Mr. Brewster the salary payroll of the mill. Mr. Brewster said that he had selected out of this payroll a group of men that he "kept his eye on." He called this his "personal payroll," and the main thing he considered when deciding to put a man on his payroll was whether or not he would continue to grow. Murray asked whether Kenyon and Duffy were on this payroll. Mr. Brewster replied,

Kenyon is on it. He's a brilliant chemist and is doing excellent work on special problems, particularly in connection with coated papers. He isn't broad enough in his point of view on management problems. He has too many outside interests —too many things that have nothing to do with the company—that's his trouble.

Duffy is in a different situation. Blanchard is very anxious to have him put on this personal payroll, and my judgment on this may be wrong. I'm holding him back for one reason. During the trouble with the union organizers at Topsfield in the early stages of the war, when I was away from the mill a good deal, I asked him to work as night inspector there and his answer was, "I don't want to be a scab." That was a foolish thing to say to me. I know that he had a brother who was sort of a leader of the employees' group at Topsfield and that he was brought up in the town. Still, I don't get his reasoning. It would have been different if I'd been asking him to take a union man's job. It all showed me that he hasn't grown up and isn't management caliber. He may grow up to become a night inspector along with Carlson and Kimball, but I don't think he will amount to much more than that. Paul Blanchard argues with me about it and thinks I'm too hard on Duffy—maybe I am. Paul says that he does good work.

# Marshall Company (F)
## A Custom Problem

IN ADDITION to its leadership in specialty items during the past 15 years, the Marshall Company, over a period of 30 years, had led the paper industry in the development of standard grades with established specifications on which its customers could rely. The company, together with six paper merchants who handled its products, formed an association to set these standard grades. The association organized three committees: an advisory committee to consider trade customs, a grading committee to study customer trends and new uses for papers, and one on merchandising to pass on all advertising. In effect, since the association based its decisions on customer requirements, they set the standard for the paper mill.

Joe Murray, a member of the Harvard Business School faculty, who was studying the operation of the Marshall Company's paper mill, found that the management gave increasing attention to the problems involved in producing specialty items and standard grades of quality satisfactory to its customers. After learning something about the connection of Paul Blanchard, the assistant production manager, with the specialty papers, Murray became interested in relating Blanchard's work to that of Fletcher, who was concerned with the quality control of the standard grades of plain papers.

Murray heard that Fletcher spent a couple of hours each morning in the control room, looking at samples of paper produced on the machines during the preceding night, checking the results of tests on the samples, and discussing with various people what should be done about the problems that cropped up. No one at the mill except Mr. Brewster himself had tried to define Fletcher's position to Murray. Mr. Brewster had said that Fletcher was the "chief inspector," but Mr. Brewster had also said that he often thought that Fletcher and Nichols should be "rolled into one."

Murray knew that Fletcher's routine included an early morning round of the machines, an hour or two in the control room, further visits to the machines and to the calendering office, the finishing department, and the beater rooms. During these trips he passed on information, looked for trouble, and discussed ways of handling it. If a machine crew saw a huge red-penciled arrow pointing at one of the specifications on the production order form or saw a heavy red line under a substandard test report on the machine data sheet by their machine, they would say, "He's been around again." One day 15 years ago Fletcher carried a pedometer with him and discovered that he had walked 12 miles through the mill. Since then, the development of the control room, the addition of three inspectors, and the increasing consciousness of quality control problems throughout the mill had made it possible for Fletcher himself to do a great deal less of the "leg work."

On a particular morning early in July, Murray found Fletcher in the control room at 8:30 A.M. At 9 o'clock, Blanchard came in and began looking at samples with Fletcher and talking them over.

The work of Blanchard and Fletcher was complicated in July 1947 by continual shortages of paper-making materials and limitations in production facilities. It was frequently necessary to ration output to customers, who were often willing to take paper even though it did not meet their stated specifications and who seldom returned it without showing a good reason. The management, however, anticipated that in the near future, as output caught up to demand throughout the industry, the customers would become increasingly particular about what they would accept.

Blanchard's contacts in the mill included daily rounds of the control room, paper mill, calendering, coating, and finishing. During these rounds he discussed customer complaints and other problems with Fletcher and his inspectors, with the quality control men, with the foremen, and directly with the men. For example, if a customer returned some defective paper, he would bring a sample back to the machine crew responsible for it, "talk it over with them," and try to figure out what had happened and how to prevent it from happening again. "Sometimes the men admit they're at fault," Blanchard said. "Sometimes they put the blame right back on management, and sometimes they figure out new ways of licking a problem we hadn't thought of before."

After Blanchard and Fletcher had talked over the samples for a while, one in particular caught their attention. This was a sample of book paper currently in production on machine Number 11. Number 11 was one of the older machines; it was used for quantity output of plain paper and of body stock for coated paper. Production costs on this machine tended to run higher than on some of the other machines. Like the others, it had acquired over the years certain characteristics of its own that created difficulties in controlling the quality of the paper.

Decisions as to what papers should run on machine Number 11 took place in the scheduling office under the direct supervision of Mr. Elcott, who reported to Mr. Graham. Elcott's knowledge of the machines and of the paper scheduled on them was so thorough that he could wake to a telephone call at 3 A.M. and tell a worried foreman who had run out of work or who was faced with a machine breakdown what to do about it.

The customer's specifications for the book paper included a maximum bulk limit, that is, a maximum thickness for the paper. The paper had consistently exceeded this limit on the current order and on several previous ones, all of which had been run on Number 11. Blanchard and Fletcher discussed various ways of reducing the bulk. One possibility was to beat the fiber longer before it went to the paper machines. This would break down the fiber, but it would also result in greater hydration of the pulp. The paper machine was adjusted to handle pulp of the present degree of hydration. If wetter pulp entered the machine, it would still be moist when it arrived at the dry end. There was no way to increase the heat in the drier rolls; the only alternative would be to slow down the machine so that the pulp would be exposed to the driers for a longer time.

Fletcher suggested slowing the speed of the machine by 100 feet per minute. Blanchard answered,

Can you imagine prevailing on anyone out there in the paper-making department to slow the machine down?

FLETCHER:    It wouldn't be easy.

BLANCHARD:    Maybe we can lick this by heavier calendering on the paper machines.

FLETCHER:    I was out by the machine yesterday and we tried that. But we started getting calender cuts in the paper, so we had to give it up. Those stacks at the machine won't take the heavier calendering.

BLANCHARD:    I guess we'll have to send it down to the supercalendering department. I don't know whether it will work or not. This is the third order of this kind of paper we've sent down there. We might as well mark the order for calendering in the first place. Mr. Goodwin will know what to do about it if anybody does.

FLETCHER:    Have you heard any more from the sales office about it?

BLANCHARD:    Yes, I got a call yesterday asking if we couldn't do something to end the trouble for good. We'll try to get by with calendering, but if I hear direct from the customer on it we're going to have to do something more. On each order we've had to notify them in advance that we're not meeting their bulk specifications. I think they've been squashing the paper to make it fit inside the book covers. There's no telling how long they'll be willing to keep that up.

MURRAY:    If supercalendering can't handle it, what could you do about it?

BLANCHARD:    Well, we could change the furnish. We're short on cellate pulp, but it certainly cuts down the fiber thickness. That's one answer.

FLETCHER:    That would be easy enough to do. I could speak to my inspectors, or the beater engineers, or Jack Dugan, who's in charge of the furnish specifications, and any one of them could make the change. But we couldn't do that. We've already promised more paper requiring cellate pulp than we can make with the cellate we have on hand plus what's been promised us, and I doubt if there'll be any more available for months. What about slowing down the machine —any chance?

BLANCHARD:    That would be a tough one to put through. The men like this paper now; they can earn a good bonus on it. They'd howl if we cut down their output. Besides, Dave Nichols is already behind on the tonnage figure that Mr. Brewster wants for this month. Dave would feel pretty bad if he had to take another slowdown. Even if we asked him, he would probably talk us out of it.

FLETCHER:    Number 11 itself might be the cause of the trouble. This order could be run on Number 14.

BLANCHARD:    Any change like that would certainly have to go through the front office. I've got another order running on Number 14 right now. The sales office is kicking about the price, and the only way we could cut the cost would be to shift it to another machine; but Elcott has already made the decision about that. If we wanted to get a change, we'd have to talk to Graham. Then it would be up to him.

MURRAY:    What are the chances of your asking the customer to put up with it the way it is?

BLANCHARD:    Not when it's a standard paper like this. Kenyon is out in Buffalo now to see if a customer can't adapt his machines to handle some heavy bulk specialty paper we're sending him. That's a new item, and it looks as if it might be easier to make some modification of the customer's equipment than to change the paper. But when we've got a standard paper like this, we should be able to put it out according to specifications.

FLETCHER:    Well, we're not going to do anything about it now, anyway.

Fletcher left the control room to go down to the mill, and Blanchard went back to his office.

# Marshall Company (G)

JOE MURRAY, a member of the Harvard Business School faculty who was making a study of the Marshall Paper Company, dropped into the office of Paul Blanchard, the assistant production manager, one morning and sat down. He had previously discussed with Blanchard in some detail Blanchard's relations with the specialty group and with the men who worked in the production office and in the papermaking department.[1]

Blanchard began the conversation casually.

BLANCHARD: Morning, Joe. I had an interesting thing happen to me a minute ago. I just finished talking to Mr. Prout on the phone about that wax-coated paper we are running. Ned Kenyon had been having some trouble with it; and when he got stuck, he finally came in to see me. We went over the situation carefully and decided what must be done. I called Mr. Prout and told him our conclusions. He just flatly refused to do it.

In July 1947 the demand for papers of all kinds heavily exceeded the supply of materials and paper-making facilities. The Marshall Company sales and production personnel frequently found it necessary to ask customers to accept paper that differed from established specifications. They were making every effort, however, to meet customer requirements in coated papers as well as other types.

Many of the high-quality papers produced by the mill, in addition to certain of the specialty papers, were coated papers. The coating department was one of the major divisions of the mill. Mr. Prout had worked in the coating and calendering department for many years while his father had been its superintendent, and had succeeded to the position when his father retired. He reported directly to John Graham. Austin Brewster considered Prout a "technically excellent man." Murray heard that Prout felt that his department was an empire separate from the rest of the mill.

Blanchard's supervisory work on the specialty papers, plain and coated,

---

[1] See Marshall Company (E) and (F).

occupied a major portion of his time and took him into most of the departments of the mill. The remainder of his supervisory work dealt largely with the quality of the standard plain papers. On this work, he dealt with the paper-making department, which was under the supervision of Dave Nichols, and with the finishing department, which was headed by Frank Goodwin. On the supervision of the coated specialty papers, however, he dealt with Prout, who was responsible to Graham for production and quality of all coated papers.

BLANCHARD:   I usually can get things done with Frank Goodwin in the finishing department. He trained me right. Over a long period of time, he taught me to be careful in the way I deal with him. I never got into any real trouble with him; but every once in a while, at first, he would call me up and say: "Paul what was that business you were talking about to so-and-so this afternoon?" After I'd explained and we had come to a conclusion, he'd make some comment such as: "It would have been easier to talk to me in the first place." For a long time now, I've always gone to him first on anything I thought ought to be done. If for any reason he is away, of course I don't hesitate to talk to Hank Crawford in the plain paper section of the finishing department, or to Allen on a coated specialty paper. I'm always careful, however, to ask them to talk to Frank about the problem when he gets back.

When I go down through the mill, naturally I see things that ought to be changed, or the men tell me about things that need improvement. I generally talk to Crawford or even to Phillips or McColl in the finishing department about things there; and in one way or another, they seem to get done. I don't know exactly what happens. I suppose they go to Frank and say something like: "I was talking to Paul Blanchard the other day, and such and such seemed like a good idea. What do you think?" Discussing a problem and leaving the conclusion for them to act upon seems to work pretty well with the men who are about my own age. With the older men, it doesn't seem to work so well.

MURRAY:   How about men like Bill Phinney, superintendent of the pulp mill? He's about your age, isn't he?

BLANCHARD:   Well, I don't see much of him, anyway. He deals directly with Mr. Brewster or Mr. Graham. My work doesn't take me into the pulp mill very much. Once in a while something comes up and I go over to see him; but that isn't often. I want to see him now on that run of dirty pulp we had the other night. We ran 80 tons of paper, as you know, on machines Number 11 and Number 14 before we stopped the run. It seems ridiculous that the people in the pulp mill would try to save 16 to 18 tons of pulp and let us spoil 80 tons of paper. If they had let us know in advance, perhaps we could have made some kind of paper where the dirt did not matter so much. The pulp mill had storage room for that much pulp, and they could have held it for a little while so that we could have had some choice of what kind of paper to use it in. You know, we could have used it in one-side coated paper, where it would have been covered up, or in paper for bottle and can labels, where the print would hide the dirt. Coming unexpectedly over the week end, as it did, it upset the night men. They are not as intimately acquainted with customer requirements as the day men and did not know exactly what ought to be done. Selling that paper to the jobbers may not be too serious a problem. We'll still make a profit on it, although a smaller one than we would have made on the original order. The worst thing is that we are behind in our allotments on that order. We can't tell the customer that we just can't make good enough paper to ship to him. We have to tell him that we are behind on our schedules; we will be, too. All the other orders will get upset.

I see Phinney on that sort of thing. I talk to him from time to time on things that affect the quality of the paper, but I don't see him regularly in the course of my ordinary work. John Graham has probably talked to Phinney about that load of dirt already, but I wouldn't expect John to talk to me about it. He would expect me to see Phinney myself to find out what it was all about and to see what can be done to stop its happening again.

Mr. Prout's department is different. I work with them all the time. I go through there every day, as I go through the paper mill and the finishing department. Naturally, I see things, and the men talk to me. I remember when I was going through the calendering department the other day. One of the rolls of paper—they weigh about two thousand pounds, you know—was propped up on the bench with a stick. It might have been kicked loose or jarred out and caused a serious accident. I talked to the man who was handling the paper and told him how dangerous it was. He told me a lot about how hard it was to handle the rolls there now, since the benches were getting worn out, and things like that. I went in to see Mr. Prout after that and discussed the situation with him, but I don't think much happened. I have no idea what he did about that particular roll or the man who was working on it. I imagine that the condition of the benches was just a temporary thing, while he was waiting for the maintenance department to get around to fixing it.

Sometimes I don't have any luck in dealing with Mr. Prout. Often I can ask him to do things in a certain way and explain the reasons and he will do it. Sometimes I can't get anywhere with him. When you came in, I had just asked him to have the machine running the light tissue shut down until we had finished running the paper that required the wax finish. I explained to him how we had tried to run them both together and couldn't make it work. He merely said to me, "I will not shut down that machine," and hung up. This is a situation where I will have to work out something with him. Both the tissue and the wax-finish paper are specialty papers, and at the present time the quality of neither of them is good enough to sell. He's running them on those two machines that have the joint temperature control, and they just won't work for those runs. If we get the temperature high enough to handle the wax on one of the machines, it's too high for that very thin paper on the other machine, and it comes through brittle. We've tried all the combinations we can think of, and there seems to be nothing we can do to run them both at once. The other machines that will take these orders are all tied up, so we have to run them on these machines.

MURRAY:    What are you going to do now?

BLANCHARD:    Well, I guess I had better go down and talk it over with Mr. Prout. We will have to work out something.

# Recent Technological Developments in the Paper Industry*

THERE HAVE BEEN a number of important developments in printing technology in the ten years from 1950 to 1960, although none of them has been important enough to change the basic process significantly. The most recent major changes are (1) the use of automatic controls to alter the pulp mixture and paper machine speeds, (2) the tremendous increase in the capability of machines to produce paper more quickly, (3) the ability to use lower and lower grades of wood to manufacture acceptable grades of paper, and (4) the beginnings of simplification of machine design.

## THE USE OF AUTOMATIC CONTROLS

About 20 years ago an old time Scotch paper maker, who was a machine tender in a small Connecticut mill, with perhaps 40 or more years of paper-making experience in the old country and here in the United States, made an observation worth remembering. He said, "There are three ways of making paper: your way, my way, and the right way." The first two ways of making paper are giving ground in an ever-accelerating manner to the right way, or to the science of making paper as opposed to the art, based on opinion, custom, and habit.

The paper-making process is subject to a great many variables. A few of the factors which affect sheet quality are: fiber length, pulp consistency, machine speed, temperature, and water flow. Each of these in combination can affect such qualities of the finished product as weight, finish, thickness, softness, and moisture. All of these can be controlled by the machine tender, who must possess rare judgment and experience in order to pick the correct set of combinations and degree of adjustment of the process variables. Inevitably, this dependence on human ability causes unwanted variations in the finished product.

---

* Reproduced by permission of the Technical Association of the Pulp and Paper Industry.

Tremendous strides have been made in the past few years toward applying to this problem scientific methods for quality measurement, recording, and control. Measurements that were formerly made by feeling the consistency of the pulp mixture or weighing a square of paper cut from the sheet are now made electronically. A stuff box consistency control has been developed which automatically adds fresh water to or removes it from the mixture of pulp and water entering the machine. In this way, the basic weight and smoothness of the end product are controlled by electronic beta-radiation gauges which constantly record the weight of the paper, and automatically compensate for any more-than-standard variations. Magnetic inductance thickness recorders similarly deal with the bulk of the sheet, while automatic pH recorders and electronic moisture meters record its acidity and water content.

In most instances, these controls not only serve as indicators to the paper maker, but actually make the machine adjustments that were formerly accomplished by the operator. Through the proper selection and application of instruments, paper can be made under measured, known, and controlled conditions. It is interesting to note that in many instances paper machine operators are not content to allow the machines to operate automatically. At one plant which recently installed a consistency control, it was found that the operators check on the accuracy of the automatic device by periodically feeling the consistency of the pulp with their hands and adding water when necessary. Commenting on this problem of operator interference, a large manufacturer of paper-making machinery stated that he believed his industry would start including entire sets of hand operated controls on new equipment which would have no effect on the actual process other than to satisfy the operator's desire to believe he is controlling the process.

## INCREASED MACHINE SPEEDS

The increases in the capability of Fourdrinier machines to produce paper at higher speeds and greater widths have been enormous in recent years. In 1951, for example, the fastest machines for book papers operated on widths of 190 inches at approximately 1125 feet per minute. At the present time, the newest machines can handle book paper widths of 220 inches at speeds up to 1400 feet per minute. Newsprint machines in 1951 were able to produce widths of 240 inches at 1600 feet per minute. Today, the newest models can produce paper as wide as 348 inches at speeds up to 2000 feet per minute. This race to higher and higher capabilities has been climaxed by the recent announcement that one major manufacturer is considering the purchase of a machine which will produce tissue at a speed of 3600 feet per minute.

This enormous increase in machine capacity is the result of a number of important innovations. First, it was necessary to develop chemicals which would impart sufficient "wet strength" to the paper so that it would not break as it travelled along the Fourdrinier wires at high speeds. Second, in order to make paper at higher speeds, methods had to be developed for increasing the ejection velocity of the pulp so that it could immediately travel at the same speed as the wires were moving. It was discovered that this factor could be effectively controlled by pressurizing the headbox from which the pulp is ejected. Finally, high velocity air driers were developed which are four times as efficient as conventional driers. In one installation, two of these new driers were installed on a machine where this operation was the only limiting factor, and production was actually increased by 50 percent.

## UTILIZATION OF LOW-COST HARDWOODS

In the recent past, the usage of paper has increased at a faster rate than ever before. As a result, many companies have been faced with the problem of dwindling supplies of the woods most commonly used to make paper. In order to meet this problem, research efforts have been focused on developing pulping processes for some of the less commonly used, and consequently less expensive, species of wood.

It has been learned that by using a semichemical process, which is a combination of the chemical and mechanical pulping processes, a low-cost pulp can be produced from abundant short-fiber hardwoods which does not have the traditionally objectionable qualities of short-fiber pulp. The practicability of this semichemical method of treating hardwoods depended on developments at two stages of this new pulping process. First, it was discovered in research laboratories that a neutral sodium sulfite solution could dissolve the bonding matter in hardwoods economically. Second, a process was developed for subjecting the pulp to mechanical fiberizing on machinery which operated in a lengthwise fashion and thus did not further shorten the natural short hardwood fibers.

This process produced low-cost pulp which can be used very advantageously in combination with regular chemical or groundwood pulp. Consequently, it has become possible to improve the physical characteristics of certain papers while replacing part of the expensive softwood pulp with more economical, semichemically prepared hardwood pulp. As a result, aspen, beech, oak, maple, and poplar can now be utilized economically.

Developments of this kind have been made at many stages of the paper-making process. For example, a radically new innovation known as chemical barking is being used to assist in the difficult job of removing bark from the lower-cost hardwoods. By this process, chemicals are injected into the tree which loosen the bark for easy removal. Another discovery, known as the chemi-groundwood process, makes it easier to grind hardwoods. By this process, four foot logs are dropped into pressure vessels and are treated with a soda solution. This softens the logs and simplifies the grinding process.

By developing methods such as these, the paper industry can now efficiently utilize enormous amounts of timber that previously could only be used in limited quantities.

## SIMPLIFICATION OF MACHINE DESIGN

The tremendous emphasis on developing higher machine speeds and increased production ratios has forced the industry to disregard, to a great extent, the introduction of machines designed for simplicity and ease of maintenance. As a result, many of the new machines have been criticized by some industry leaders for being over-designed and complicated. The reversal of this trend has been signaled by several new developments, of which the most important is the cantilevered Fourdrinier.

On the normal paper machine, the wires wear out frequently and sometimes must be replaced as often as once each week. Before the development of the cantilevered Fourdrinier design, it was necessary to remove all the wire and guide rolls from the machine in order to replace the wire. Before the machine could be started up again, each roll had to be refitted. The new cantilevered design makes it possible to slide the entire wire section from the machine without touching the rolls. Once the damaged wires are replaced, the entire section can be placed back into the machine and it can be started up immediately. In effect, the cantilevered design eliminates the necessity for moving 500 tons of machinery into the aisles in order to replace a few hundred pounds of wire.

More developments of this kind can be expected for the future at practically all stages of the paper-making process.

# READINGS

## Criteria for Organizational Planning*

### GENE W. DALTON

THE ADMINISTRATOR MUST, more or less frequently, make a commitment to introduce an important change into the organization or segment of the organization he is concerned with. As students of business administration, you have been asked to make such a commitment to a change proposal in regard to the cases you have studied. This process is not new, but it is particularly highlighted by cases that emphasize change.

When we begin to discuss and assess recommended changes and action proposals, however, we find ourselves immediately faced with a normative problem. What is our purpose in recommending the actions we propose? What ends do we seek to attain? Against what criteria shall we measure the outcomes? These questions are neither naïve nor are their answers obvious. Every person involved in planning organizational changes must address these questions in some way. Part of the complexity of the problem arises from the fact that any behavioral act and its consequences can fruitfully be examined and evaluated from a number of different viewpoints. One way of bringing some of the viewpoints into focus is to examine the event or proposal in terms of its functional or dysfunctional effects for different operating systems. In this paper we shall examine three types of relevant operating systems—the total organization, the small face-to-face work group, and the individual. We will be considering the factors which work to maintain the effective operation of these systems, as well as some of the problems and possibilities for facilitating their growth and development. We shall examine each of these systems separately, but first let us make note of some general tendencies and potentialities of human behavioral systems.

---

* Originally presented as "Criteria for Planning Organizational Change," in Lawrence, et al. (Eds.) *Organizational Behavior and Administration* (Rev. ed., Homewood, Ill.: Richard D. Irwin, Inc. and The Dorsey Press, 1965).

## MAINTENANCE AND GROWTH

Investigators from a variety of disciplines have reported the tendency for human behavioral systems to *maintain* and *preserve* themselves. Given sufficiently effective mechanisms within a system and a sufficiently favorable environment, the system will tend to maintain a steady state or a *moving equilibrium*. When parts of the system are pulled out of balance, or when some of its essential operations are blocked or threatened, the system *reacts* and mobilizes to restore the system to its prior balance. This "homeostatic tendency" was first noted and explicated by students of biological systems, but has also come to be an essential conceptual tool for those trying to understand the behavior of social systems.

Another characteristic of individuals, groups, and organizations which is sometimes overlooked by those who focus on the reactive tendencies of human systems is the potential which these systems have to *grow* and *develop*. Human systems have in common the *potential for increasing internal complexity* and for expanding their capacity to influence their environment. They can "learn" from their transactions with their environment and thus increase their capacity to act on their environment—to become *proactive* as well as reactive. That all such systems do not grow and develop does not deny the existence of this potential. Rather it points to the fact that growth takes place only when certain factors are present and under certain favoring circumstances.

We shall not try to draw a falsely concrete demarcation between maintenance and growth, between reaction and proaction.[1] An action or a series of acts may have both reactive and proactive elements. It is often difficult to distinguish between maintenance and growth. Without trying to draw any artificial distinctions, let us keep in mind these two general characteristics of human behavioral systems as we examine separately each of the three systems listed in the second paragraph of this paper.

## THE TOTAL ORGANIZATION

For an organization to maintain itself and function effectively, it must have a number of different well-understood sets of activities. It must have a production system—a set of activities for producing goods, services, or ideas which the organization seeks to provide for its environment. Ideally, the best technological knowledge would be used in designing these activities. It must have a marketing and distribution system, which again would

---

[1] For a more detailed description of reactive and proactive tendencies in organizational systems, see J. V. Clark, "A Healthy Organization," *California Management Review*, Vol. 4, No. 4 (Summer, 1962), pp. 16–30.

ideally use the best available knowledge in promoting and distributing the product. It must have a product designing system to create technically practical and commercially useful products. To bind these required activities together, it must have a communication-decision system. Ideally, necessary choices and decisions would be made for the organization by the individual most expert on the issue involved. A set of rewards and punishments (financial and nonfinancial) is also needed. Ideally, the rewards would be highly valued by the members of the organization and would be administered in such a way as to reinforce those activities which contribute to organizational purpose and extinguish those activities which do not. Finally, a set of sentiments is needed which function to insure the full contribution of those who work in the organization. Ideally, the dominant sentiment would be unswerving loyalty to the purpose of the organization. When any of the elements described above is completely inoperative in an organization, the system will have difficulty maintaining itself and will tend to disintegrate or go through a series of convulsive reorganizations or both.

We also noted that human systems have the potential to grow and complicate as well as maintain themselves. Full achievement of organizational purpose is impossible without such growth. (We defined growth as an increasing capacity to cope with the environment rather than in terms of increasing size.) Where this potential is not realized, we find organizations which tend to become primarily defensive and inflexible in their strategies and highly vulnerable to environmental shifts.

What are the features of an organization which tends to realize this potential? These are more difficult to state. Less is known about organizational growth than about organizational maintenance, but at least three features appear to be necessary. First there has to be a system for gathering information from the outside—for sensing and anticipating customer needs and ways of filling them. In effect, they must be "open-ended" rather than "closed" systems. However, new information, ideas, and technology are not useful unless the organization has a second feature—a built-in set of procedures for changing itself and a set of attitudes which tolerate and facilitate change. The Scottish firms studied by Burns and Stalker,[2] which brought in a new electronic technology but were unable to incorporate the change into the *existing* organizational framework, were finally unable to utilize the new technology. Third, some mechanisms and attitudes have to be developed and maintained which facilitate the confrontation of and integration of divergent ideas.[3]

As we have described a model of an organization oriented entirely

---

[2] T. Burns and G. M. Stalker, *The Management of Innovation.* Chicago: Quadrangle Books, 1962.

[3] M. P. Follett, *Dynamic Administration.* New York: Harper & Bros., 1940, pp. 30–49.

toward the achievement of organizational purposes, the reader may have begun to share some of William Whyte's concern about the rise of the "organization man."[4] Nevertheless, we need to be reminded, occasionally, of the obvious fact that the achievements of large-scale healthy organizations constitute an essential ingredient in modern civilized life. If our business organizations did not do a reasonable job of achieving their purpose, we would not have the material means to sustain our complex society.

The limits of this model lie in the fact that it takes into account only one system—the organization itself. Our purpose is to explore some of the other systems which must also be taken into account in building a model for a healthy organization.

## THE WORK GROUP

One of the richest of man's experiences derives from working together with others to achieve a common end. In almost every known culture, men have been known to seek out these experiences. In our own society, an expanding body of literature[5] attests to the fact that people in larger organizations tend to form small, informal work groups even in circumstances where their formation would appear to be difficult and unlikely. These groups provide their members an opportunity for social exchange, for gaining esteem and emotional support. These groups spontaneously develop a system of interactions and activities and develop norms which influence the behavior of their members.

For an organization to be most functional at this level, the members would have to have a set of activities in which they could jointly engage and have the opportunity to interact around these activities. From these minimal conditions, a system of activities and interactions will tend to emerge and provide its members with the satisfactions of membership. The organization need not provide the detailed procedures, only the conditions.

The question may be posed as to why an organizational planner should take this dimension into account. If these systems tend to form spontaneously and maintain themselves, why should they be planned for? Moreover, is it not true that they have often been known to work at cross-purposes to organizational goals? The answer to this latter question is,

---

[4] William H. Whyte, Jr., *The Organization Man.* New York: Simon and Schuster, Inc., 1956.

[5] P. M. Blau, *The Dynamics of Bureaucracy.* Chicago: University of Chicago Press, 1955; G. Homans, *The Human Group.* New York: Harcourt Brace & Co., 1950; G. F. F. Lombard, *Behavior in a Selling Group.* (Boston: Harvard Business School, Division of Research, 1955; A. Zaleznik, *Worker Satisfaction and Development.* Boston: Harvard Business School, Division of Research, 1956; A. Zaleznik *et al., The Motivation, Productivity and Satisfaction of Workers: A Prediction Study.* Boston: Harvard Business School, Division of Research, 1958.

of course, in the affirmative. In fact, a large part of the organizational planning in the past has sought to prevent the formation of such groups. These efforts to isolate individual activity and to prevent joint efforts have proved enlightening. When isolation is successful, investigators have often found high employee dissatisfaction, and high turnover.[6] More frequently, however, groups have formed around a set of collusive relationships (i.e., rate restriction) or purely social activities (i.e., betting pools, collections, horseplay, etc.). The primary question is often not whether a group will form and provide some social satisfactions for its members, but whether these satisfactions will be derived from relationships built around task accomplishment or whether the time and energy invested in obtaining these satisfactions are drained off into nontask-related and ritualistic activities.

Are groups to be taken into account, however, only because they are a necessary evil? What about the potential capacity for the small group to complicate and exert an increasingly effective and positive influence in the organization? We are aware of the contribution of the highly effective paper-machine crews in the Marshall Company. Barnes[7] reports the development of a highly creative engineering group which was given relatively great freedom to develop its own work patterns. Clark[8] reports a work group which spent a year meeting in the members' homes to design a whole new methods-handling system in its department. For most of this time its work was unknown to management.

This potential is too often unrealized, however. Many, if not most, work groups in American industry could be described as "frozen" groups. Let us examine the way this term was used by Zaleznik, Christensen, and Roethlisberger to describe industrial work groups they had observed carefully. They described the characteristics of these work groups as follows:

1. These groups have few, if any, ways of relating themselves in a positive fashion to the organizational settings in which they live. They seem to be able to develop only in one direction, i.e., in the direction of maintaining their values in an environment which seems to be indifferent to them.
2. Their regular members and leaders have little opportunity to exercise their influence, leadership, and responsibilities except in the direction of maintaining the group's social life and organization. Excluded from participation in the setting, planning, and implementation of production goals, they devote most of their energies to the maintenance of production norms.
3. But even the internal developments of their social life become merely endless

---

[6] E. Mayo, *The Human Problems of an Industrial Civilization.* New York: Viking Press, 1960; C. R. Walker, and R. H. Guest, *The Man on the Assembly Line.* Cambridge, Mass.: Harvard University Press, 1952.

[7] L. B. Barnes, *Organizational Systems and Engineering Groups.* Boston: Harvard Business School, Division of Research, 1960.

[8] Clark, *op. cit.*

one-level elaborations of existing values that stay at constant levels of sameness
—same routine activities, same routine conversational topics, same patterns of
"on-the-line" output, same collective beliefs, same "gripes," same problems,
and the same resolution of them.

4. Thus these groups offer few opportunities for the self-development of their
members. If the individual in such a group identifies with the regular social
subgroups, he is bound by their norms, values, and limited aspirations. In
terms of self-development the price paid for regular membership is high. But
also high are the costs of nonconformity. The deviants and isolates incur not
only the penalties of social isolation but the penalties of social antagonisms as
well. They become the butt of jokes and the victims of horseplay. In this situation their chances to influence change in others or in themselves are limited.
Thus under both circumstances the opportunities for doing new things, for
developing new ways for doing them, for assuming increased personal responsibility, and for personal self-development are seriously limited.

To such groups that have lost their organizational health, i.e., that are incapable
of development except in the lopsided way we have described, we shall give the
name "frozen." Such groups appear in many businesses at different organizational
levels but, as many studies have shown, they flourish at the work level. The social
pathology they manifest is one of incomplete growth and development. Although
they can and do develop along one dimension, this very internal dead-level
elaboration prevents and works against their external development.[9]

Guidelines for "unfreezing" such groups or for preventing their crystal-
lization are not fully defined. Still, you have two points from which to
begin your analysis. First you can examine some of the conditions of
"frozenness" and explore how each might be altered. Second, you have
your own experiences in groups from which you might be able to draw.

## THE INDIVIDUAL

We turn now to the individual. The individual comes to the organization to satisfy a number of complex needs. We are forced to oversimplify
in describing these, but we might begin by stating that the individual seeks
from the organization the means with which to provide economically for
himself and his family. This, however, is only a beginning. He has needs
for safety and security. We have mentioned the social needs which he
brings with him to the organization. He also has needs to maintain some
level of self-esteem and a sense of personal accomplishment. He seeks,
not always successfully, to achieve some kind of esteem in the eyes of
others. When these needs listed here are frustrated, we often find patterns
of high turnover of personnel, or militant unionism, or both. Ideally, for
an organization to be functional at this level, it would be designed so as to
fulfill each of these needs for the contributing members of the organization.

---

[9] Zaleznik et al., op. cit., pp. 390–91.

It would also provide something more. It would provide those conditions which would facilitate individual growth and development. There is a great deal of ferment and controversy among psychologists concerning the nature and the determinants of individual growth. Allport,[10] Rogers,[11] and Bronfenbrenner[12] postulate a persistent *tendency* among individuals in the direction of growth, increased capacity, and self-determination. Robert White[13] has gathered considerable research evidence to support his theory of a universal human *need* for increased competence. Maslow[14] describes a need for what he calls "self-actualization." Argyris[15] goes so far as to make organizations responsible for much of the neurosis of our time because they frustrate the needs of the individual for growth and self-determination.

We need not enter into the controversy. There *is* general agreement that the individual has the *potential* capacity to learn, complicate, and take greater responsibility for his own behavior. For an organization to be fully functional along this dimension, it must provide conditions which facilitate individual growth. What are these conditions? Again there is a wide range of formulations among those interested in individual growth, but a few ideas tend to be held in common. First, there is sufficient opportunity and encouragement to take self-determined action and take responsibility for this action. Second, the environment is sufficiently supportive so that taking such action is not seen as too dangerous, and third, the individual is able to obtain clear-cut and valid feedback regarding the consequences of this action.

## A MULTIFUNCTIONAL APPROACH TO ANALYSIS AND PLANNING

Our examination of these three levels of behavioral systems points up two things. First, it illustrates that the human values represented in each level are both real and important. Second, and perhaps more significant, it provides us with a scheme which will help us in explaining and even predicting problems in organizations where behavior is functional at only one of these levels. It provides us with a multifunctional approach to the evaluation of behavior and behavioral change in organizations. Using this approach, we are led to examine an act or a proposal in terms of its function for each system and in terms of its probable effect on the system's

---

10 G. Allport, "The Open System in Personality Theory," in *Personality and Social Encounter.* Boston: Beacon Press, 1960.

11 C. Rogers, *On Becoming a Person.* Cambridge, Mass.: Riverside Press, 1961.

12 U. Bronfenbrenner, "Toward an Integrated Theory of Personality," in Robert R. Blake and Glenn Ramsey, *Perception.* New York: Ronald Press, 1951.

13 Robert White, "Motivation Reconsidered, The Concept of Competence," *Nebraska Symposium on Motivation,* 1960.

14 A. H. Maslow, *Motivation and Personality.* New York: Harper & Bros., 1954.

15 Chris Argyris, *Personality and Organization.* New York: Harper & Row, 1957.

reactive tendencies and its potential for growth. Let us try out our scheme by examining three instances of behavior in organizations which tend to be aimed at achievement at only one or two of these levels.

Perhaps the movement which is, in the mind of many persons, most closely identified with the first level, achievement of organizational purpose, is the scientific management movement. Frederick W. Taylor, one of the founders and leading exponents of scientific management, described an incident showing how he went about trying to change organizational behavior.[16] Taylor himself stated that he was trying to effect change at two levels, "to secure the maximum prosperity for the employer, coupled with the maximum prosperity for each employee." Taylor found a gang loading on the average of about 12½ tons of pig iron per man per day. He estimated that each man ought to be able to handle 48 tons per day instead. Following his own "inflexible rule to talk and deal with only one man at a time," Taylor sought out a Pennsylvania Dutchman named Schmidt and spoke to him as follows:

> Schmidt, are you a high-priced man?
>
> Vell, I don't know vat you mean.
>
> Oh yes, you do. What I want to know is whether you are a high-priced man or not.
>
> Vell, I don't know vat you mean.
>
> Oh, come now, you answer my questions. What I want to find out is whether you are a high-priced man or one of these cheap fellows here. What I want to find out is whether you want to earn $1.85 a day or whether you are satisfied with $1.15, just the same as all those cheap fellows are getting.
>
> Did I vant $1.85 a day? Vas dot a high-priced man? Vell, yes, I vas a high-priced man. . . .
>
> Well, if you are a high-priced man, you will do exactly as this man tells you tomorrow, from morning till night. When he tells you to pick up a pig and walk, you pick it up and you walk, and when he tells you to sit down and rest, you sit down. You do that right straight through the day. And what's more, no back talk. Now a high-priced man does just what he's told to do, and no back talk. Do you understand that? When this man tells you to walk, you walk; when he tells you to sit down, you sit down, and you don't talk back to him. Now you come on to work here tomorrow morning and I'll know before night whether you are really a high-priced man or not. . . .[17]

Taylor reports that indeed Schmidt did do exactly as he was told. He moved 47 tons and earned $1.85 per day. Immediately, Schmidt's earning *did* rise and the profits for the company *increased*. But when we examine this change from a multifunctional point of view, other factors are brought into focus. If Taylor's approach is taken with each member of the

---

[16] F. W. Taylor, *The Principles of Scientific Management.* New York: Harper & Bros., 1911.

[17] *Ibid.*

firm, what effects does it have on individual learning and growth? If individual growth is blocked, what effect will this have on organizational growth? What kinds of response might we expect from the work groups affected? How might the groups act to protect and maintain themselves? How would defensive group action affect the profitability of the firm?

Let us turn to another example. In the case Work Group Ownership of an Improved Tool,[18] we find an instance of strong group development. Two workers having developed a new high-speed tool bit shared it only with the members of their work group, keeping it hidden from management. The members of the group were able to "peg production" and still earn incentive earnings. With their extra time, they applied greater care and workmanship to their other products. They established a reputation for accuracy and low spoilage. At the group level, we find high functionality. We find cohesion, loyalty, and cooperation around a task. The group was not only maintaining itself but was becoming more capable of dealing with its environment. Individual members were being rewarded by the group not only for conformity but for creativeness and skill. But the company, which was planning to set up a new plant unit making the same product, was deprived of the benefit of the innovation.

To fill out our triad, we turn to a poignant account of a utopian society, the Fruitlands experiment, made famous by the skillful pen of Louisa May Alcott.[19] Here was an organization created to maximize individual growth. However, the features which we described earlier as essential for the maintenance of an organization were never developed. Hence, Fruitlands failed as a productive organization and thus became dysfunctional at all three levels.

Before we leave our examination of changes which were functional at only one or two levels and their consequences, let us also take the time factor into account. A change which is functional at only one level may appear to be successful because its dysfunctional effects at other levels are not immediately apparent. Likert[20] points to an unrecognized dysfunctionality in a number of cost-reduction drives and crash programs for immediate productivity increases. Research indicated that pressure drives for increased production in a well-established organization yielded substantial and immediate increases in productivity. Hidden, however, was the fact that these gains came through a "liquidation of human assets." Hostilities increased, there was a greater reliance upon authority, loyalties declined,

[18] P. R. Lawrence, et al., *Organizational Behavior and Administration*. Rev. ed. Homewood, Ill.: Irwin-Dorsey, 1965, p. 405.

[19] L. M. Alcott, "Transcendental Wild Oats," from *Silver Pitchers*, 1876. Reprinted in *The Transcendentalist Revolt Against Materialism*, G. F. Whicher, ed. Boston: D.C. Heath & Co., 1949.

[20] R. Likert, *New Patterns of Management*. New York: McGraw Hill Book Co., Inc., 1961, pp. 61–76. Also see R. Likert and S. Seashore, "Making Cost Control Work," *Harvard Business Review*, November–December, 1963.

motivation to restrict production began to increase and eventually turnover increased. The liquidation of these assets was not reflected in standard organizational measures of profit and loss for several quarters. Yet
eventually even these measures came to show that the cost to the organization had been much higher than the initial savings.

When we begin to raise into question such "good" things as cost reduction and drives for greater productivity, we must underscore a point
which may have already become apparent to the reader. We should be
forewarned when we try to take a multifunctional approach to organizational analysis and planning that a certain amount of "tough-mindedness"
will be required. We may have to reexamine some of our most cherished
beliefs. Old friends such as "management prerogatives," "span of control,"
"good human relations," "line-staff," etc., will have to prove themselves
again. Some of our pet antipathies toward organizations, groups, and
individuals will have to be recognized and corrected for. All of us, including the writer, have our hobbyhorses, which we like to ride. But if we are
in earnest about seeking multifunctionality, we cannot take sides with the
organization, the group, or the individual. Instead we shall be forced to
face up to their interdependence.

Let us now turn to the idea of synthesis. We have seen how a recognition
of the interdependence of the parts of an organization complicates our
view of organizational change. Because the actions of any part of the
organization affect all other parts, our analysis of the consequences of
any behavior must take into account a number of things at once. Yet the
very interconnectedness of the parts of the organization and the overlapping of the systems we have mentioned raise the possibility of reducing
this complexity through a process of *synthesis*. Some procedures, norms,
practices, and rules tend to be functional at all three levels *at once*. They
do several pieces of work simultaneously. The needs of the organization,
the group, and the individual are all addressed by a single act. Thus a
real economy is achieved.

To illustrate such a synthesis, we shall return to the Marshall Company.
We shall examine the norms and mechanisms related to training, learning,
and promotion. We watched Nichols both training and being trained as he
helped to start up machine Number 9. Graham stood in the background
and watched. Nichols reported that:

Graham doesn't say much to me when I'm starting up a machine. Later on,
he will tell me things he thought might have been improved—even some of the
little things. But now, he won't bother me.

We read how Nichols allowed the second hand to try to thread the
paper on the thread rolls till it became fairly clear that he was temporarily
"in over his head" and needed help. Next, we noted that the second hand

allowed the third hand to try out the second hand's tasks, *if he showed an interest*. The second hand describes what he was doing as follows:

You really just learn by doing. You master your own job, and then you watch the next fellow working, and do as much as you can. Of course, some of the guys think if you do your own job and then stop, that's what you get paid for. But you don't learn anything that way.

MURRAY:    Isn't there any feeling that you cut in on someone else's job by learning it?

BOLTON:    Oh, no. You can do as much as you know how. A good man will keep you busy answering his questions, and when he does that, you bring him along. Of course, the thing is, you've gotta keep learning so you know more than the other guys. (Al paused and seemed for several seconds to be thinking intently.) There's one fellow—he's no good. He came over from the other side of the river during the war and worked up to be second hand. Now, guys are coming back from the service who know more than he does. Men under him are better than he is, but he gives orders and pretends to know more than anyone else. No one likes him.

The same procedure worked at all levels in the organization. Dudley, talking about people at the management level, informed the researcher that a man is allowed to take on as much responsibility as he thinks he can handle. He promotes himself. He is not pushed. But he *is* held responsible for his performance. He can get help and coaching when he wants it, but it isn't pushed on him. If he is able to handle the new responsibility, his reputation and influence increase and he can take on more responsibility. If he tries to move beyond his capacity, he loses reputation and influence.

What kind of synthesis do we observe? Along the individual dimension, an employee is allowed to seek security at the level he finds comfortable. He isn't pushed or punished for staying there. But he also has the opportunity to learn, grow, and test himself. The group activities and norms are built around the helping, teaching exchange. Douglas was being ostracized for giving orders rather than learning and teaching. Trying to move too fast without learning the skills involved was similarly punished. Social satisfactions were derived from the exchange of knowledge and skill for esteem. The learner was obligated to ask for help, the person with greater knowledge was obligated to help. The organization was served well by an effective placement-training system, an effective reward system (taking responsibility, high performance, teaching, and learning were rewarded), and a set of attitudes which stressed organizational loyalty and fostered change.

The more dramatic synthesis is illustrated in the British Coal Industries case.[21] The workers on one shift (the fillers) were dependent on the

---

[21] P. R. Lawrence, *et al., Organizational Behavior and Administration*. Homewood, Ill.: Irwin-Dorsey, 1961 p. 107.

workers on a prior shift with little interaction and no control over the men in the prior shift. In their dependent isolation, the fillers were often depressed and outraged. To protect themselves, they formed collusive small groups, leaving the old, ill, and helpless without support. Secrecy, mistrust, and mutual scapegoating prevailed. Absenteeism was high, productivity was low, and the miners were leaving the coal fields.

Finally, an organizational innovation was discovered at one mine and applied to others. Under the new composite system, instead of one shift doing all the cutting and another shift doing all the filling, each shift took up the work where the group from the previous shift left off. When they completed that phase, they redeployed to the next task. Moreover, all the men from the three shifts were formed into a single self-selected composite group. The members were given the responsibility for distributing the task and shifts among themselves. Control over the interaction between men on different parts of the cycle was now in the hands of the cycle group.

Partly because the new pattern followed an earlier tradition and partly because the new pattern met the needs of the men in the situation, the new pattern produced significant changes. Individual isolation and victimization dropped. Absenteeism declined. The composite group developed a sense of mutual responsibility and the amount of unnecessary work created by one shift for another by careless work or from technical breakdowns dropped from 25 percent to 5 percent of the men's time. Less supervision was required, and productivity was 17 percent greater. Thus improvement along all three dimensions was synthesized in one change.

The illustrations from the Marshall and British Coal cases, as reported here, do not reflect the painful difficulty or the drain on time involved in working out this synthesis. They are in no way meant to minimize the difficulty of finding multifunctional solutions to organizational problems. On the contrary, they are cited to illustrate some kinds of creative solutions to problems.

## THE LEGITIMACY OF ORGANIZATIONAL PLANNING

Having gotten more deeply into the criteria for planning and instituting organizational change, a number of readers may have come face-to-face with an uneasy feeling about the legitimacy of planning at all. Isn't this manipulation? Instead of leaving this as an uneasy feeling, let us confront it. In fact, we are all constantly engaged in the process of influencing those around us, though we may not admit it. As long as we keep this process intuitive and the criteria implicit, the question of manipulation does not seem to arise. But when we try to state explicit criteria, questions concerning Machiavellianism and manipulation immediately appear. We tend to feel no concern about introducing a new budgetary control system until we explicitly take into account how it will change behavior. Yet attempts to influence others when we do not consciously consider our effect are more likely to be detrimental than open conscious planning. There is nothing humanistically wrong with planning per se. It is planning without knowledge or awareness which is humanistically wrong, to say nothing of inefficient.

The problem of excessive conformity in our society, if there is one, is not fostered by organizational planning per se, but by the kinds of models used. The reader may take issue with the organizational model presented here, but not with the process of conscious planning. This discussion has advocated a multifunctional planning model which addresses simultaneously the needs of the organization, the work group, and the individual. It provides one model which we may find useful. But whether this exact scheme is personally useful to each reader is secondary. More important is that each of us adopts some point of view large enough to include the other points of view which exist in any situation.

# The Human Side of Enterprise*

## DOUGLAS MURRAY McGREGOR

It has become trite to say that industry has the fundamental know-how to utilize physical science and technology for the material benefit of mankind, and that we must now learn how to utilize the social sciences to make our human organizations truly effective.

To a degree, the social sciences today are in a position like that of the physical sciences with respect to atomic energy in the thirties. We know that past conceptions of the nature of man are inadequate and, in many ways, incorrect. We are becoming quite certain that, under proper conditions, unimagined resources of creative human energy could become available within the organizational setting.

We cannot tell industrial management how to apply this new knowledge in simple, economic ways. We know it will require years of exploration, much costly development research, and a substantial amount of creative imagination on the part of management to discover how to apply this growing knowledge to the organization of human effort in industry.

### MANAGEMENT'S TASK: THE CONVENTIONAL VIEW

The conventional conception of management's task in harnessing human energy to organizational requirements can be stated broadly in terms of three propositions. In order to avoid the complications introduced by a label, let us call this set of propositions *Theory X*:

1. Management is responsible for organizing the elements of productive enterprise—money, materials, equipment, people—in the interest of economic ends.

* Adventures in Thought and Action: Proceedings of the Fifth Anniversary Convocation of the School of Industrial Management, M.I.T., Cambridge, Mass., April 9, 1957 (Cambridge, Mass.: Technology Press, 1957), by permission.

2. With respect to people, this is a process of directing their efforts, motivating them, controlling their actions, modifying their behavior to fit the needs of the organization.
3. Without this active intervention by management, people would be passive, even resistant, to organizational needs. They must therefore be persuaded, rewarded, punished, controlled—their activities must be directed. This is management's task. We often sum it up by saying that management consists of getting things done through other people.

Behind this conventional theory there are several additional beliefs—less explicit, but widespread:

4. The average man is by nature indolent—he works as little as possible.
5. He lacks ambition, dislikes responsibility, prefers to be led.
6. He is inherently self-centered, indifferent to organizational needs.
7. He is by nature resistant to change.
8. He is gullible, not very bright, the ready dupe of the charlatan and the demagogue.

The human side of economic enterprise today is fashioned from propositions and beliefs such as these. Conventional organization structures and managerial policies, practices, and programs reflect these assumptions. In accomplishing its task, with these assumptions as guides, management has conceived of a range of possibilities.

At one extreme, management can be "hard" or "strong." The methods for directing behavior involve coercion and threat (usually disguised), close supervision, tight controls over behavior. At the other extreme, management can be "soft" or "weak." The methods for directing behavior involve being permissive, satisfying people's demands, achieving harmony. Then they will be tractable, accept direction.

This range has been fairly completely explored during the past half century, and management has learned some things from the exploration. There are difficulties in the "hard" approach. Force breeds counter forces: restriction of output, antagonism, militant unionism, subtle but effective sabotage of management objectives. This "hard" approach is especially difficult during times of full employment.

There are also difficulties in the "soft" approach. It leads frequently to the abdication of management—to harmony, perhaps, but to indifferent performance. People take advantage of the soft approach. They continually expect more, but they give less and less.

Currently, the popular theme is "firm but fair." This is an attempt to gain the advantages of both the hard and the soft approaches. It is reminiscent of Teddy Roosevelt's "speak softly and carry a big stick."

## IS THE CONVENTIONAL VIEW CORRECT?

The findings which are beginning to emerge from the social sciences challenge this whole set of beliefs about man and human nature and about the task of management. The evidence is far from conclusive, certainly, but it is suggestive. It comes from the laboratory, the clinic, the schoolroom, the home, and even to a limited extent from industry itself.

The social scientist does not deny that human behavior in industrial organization today is approximately what management perceives it to be. He has, in fact, observed it and studied it fairly extensively. But he is pretty sure that this behavior is *not* a consequence of man's inherent nature. It is a consequence rather of the nature of industrial organizations, of management philosophy, policy, and practice. The conventional approach of Theory X is based on mistaken notions of what is cause and what is effect.

Perhaps the best way to indicate why the conventional approach of management is inadequate is to consider the subject of motivation.

### Physiological Needs

Man is a wanting animal; as soon as one of his needs is satisfied, another appears in its place. This process is unending. It continues from birth to death.

Man's needs are organized in a series of levels—a hierarchy of importance. At the lowest level, but preeminent in importance when they are thwarted, are his *physiological needs*. Man lives for bread alone when there is no bread. Unless the circumstances are unusual, his needs for love, for status, for recognition are inoperative when his stomach has been empty for a while. But when he eats regularly and adequately, hunger ceases to be an important motivation. The same is true of the other physiological needs of man—rest, exercise, shelter, protection from the elements.

A *satisfied need is not a motivator of behavior!* This is a fact of profound significance that is regularly ignored in the conventional approach to the management of people. Consider your own need for air: Except as you are deprived of it, it has no appreciable motivating effect upon your behavior.

### Safety Needs

When the physiological needs are reasonably satisfied, needs at the next higher level begin to dominate man's behavior—to motivate him. These are called *safety needs*. They are needs for protection against danger, threat, deprivation. Some people mistakenly refer to these as needs for security. However, unless man is in a dependent relationship where he fears arbitrary deprivation, he does not demand security. The need is for the "fairest possible break." When he is confident of this, he is more than willing to take risks. But when he feels threatened or dependent, his greatest need is for guarantees, for protection, for security.

The fact needs little emphasis that, since every industrial employee is in a dependent relationship, safety needs may assume considerable importance. Arbitrary management actions, behavior which arouses uncertainty with respect to continued employment or which reflects favoritism or discrimination, unpredictable administration of policy—these can be powerful motivators of the safety needs in the employment relationship *at every level,* from worker to vice president.

## Social Needs

When man's physiological needs are satisfied and he is no longer fearful about his physical welfare, his *social needs* become important motivators of his behavior—needs for belonging, for association, for acceptance by his fellows, for giving and receiving friendship and love.

Management knows today of the existence of these needs, but it often assumes quite wrongly that they represent a threat to the organization. Many studies have demonstrated that the tightly knit, cohesive work group may, under proper conditions, be far more effective than an equal number of separate individuals in achieving organizational goals.

Yet management, fearing group hostility to its own objectives, often goes to considerable lengths to control and direct human efforts in ways that are inimical to the natural "groupiness" of human beings. When man's social needs—and perhaps his safety needs, too—are thus thwarted, he behaves in ways which tend to defeat organizational objectives. He becomes resistant, antagonistic, uncooperative. But this behavior is a consequence, not a cause.

## Ego Needs

Above the social needs, in the sense that they do not become motivators until lower needs are reasonably satisfied, are the needs of greatest significance to management and to man himself. They are the *egoistic needs,* and they are of two kinds:

1. Those needs that relate to one's self-esteem—needs for self-confidence, for independence, for achievement, for competence, for knowledge.
2. Those needs that relate to one's reputation—needs for status, for recognition, for appreciation, for the deserved respect of one's fellows.

Unlike the lower needs, these are rarely satisfied; man seeks indefinitely for more satisfaction of these needs once they have become important to him. But they do not appear in any significant way until physiological, safety, and social needs are all reasonably satisfied.

The typical industrial organization offers few opportunities for the satisfaction of these egoistic needs to people at lower levels in the hierarchy. The conventional methods of organizing work, particularly in mass-production industries, give little heed to these aspects of human motivation. If the practices of scientific management were deliberately calculated to thwart these needs, they could hardly accomplish this purpose better than they do.

### Self-Fulfillment Needs

Finally—a capstone, as it were, on the hierarchy of man's needs—there are what we may call the *needs for self-fulfillment*. These are the needs for realizing one's own potentialities, for continued self-development, for being creative in the broadest sense of that term.

It is clear that the conditions of modern life give only limited opportunity for these relatively weak needs to obtain expression. The deprivation most people experience with respect to other lower-level needs diverts their energies into the struggle to satisfy *those* needs, and the needs for self-fulfillment remain dormant.

### MANAGEMENT AND MOTIVATION

We recognize readily enough that a man suffering from a severe dietary deficiency is sick. The deprivation of physiological needs has behavioral consequences. The same is true—although less well recognized—of deprivation of higher-level needs. The man whose needs for safety, association, independence, or status are thwarted is sick just as surely as the man who has rickets. And his sickness will have behavioral consequences. We will be mistaken if we attribute his resultant passivity, his hostility, his refusal to accept responsibility to his inherent "human nature." These forms of behavior are *symptoms* of illness—of deprivation of his social and egoistic needs.

The man whose lower-level needs are satisfied is not motivated to satisfy those needs any longer. For practical purposes they exist no longer. Management often asks, "Why aren't people more productive? We pay good wages, provide good working conditions, have excellent fringe benefits and steady employment. Yet people do not seem to be willing to put forth more than minimum effort."

The fact that management has provided for these physiological and safety needs has shifted the motivational emphasis to the social and perhaps to the egoistic needs. Unless there are opportunities *at work* to satisfy these higher-level needs, people will be deprived, and their behavior will reflect this deprivation. Under such conditions, if management continues to focus its attention on physiological needs, its efforts are bound to be ineffective.

People *will* make insistent demands for more money under these conditions. It becomes more important than ever to buy the material goods and services which can provide limited satisfaction of the thwarted needs. Although money has only limited value in satisfying many higher-level needs, it can become the focus of interest if it is the *only* means available.

## The Carrot-and Stick Approach

The carrot-and-stick theory of motivation (like Newtonian physical theory) works reasonably well under certain circumstances. The *means* for satisfying man's physiological and (within limits) his safety needs can be provided or withheld by management. Employment itself is such a means, and so are wages, working conditions, and benefits. By these means the individual can be controlled so long as he is struggling for subsistence.

But the carrot-and-stick theory does not work at all once man has reached an adequate subsistence level and is motivated primarily by higher needs. Management cannot provide a man with self-respect, or with the respect of his fellows, or with the satisfaction of needs for self-fulfillment. It can create such conditions that he is encouraged and enabled to seek such satisfactions *for himself,* or it can thwart him by failing to create those conditions.

But this creation of conditions is not "control." It is not a good device for directing behavior. And so management finds itself in an odd position. The high standard of living created by our modern technological knowhow provides quite adequately for the satisfaction of physiological and safety needs. The only significant exception is where management practices have not created confidence in a "fair break"—and thus where safety needs are thwarted. But by making possible the satisfaction of low-level needs, management has deprived itself of the ability to use as motivators the devices on which conventional theory has taught it to rely—rewards, promises, incentives, or threats and other coercive devices.

The philosophy of management by direction and control—*regardless of whether it is hard or soft*—is inadequate to motivate because the human needs on which this approach relies are today unimportant motivators of behavior. Direction and control are essentially useless in motivating people whose important needs are social and egoistic. Both the hard and the soft approach fail today because they are simply irrelevant to the situation.

People, deprived of opportunities to satisfy at work the needs which are now important to them, behave exactly as we might predict—with indolence, passivity, resistance to change, lack of responsibility, willingness to follow the demagogue, unreasonable demands for economic benefits. It would seem that we are caught in a web of our own weaving.

## A NEW THEORY OF MANAGEMENT

For these and many other reasons, we require a different theory of the task of managing people based on more adequate assumptions about human nature and human motivation. I am going to be so bold as to suggest the broad dimensions of such a theory. Call it *Theory Y*, if you will.

1. Management is responsible for organizing the elements of productive enterprise—money, materials, equipment, people—in the interest of economic ends.
2. People are *not* by nature passive or resistant to organizational needs. They have become so as a result of experience in organizations.
3. The motivation, the potential for development, the capacity for assuming responsibility, the readiness to direct behavior toward organizational goals are all present in people. Management does not put them there. It is a responsibility of management to make it possible for people to recognize and develop these human characteristics for themselves.
4. The essential task of management is to arrange organizational conditions and methods of operation so that people can achieve their own goals *best* by directing *their own* efforts toward organizational objectives.

This is a process primarily of creating opportunities, releasing potential, removing obstacles, encouraging growth, providing guidance. It is what Peter Drucker has called "management by objectives" in contrast to "management by control." It does *not* involve the abdication of management, the absence of leadership, the lowering of standards, or the other characteristics usually associated with the "soft" approach under Theory X.

### Some Difficulties

It is no more possible to create an organization today which will be a full, effective application of this theory than it was to build an atomic power plant in 1945. There are many formidable obstacles to overcome.

The conditions imposed by conventional organization theory and by the approach of scientific management for the past half century have tied men to limited jobs which do not utilize their capabilities, have discouraged the acceptance of responsibility, have encouraged passivity, have eliminated meaning from work. Man's habits, attitudes, expectations—his whole conception of membership in an industrial organization—have been conditioned by his experience under these circumstances.

People today are accustomed to being directed, manipulated, controlled in industrial organizations and to finding satisfaction for their social, egoistic, and self-fulfillment needs away from the job. This is true of much of management as well as of workers. Genuine "industrial citizenship" (to borrow again a term from Drucker) is a remote and unrealistic idea, the meaning of which has not even been considered by most members of industrial organizations.

Another way of saying this is that Theory X places exclusive reliance upon external control of human behavior, while Theory Y relies heavily on self-control and self-direction. It is worth noting that this difference is the difference between treating people as children and treating them as mature adults. After generations of the former, we cannot expect to shift to the latter overnight.

### Steps in the Right Direction

Before we are overwhelmed by the obstacles, let us remember that the application of theory is always slow. Progress is usually achieved in small steps. Some innovative ideas which are entirely consistent with Theory Y are today being applied with some success.

*Decentralization and Delegation.*   These are ways of freeing people from the too-close control of conventional organization, giving them a degree of freedom to direct their own activities, to assume responsibility, and, importantly, to satisfy egoistic needs. In this connection, the flat organization of Sears, Roebuck and Company provides an interesting example. It forces "management by objectives," since it enlarges the number of people reporting to a manager until he cannot direct and control them in the conventional manner.

*Job Enlargement.*   This concept, pioneered by I.B.M. and Detroit Edison, is quite consistent with Theory Y. It encourages the acceptance of responsibility at the bottom of the organization; it provides opportunities for satisfying social and egoistic needs. In fact, the reorganization of work at the factory level offers one of the more challenging opportunities for innovation consistent with Theory Y.

*Participation and Consultative Management.*   Under proper conditions, participation and consultative management provide encouragement to people to direct their creative energies toward organizational objectives, give them some voice in decisions that affect them, provide significant opportunities for the satisfaction of social and egoistic needs. The Scanlon Plan is the outstanding embodiment of these ideas in practice.

*Performance Appraisal.*   Even a cursory examination of conventional programs of performance appraisal within the ranks of management will reveal how completely consistent they are with Theory X. In fact, most such programs tend to treat the individual as though he were a product under inspection on the assembly line.

A few companies—among them General Mills, Ansul Chemical, and

General Electric—have been experimenting with approaches which involve the individual in setting "targets" or objectives *for himself* and in a *self-evaluation* of performance semiannually or annually. Of course, the superior plays an important leadership role in this process—one, in fact, which demands substantially more competence than the conventional approach. The role is, however, considerably more congenial to many managers than the role of "judge" or "inspector" which is usually forced upon them. Above all, the individual is encouraged to take a greater responsibility for planning and appraising his own contribution to organizational objectives; and the accompanying effects on egoistic and self-fulfillment needs are substantial.

### Applying the Ideas

The not infrequent failure of such ideas as these to work as well as expected is often attributable to the fact that a management has "bought the idea" but applied it within the framework of Theory X and its assumptions.

Delegation is not an effective way of exercising management by control. Participation becomes a farce when it is applied as a sales gimmick or a device for kidding people into thinking they are important. Only the management that has confidence in human capacities and is itself directed toward organizational objectives rather than toward the preservation of personal power can grasp the implications of this emerging theory. Such management will find and apply successfully other innovative ideas as we move slowly toward the full implementation of a theory like Y.

### THE HUMAN SIDE OF ENTERPRISE

It is quite possible for us to realize substantial improvements in the effectiveness of industrial organizations during the next decade or two. The social sciences can contribute much to such developments; we are only beginning to grasp the implications of the growing body of knowledge in these fields. But if this conviction is to become a reality instead of a pious hope, we will need to view the process much as we view the process of releasing the energy of the atom for constructive human ends—as a slow, costly, sometimes discouraging approach toward a goal which would seem to many to be quite unrealistic.

The ingenuity and the perseverance of industrial management in the pursuit of economic ends have changed many scientific and technological dreams into commonplace realities. It is now becoming clear that the application of these same talents to the human side of enterprise will not only enhance substantially these materialistic achievements, but will bring us one step closer to "the good society."

# One More Time: How Do You Motivate Employees?*

FREDERICK HERZBERG

How MANY ARTICLES, books, speeches, and workshops have pleaded plaintively, "How do I get an employee to do what I want him to do?" The psychology of motivation is tremendously complex, and what has been unraveled with any degree of assurance is small indeed. But the dismal ratio of knowledge to speculation has not dampened the enthusiasm for new forms of snake oil that are constantly coming on the market, many of them with academic testimonials. Doubtless this article will have no depressing impact on the market for snake oil, but since the ideas expressed in it have been tested in many corporations and other organizations, it will help—I hope—to redress the imbalance in the aforementioned ratio.

## "MOTIVATING" WITH KITA

In lectures to industry on the problem, I have found that the audiences are anxious for quick and practical answers, so I will begin with a straight-forward, practical formula for moving people.

What is the simplest, surest, and most direct way of getting someone to do something? Ask him? But if he responds that he does not want to do it, then that calls for a psychological consultation to determine the reason for his obstinacy. Tell him? His response shows that he does not understand you, and now an expert in communication methods has to be brought in to show you how to get through to him. Give him a monetary incentive? I do not need to remind the reader of the complexity and difficulty involved in setting up and administering an incentive system. Show him? This means a costly training program. We need a simple way.

Every audience contains the "direct action" manager who shouts, "Kick him!" And this type of manager is right. The surest and least circumlocuted

* Reprinted by permission from *Harvard Business Review*, January–February issue 1968, pp. 53–62.

way of getting someone to do something is to kick him in the pants—give him what might be called the KITA.

There are various forms of KITA, and here are some of them:

**Negative Physical KITA.**  This is a literal application of the term and was frequently used in the past. It has, however, three major drawbacks: (1) it is inelegant; (2) it contradicts the precious image of benevolence that most organizations cherish; and (3) since it is a physical attack, it directly stimulates the automatic nervous system, and this often results in negative feedback—the employee may just kick you in return. These factors give rise to certain taboos against negative physical KITA.

The psychologist has come to the rescue of those who are no longer permitted to use negative physical KITA. He has uncovered infinite sources of psychological vulnerabilities and the appropriate methods to play tunes on them. "He took my rug away"; "I wonder what he meant by that"; "the boss is always going around me"—these symptomatic expressions of ego sores that have been rubbed raw are the result of application of:

**Negative Psychological KITA.**  This has several advantages over negative physical KITA. First, the cruelty is not visible; the bleeding is internal and comes much later. Second, since it affects the higher cortical centers of the brain with its inhibitory powers, it reduces the possibility of physical backlash. Third, since the number of psychological pains that a person can feel is almost infinite, the direction and site possibilities of the KITA are increased many times. Fourth, the person administering the kick can manage to be above it all and let the system accomplish the dirty work. Fifth, those who practice it receive some ego satisfaction (one-upmanship), whereas they would find drawing blood abhorrent. Finally, if the employee does complain, he can always be accused of being paranoid, since there is no tangible evidence of an actual attack.

Now, what does negative KITA accomplish? If I kick you in the rear (physically or psychologically), who is motivated? *I* am motivated; *you* move! Negative KITA does not lead to motivation, but to movement. So:

**Positive KITA.**  Let us consider motivation. If I say to you, "Do this for me or the company, and in return I will give you a reward, an incentive, more status, a promotion, all the quid pro quos that exist in the industrial organization," am I motivating you? The overwhelming opinion I receive from management people is, "Yes, this is motivation."

I have a year-old Schnauzer. When it was a small puppy and I wanted it to move, I kicked it in the rear and it moved. Now that I have finished its obedience training, I hold up a dog biscuit when I want the Schnauzer to move. In this instance, who is motivated—I or the dog? The dog wants the biscuit, but it is I who want it to move. Again, I am the one who is motivated, and the dog is the one who moves. In this instance all I did was apply KITA frontally; I exerted a pull instead of a push. When industry wishes to use such positive KITA's, it has available an incredible number and variety of dog biscuits (jelly beans for humans) to wave in front of the employee to get him to jump.

Why is it that managerial audiences are quick to see that negative KITA is *not* motivation, while they are almost unanimous in their judgment that positive KITA *is* motivation? It is because negative KITA is rape, and positive KITA is seduction. But it is infinitely worse to be seduced than to be raped; the latter is an unfortunate occurrence, while the former signifies that you were a party to your own downfall. This is why positive KITA is so popular: it is a tradition; it is in the American way. The organization does not have to kick you; you kick yourself.

## Myths about Motivation

Why is KITA not motivation? If I kick my dog (from the front or the back), he will move. And when I want him to move again, what must I do? I must kick him again. Similarly, I can charge a man's battery, and then recharge it, and recharge it again. But it is only when he has his own generator that we can talk about motivation. He then needs no outside stimulation. He *wants* to do it.

With this in mind, we can review some positive KITA personnel practices that were developed as attempts to instill "motivation":

1. *Reducing Time Spent at Work.*   This represents a marvelous way of motivating people to work—getting them off the job! We have reduced (formally and informally) the time spent on the job over the last 50 or 60 years until we are finally on the way to the "6½-day weekend." An interesting variant of this approach is the development of off-hour recreation programs. The philosophy here seems to be that those who play together, work together. The fact is that motivated people seek more hours of work, not fewer.

2. *Spiraling Wages.*   Have these motivated people? Yes, to seek the next wage increase. Some medievalists still can be heard to say that a good depression will get employees moving. They feel that if rising wages don't or won't do the job, perhaps reducing them will.

3. *Fringe Benefits.*   Industry has outdone the most welfare-minded of welfare states in dispensing cradle-to-the-grave succor. One company I know of had an informal "fringe benefit of the month club" going for a while. The cost of fringe benefits in this country has reached approximately 25 percent of the wage dollar, and we still cry for motivation.

People spend less time working for more money and more security than ever before, and the trend cannot be reversed. These benefits are no longer rewards; they are rights. A 6-day week is inhuman, a 10-hour day is exploitation, extended medical coverage is a basic decency, and stock options are the salvation of American initiative. Unless the ante is continuously raised, the psychological reaction of employees is that the company is turning back the clock.

When industry began to realize that both the economic nerve and the lazy nerve of their employees had insatiable appetites, it started to listen to the behavioral scientists who, more out of a humanist tradition than from scientific study, criticized management for not knowing how to deal with people. The next KITA easily followed.

**4. Human Relations Training.** Over 30 years of teaching and, in many instances, of practicing psychological approaches to handling people have resulted in costly human relations programs and, in the end, the same question: How do you motivate workers? Here, too, escalations have taken place. Thirty years ago it was necessary to request, "Please don't spit on the floor." Today the same admonition requires three "please"s before the employee feels that his superior has demonstrated the psychologically proper attitudes toward him.

The failure of human relations training to produce motivation led to the conclusion that the supervisor or manager himself was not psychologically true to himself in his practice of interpersonal decency. So an advanced form of human relations KITA, sensitivity training, was unfolded.

**5. Sensitivity Training.** Do you really, really understand yourself? Do you really, really, really trust the other man? Do you really, really, really, really cooperate? The failure of sensitivity training is now being explained, by those who have become opportunistic exploiters of the technique, as a failure to really (five times) conduct proper sensitivity training courses.

With the realization that there are only temporary gains from comfort and economic and interpersonal KITA, personnel managers concluded that the fault lay not in what they were doing, but in the employee's failure to appreciate what they were doing. This opened up the field of communications, a whole new area of "scientifically" sanctioned KITA.

**6. Communications.** The professor of communications was invited to join the faculty of management training programs and help in making employees understand what management was doing for them. House organs, briefing sessions, supervisory instruction on the importance of communication, and all sorts of propaganda have proliferated until today there is even an International Council of Industrial Editors. But no motivation resulted, and the obvious thought occurred that perhaps management was not hearing what the employees were saying. That led to the next KITA.

**7. Two-Way Communication.** Management ordered morale surveys, suggestion plans, and group participation programs. Then both employees and management were communicating and listening to each other more than ever, but without much improvement in motivation.

The behavioral scientists began to take another look at their conceptions and their data, and they took human relations one step further. A glimmer of truth was beginning to show through in the writings of the so-called higher-order-need psychologists. People, so they said, want to actualize themselves. Unfortunately, the "actualizing" psychologists got mixed up with the human relations psychologists, and a new KITA emerged.

**8. Job Participation.** Though it may not have been the theoretical intention, job participation often became a "give them the big picture" approach. For example, if a man is tightening 10,000 nuts a day on an assembly line with a torque wrench, tell him he is building a Chevrolet. Another approach had the goal of giving the employee a *feeling* that he is determining, in some measure, what he does on his job. The goal was to provide a *sense* of achievement rather than a substantive achievement in his task. Real achievement, of course, requires a task that makes it possible.

But still there is no motivation. This led to the inevitable conclusion that the employees must be sick, and therefore to the next KITA.

**9. Employee Counseling.** The initial use of this form of KITA in a systematic fashion can be credited to the Hawthorne experiment of the Western Electric Company during the early 1930's. At that time, it was found that the employees harbored irrational feelings that were interfering with the rational operation of the factory. Counseling in this instance was a means of letting the employees unburden themselves by talking to someone about their problems. Although the counseling techniques were primitive, the program was large indeed.

The counseling approach suffered as a result of experiences during World War II, when the programs themselves were found to be interfering with the operation of the organizations; the counselors had forgotten their role of benevolent listeners and were attempting to do something about the problems that they heard about. Psychological counseling, however, has managed to survive the negative impact of World War II experiences and today is beginning to flourish with renewed sophistication. But, alas, many of these programs, like all the others, do not seem to have lessened the pressure of demands to find out how to motivate workers.

Since KITA results only in short-term movement, it is safe to predict that the cost of these programs will increase steadily and new varieties will be developed as old positive KITA's reach their satiation points.

## HYGIENE VS. MOTIVATORS

Let me rephrase the perennial question this way: How do you install a generator in an employee? A brief review of my motivation-hygiene theory of job attitudes is required before theoretical and practical suggestions can be offered. The theory was first drawn from an examination of events in the lives of engineers and accountants. At least 16 other investigations, using a wide variety of populations (including some in the Communist countries), have since been completed, making the original research one of the most replicated studies in the field of job attitudes.

The findings of these studies, along with corroboration from many other investigations using different procedures, suggest that the factors involved in producing job satisfaction (and motivation) are separate and distinct from the factors that lead to job dissatisfaction. Since separate factors need to be considered, depending on whether job satisfaction or job dissatisfaction is being examined, it follows that these two feelings are not opposites of each other. The opposite of job satisfaction is not job dissatisfaction but, rather, *no* job satisfaction; and, similarly, the opposite of job dissatisfaction is not job satisfaction, but *no* job dissatisfaction.

Stating the concept presents a problem in semantics, for we normally think of satisfaction and dissatisfaction as opposites—i.e., what is not satisfying must be dissatisfying, and vice versa. But when it comes to understanding the behavior of people in their jobs, more than a play on words is involved.

Two different needs of man are involved here. One set of needs can be thought of as stemming from his animal nature—the built-in drive to avoid pain from the environment, plus all the learned drives which become conditioned to the basic biological needs. For example, hunger, a basic biological drive, makes it necessary to earn money, and then money becomes a specific drive. The other set of needs relates to that unique human characteristic, the ability to achieve and, through achievement, to experience psychological growth. The stimuli for the growth needs are tasks that induce growth; in the industrial setting, they are the *job content*. Contrariwise, the stimuli inducing pain-avoidance behavior are found in the *job environment*.

The growth or *motivator* factors that are intrinsic to the job are: achievement, recognition for achievement, the work itself, responsibility, and growth or advancement. The dissatisfaction-avoidance or *hygiene* (KITA) factors that are extrinsic to the job include: company policy and administration, supervision, interpersonal relationships, working conditions, salary, status, and security.

A composite of the factors that are involved in causing job satisfaction and job dissatisfaction, drawn from samples of 1,685 employees, is shown in Exhibit 1. The results indicate that motivators were the primary cause of satisfaction, and hygiene factors the primary cause of unhappiness on the job. The employees, studied in 12 different investigations, included lower-level supervisors, professional women, agricultural administrators, men about to retire from management positions, hospital maintenance personnel, manufacturing supervisors, nurses, food handlers, military officers, engineers, scientists, housekeepers, teachers, technicians, female assemblers, accountants, Finnish foremen, and Hungarian engineers.

They were asked what job events had occurred in their work that had

## EXHIBIT 1

Factors Affecting Job Attitudes, as Reported in 12 Investigations

Factors characterizing 1844 events on the job that led to *extreme dissatisfaction*
Percentage frequency

Factors characterizing 1753 events on the job that led to *extreme satisfaction*
Percentage frequency

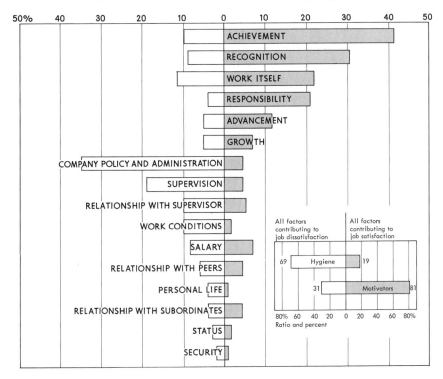

led to extreme satisfaction or extreme dissatisfaction on their part. Their responses are broken down in the exhibit into percentages of total "positive" job events and of total "negative" job events. (The figures total more than 100 percent on both the "hygiene" and "motivators" sides because often at least two factors can be attributed to a single event; advancement, for instance, often accompanies assumption of responsibility.)

To illustrate, a typical response involving achievement that had a negative effect for the employee was, "I was unhappy because I didn't do the job successfully." A typical response in the small number of positive job events in the Company Policy and Administration grouping was, "I was happy because the company reorganized the section so that I didn't report any longer to the guy I didn't get along with."

As the lower right-hand part of the exhibit shows, of all the factors contributing to job satisfaction, 81 percent were motivators. And of all the factors contributing to the employees' dissatisfaction over their work, 69 percent involved hygiene elements.

### Eternal Triangle

There are three general philosophies of personnel management. The first is based on organizational theory, the second on industrial engineering, and the third on behavioral science.

The organizational theorist believes that human needs are either so irrational or so varied and adjustable to specific situations that the major function of personnel management is to be as pragmatic as the occasion demands. If jobs are organized in a proper manner, he reasons, the result will be the most efficient job structure, and the most favorable job attitudes will follow as a matter of course.

The industrial engineer holds that man is mechanistically oriented and economically motivated and his needs are best met by attuning the individual to the most efficient work process. The goal of personnel management therefore should be to concoct the most appropriate incentive system and to design the specific working conditions in a way that facilitates the most efficient use of the human machine. By structuring jobs in a manner that leads to the most efficient operation, the engineer believes that he can obtain the optimal organization of work and the proper work attitudes.

The behavioral scientist focuses on group sentiments, attitudes of individual employees, and the organization's social and psychological climate. According to his persuasion, he emphasizes one or more of the various hygiene and motivator needs. His approach to personnel management generally emphasizes some form of human relations education, in the hope of instilling healthy employee attitudes and in organizational climate which he considers to be felicitous to human values. He believes that proper attitudes will lead to efficient job and organizational structure.

There is always a lively debate as to the overall effectiveness of the approaches of the organizational theorist and the industrial engineer. Manifestly they have achieved much. But the nagging question for the behavioral scientist has been: What is the cost in human problems that eventually cause more expense to the organization—for instance, turnover, absenteeism, errors, violation of safety rules, strikes, restriction of output, higher wages, and greater fringe benefits? On the other hand, the behavioral scientist is hard put to document much manifest improvement in personnel management using his approach.

The three philosophies can be depicted as a triangle, as is done in Exhibit 2, with each persuasion claiming the apex angle. The motivation-hygiene theory claims the same angle as industrial engineering, but for opposite goals. Rather than rationalizing the work to increase efficiency, the theory suggests that work be *enriched* to bring about effective utiliza-

EXHIBIT 2

"Triangle" of Philosophies of Personnel Management

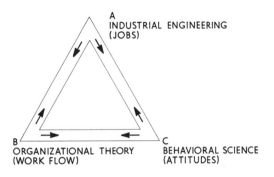

A
INDUSTRIAL ENGINEERING
(JOBS)

B
ORGANIZATIONAL THEORY
(WORK FLOW)

C
BEHAVIORAL SCIENCE
(ATTITUDES)

tion of personnel. Such a systematic attempt to motivate employees by manipulating the motivator factors is just beginning.

The term *job enrichment* describes this embryonic movement. An older term, job enlargement, should be avoided because it is associated with past failures stemming from a misunderstanding of the problem. Job enrichment provides the opportunity for the employee's psychological growth, while job enlargement merely makes a job structurally bigger. Since scientific job enrichment is very new, this article only suggests the principles and practical steps that have recently emerged from several successful experiments in industry.

### Job Loading

In attempting to enrich an employee's job, management often succeeds in reducing the man's personal contribution, rather than giving him an opportunity for growth in his accustomed job. Such an endeavor, which I shall call horizontal job loading (as opposed to vertical loading, or providing motivator factors), has been the problem of earlier job enlargement programs. This activity merely enlarges the meaninglessness of the job. Some examples of this approach, and their effect, are:

1. Challenging the employee by increasing the amount of production expected of him. If he tightens 10,000 bolts a day, see if he can tighten 20,000 bolts a day. The arithmetic involved shows that multiplying zero by zero still equals zero.
2. Adding another meaningless task to the existing one, usually some routine clerical activity. The arithmetic here is adding zero to zero.
3. Rotating the assignments of a number of jobs that need to be enriched. This means washing dishes for a while, then washing silverware. The arithmetic is substituting one zero for another zero.

4. Removing the most difficult parts of the assignment in order to free the worker to accomplish more of the less challenging assignments. This traditional industrial engineering approach amounts to subtraction in the hope of accomplishing addition.

These are common forms of horizontal loading that frequently come up in preliminary brainstorming sessions on job enrichment. The principles of vertical loading have not all been worked out as yet, and they remain rather general, but I have furnished seven useful starting points for consideration in Exhibit 3.

## EXHIBIT 3

### Principles of Vertical Job Loading

| Principle | Motivators Involved |
|---|---|
| A. Removing some controls while retaining accountability | Responsibility and personal achievement |
| B. Increasing the accountability of individuals for own work | Responsibility and recognition |
| C. Giving a person a complete natural unit of work (module, division, area, and so on) | Responsibility, achievement, and recognition |
| D. Granting additional authority to an employee in his activity; job freedom | Responsibility, achievement, and recognition |
| E. Making periodic reports directly available to the worker himself rather than to the supervisor | Internal recognition |
| F. Introducing new and more difficult tasks not previously handled | Growth and learning |
| G. Assigning individuals specific or specialized tasks, enabling them to become experts | Responsibility, growth, and advancement |

### A Successful Application

An example from a highly successful job enrichment experiment can illustrate the distinction between horizontal and vertical loading of a job. The subjects of this study were the stockholder correspondents employed by a very large corporation. Seemingly, the task required of these carefully selected and highly trained correspondents was quite complex and challenging. But almost all indexes of performance and job attitudes were low, and exit interviewing confirmed that the challenge of the job existed merely as words.

A job enrichment project was initiated in the form of an experiment with one group, designated as an achieving unit, having its job enriched by the principles described in Exhibit 3. A control group continued to do its job in the traditional way. (There were also two "uncommitted" groups

of correspondents formed to measure the so-called Hawthorne Effect—
that is, to gauge whether productivity and attitudes toward the job
changed artificially merely because employees sensed that the company
was paying more attention to them in doing something different or novel.
The results for these groups were substantially the same as for the control group, and for the sake of simplicity I do not deal with them in this
summary.) No changes in hygiene were introduced for either group other
than those that would have been made anyway, such as normal pay
increases.

The changes for the achieving unit were introduced in the first two
months, averaging one per week of the seven motivators listed in Exhibit
3. At the end of six months the members of the achieving unit were found
to be outperforming their counterparts in the control group, and in addition indicated a marked increase in their liking for their job. Other results
showed that the achieving group had lower absenteeism and, subsequently, a much higher rate of promotion.

Exhibit 4 illustrates the changes in performance, measured in February
and March, before the study period began, and at the end of each month
of the study period. The shareholder service index represents quality of
letters, including accuracy of information, and speed of response to stock-
holders' letters of inquiry. The index of a current month was averaged

**EXHIBIT 4**

Shareholder Service Index in Company Experiment
(three-month cumulative average)

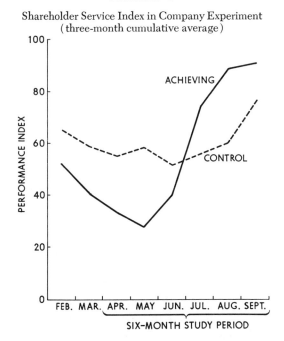

into the average of the two prior months, which means that improvement was harder to obtain if the indexes of the previous months were low. The "achievers" were performing less well before the six-month period started, and their performance service index continued to decline after the introduction of the motivators, evidently because of uncertainty over their newly granted responsibilities. In the third month, however, performance improved, and soon the members of this group had reached a high level of accomplishment.

Exhibit 5 shows the two groups' attitudes toward their job, measured at

**EXHIBIT 5**

Changes in Attitudes toward Tasks in Company Experiment
( changes in mean scores over six-month period )

the end of March, just before the first motivator was introduced, and again at the end of September. The correspondents were asked 16 questions, all involving motivation. A typical one was, "As you see it, how many opportunities do you feel that you have in your job for making worthwhile contributions?" The answers were scaled from 1 to 5, with 80 as the maximum possible score. The achievers became much more positive about their job, while the attitude of the control unit remained about the same (the drop is not statistically significant).

How was the job of these correspondents restructured? Exhibit 6 lists the suggestions made that were deemed to be horizontal loading, and the actual vertical loading changes that were incorporated in the job of the achieving unit. The capital letters under "Principle" after "Vertical Loading" refer to the corresponding letters in Exhibit 3. The reader will note that the rejected forms of horizontal loading correspond closely to the list

**EXHIBIT 6**

Enlargement vs. Enrichment of Correspondents' Tasks in Company Experiment

| Horizontal Loading Suggestions (Rejected) | Vertical Loading Suggestions (Adopted) | Principle |
|---|---|---|
| Firm quotas could be set for letters to be answered each day, using a rate which would be hard to reach. | Subject matter experts were appointed within each unit for other members of the unit to consult with before seeking supervisory help. (The supervisor had been answering all specialized and difficult questions.) | G |
| The women could type the letters themselves, as well as compose them, or take on any other clerical functions. | Correspondents signed their own names on letters. (The supervisor had been signing all letters.) | B |
| All difficult or complex inquiries could be channeled to a few women so that the remainder could achieve high rates of output. These jobs could be exchanged from time to time. | The work of the more experienced correspondents was proofread less frequently by supervisors and was done at the correspondents' desks, dropping verification from 100% to 10%. (Previously, all correspondents' letters had been checked by the supervisor.) | A |
| | Production was discussed, but only in terms such as "a full day's work is expected." As time went on, this was no longer mentioned. (Before, the group had been constantly reminded of the number of letters that needed to be answered.) | D |
| The women could be rotated through units handling different customers, and then sent back to their own units. | Outgoing mail went directly to the mailroom without going over supervisors' desks. (The letters had always been routed through the supervisors.) | A |
| | Correspondents were encouraged to answer letters in a more personalized way. (Reliance on the form-letter approach had been standard practice.) | C |
| | Each correspondent was held personally responsible for the quality and accuracy of letters. (This responsibility had been the province of the supervisor and the verifier.) | B, E |

of common manifestations of the phenomenon enumerated under "Job Loading."

## STEPS TO JOB ENRICHMENT

Now that the motivator idea has been described in practice, here are the steps that managers should take in instituting the principle with their employees:

1. Select those jobs in which (a) the investment in industrial engineering does not make changes too costly, (b) attitudes are poor, (c) hygiene is becoming very costly, and (d) motivation will make a difference in performance.

2. Approach these jobs with the conviction that they can be changed. Years of tradition have led managers to believe that the content of the jobs is sacrosanct and the only scope of action that they have is in ways of stimulating people.

3. Brainstorm a list of changes that may enrich the jobs, without concern for their practicality.

4. Screen the list to eliminate suggestions that involve hygiene, rather than actual motivation.

5. Screen the list for generalities, such as "give them more responsibility," that are rarely followed in practice. This might seem obvious, but the motivator words have never left industry; the substance has just been rationalized and organized out. Words like "responsibility," "growth," "achievement," and "challenge," for example, have been elevated to the lyrics of the patriotic anthem for all organizations. It is the old problem typified by the pledge of allegiance to the flag being more important than contributions to the country—of following the form, rather than the substance.

6. Screen the list to eliminate any *horizontal* loading suggestions.

7. Avoid direct participation by the employees whose jobs are to be enriched. Ideas they have expressed previously certainly constitute a valuable source for recommended changes, but their direct involvement contaminates the process with human relations *hygiene* and, more specifically, gives them only a *sense* of making a contribution. The job is to be changed, and it is the content that will produce the motivation, not attitudes about being involved or the challenge inherent in setting up a job. That process will be over shortly, and it is what the employees will be doing from then on that will determine their motivation. A sense of participation will result only in short-term movement.

8. In the initial attempts at job enrichment, set up a controlled experiment. At least two equivalent groups should be chosen, one an experimental unit in which the motivators are systematically introduced over a period of time, and the other one a control group in which no changes are

made. For both groups, hygiene should be allowed to follow its natural course for the duration of the experiment. Pre- and post-installation tests of performance and job attitudes are necessary to evaluate the effectiveness of the job enrichment program. The attitude test must be limited to motivator items in order to divorce the employee's view of the job he is given from all the surrounding hygiene feelings that he might have.

9. Be prepared for a drop in performance in the experimental group the first few weeks. The changeover to a new job may lead to a temporary reduction in efficiency.

10. Expect your first-line supervisors to experience some anxiety and hostility over the changes you are making. The anxiety comes from their fear that the changes will result in poorer performance for their unit. Hostility will arise when the employees start assuming what the supervisors regard as their own responsibility for performance. The supervisor without checking duties to perform may then be left with little to do.

After a successful experiment, however, the supervisor usually discovers the supervisory and managerial functions he has neglected, or which were never his because all his time was given over to checking the work of his subordinates. For example, in the R&D division of one large chemical company I know of, the supervisors of the laboratory assistants were theoretically responsible for their training and evaluation. These functions, however, had come to be performed in a routine, unsubstantial fashion. After the job enrichment program, during which the supervisors were not merely passive observers of the assistants' performance, the supervisors actually were devoting their time to reviewing performance and administering thorough training.

What has been called an employee-centered style of supervision will come about not through education of supervisors, but by changing the jobs that they do.

## CONCLUDING NOTE

Job enrichment will not be a one-time proposition, but a continuous management function. The initial changes, however, should last for a very long period of time. There are a number of reasons for this:

1. The changes should bring the job up to the level of challenge commensurate with the skill that was hired.
2. Those who have still more ability eventually will be able to demonstrate it better and win promotion to higher-level jobs.
3. The very nature of motivators, as opposed to hygiene factors, is that they have a much longer-term effect on employees' attitudes. Perhaps the job will have to be enriched again, but this will not occur as frequently as the need for hygiene.

Not all jobs can be enriched, nor do all jobs need to be enriched. If only a small percentage of the time and money that is now devoted to hygiene, however, were given to job enrichment efforts, the return in human satisfaction and economic gain would be one of the largest dividends that industry and society have ever reaped through their efforts at better personnel management.

The argument for job enrichment can be summed up quite simply: If you have someone on a job, use him. If you can't use him on the job, get rid of him, either via automation or by selecting someone with lesser ability. If you can't use him and you can't get rid of him, you will have a motivation problem.

# Achievement Motivation and Management Control*

## ROBERT A. STRINGER, JR.

Most adults carry around with them the potential energy to behave in a variety of ways. Whether or not they do behave in these ways depends on (1) the kinds of motives or needs a person has, and (2) the characteristics of the environment.

A person's motivation is said to depend on three factors. First, the "basic" strength of the particular motive; second, the person's expectation that he can satisfy the motive in this situation; and third, the amount of satisfaction the person anticipates.

The final two determinants of aroused motivation are not part of a person's personality. They are not inside the person. They can be considered characteristics of the environment, because they change as the person moves from situation to situation. Different work settings signal to the individual that different kinds of satisfactions can be gained by behaving in certain ways. These signals (or cues) lead to different kinds of motivation. By understanding the varieties of human motivation, managers will be in a better position to control the activities of their subordinates.

It is assumed that every individual personality is composed of a network of these basic motives. Some of the more important motives that have been studied are:

1. Need for achievement—the need for competitive success as measured against some standard of excellence.
2. Need for power—the need for personal influence and control over the means of influencing others.
3. Need for affiliation—the need for close interpersonal relationships and friendships.

* Reprinted from the November–December 1966 issue of *Personnel Administration.* Copyright 1966, by permission from the Society for Personnel Administration, 485–487 National Press Building, 14th and F Street, N.W., Washington, D.C. 20004.

4. Fear of failure—the fear of competition or criticism when involved in an activity that is to be evaluated.

*Motives* are generally acquired during a person's early years, and they remain relatively unchanged in adult life. *Motivation,* however, is determined by the interplay between a person and his environment. Thus a man's *motivated behavior* may change radically throughout his adult life.

## ACHIEVEMENT MOTIVATION

Managers must concern themselves with *motivation to accomplish results.* When a man's motivation to achieve is aroused, accomplishment of the task will be its own best reward. The significance of achievement motivation revolves around this notion of self-reinforcing performance. When we speak of "self-motivated" men, we refer to men who are acting to satisfy their need to achieve.

It is not surprising that McClelland found high levels of achievement motivation associated with entrepreneurial behavior, innovative risk-taking, and business success.[1] Men with a high need to achieve ("high achievers") tend to:

1. Seek and assume high degrees of personal responsibility.
2. Take calculated risks.
3. Set challenging but realistic goals for themselves.
4. Develop comprehensive plans to help them attain their goals.
5. Seek and use concrete, measurable feedback of the results of their actions.
6. Seek out business opportunities where their desires to achieve will not be thwarted.

McClelland has also pointed out that environmental factors greatly influence achievement motivation.[2] This, of course, is consistent with our principles of motivation. But what are the critical dimensions of the environment that influence motivation to achieve? Recent research has sought to answer this question.[3] The implications of this research, although tentative, seem clear. High achievers will be attracted to those business environments which offer:

---

[1] McClelland, D. C., *The Achieving Society.* Princeton, N.J.: Van Nostrand, 1961.

[2] McClelland, D. C., "Toward a Theory of Motive Acquisition," *American Psychologist,* May 1965; "Achievement Motivation Can Be Developed," *Harvard Business Review,* Nov.-Dec. 1965.

[3] Litwin, G. H., & Stringer, R. A., *Motivation and Organizational Climate,* Harvard Graduate School of Business Administration Division of Research (in process); *The Influence of Organizational Climate on Human Motivation,* unpublished monograph, 1966.

1. Personal responsibility for accomplishments.
2. Freedom to pursue goals by means of one's own choosing.
3. Prompt and unbiased feedback of the results of action.
4. Moderately risky situations.
5. Consistent rewards and recognition for jobs well done.

These climatic factors seem to stimulate achievement motivation in the individual. They add up to excitement and satisfaction.

## CLIMATE AND CONTROL

By creating the right kind of climate, managers can have a very definite impact on the achievement motivation of their subordinates. They can present these individuals with new sources of satisfaction and new opportunities to achieve, thereby arousing achievement motivation. Once aroused, achievement-oriented behavior will be self-rewarding. Thus, the manager need not exercise constant and forceful restraint on his subordinate's activities.

An important tool in the hands of management to influence the climate of their organizations and the motivation of their subordinates is the management control system. We will define control systems as those processes and structures by which managers assure that resources and energies are put to work serving the objectives of the organization.

Every individual interprets or perceives the control system differently, and therefore the concept of "organizational climate" is needed. When we speak of environmental influences on human motivation, we are referring to the perceived environment, that is, the climate. (See Exhibit 1.)

**EXHIBIT 1**

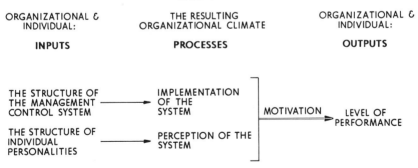

Climate is determined by the structure *and* the implementation of the control system, and the values and attitudes that each manager brings to the job of control. For example, the managers in Division A might be

sticklers for detail and insist on following the prescribed control procedures exactly. Managers in Division B, operating under a very similar structure, may choose to ignore a lot of the detailed rules or procedures. In this
kind of organization, the two divisions may perform very differently. Why?
The answers, on the surface, seem to be obvious. "People in Division A
resent all the rules and regulations." Or, "Division B performs well because
the workers are 'motivated' to do a better job."

Such explanations do not help the manager do his job better. Such
explanations describe, rather than analyze, the causal factors involved.
Analysis requires understanding. This article aims to provide a basis for
better understanding of the dynamics of human motivation in work situations. We will present eight propositions about motivation to achieve.

It is assumed that there is a certain "base level" of motivation to achieve
operative at the present time, but that the full potential of this achievement
motivation is going unrealized. The basic strategy of these eight propositions is to program the management control processes in such a way that
achievement-oriented behavior is reinforced and rewarded.

*Proposition 1.  Achievement motivation will tend to be aroused if the
goals of the responsibility center are made explicit.*

Achievement motivation, by definition, refers to competition with a standard of excellence. This standard may be internal (within the individual's
own mind) or external (stated by the organization within which he works).
By making external performance standards explicit, individuals can include
them in their internal frame of reference. The specific goals and objectives
of the responsibility center can become part of each individual's future
plans. Personal achievement can be defined in terms of the yardsticks and
measurements which are most important to the organization. That is, if
quality is less important than pure volume, it would be dysfunctional for
workers to strive for 100 percent perfect quality. By making the quality
standards explicit—both as to the specific level *and* the relative importance
of other goals—achievement energies can be channeled into more useful
pursuits.

*Proposition 2.  Achievement motivation will tend to be aroused if goals
represent a moderate degree of risk for the individuals involved.*

Individuals with high motivation prefer to work under conditions of
moderate risk. That is, the subjective probabilities of success should be
about 50–50. If goals seem to be speculative and the likelihood of success
is very low, motivation to achieve will not be aroused. If the goals are too
conservative and the likelihood of success is quite high, motivation will not
be aroused. Moderately risky goals represent a continuing challenge, and
it is this element of challenge that must be stated in the goals of the responsibility center and the goals of the individual.

Several alternatives are open to the manager in implementing this proposition. He may assess the chances of success and failure for his subordi-

nates and impose a goal that, in his mind, seems like a moderately risky one. Or he may rely on his subordinate's judgment and opinion, and allow the subordinate some freedom in setting his goals. (See Exhibit 2.)

**EXHIBIT 2**

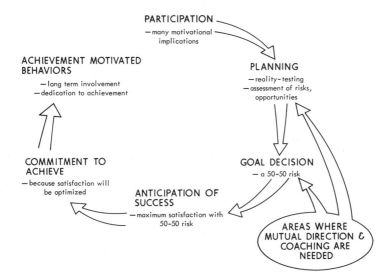

*Proposition 3.* *A higher level of achievement motivation will tend to be aroused if provision is made in the management control process for adjusting specific goals when the chances of goal-accomplishment change significantly (from the 50–50 level).*

The facts of business life are clear: environments are continually changing, and the chances of success change with each change in the environment. Even without any significant change in the environment, the odds of success may change as additional information about the tasks and the critical skills become known. A calculated risk in January may become an impossible goal by May.

To achieve flexibility, there are at least two alternatives open to management. First, the formal reward system could be adjusted to account for the risk elements of performance. Subordinates who succeeded in accomplishing goals that were judged to be 50–50 risks could be paid more than subordinates who worked toward conservative or speculative goals. A second alternative could be to have a provision for systematic review and adjustment of goals when the odds of success deviate significantly from the 50–50 criteria.

The second alternative is the most desirable. By providing for changes in individual and responsibility center goals, the control process will be facilitating the development of achievement motivation. By forcing managers and their subordinates to examine their objectives and by insisting that these objectives remain challenging (that is, with 50–50 odds of accomplishment), the entire climate of the organization can be injected with new excitement and achievement.

**Proposition 4.** *Achievement motivation will tend to be aroused if managers are evaluated in terms of their goal setting behaviors.*

Because of the central importance of goal setting, the creation of an achieving climate will be furthered by zeroing in on this activity when evaluating individual managers.

We are not suggesting that managers be rewarded in proportion to their *performance* compared to the degree of risk (this idea was rejected in 3). Rather, we are suggesting that they be rewarded for setting moderately risky goals.

**Proposition 5.** *Achievement motivation will tend to be aroused if individuals are given feedback of the progress they are making toward their goals.*

Empirical research has found that high achievers characteristically desire concrete feedback of the results of their actions. This feedback not only gives them achievement satisfaction, but it helps them plan ahead and set more realistic goals in the future. Further proof of this point is that high achievers tend to *seek* jobs which provide for immediate and tangible feedback, such as sales positions.

Several aspects of performance feedback are especially important. It should be: (a) prompt, (b) unbiased, and (c) relevant. The implications of these aspects of the feedback process on management control are far-reaching.

When feedback of performance is given, only pertinent information should be used. A wealth of data tends to confuse, rather than motivate, managers. One successful attempt to solve this problem involves the extensive use of graphic presentations.

**Proposition 6.** *Achievement motivation will tend to be aroused if there is a climate that emphasizes individual responsibility.*

High achievers seek success, and unless they can plainly see that their success is truly theirs, little achievement satisfaction can be gained. To increase the opportunity for achievement satisfactions, the organization must place a premium on the assumption of personal responsibility at all levels of management.

In both the goal setting and performance review processes, a climate of responsibility will be created if (1) there is a "results orientation" and (2) there is sufficient "coaching." By focusing on the desired results, the entire achievement syndrome is forced upon the manager, for *a results orientation focuses on those aspects of the subordinate's behavior which are critical to his personal achievement and the achievement of the firm.* Other issues will be placed in secondary positions.

*Proposition 7. Achievement motivation will be aroused if the rewards and punishments formally provided for as part of the management control system are perceived as consistent with achievement goals.*

One consequence of the development of high levels of achievement motivation is that achievement itself becomes the most important reward. High achievers derive most of their satisfaction out of doing a good job, not out of receiving the external rewards associated with success. Formal organizational rewards are important, however, for they satisfy other personal needs and they may *symbolize success.* Thus, careful control of organizational rewards and punishments may be useful in arousing achievement.

Researchers have found that high achievers *expect to be punished* when they fail to achieve their goals. Such expectations seem to make success all the more satisfying. If organizations fail to discriminate between success and failure, or if punishments are not associated with failure to accomplish results, the entire reward system will have relatively little effect on achievement.

The fourth consideration raises important theoretical and practical questions. Rewards and punishments should be dispensed to individuals, not to groups or responsibility centers.

When rewards are given to groups rather than to individuals, personal accomplishments may be buried, making it difficult to arouse entrepreneurial spirit. A formal reward system built around individual rewards for individual accomplishments is more consistent with the six preceding propositions.

*Proposition 8. Achievement motivation will tend to be increased when there is a climate of mutual support and encouragement.*

The theoretical support for this proposition goes beyond the relatively simple concepts of achievement motivation that have been presented earlier. Briefly, it has been found that the motive, fear of failure (or need to avoid failure) debilitates motivation to achieve. A high level of the failure motive will proportionately weaken the resultant achievement motivation.

The creation of a supportive climate tends to reduce anxiety and negate many of the dysfunctional effects that anxiety is likely to have on continued high performance. To stimulate achievement motivation, support must be task-oriented. If task-related support and encouragement is stressed, the entire organizational climate can become "self-generating." That is, *mutual support* will act as a powerful reinforcement device. Coaching, helping, informal encouragements, and other reciprocal supportive relationships can solidify the arousal effects of Propositions 1 through 7.

## SUMMARY

Arousal of achievement motivation is desirable *when there is an entrepreneurial function to be performed.* When risks must be taken, when specific objectives must be set and met, and when individuals must act on their own initiative and live with their results, the proper framework for control revolves around these eight propositions.

The ultimate responsibility for implementation of these new management control processes must lie with line managers. Control personnel can describe and initiate the framework, but they cannot create the on-going working climate that is required. If management succeeds in altering the climate and management control processes, what can be expected? If motivation is aroused and if achievement successes begin to reinforce this arousal, a new spirit of dynamic growth can be fostered. With growth will come new challenges and new risks. But the high achiever can be a selfish soul. Once he tastes success, his appetite is nearly insatiable. Unless the firm can continue to present him with challenges and responsibility, he may seek them elsewhere.

> In vain the sage, with retrospective eye,
> Would from the apparent conclude the why,
> Infer the motive from the deed, and show
> That what we chanced was what we meant to do.
> ALEXANDER POPE, *Moral Essays*

# The New Look in Motivational Theory for Organizational Research*

## J. G. HUNT
## J. W. HILL

DURING THE LAST FEW YEARS the treatment of motivation with respect to industrial and other formal organizations has more often than not been in terms of models by Maslow or Herzberg.[1] Where theories are apparently so thoroughly accepted, one naturally assumes a fairly substantial amount of data leading to empirical verification. However, as we shall show, there is relatively little empirical evidence concerning Maslow's theory; and while there are many studies bearing on Herzberg's theory, it remains controversial. After comparing these two approaches and reviewing their present status, we will describe a newer motivation theory developed by Vroom, which is similar to those developed by Atkinson *et al.* and Edwards in experimental psychology, and Peak, Rosenberg and Fishbein in social psychology.[2] It is our contention, on both theoretical and empirical grounds, that Vroom's theory, more than Maslow's or Herzberg's, is in line with the thinking of contemporary psychologists and industrial sociologists and is the best yet developed for organizational use.

* Reprinted with permission from *Human Organization*, Vol. 28, No. 2 (Summer, 1969), pp. 100–109.

[1] A. H. Maslow, *Motivation and Personality*, New York: Harper and Row, 1954; "A Theory of Human Motivation," *Psychological Review*, Vol. 50, 1943, pp. 370–396; and *Eupsychian Management*, Homewood, Illinois: Irwin-Dorsey, 1965; F. Herzberg, B. Mausner, and B. B. Snyderman, *The Motivation to Work*. New York: Wiley, 1959; and F. Herzberg, *Work and the Nature of Man*. Cleveland, Ohio: World Publishing Co., 1966, pp. 130–131. V. H. Vroom, *Work and Motivation*. New York: Wiley, 1964.

[2] J. W. Atkinson, J. R. Bastian, R. W. Earl, and G. H. Litwin, "The Achievement Motive, Goal Setting, and Probability Preferences," *Journal of Abnormal and Social Psychology*, Vol. 60, 1960, pp. 27–36; W. Edwards, "Behavioral Decision Theory," *Annual Review of Psychology*. Palo Alto, California: Annual Reviews Inc., 1961, pp. 473–499; H. Peak, "Attitude and Motivation," *Nebraska Symposium on Motivation*. Lincoln, Nebraska: University of Nebraska Press, 1955, pp. 148–184. M. Rosenberg, "Cognitive Structure and Attitudinal Affect," *Journal of Abnormal and Social Psychology*, Vol. 53, 1956, pp. 367–372; M. Fishbein, "An Operational Definition of Belief and Attitude," *Human Relations*, Vol. 15, 1962, pp. 35–43.

## THE MASLOW MODEL

Maslow's theory hypothesizes five broad classes of needs arranged in hierarchical levels of prepotency so that when one need level is satisfied, the next level is activated. The levels are: (1) physiological needs; (2) security or safety needs; (3) social, belonging, or membership needs; (4) esteem needs further subdivided into esteem of others and self-esteem including autonomy; and (5) self-actualization or self-fulfillment needs.

The original papers present very little empirical evidence in support of the theory and no research at all that tests the model in its entirety. Indeed, Maslow argues that the theory is primarily a framework for future research. He also discusses at length some of the limitations of the model and readily admits that these needs may be unconscious rather than conscious. While Maslow discusses his model and its limitations in detail, a widely publicized paper by McGregor gives the impression that the model can be accepted without question and also that it is fairly easy to apply.[3] In truth, the model is difficult to test, which is probably why there are so few empirical studies to either prove or refute the theory.

Porter provides the most empirical data concerning the model.[4] At the conscious level he measures all except the physiological needs. His samples are based only on managers, but they cover different managerial levels in a wide range of business organizations in the United States and thirteen other countries. Porter's studies have a number of interesting findings, but here we are primarily concerned with two: (1) in the United States and Britain (but not in the other twelve countries) there tends to be a hierarchical satisfaction of needs as Maslow hypothesizes; and (2) regardless of country or managerial level there is a tendency for those needs which managers feel are most important to be least satisfied.

A study by Beer of female clerks provides additional data concerning the model.[5] He examines the relationship between participative and considerate or human relations oriented supervisory leadership styles and satisfaction of needs. He also goes one step further and argues that need satisfaction, as such, does not necessarily lead to motivation. Rather, motivation results only from need satisfaction which occurs in the process of task-

[3] D. McGregor, "Adventure in Thought and Action," *Proceedings of the Fifth Anniversary Convocation of the School of Industrial Management, Massachusetts Institute of Technology*. Cambridge, Massachusetts: Massachusetts Institute of Technology, 1957, pp. 23–30.

[4] L. W. Porter, *Organizational Patterns of Managerial Job Attitudes*. New York: American Foundation for Management Research, 1964. See also M. Haire, E. Ghiselli and L. W. Porter, *Managerial Thinking: An International Study*. New York: Wiley, 1966, especially chapters 4 and 5.

[5] M. Beer, *Leadership, Employee Needs, and Motivation*. Columbus, Ohio: Bureau of Business Research, Ohio State University, 1966.

oriented work. He reasons that a participative leadership style should meet this condition since it presumably allows for the satisfaction of the higher order needs (self-actualization, autonomy, and esteem). Beer found that workers forced to arrange needs in a hierarchy (as required by his ranking method) tend to arrange them as predicted by Maslow. He also found that self-actualization, autonomy, and social needs were most important, while esteem and security needs were least important, although his method (unlike Porter's) did not allow a consideration of the relationship between importance and need satisfaction. Interestingly enough, there was no significant relationship between need satisfaction and Beer's measure of motivation nor between any of the leadership style dimensions and motivation. There were, however, significant relationships between leadership style dimensions and need satisfaction. Beer concludes that the model has questionable usefulness for a theory of industrial motivation although it may provide a fairly reliable measurement of the *a priori* needs of industrial workers.

We have found only three studies that systematically consider the Maslow theory in terms of performance.[6]

The first of these, by Clark, attempts to fit a number of empirical studies conducted for different purposes into a framework which provides for progressive activation and satisfaction of needs at each of the hierarchical levels. The findings are used to make predictions concerning productivity, absenteeism, and turnover as each need level is activated and then satisfied. While the article does not explicitly test the Maslow model, it is highly suggestive in terms of hypotheses for future research that might relate the theory to work group performance.

A second study, by Lawler and Porter, correlates satisfaction of managers' needs (except physiological) with rankings of their performance by superiors and peers. All correlations are significant but low, ranging from 0.16 to 0.30. Lawler and Porter conclude that satisfaction of higher order needs is more closely related to performance than satisfaction of lower order needs. However, the differences are not very great and they are not tested for significance. For example, correlations of superior ratings for the lower order security and social needs are 0.21 and 0.23, while for the higher order esteem, autonomy, and self-actualization needs they are 0.24, 0.18, and 0.30. Peer correlations are similar. Thus, unlike Lawler and Porter, we conclude that in this study the correlations for lower order needs are about the same as for higher order needs.

A more recent Porter and Lawler investigation seems to provide addi-

---

[6] J. V. Clark, "Motivation in Work Groups: A Tentative View," *Human Organization*, Vol. 19, 1960, pp. 199–208. E. E. Lawler and L. W. Porter, "The Effect of Performance on Job Satisfaction," *Industrial Relations*, Vol. 7, No. 1, 1967, pp. 20–28. L. W. Porter and E. E. Lawler, *Managerial Attitudes and Performance.* Homewood, Illinois: Irwin-Dorsey, 1968, pp. 148, 150.

tional support for their earlier findings by showing that higher order needs accounted for more relationships significant at the 0.01 level than lower order needs. However, they do not report correlations between these needs and performance and so we cannot evaluate their conclusion as we did for their earlier study.

## THE HERZBERG MODEL

A second frequently mentioned motivational model is that proposed by Herzberg and his associates in 1959.[7] They used a semi-structured interview technique to get respondents to recall events experienced at work which resulted in a marked improvement or a marked reduction in their job satisfaction. Interviewees were also asked, among other things, how their feelings of satisfaction or dissatisfaction affected their work performance, personal relationships, and well-being. Content analysis of the interviews suggested that certain job characteristics led to job satisfaction, while *different* job characteristics led to job dissatisfaction. For instance, job achievement was related to satisfaction while working conditions were related to dissatisfaction. Poor conditions led to dissatisfaction, but good conditions did not necessarily lead to satisfaction. Thus, satisfaction and dissatisfaction are not simple opposites. Hence a two-factor theory of satisfaction is needed.

The job content characteristics which produced satisfaction were called "motivators" by Herzberg and his associates because they satisfied the individual's need for self-actualization at work. The job environment characteristics which led to dissatisfaction were called "hygienes" because they were work-supporting or contextual rather than task-determined and hence were analogous to the "preventative" or "environmental" factors recognized in medicine. According to this dichotomy, motivators include achievement, recognition, advancement, possibility of growth, responsibility, and work itself. Hygienes, on the other hand, include salary; interpersonal relations with superiors, subordinates, and peers; technical supervision; company policy and administration; personal life; working conditions; status; and job security.

There is considerable empirical evidence for this theory. Herzberg himself, in a summary of research through early 1966, includes ten studies of seventeen populations which used essentially the same method as his original study.[8] In addition, he reviews twenty more studies which used a variety of methodologies to test the two-factor theory. Of the studies included in his review, those using his critical incident method generally

---

[7] Herzberg, Mausner and Snyderman, *op. cit.*

[8] Herzberg, *op cit.*, chapters 7, 8. See also K. Davis, *Human Relations at Work* (third edition). New York: McGraw-Hill, 1967, pp. 32–36; and, R. J. Burke, "Are Herzberg's Motivators and Hygienes Undimensional?" *Journal of Applied Psychology*, Vol. 50, 1966, pp. 217–321.

confirm the theory. Those using other methods give less clear results, which Herzberg acknowledges but attempts to dismiss for methodological reasons. At least nine other studies, most of which have appeared since Herzberg's 1966 review, raise even more doubts about the theory.[9]

While it is beyond the scope of the present article to consider these studies in detail, they raise serious questions as to whether the factors leading to satisfaction and dissatisfaction are really different from each other. A number of the studies show that certain job dimensions appear to be more important for *both* satisfaction and dissatisfaction. Dunnette, Campbell, and Hakel, for example, conclude from these and also from their own studies that Herzberg is shackled to his method and that achievement, recognition, and responsibility seem important for both satisfaction *and* dissatisfaction, while such dimensions as security, salary, and working conditions are less important.[10] They also raise by implication an issue concerning Herzberg's methodology which deserves further comment. That is, if data are analyzed in terms of percentage differences between groups, one result is obtained; if they are analyzed in terms of ranks within groups, another result occurs. The first type of analysis is appropriate for identifying factors which account for differences between events (as Herzberg did in his original hypothesis). The second type of analysis is appropriate if we want to know the most important factors within the event categories (which is what Herzberg claims he was doing). Analyzing the findings of Dunnette and his colleagues by the first method, we confirm Herzberg's theory; but if we rank the findings within categories, as Dunnette *et al.* also did, we find no confirmation. If we want to know whether "achievement" is important in job satisfaction we must look at its relative rank among other factors mentioned in the events leading to satisfaction, not whether it is mentioned a greater percentage of the time in satisfying events than in dissatisfying events. This distinction in analytical methods was discussed several years ago by Viteles and even earlier by Kornhauser.[11]

---

[9] For a review of six of these studies as well as a report on their own similar findings see M. D. Dunnette, J. P. Campbell, and M. D. Hakel, "Factors Contributing to Job Satisfaction and Job Dissatisfaction in Six Occupational Groups," *Organizational Behavior and Human Performance*, Vol. 2, 1967, pp. 143–174. See also C. L. Hulin and P. A. Smith, "An Empirical Investigation of Two Implications of the Two-Factor Theory of Job Satisfaction," *Journal of Applied Psychology*, Vol. 51, 1967, pp. 396–402; C. A. Lindsay, E. Marks, and L. Gorlow, "The Herzberg Theory: A Critique and Reformulation," *Journal of Applied Psychology*, Vol. 51, 1967, pp. 330–339. This latter study and one by J. R. Hinrichs and L. A. Mischkind, "Empirical and Theoretical Limitations of the Two-Factor Hypothesis of Job Satisfacton," *Journal of Appled Psychology*, Vol. 51, 1967, pp. 191–200, are especially useful for suggesting possible reformulations and extensions of the theory which may help overcome some the objections voiced in the studies mentioned above.

[10] Dunnette, Campbell and Hakel, *op. cit.*, pp. 169–173.

[11] M. S. Viteles, *Motivation and Morale in Industry*. New York: Norton, 1953, chapter 14: A. Kornhauser, "Psychological Studies of Employee Attitudes," *Journal of Consulting Psychology*, Vol. 8, 1944, pp. 127–143.

We conclude that any meaningful discussion of Herzberg's theory must recognize recent negative evidence even though the model seems to make a great deal of intuitive sense. Much the same can be said of Maslow's theory.

## FURTHER CONSIDERATIONS IN USING THE MASLOW AND HERZBERG THEORIES

Putting aside for the moment the empirical considerations presented by the two models, it is instructive to compare them at the conceptual level suggested in Figure 1. While the figure shows obvious similarities be-

FIGURE 1

Maslow's Need-Priority Model Compared with Herzberg's
Motivation-Hygiene Model*

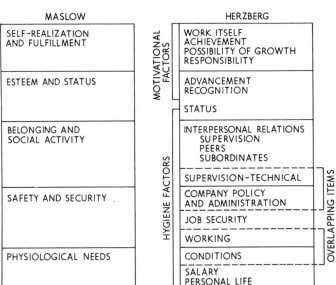

* Adapted from K. Davis, *Human Relations at Work*. New York: McGraw-Hill, 1967, p. 37.

tween the Maslow and Herzberg models, there are important differences as well. Where Maslow assumes that any need can be a motivator if it is relatively unsatisfied, Herzberg argues that only the higher order needs serve as motivators and that a worker can have unsatisfied needs in both the hygiene and motivator areas simultaneously. One might argue that the reason higher order needs are motivators is that lower order needs have essentially been satisfied. However, Herzberg presents some evidence that even in relatively low level blue collar and service jobs, where presumably lower order needs are less well-satisfied, the higher order needs are still the only ones seen by the workers as motivators.[12]

Another important consideration is the relationship of these models to the accomplishment of organizational objectives. Even if there were unequivocal empirical support for the theories, there is need to translate the findings into usable incentives for promoting such objectives as superior performance, lower turnover, lower absenteeism, etc. If not, they are of little use to industrial organizations. As indicated earlier, there is relatively little evidence empirically relating Maslow's model to performance, or even to psychological well-being. Furthermore, the one Lawler and Porter study seems to show that satisfaction of higher and lower order needs are about equally related to performance, although their later investigation suggests that the former are more strongly related to performance than the latter. But we cannot tell for sure because correlations and differences between correlations are not reported.

Similarly, although Herzberg asked his respondents for effects of job events on their performance, he reports only two studies which attempt to measure performance independent of the respondent's estimate. These seem to show the performance is favorably influenced as more "motivators" are provided in the job.[13] However, insufficient data are presented to permit evaluation of the adequacy of the experimental design and performance measures. A study by Friedlander and Walton that considered employee turnover used a modification of Herzberg's technique and found that employees' reasons for staying on the job were different from their reasons for leaving.[14] The reasons for staying would be called "motivators" while those for leaving were "hygiene" factors.

We conclude that Herzberg's two-factor theory *may* be related to turnover and performance; but present studies are subject to serious criticisms. And we could find only two empirical investigations which related Maslow's model to any of these outputs.

In addition, it should be noted that neither model adequately handles the theoretical problem of some kind of linkage by which individual need satisfaction is related to the achievement of organizational objectives. Given the present formulation, it is entirely possible that there can be need satisfaction which is *not necessarily* directed toward the accomplishment of organizational goals. For example, an important organizational objective might be increased production, but workers might conceivably receive more need satisfaction from turning out a higher quality product at a sacrifice in quantity. They might also be meeting their social needs

---

[12] Herzberg, *op. cit.*, chapters 7–9.

[13] Herzberg, *op. cit.*, chapter 8.

[14] F. Friedlander and E. Walton, "Positive and Negative Motivations Toward Work," *Administrative Science Quarterly*, Vol. 9, 1964, pp. 194–207.

through identification with a work group with strong sanctions against "rate busting."

Finally, neither of these theories as they stand can really handle the problem of individual differences in motivation. Maslow, for example, explains that his model may not hold for persons with particular experiences. His theory is therefore nonpredictive because data that do not support it can be interpreted in terms of individual differences in previous need gratification leading to greater or lesser prepotency of a given need category.[15] Herzberg, in similar fashion, describes seven types of people differentiated by the extent to which they are motivator or hygiene seekers, or some combination of the two, although he never relates these differences empirically to actual job performance. We turn then to a model which explicitly recognizes these issues and appears to offer great potential for understanding motivation in organizations.

## THE VROOM MODEL

Brayfield and Crockett as long ago as 1955 suggested an explicit theoretical linkage between satisfaction, motivation, and the organizational goal of productivity. They said:

> It makes sense to us to assume that individuals are motivated to achieve certain environmental goals and that the achievement of these goals results in satisfaction. Productivity is seldom a goal in itself but is more commonly a means to goal attainment. Therefore, . . . we might expect high satisfaction and high productivity to occur together when productivity is perceived as a path to certain important goals and when these goals are achieved.[16]

Georgopoulas, Mahoney, and Jones provide some early empirical support for this notion in their test of the "path-goal hypothesis."[17] Essentially, they argue that an individual's motivation to produce at a given level depends upon his particular needs as reflected in the goals toward which he is moving *and* his perception of the relative usefulness of productivity behavior as a path to attainment of these goals. They qualify this, however, by saying that the need must be sufficiently high, no other economical paths must be available to the individual, and there must be a lack of restraining practices.

More recently, Vroom has developed a motivational model which ex-

---

[15] It should be noted that the Porter and Lawler research reported above extends the Maslow model by providing an explicit linkage between need satisfaction and performance and also implicitly recognizes individual motivational differences. To do these things, their research makes use of Vroomian concepts discussed in the next section.

[16] A. H. Brayfield and W. H. Crockett, "Employee Attitudes and Employee Performance," *Psychological Bulletin*, Vol. 52, 1955, p. 416.

[17] B. S. Georgopoulas, G. M. Mahoney, and N. W. Jones, "A Path-Goal Approach to Productivity," *Journal of Applied Psychology*, Vol. 41, 1957, pp. 345–353.

tends the above concepts and is also related to earlier work of experimental and social psychologists.[18] He defines motivation as a "process governing choices, made by persons or lower organisms, among alternative forms of voluntary activity."[19] The concept is incorporated in Figure 2, which

**FIGURE 2**

Vroom's Motivational Model*

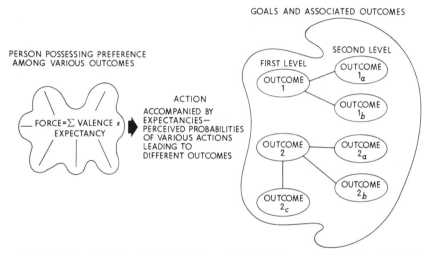

* Adapted from M. D. Dunnette, "The Motives of Industrial Managers," *Organizational Behavior and Human Performance,* Vol. 2, 1967, p. 178. (Copyright, Academic Press, Inc.)

depicts Vroom's model graphically. Here, the individual is shown as a role occupant faced with a set of alternative "first-level outcomes." His preference choice among these first-level outcomes is determined by their expected relationship to possible "second-level outcomes."

Two concepts are introduced to explain the precise method of determining preferences for these first-level outcomes. These concepts are *valence* and *instrumentality*. Valence refers to the strength of an individual's desire for a particular outcome. Instrumentality indicates an individual's perception of the relationship between a first-level outcome and a second-level outcome or, in other words, the extent to which a first-level outcome is seen as leading to the accomplishment of a second-level outcome.

Valence is measured by instructing workers to rank important individual goals in order of their desirability, or they may rate goals on Likert-type

---

[18] This section is based especially on discussions in Vroom, *op. cit.,* Chapters 2 and 7. See also J. Galbraith and L. L. Cummings, "An Empirical Investigation of the Motivational Determinants of Task Performance: Interactive Effects between Instrumentality—Valence and Motivation—Ability," *Organizational Behavior and Human Performance,* Vol. 2, 1967, pp. 237–257.

[19] Vroom, *op. cit.,* p. 6.

scales. Instrumentality can be measured by rating scales which involve perceived differences in the direction and strength of relationships between various first- and second-level outcomes. Important goals of industrial workers often cited in the empirical behavioral science literature are promotion, pay, pleasant working conditions, and job security. The goals can be ranked by individual workers in terms of their desirability. The resulting scores are measures of valence. In addition, each individual can be instructed to indicate on an appropriate scale the likelihood that a certain job behavior, e.g., high productivity, will lead to each of the four goals described. This score is the instrumental relationship between productivity and a specified goal. Obviously there are alternative methods of measurement available for the concepts; we will leave these for a more detailed discussion later.

Vroom expresses the valence of a first-level outcome to a person "as a monotonically increasing function of an algebraic sum of the products of the valences of all [second-level] outcomes and his conceptions of its instrumentality for the attainment of the [second-level] outcomes."[20]

For example, assume that an individual desires promotion and feels that superior performance is a very strong factor in achieving that goal. His first-level outcomes are then superior, average, or poor performance. His second-level outcome is promotion. The first-level outcome of high performance thus acquires a positive valence by virtue of its expected relationship to the preferred second-level outcome of promotion. Assuming no negative second-level outcomes associated with high performance and no other first-level outcomes that contribute to promotion, we expect motivation toward superior performance because promotion is important and superior performance is seen as instrumental in its accomplishment. Or, to put it in Vroom's terms, performance varies directly with the product of the valence of the reward (promotion) and the perceived instrumentality of performance for the attainment of the reward.

An additional concept in Vroom's theory is *expectancy*. This is a belief concerning the likelihood that a particular action or effort will be followed by a particular first-level outcome and can be expressed as a subjective probability ranging from 0 to 1. Expectancy differs from instrumentality in that it relates *efforts* to first-level outcomes where instrumentality relates first- and second-level outcomes to each other. Vroom ties this concept to his previous one by stating, "the force on a person to perform an [action] is a monotonically increasing function of the algebraic sum of the products of the valences of all [first-level] outcomes and the strength of his expectancies that the [action] will be followed by the attainment of these outcomes."[21] "Force" here is similar to our concept of motivation.

---

[20] Vroom, *op. cit.*, p. 17.
[21] Vroom, *op. cit.*, p. 18.

This motivational model, unlike those discussed earlier, emphasizes individual differences in motivation and makes possible the examination of very explicit relationships between motivation and the accomplishment of organizational goals, whatever these goals may be. Thus instead of assuming that satisfaction of a specific need is likely to influence organizational objectives in a certain way, we can find out how important to the employees are the various second-level outcomes (worker goals), the instrumentality of various first-level outcomes (organizational objectives) for their attainment, and the expectancies that are held with respect to the employees' ability to influence the first-level outcomes.

## EMPIRICAL TESTS OF VROOM'S MODEL

Vroom has already shown how his model can integrate many of the empirical findings in the literature on motivation in organizations.[22] However, because it is a relatively recent development, empirical tests of the model itself are just beginning to appear. Here we shall consider four such investigations.

In the first study, Vroom is concerned with predicting the organizational choices of graduating college students on the basis of their instrumentality-goal index scores.[23] These scores reflect the extent to which membership in an organization was perceived by the student as being related to the acquisition of desired goals. According to the theory, the chosen organization should be the one with the highest instrumentality-goal index. Ratings were used to obtain preferences for fifteen different goals and the extent to which these goals could be attained through membership in three different organizations. These two ratings were thus measures of the valences of second-level outcomes and the instrumentality of organizational membership for attainment of these outcomes, respectively. The instrumentality-goal index was the correlation between these two measures. But Vroom's theory also involves consideration of expectancy, i.e., how probable is it that the student can become a member of a particular organization. The choice is not his alone but depends upon whether he is acceptable to the organization. A rough measure of expectancy in this study was whether or not the student had received an offer by the organization. If he had received an offer, expectancy would be high; if not, it would be low. The results show that, considering only organizations from which offers of employment were actually received, 76 percent of the students chose the organization with the highest instrumentality-goal index score. The evidence thus strongly supports Vroom's theory.

[22] Vroom, *op. cit.*

[23] V. H. Vroom, "Organizational Choice: A Study of Pre- and Postdecision Processes," *Organizational Behavior and Human Performance,* Vol. 1, 1966, pp. 212–225.

The next study, by Galbraith and Cummings, utilizes the model to predict the productivity of operative workers.[24] Graphic rating scales were used to measure the instrumentality of performance for five goals—money, fringe benefits, promotion, supervisor's support, and group acceptance. Similar ratings were used for measuring the desirability of each of the goals for the worker. The authors anticipated that a worker's expectation that he could produce at a high level would have a probability of one because the jobs were independent and productivity was a function of the worker's own effort independent of other human or machine pacing. Figure 3 outlines the research design.

**FIGURE 3**

Individual Goals and Productivity as Measured by Vroom's
Model in One Industrial Plant*

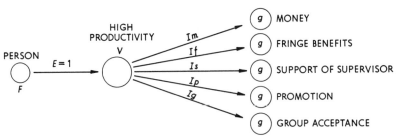

$g$ = Desirability of a particular outcome (rating).
$I$ = Instrumentality of production for particular outcomes (rating of relationship).
$E$ = Expectancy (=1 here because worker sets own pace and is assumed to be capable of high productivity).
$V$ = (Valence) the sum of the cross products of instrumentality and $g$.
$F$ = (Force) expectency times the valence of productivity.
Productivity = Objective measures of amount of production in relation to the production standard.

* Based on data from J. Galbraith and L. L. Cummings. See footnote 23.

Multiple regression analysis showed that productivity was significantly related positively to the instrumentality-goal interactions for supervisor support and money, and there was an almost significant ($p < 0.10$) relationship with group acceptance. The other factors did not approach significance and the authors explain this lack of significance in terms of the situational context. That is, fringe benefits were dependent not so much on productivity as on a union/management contract, and promotion was based primarily on seniority. Thus the instrumentality of productivity for the attainment of these goals was low and the model would predict no

---

[24] Galbraith and Cummings, *op. cit.*, pp. 237–257.

relationship. The Galbraith and Cummings study thus supports Vroom's contention that motivation is related to productivity in those situations where the acquisition of desired goals is dependent upon the individual's production and not when desired outcomes are contingent on other factors.

A third study is that of Hill relating a model similar to Vroom's to behavior in a utility company.[25] Hill's model is based upon Edward's subjective expected utility maximization theory of decision making.[26] Here one given a choice between alternatives A and/or B will select that alternative which maximizes his subjective expected utility or expected value. If the outcomes associated with action A are more desirable than those associated with B, and their probability of occurrence is greater than or equal to those associated with B, then an individual will choose behavior A over behavior B. The basic concepts are subjective expectation and subjective utility or valence. Expectation and utility are multiplicatively related and can be measured by the same techniques used to test Vroom's theory. Where a relationship is found between Subjective Expected Utility (SEU) and overt behavior, it can be interpreted as support for Vroom.

The behavior considered in Hill's study is that of job bidding. This behavior is encountered in organizations that post descriptions of job openings on employee bulletin boards and encourage qualified employees to "bid" (apply) for them. Here records were kept of the number of bids made over a three-year period by groups of semiskilled electrical repairmen matched in learning ability, seniority in grade, and age. The men were asked about the consequences of bidding and not bidding on the next higher grade job, and rated the consequence on a seven-point scale of desirability and a similar scale of probability of occurrence. Bidders were those who had bid three or more times during that time.

Fourteen different SEU indices were computed from interview data to determine the relative validity of each in predicting bidding behavior. Typical of these indices were: (1) the sums of the cross products of expectation and utility for the positive consequences of bidding ($\Sigma \overset{+}{\text{SEU}}$); (2) the same score for the negative consequences of bidding ($\Sigma \overset{-}{\text{SEU}}$); and (3) the cross products of the *mean* expectation and utility scores for positive and negative consequences $\left( \dfrac{\Sigma \overset{+}{\text{SEU}}}{N}, \dfrac{\Sigma \overset{-}{\text{SEU}}}{N} \right)$. In addition to these SEU indices, two traditional attitudinal and motivational measures were used. Semantic differential scales measured each subject's respective evaluation of bidding

[25] J. W. Hill, "An Application of Decision Theory to Complex Industrial Behavior," unpublished dissertation, Wayne State University, Detroit, Michigan, 1965.

[26] Edwards, *op. cit.*, pp. 473–499.

and the next higher grade job and each subject's need for achievement was obtained.[27]

It was hypothesized that: (1) there would be a positive correlation between the SEU indices and bidding; and (2) the SEU indices would be more highly related to bidding behavior than the traditional measures.

We do not discuss relationships for all of the indices here but do consider results for one of the more comprehensive indices and those from multiple regression analysis. This index is the algebraic sum of the cross products of the positive and negative consequences of bidding minus the same score for not bidding for each individual. The correlation of this index with bidding was 0.26, $p < 0.05$ for a one-tailed test. The correlations between the two semantic differential scales and bidding were $-0.09$ and $-0.25$, respectively. Neither of these is significant for a one-tailed test predicting a positive correlation. The correlation between need for achievement and bidding was a nonsignificant 0.17. A multiple regression analysis determined the relative contribution of the SEU indices to the prediction of bidding. A variable was selected for analysis on the basis of its relationship to the criterion and its intercorrelation with the other predictors. The multiple correlation for bidding and seven selected variables was 0.61, $p < 0.05$. This correlation included four SEU indices, all of which had higher beta weights than the semantic differentials or need for achievement. Thus these variables accounted for more variance in the criterion than did the traditional attitudinal and motivational measures. Both hypotheses were therefore confirmed. This study adds support to the usefulness of this type of model in the study of motivation.

Finally, Lawler and Porter report a study that attempts to relate managerial attitudes to job performance rankings by superiors and peers.[28] In it, 145 managers from five different organizations completed questionnaires concerning seven kinds of rewards, and their expectations that different kinds of behavior would lead to these rewards. The expectations and the ratings of the importance of instrumentality and valence, respectively, were combined multiplicatively to yield multiple correlations which were significantly related to supervisor and peer rankings of the manager's effort to perform his job well. The correlations were higher with effort to perform the job than with the rankings of job performance. Lawler and Porter predicted this result because they reasoned that job performance is influenced by variables other than motivation, e.g., by ability and role perceptions. Of course, Vroom's model is not a behavioral theory but one of motivation

---

[27] For discussions of these measures see C. Osgood, G. Suci, and P. Tannenbaum, *The Measurement of Meaning* Urbana, Ill.: University of Illinois Press, 1957; A. L. Edwards, *Personal Preference Schedule Manual.* New York: Psychological Corporation, 1959.

[28] E. E. Lawler and L. W. Porter, "Antecedent Attitudes of Effective Managerial Performance," *Organizational Behavior and Human Performance,* Vol. 2, 1967, pp. 122–142.

only. Motivation is not going to improve performance if ability is low or role perceptions are inaccurate. Vroom's model explains how goals influence effort and that is exactly the relationship found by Lawler and Porter.

## CONCLUSION

Taken together, the four studies discussed in the previous section seem to show that Vroom's model holds great promise for predicting behavior in organizations. There still remain some unanswered questions. We do not know all of the goals that have positive valence in a work situation. We do not know how much of a difference in force is necessary before one kind of outcome is chosen over another. Nor do we know what combination of measures yields the best prediction in a given situation. The answers to these and other questions await further research.

One more point should perhaps be made concerning the four studies and their measurement of Vroom's concepts. While it is true that all of them used subjective measures, the model can in fact be tested with more objective devices. Instrumentality can be inferred from organization practices, expectations can be manipulated by instructions, and goals can be inferred from observed approach and avoidance behaviors. Of course, all of these techniques require assumptions concerning their relationship to the worker's subjective perceptions of the situation; but the model is certainly not bound to the methods of measurement used so far. In fact, Vroom specifies in considerable detail the different kinds of techniques that might be used to test his model.[29]

More work must be done before we can make any statements concerning the overall validity of Vroom's model. But the rigor of his formulation, the relative ease of making the concepts operational, and the model's emphasis on individual differences show considerable promise. We are also encouraged by the results of relatively sophisticated studies testing the theory. We believe it is time for those interested in organizational behavior to take a more thoroughly scientific look at this very complex subject of industrial motivation, and Vroom's model seems a big step in that direction.

---

[29] Vroom, *Work and Motivation, op. cit.,* chapter 2.

# Beyond the Teaching Machine: The Neglected Area of Operant Conditioning in the Theory and Practice of Management*

WALTER R. NORD

This paper maintains that the work of B. F. Skinner has not been recognized in the administrative and management literature to the extent that it deserves. The work of Skinner is highly consistent with that of many widely accepted students of management, except that Skinner's work deals specifically with scheduling reinforcements, does not require acceptance of the metaphysics of many of the "humanistic" psychologists, and is based on considerable empirical evidence. The power of positive reinforcement, the unanticipated consequences of punishment, and the value of partial reinforcement are stressed. Finally, the operant view is applied to some managerial problems. It seems clear that the conditioning approach can meaningfully integrate much of the behavioral science literature and serve organizations in the areas of personnel development, job design, compensation and alternative rewards, and organizational design.

THE WORK of B. F. Skinner and the operant conditioners has been neglected in management and organizational literature. The present paper is an attempt to eliminate this lacuna. When most students of management and personnel think of Skinner's work, they begin and end with programmed instruction. Skinner's ideas, however, have far greater implications for the design and operation of social systems and organizations than just the teaching machine. These additional ideas could be of great practical value.

While neglecting conditioning, writers in the administrative, management, and personnel literature have given extensive attention to the work of other behavioral scientists. McGregor and Maslow are perhaps the behavioral scientists best known to practitioners and students in the area

* Organizational Behavior and Human Performance, Vol. 4, 1969.

of business and management. Since the major concern of managers of human resources is the prediction and control of the behavior of organizational participants, it is curious to find that people with such a need are extremely conversant with McGregor and Maslow and totally ignorant of Skinner. This condition is not surprising since leading scholars in the field of what might be termed the applied behavioral sciences have turned out book after book, article after article, and anthology after anthology with scarcely a mention of Skinner's contributions to the design of social systems. While many writers who deal with the social psychology of organizations are guilty of the omission, this paper will focus primarily on the popular positions of Douglas McGregor, Abraham Maslow, and Frederick Herzberg to aid in exposition.

Almost every book in the field devotes considerable attention to Maslow and McGregor. These men have certainly contributed ideas which are easily understood and "make sense" to practitioners. Also, many practitioners have implemented some of these ideas successfully. However, the belief in the Maslow–McGregor creed is not based on a great deal of evidence. This conclusion is not mine alone, but in fact closely parallels Maslow's (1965) own thoughts. He wrote:

> After all, if we take the whole thing from McGregor's point of view of a contrast between a Theory X view of human nature, a good deal of the evidence upon which he bases his conclusions comes from my researches and my papers on motivations, self-actualization, et cetera. But I of all people should know just how shaky this foundation is as a final foundation. My work on motivations came from the clinic, from a study of neurotic people. The carry-over of this theory to the industrial situation has some support from industrial studies, but certainly I would like to see a lot more studies of this kind before feeling finally convinced that this carry-over from the study of neurosis to the study of labor in factories is legitimate. The same thing is true of my studies of self-actualizing people— there is only this one study of mine available. There were many things wrong with the sampling, so many in fact that it must be considered to be, in the classical sense anyway, a bad or poor or inadequate experiment. I am quite willing to concede this—as a matter of fact, I am eager to concede it—because I'm a little worried about this stuff which I consider to be tentative being swallowed whole by all sorts of enthusiastic people, who really should be a little more tentative in the way that I am (p. 55–56).

By contrast, the work of Skinner (1953) and his followers has been supported by millions of observations made on animals at all levels of the phylogenetic scale, including man. Over a wide variety of situations, behavior has been reliably predicted and controlled by operant and classical conditioning techniques.

Why then have the applied behavioral sciences followed the McGregor-Maslow approach and ignored Skinner? Several reasons can be suggested. First is the metaphysical issue. Modern Americans, especially of the managerial class, prefer to think of themselves and others as being self-actualizing creatures operating near the top of Maslow's need-hierarchy, rather than as animals being controlled and even "manipulated" by their environment. McGregor (1960) developed his argument in terms of Maslow's hierarchy. Skinner's position is unattractive in the same way the Copernican theory was unattractive. Second, Skinner's work and stimulus–response psychology in general appear too limited to allow appplication to complex social situations. Certainly, this point has much merit. The application of S–R theory poses a terribly complex engineering problem, perhaps an insoluble one in some areas. Nevertheless, the designs of some experimental social systems, which will be discussed later in this paper, demonstrate the feasibility of the practical application of Skinnerian psychology to systems design. A third possible reason for the acceptance of the McGregor and Maslow school and rejection of Skinner may stem from the fact that the two approaches have considerable, although generally unrecognized overlap. As will be shown below, McGregor gave primary importance to the environment as the determinant of individual behavior. Similarly, although not as directly, so does Maslow's hierarchy of needs. The major issue between Skinner and McGregor–Maslow has to do with their models of man. Skinner focuses on man being totally shaped by his environment. Maslow–McGregor see man as having an essence or intrinsic nature which is only congruent with certain environments. The evidence for any one set of metaphysical assumptions is no better than for almost any other set. Empirically, little has been found which helps in choosing between Skinner's and McGregor's assumptions. Further, since most managers are concerned mainly with behavior, the sets of assumptions are of limited importance. It should be noted, however, that if McGregor's writings were stipped of Maslow's model of man, his conclusions on the descriptive and proscriptive levels would remain unchanged. Such a revision would also make McGregor's ideas almost identical with Skinner's. With more attention to contingencies of reinforcement and a broader view of the possibilities of administering reinforcement, the two sets of ideas as they apply to prediction and control of action would be virtually indistinguishable.

The remainder of this paper will be devoted to three areas. First, the similarities and differences between McGregor and Skinner will be discussed. Then a summary of the Skinnerian position will be presented. Finally, the potential of the Skinnerian approach for modern organizations will be presented with supporting evidence from social systems in which it has already been applied.

## McGREGOR AND SKINNER COMPARED

The importance of environmental factors in determining behavior is the crucial and dominant similarity between Skinner and McGregor. As will be shown below, environmental determination of behavior is central to both men.

McGregor (1960) gave central importance to environmental factors in determining how a person behaves. For example, he saw employee behavior as a consequence of organizational factors which are influenced by managerial strategy. In a sense, Theory X management leads to people behaving in a way which confirms Theory X assumptions, almost as a self-fulfilling prophecy. In addition, McGregor's statement of Theory Y assumptions places stress on "proper conditions," rewards and punishments, and other environmental factors. Further, he recognized the importance of immediate feedback in changing behavior. Also, he noted that failure to achieve results is often due to inappropriate methods of control. These are the very terms a behaviorist such as Skinner uses in discussing human actions. Finally, McGregor (1966) noted stimulus-response psychology as a possible model for considering organizational behavior. However, he discarded the reinforcement approach because it did not permit intrinsic rewards to be dealt with. Such a view not only led him to discard a model which describes, by his own admission, important behaviors, but is based on an incomplete view of reinforcement.

McGregor's basic arguments could have been based on Skinner rather than Maslow. The major difference would be the assumption of fewer givens about human nature. In view of this similarity one need not choose either Skinner or McGregor. Rather, there is considerable overlap in that both focus on changing the environmental conditions to produce changes in behavior. Further, both writers place substantial emphasis on the goals of prediction and control. Both are quite explicit in suggesting that we often get undesired results because we use inappropriate methods of control. In fact, the emphasis that McGregor's (1960) first chapter gives to the role of environment in controlling behavior seems to place him clearly in the behavioral camp.

Certainly there are important differences between Skinner and McGregor as well as the marked similarities noted above. For example, McGregor's (1960) use of Maslow's hierarchy of needs implies a series of inborn needs as a focus of the causal factors of behavior whereas Skinner (1953) views environmental factors as the causes of behavior. This difference does not, however, suggest an unresolvable conflict on the applied level. Skinner too allows for satiation on certain reinforcers which will be subject to species and individual differences. Proceeding from this premise, Skinner focuses on the environmental control of behavior in a more rigorous and specific fashion than did McGregor. For example, McGregor (1960) advocated an agricultural approach to development which emphasizes the provision of the conditions for behavioral change as a management responsibility. He noted in a general way that features of the organization, such as a boss, will influence behavioral change. He added that the change would not be per-

manent unless the organizational environment reinforced the desired behavior pattern. Such a general approach is an assumed basis for Skinner,
who proceeds to focus on the types of reinforcement, the details of the administration of reinforcement, and the outcomes which can be expected
from the administration of various types of reinforcement. Thus, changes
in behavior which are predicted and achieved by Skinnerian methods can
be viewed as empirical support for the work of McGregor.

There are other commonalities in the thinking of the two men. Both
assume that there are a wide number of desirable responses available
to a person which he does not make because the responses are not rewarded
in the environment. Both suggest that many undesired responses are repeated because they are rewarded. Both are clearly advocating a search
for alternatives to controlling behavior which will be more effective in
developing desired responses.

At this same level of analysis, there seems to be one major difference
which revolves around the issue of self-control. However, this difference
may be more apparent than real. Skinner (1953) wrote "It appears, therefore, that society is responsible for the larger part of the behavior of self-
control. If this is correct, little ultimate control remains with the individual
(p. 240)." Continuing on self-control, Skinner adds: "But it is also behavior;
and we account for it in terms of other variables in the environment and
history of the individual. It is these variables which provide the ultimate
control (p. 240)."

In apparent contrast, McGregor (1960) stated: "Theory Y assumes that
people will exercise self-direction and self-control in the achievement of
organizational objectives *to the degree that they are committed to those
objectives* (p. 56)." Seemingly this statement contradicts Skinner in placing
the locus of control inside the individual. However, this conflict is reduced
a few sentences later when McGregor (1960) added "Managerial policies
and practices materially affect this degree of commitment (p. 56)." Thus,
both writers, Skinner far more unequivocally than McGregor, see the
external environment as the primary factor in self-control. While McGregor
polemicized against control by authority, he was not arguing that man is
"free." Perhaps the more humanistic tone of McGregor's writing or his
specific attention to managerial problems faced in business is responsible
for his high esteem among students of management relative to that accorded
Skinner. While metaphorically there is great difference, substantively there
is little. It would seem, however, that metaphors have led practitioners and
students of applied behavioral science to overlook some valuable data and
some creative management possibilities.

One major substantive difference between the two approaches exists:
it involves intrinsic rewards. McGregor (1966) saw a dicotomy in the effects
of intrinsic and extrinsic rewards, noting research which has shown intrinsic
ones to be more effective. He concludes the "mechanical" view (reinforce-

ment theory) is inadequate, because it does not explain the superior out-comes of the use of "intrinsic" over "extrinsic" rewards. Here, as will be dis-cussed in more detail later in connection with Herzberg, the problem is McGregor's failure to consider scheduling of reinforcement. "Intrinsic" rewards in existing organizations may be more effective because they occur on a more appropriate schedule for sustaining behavior than do "extrinsic" rewards. Intrinsic rewards are given by the environment for task completion or a similar achievement, and often occur on a ratio schedule. The impli-cations of this crucial fact will be discussed shortly in considering Skinner's emphasis on the scheduling of rewards. For the present, it is suggested that McGregor gave little attention to reinforcement schedules and made a qualitative distinction between external and internal rewards. He seems to agree with Skinner that achievement, task completion, and control of the environment are reinforcers in themselves. Skinner's work suggests, how-ever, that these rewards have the same consequences as "extrinsic" rewards, if they are given on the same schedule.

By way of summary to this point, it appears that more humanistic social scientists have been preferred by managers to behaviorists such as Skinner in their efforts to improve the management of human resources. Perhaps the oversight has been due to the congruence between their values and the metaphysics of people such as McGregor and Maslow. The dif-ferences between McGregor and Skinner do not appear to involve open conflict.

To the extent the two approaches agree, the major criterion in employing them would seem to be the degree to which they aid in predicting and controlling behavior toward organizational goals. The work of Skinner and his followers has much to offer in terms of the above criterion. In particular, McGregor's followers might find Skinner's work an asset in implementing Theory Y. The remainder of this paper will develop some of the major points of the Skinnerian approach and seek to explore their potential for industrial use.

## CONDITIONING—A SYNTHESIS FOR ORGANIZATIONAL BEHAVIOR

The behavioral psychology of Skinner assumes, like Theory Y, that rate of behavior is dependent on the external conditions in which the behavior takes place. Like Theory X, it stresses the importance of the administration of rewards and punishments. Unlike Theory X, Skinnerian psychology places emphasis on rewards. Like Theory Y it emphasizes the role of inter-dependence between people in a social relationship and thus views the administration of rewards and punishments as an exchange. For those who are unfamiliar with the work of Skinner and his followers, a brief summary follows. Like any summary of an extensive body of work, this review omits a lot of important material. A more detailed, yet simple, introduction to conditioning can be found in Bijou and Baer (1961) and Skinner (1953). Extensions of this work by social exchange theorists such as Homans (1961) suggest that the conditioning model can be extended to a systems approach, contrary to McGregor's (1966) belief.

Generally, conditioned responses can be divided into two classes. Each class is acquired in a different fashion. The first class, generally known as respondent or classically conditioned behavior, describes the responses which are controlled by prior stimulation. These responses, generally thought of as being involuntary or reflexive, are usually made by the "smooth muscles." Common ones are salivation and emotional responses. Initially, the presentation of an unconditioned stimulus will elicit a specific response. For example, food placed on one's tongue will generally cause salivation. If a bell is sounded and then food is placed on the tongue, and this process is repeated several times, the sound of the bell by itself will elicit salivation. By this process, stimuli which previously did not control behavior such as the bell, can become a source of behavior control. Many of our likes and dislikes, our anxieties, our feelings of patriotism, and other emotions can be thought of as such involuntary responses. The implications of emotional responses are of major importance to the management of human resources and more will be said about them later. However, the second class of responses, the operants, are of even greater importance.

The rate of operant responses is influenced by events which follow them. These events are considered to be the consequences of behavior. The responses, generally thought to be voluntary, are usually made by striped muscles. All that is necessary for the development of an operant response is that the desired response has a probability of occurring which is greater than zero for the individual involved. Most rapid conditioning results when the desired response is "reinforced" immediately (preferably about one-half second after the response). In other words, the desired response is followed directly by some consequence. In simple terms, if the outcome is pleasing to the individual, the probability of his repeating the response is apt to be increased. If the consequence is displeasing to the individual, the probability of his repeating the response is apt to be decreased. The process of inducing such change (usually an increase) in the response rate, is called operant conditioning. In general, the frequency of a behavior is said to be a function of its consequences.

The above description of operant conditioning is greatly simplified. The additional considerations which follow will only partially rectify this state. One crucial factor has to do with the frequency with which a given consequence follows a response. There are several possible patterns. Most obviously, the consequence can be continuous (for example, it follows the response every time the response is made). Alternatively a consequence might follow only some of the responses. There are two basic ways in which such partial reinforcement can be administered. First, the consequence can be made contingent on a certain number of responses. Two sub-patterns are possible. Every $n$th response may be reinforced or an average of $1/n$ of the responses may be reinforced in a random pattern. These two related patterns are called ratio schedules. The former is known as a fixed ratio and the latter is known as a variable ratio. Ratio schedules tend to generate a high rate of response, with the variable ratio schedule leading to a more durable response than both the fixed-ratio and continuous patterns. A second technique of partial reinforcement can be designed where the consequence follows the response only after a certain amount of time has elapsed. The first response made after a specified interval is then reinforced, but all other responses produce neutral stimulus outcomes. This pattern can also be either fixed or variable. Generally, interval schedules develop responses which are quite long lasting when reinforcement is no longer given, but do not yield as rapid a response rate as ratio schedules do. Obviously, mixed patterns of ratio and interval schedules can also be designed.

A second consideration about operant conditioning which deserves brief mention is the concept of a response hierarchy. All the responses which an individual could make under a given set of conditions can be placed in order according to probability that they will be made. In this view, there are two basic strategies for getting an individual to make the desired response. First, one could attempt to reduce the probability of all the more probable responses. Second, one could attempt to increase the probability of the desired response. Of course, some combination of these two approaches may often be used.

Strategies for changing the probability of a response can be implemented by punishment, extinction, and positive reinforcement. Generally punishment and extinction are used to decrease the occurrence of a response whereas positive reinforcement is used to increase its probability. An understanding of these three operations in behavior control is important, not only for knowing how to use them, but chiefly because of their unanticipated consequences or their side-effects.

Punishment is the most widely used technique in our society for behavior control. Perhaps, as Reese (1966) said, the widespread use of punishment is due to the immediate effects it has in stopping or preventing the undesired response. In this sense, the punisher is reinforced for punishing. Also, many of us seem to be influenced by some notion of what Homans (1961) called distributive justice. In order to reestablish what we believe to be equity, we may often be led to punish another person. This ancient assumption of ". . . an eye for an eye . . ." has been widely practiced in man's quest for equity and behavior control.

Whatever the reason for punishing, it can be done in two ways, both of which have unfortunate side-effects. First, punishment can be administered in the form of some aversive stimulus such as physical pain or social disapproval. Secondly, it can be administered by withdrawing a desired stimulus. The immediate effect is often the rapid drop in frequency of the punished response. The full effects, unfortunately, are often not clearly recognized. Many of these consequences are crucial for managers of organizations.

Punishment may be an inefficient technique for controlling behavior for a number of reasons. First, the probability of the response may be reduced only when the threat of punishment is perceived to exist. Thus, when the punishing agent is away, the undesired response may occur at its initial rate. Secondly, punishment only serves to reduce the probability of the one response. This outcome does not necessarily produce the desired response, unless that response is the next most probable one in the response hierarchy. Really, what punishment does is to get the individual to do something other than what he has been punished for. A third effect is that the punishment may interfere with the responses being made under desired circumstances. For example, if an organizational member attempts an innovation which is met with punishment by his superiors because they did not feel he had the authority to take the step, it is quite possible that his creative behavior will be reduced even in those areas where his superiors expect him to innovate.

In addition to these effects there are some other important byproducts of punishment. Punishment may result in a person's making responses which are incompatible with the punished response. Psychological tension, often manifested in emotional behavior such as fear or anxiety, is often the result. Secondly, punishment may lead to avoidance and dislike of the punishing agent. This effect can be especially important to managers who are attempting to build open, helping relationships with subordinates. The roles of punishing agent and helper are often incompatible. Many line-staff conflicts in organizations undoubtedly can be explained in these terms. Finally, punishment may generate counter-aggression. Either through a modeling effect or a justice effect, the punished person may respond with aggressive responses towards the punishing agent or towards some other stimulus.

The second technique for behavior change, commonly called extinction, also focuses primarily on reducing the probability of a response. Extinction arises from repeated trials where the response is followed by a neutral stimulus. This technique generates fewer byproducts than punishment. However, like punishment, it does not lead to the desired responses being developed. Furthermore, to the extent that one has built up an expectation of a reward for a certain response, a neutral consequence may be perceived as punishing. Thus, extinction may have some advantages over punishment, but has many of the same limitations.

Positive reinforcement is the final technique for changing behavior. Under conditions of positive reinforcement, the response produces a consequence that results in an increase in the frequency of the response. It is commonly stated that such a consequence is rewarding, pleasing, or drive-reducing for the individual. The operant conditioners, however, avoid such inferences and define positive reinforcers as stimuli which increase the probability of a preceding response. Positive reinforcement is efficient for several reasons. First, it increases the probable occurrence of the desired response. The process involves rewarding approximations to the direct response itself immediately after it is made. The desired behavior is being directly developed as opposed to successive suppression of undesired acts. Secondly, the adverse emotional responses associated with punishment and extinction are apt to be reduced, and in fact favorable emotions may be developed. Since people tend to develop positive affect to others who reward them, the "trainer" is apt to become positively valenced in the eyes of the "learner."

By way of summary, Skinner's (1953) approach suggested that the control of behavior change involves a reduction in the probability of the most prepotent response and/or an increase in the probability of some desired response. Punishment and extinction may be used. These means can only reduce the probability of the unwanted responses being made. Also, they may have undesired side effects. The third technique, positive reinforcement, has the important advantage of developing the desired response rather than merely reducing the chances of an undesired one. Also, positive reinforcement is apt to produce favorable rather than unfavorable "side effects" on organizational relationships.

This approach seems to suggest that both or neither Theory X and Theory Y assumptions are useful. This section suggested that conditioning may be both Theory X and Theory Y. Perhaps since the operant view does not make either set of assumptions, it is neither Theory X nor Theory Y. Operant conditioning is consistent with Theory Y in suggesting that the limits on human beings are a function of the organizational setting, but like Theory X, implies something about human nature; namely that deprivation or threat of some sort of deprivation is a precondition for behavior to be controlled. From the managerial perspective, however, the nomonological question is of little significance. The important thing to managers is behavior and the major point of this approach is that behavior is a function of its consequences. Good management is that which leads to the desired behavior by organizational members. Management must see to it that the consequences of behavior are such as to increase the frequency of desired behavior and decrease the frequency of undesired behaviors. The question becomes, how can managers develop a social system which provides the appropriate consequences? In many ways the answer to this question is similar to what Theory Y advocates have suggested. However, there are some new possibilities.

## APPLICATIONS OF CONDITIONING IN ORGANIZATIONS

The potential uses of the Skinnerian framework for social systems are increasing rapidly. The approach has far more applicability to complex social systems than has often been recognized. McGregor's rejection of the stimulus-response or the reward-punishment approach as inadequate for management because it does not allow for a systems approach is quite inconsistent with this general trend and his own environmentally based approach. Recent work in the field of behavioral control has begun to refute McGregor's position. The Skinnerian view can be and has been used to redesign social systems.

The most complete redesign was envisioned by Skinner (1948) in his novel, *Walden Two*. In this book, Skinner developed a society based on the use of positive reinforcement and experimental ethics geared to the goal of competition of a coordinated social unit with its environment. In other words, the system is designed to reward behaviors which are functional for the whole society. Social change is introduced on the basis of empirical data. As a result of the success of this system, man is enabled to pursue those activities which are rewarding in themselves. Although the book is a novel, it can be a valuable stimulus for thought about the design of social organization.

In addition, Skinner (1954) has taken a fresh look at teaching and learning in conventional educational systems. He noted that the school system depends heavily on aversive control or punishment. The use of low marks and ridicule have merely been substituted for the "stick." The teacher, in Skinner's view, is an out of date reinforcing mechanism. He suggested the need to examine the reinforcers which are available in the system and to apply them in a manner which is consistent with what is known about learning. For example, control over the environment itself may be rewarding. Perhaps grades reinforce the wrong behavior and are administered on a rather poor schedule. It would seem that a search for new reinforcers and better reinforcement schedules is appropriate for all modern organizations.

These speculations suggest the potential for great advances. *Walden Two* is in many ways an ideal society but has been a source of horror to many readers. The thoughts about changes in teaching methods are also a subject of controversy. However, the environment can be designed to aid in the attainment of desired ends. People resist the idea that they can be controlled by their environment. This resistance does not change the fact that they are under such control. Recently, evidence has begun to accumulate that the Skinnerian approach can be employed to design social systems.

Much of this evidence was collected in settings far removed from modern work organizations. The reader's initial response is apt to be, "What relevance do these studies have to my organization?" Obviously, the relation-ship is not direct. However, if, as the operant approach maintains, the con-ditioning process describes the acquisition and maintenance of behavior, the same principles can be applied to any social organization. The prob-lem of application becomes merely that of engineering. The gains may well be limited only by an administrator's ingenuity and resources.

Much of the evidence comes from studies of hospitalized mental patients and autistic children, although some has been based on normal lower class children. A few examples from these studies will serve to document the great potential of the conditioning methods for social systems. Allyon and Azrin (1965) observed mental patients' behavior to determine what activities they engaged in when they had a chance. They then made tokens contingent on certain responses such as work on hospital tasks. These tokens could be exchanged for the activities the patients preferred to en-gage in. The results of this approach were amazing. In one experiment five schizophrenics and three mental defectives served as Ss. They did jobs regularly and adequately when tokens were given for the job. Such per-formance was reported to be in sharp contrast to the erratic and inconsistent behavior characteristic of such patients. When the tokens were no longer contingent on the work, the performance dropped almost to zero. In a second experiment, a whole ward of 44 patients served as Ss. A similar pro-cedure was followed and 11 classes of tasks observed. When tokens were contingent upon the desired responses, the group spent an average of 45 hours on the tasks daily. When tokens were not contingent on responses, almost no time was spent on the tasks. The implications seem rather clear. When desired behavior is rewarded, it will be emitted, when it is not re-warded, it will not be emitted.

A great deal of related work has been reported. Allyon (1966) and Wolf, Risley, and Mees (1966) have shown how a reinforcement procedure can be effective in controlling the behavior of a psychotic patient and of an autistic child respectively. These are but a few of the many studies in a growing body of evidence.

More important for present purposes are the applications of this ap-proach in more complex social situations. The work of Hamblin et al. (1967) shows some of the interesting possibilities of the conditioning ap-proach for school classes and aggressive children. A token system was used to shape desired behavior. Through the application of the conditioning approach to the school system, gains may be made in educating children from deprived backgrounds. Two examples will illustrate these possibilities.

The first example comes from a recent newspaper story. A record shop owner in a Negro area of Chicago reported seeing the report card of a Negro boy. The owner thought the boy was bright, but the report card showed mostly unsatisfactory performance. He told the boy he would give him $5 worth of free records if he got all "excellents" on the next report card. Ten weeks later the boy returned with such a card to collect his reward. The owner reported that similar offers to other children had a remarkable effect in getting them to study and do their homework. The anecdote demonstrates what everyone knows anyway: people will work for rewards. It also suggests the converse: people will not work if rewards do not exist. The problems of education in the ghetto, and motivation to work in general, may be overcome by appropriate reinforcement. Further support for this statement comes from the work of Montrose Wolf.

Wolf (1966) ran a school for children, most of whom were sixth graders, in a lower class Negro area of Kansas City. The children attended this school for several hours after school each day and on Saturday. Rewards were given in the form of tickets which could be saved and turned in for different kinds of things like toys, food, movies, shopping trips, and other activities. Tickets were made contingent on academic performance within the remedial school itself, and on performance in the regular school system. The results were remarkable. The average school grade of the students was raised to C from D. The results on standard achievement tests showed the remedial group progressed over twice as much in one year as they had done the previous year. They showed twice as much progress as a control group. Other gains were also noted. Wolf reported that a severe punishment was not to let the children attend school. They expressed strong discontent when school was not held because of a holiday. He further noted that when reading was no longer rewarded with tickets, the students still continued to read more than before the training. Arithmetic and English did not maintain these increments. Thus, to some extent, reading appeared to be intrinsically rewarding.

A final point concerns the transferability of skills learned in such a school to society at large. Will the tasks that are not rewarding in themselves be continued? The answer is probably not, unless other rewards are provided. The task then becomes to develop skills and behavior which society itself will reward. If this method is applied to develop behavior which is rewarded by society, the behavior is apt to be maintained. The same argument holds for organizational behavior. It will be fruitless to develop behavior which is not rewarded in the organization.

In summary, evidence has been presented to show the relevance of the Skinnerian approach to complex social systems. Certainly the evidence is only suggestive of future possibilities. The rest of this paper attempts to suggest some of these implications for organizational management.

## MANAGEMENT THROUGH POSITIVE REINFORCEMENT

The implications of the systematic use of positive reinforcement for management range over many traditional areas. Some of the more important areas include training and personnel development, compensation and alternative rewards, supervision and leadership, job design, organizational design, and organizational change.

## Training and Personnel Development

The area of training has been the first to benefit from the application of conditioning principles with the use of programmed learning and the teaching machine. An example of future potential comes from the Northern Systems Company Training Method for assembly line work. In this system, the program objectives are broken down into subobjectives. The training employs a lattice which provides objective relationships between functions and objectives, indicates critical evaluation points, and presents a visual display of go-no-go functions. Progress through various steps is reinforced by rewards. To quote from a statement of the training method ". . . the trainee gains satisfaction only by demonstrated performance at the tool stations. Second, he quickly perceives that correct behaviors obtain for him the satisfaction of his needs, and that incorrect behaviors do not (p. 20)." Correct performance includes not only job skills, but also the performance of social interaction which is necessary in a factory setting. The skills taught are designed to allow for high mobility in the industrial world. The Northern Systems' method develops behavior which the economic and social system will normally reinforce, and has been successful in training people in a wide variety of skills. Its potential in training such groups as the "hard-core" unemployed seems to be limited only by the resources and creativity of program designers.

The Skinnerian approach seems to have potential for all areas of personnel development, not only for highly programmed tasks. Reinforcement theory may be useful in the development of such behaviors as creativity. The work of Maltzman, Simon, Raskin, and Licht (1960) demonstrated this possibility. After a series of experiments employing a standard experimental training procedure with free association materials, these investigators concluded that a highly reliable increase in uncommon responses could be produced through the use of reinforcement. The similarity of their results to those of operant experiments with respect to the persistence of the responses and the effect of repetitions led them to conclude that originality is a form of operant behavior. Positive reinforcement increased the rate at which original responses were emitted.

Support is also available for the efficacy of operant conditioning to more conventional personnel and leadership development. Three such contributions are discussed below. The first concerns the organizational environment as a shaper of behavior of which Fleishman's (1967) study is a case in point. He found that human relations training programs were only effective in producing on-the-job changes if the organizational climate was supportive of the content of the program. More generally it would appear that industrial behavior is a function of its consequences. Those responses which are rewarded will persist; those responses which are not rewarded or are punished will decrease in frequency. If the organizational environment does not reward responses developed in a training program, the program will be, at best, a total waste of time and money. As Sykes (1962) has shown, at worst such a program may be highly disruptive. A second implication of operant conditioning concerns the content of personnel development programs in the area of human relations. If, as Homans (1961) and others have suggested, social interaction is also influenced by the same operant principles, then people in interaction are constantly "shaping" or conditioning each other. The behavior of a subordinate is to some degree developed by his boss and vice-versa. What more sensible, practical point could be taught to organizational members than that they are teaching their fellow participants to behave in a certain manner? What more practical, sensible set of principles could be taught than that, due to latent dysfunctions generated, punishment and extinction procedures are less efficient ways to influence behavior than positive reinforcement? Clearly, the behavioral scientists who have contributed so greatly to organizational practice and personnel development have not put enough emphasis on these simple principles. The third implication for personnel development is added recognition that annual merit interviews and salary increments are very inefficient development techniques. The rewards or punishments are so delayed that they can be expected to have little feedback value for the employees involved. More frequent appraisals and distribution of rewards are apt to be far more effective, especially to the degree that they are related to specific tasks or units of work.

### Job Design

Recently, behavioral scientists have emphasized the social psychological factors which need to be attended to in job design. McGregor and others have suggested job enlargement. Herzberg (1968) has argued that job enlargement just allows an individual to do a greater variety of boring jobs and suggests that "job enrichment" is needed. For present purposes, job enlargement and job enrichment will be lumped together. Both of these approaches are consistent with the conditioning view if two differences can be resolved. First, the definitions of motivation must be translated into common terms. Second, reinforcers operating in the newly designed jobs must be delineated and tested to see if the reinforcers postulated in the newly designed jobs are really responsible for behavioral changes or if there are other reinforcers operating.

With respect to the definitions of motivation, the two approaches are really similar in viewing the rate of behavior as the crucial factor. The major differences exist on the conceptual level. Both job enlargement and job enrichment are attempts to increase motivation. Conceptually, McGregor and Herzberg tend to view motivation as some internal state. The conditioning approach does not postulate internal states but rather deals with the manipulation of environmental factors which influence the rate of behavior. Actually, some combination of the two approaches may be most useful theoretically as Vinacke (1962) has suggested. However, if both approaches are viewed only at the operational level, it is quite probable that rates of behavior could be agreed on as an acceptable criterion. Certainly from the practitioners viewpoint, behavior is the crucial variable. When a manager talks about a motivated worker, he often means one who frequently makes desired responses at a high rate without external prompting from the boss. The traditional view of motivation as an inner drive is of limited practical and theoretical value.

If both approaches could agree on the behavioral criterion, at least on an operational level, the operant approach could be employed to help resolve some practical and theoretical problems suggested by the work of McGregor and Herzberg. Since, generally speaking, the external conditions are most easily manipulated in an organization, attention can be focused on designing an environment which increases the frequency of the wanted responses. As a result, practitioners and students of organization could deal with motivation without searching for man's essence. We can avoid the metaphysical assumptions of Maslow and McGregor until they are better documented. The issue of a two-factor theory of motivation proposed by Herzberg, which recently has been severely challenged by Lindsay, Marks, and Gorlow (1967) and Hulin and Smith (1967), among others, can also be avoided. Attention can be confined to developing systems which produce high rates of desired behavior. Thus the conceptual differences about motivation do not cause unresolvable conflict at the present time.

The second area of difference between McGregor–Herzberg and the operant explanation of the effects of job enrichment stems from the failure of Herzberg and McGregor to recognize the great variety of possible rewards available in job design. The Skinnerian approach leads to the development of a more comprehensive discussion of the rewards from enriched or enlarged jobs. In terms of the operant approach, both job enrichment and job enlargement are apt to lead to what would generally be called greater motivation or what we will call higher rates of desired behavior. McGregor and Herzberg suggest feelings of achievement and responsibility explain these results. The reinforcement approach leads to a search for specific rewards in these newly designed jobs.

Job enlargement can be viewed simply as increasing the variety of tasks a person does. Recent research on self-stimulation and sensory deprivation has suggested that stimulation itself is reinforcing, especially when one has been deprived of it. The increased variety of tasks due to job enlargement may thus be intrinsically rewarding due to a host of reinforcers in the work itself rather than to any greater feeling of responsibility or achievement. These feelings may be a cause of greater productivity or merely correlates of the receipt of these intrinsic rewards from stimulation. The evidence is not clear, but the effects of job enlargement can at least be partially explained in operant terms.

Some additional support from this idea comes from Schultz's (1964) work on spontaneous alternation of behavior. Schultz suggested that spontaneous alteration of human behavior is facilitated (1) when responses are not reinforced and/or are not subjected to knowledge of correctness, (2) by the amount of prior exercise of one response alternative, and (3) by a short interval. Low feedback and reinforcement, short intervals between responses, and the frequent repetition of one response are all characteristic of many jobs which need enlargement. Merely making different responses may be rewarding to a worker, thereby explaining some of the benefits noted from job enlargement. It has also been noted that people create variation for themselves in performing monotonous tasks. For example, ritualized social interaction in the form of social "games" is a form of such alternation workers developed noted by Roy (1964).

By way of summary, much of the current work on job enlargement and enrichment has attributed the effects to feelings of achievement or responsibility, without taking into account numerous other possible reinforcers which may be more basic. Further research to determine the efficacy of these various possibilities is needed before definite conclusions can be drawn. Do the feelings of achievement or responsibility operate as reinforcers in an operant manner? Do these feelings come from other more basic rewards as task variety? Present data do not permit answers to these questions.

With respect to the benefits noted from job enrichment, an operant model may provide further insights. Herzberg (1968) maintained that some jobs can not be "enriched" or made more motivating in themselves. It is the contention of this paper that it is not the tasks which are the problem, but it is the reinforcement schedules. For example, what could be more boring, have less potential for achievement and realization of Herzberg's satisfiers than the game of bingo? Yet people will sit for hours at bingo, often under punishing conditions (since the house takes in more than it pays out) and place tokens on numbers. Similar behavior is exhibited at slot machines and other gambling devices. Most operational definitions of motivation would agree that these players are highly motivated. The reason is clear from the operant viewpoint. The reinforcement schedule employed in games of chance, the variable ratio schedule, is a very powerful device for maintaining a rapid rate of response. With respect to job design, the important requirement is that rewards follow performance on an effective schedule.

The type of rewards Herzberg (1968) called satisfiers may be important motivators because they are distributed on a variable ratio schedule. Herzberg's data does not rule out this explanation. Take achievement, for example. If a person is doing a job from which it is possible to get a feeling of achievement, there must be a reasonably large probability that a person will not succeed on the task. Often times, this condition means that some noncontinuous schedule or reinforcement is operating. An individual will succeed only on some variable ratio schedule. In addition, successful completion of the task is often the most important reward. The reward is, of course, immediate. A similar statement could be made about tasks which are said to yield intrinsic satisfaction, such as crossword puzzles or enriched jobs. Thus the factors Herzberg called motivators may derive their potency from the manner in which the rewards are administered. The task is immediately and positively reinforced by the environment on a variable ratio schedule. Often the schedule is one which rewards a very small fraction of a large number of responses. Since behavior is a function of its consequences, if jobs can be designed to reinforce desired behavior in the appropriate manner, "motivated" workers are apt to result. Some of Herzberg's results may be explained without resort to a two-factor theory more parsimoniously in terms of schedules of reinforcement. Herzberg's (1966) finding that recognition is only a motivator if it is contingent on performance further documents the operant argument.

Another suggestion for job design from the operant tradition was suggested by Homans. He explored the relationship of the frequency of an activity and satisfaction to the amount of a reward. He concluded that satisfaction is generally positively related to the amount of reward whereas frequency of an activity is negatively related to the amount of reward the individual has received in the recent past. In order to have both high satisfaction and high activity, Homans (1961) suggested that tasks need to be designed in a manner such that repeated activities lead up to the accomplishment of some final result and get rewarded at a very low frequency until just before the final result is achieved. Then the reinforcement comes often. For example, consider the job of producing bottled soda. An optimal design would have the reward immediately on the completion of putting the caps on the bottles, but the task would be designed such that all the operations prior to capping were completed before any capping was done. Near the end of a work day, all the capping could be done. High output and satisfaction might then exist simultaneously. In general then, the operant approach suggests some interesting possibilities for designing jobs in ways which would maximize the power of reinforcers in the job itself.

A similar argument can be applied to some problems faced in administration and management. For example, it is commonly recognized that programmed tasks tend to be attended to before unprogrammed ones. It is quite obvious that programmed functions produce a product which is often tangible. The product itself is a reinforcer. An unprogrammed task often requires behavior which has not been reinforced in the past and will not produce a reward in the near future. It may be beneficial to provide rewards relatively early for behavior on unprogrammed tasks. This suggestion will be difficult to put into practice because of the very nature of unprogrammed tasks. Perhaps the best that can be done is to reward the working on such tasks.

### Compensation and Alternative Rewards

Although whether money is a true "generalized reinforcer," as Skinner suggests, has not been demonstrated conclusively, for years operant principles have been applied in the form of monetary incentive systems. Opsahl and Dunnette (1966) concluded that such programs generally do increase output. However, the restriction of output and other unanticipated consequences are associated with these programs. Many writers have attributed these consequences to social forces, such as the desire for approval from one's peers. Gewitz and Baer (1958), for example, have shown that social approval has the same effects as other reinforcers in an operant situation. Dalton's (1948) famous study on rate-busters may be interpreted to show that people who are more "group-oriented" may place a higher value on social approval and hence are more apt to abide by group production norms than are less "group-oriented" people. Thus, it is not that money in piece-rate systems is not a potential reinforcer, but rather other reinforcers are more effective, at least after a certain level of monetary reward.

The successful use of the Scanlon Plan demonstrates the value of combining both economic and social rewards. This plan rewards improved work with several types of reinforcers, and often more immediately and directly than many incentive systems. The Scanlon Plan combines economic rewards, often given monthly, with social rewards. The latter are given soon after an employee's idea has been submitted or used.

Related arguments can be made for other group incentive programs. Often jobs are interdependent. The appropriate reinforcement for such tasks should be contingent upon interdependent responses, not individual ones. Even if the jobs are independent, the workers are social-psychologically interdependent. Social rewards are often obtainable by restricting output. It is hardly surprising that individual incentive programs have produced the unanticipated consequences so often noted. Further, since rewards and punishments from the informal group are apt to be administered immediately and frequently they are apt to be very powerful in controlling behavior.

In general, then, money and other rewards must be made contingent on the desired responses. Further, the importance of alternative rewards to money must be recognized in incorporated into the design of the work environment. The widely known path-goal to productivity model expresses a similar point.

Another problem of compensation in organizations is also apparent in an operant context. Often, means of compensation, especially fringe benefits, have the unanticipated consequences of reinforcing the wrong responses. Current programs of sick pay, recreation programs, employee lounges, work breaks, and numerous other personnel programs all have one point in common. They all reward the employee for not working or for staying away from the job. These programs are not "bad," since often they may act to reduce problems such as turnover. However, an employer who relies on them should realize what behavior he is developing by establishing these costly programs. Alternative expenditures must be considered. If some of the money that was allocated for these programs were used to redesign jobs so as to be more reinforcing in themselves, more productive effort could be obtained. This idea is certainly not new. A host of behavioral scientists have suggested that resources devoted to making performance of the job itself more attractive will pay social and/or economic dividends.

Another interesting application of conditioning principles has to do with the schedule on which pay is distributed. The conventional pay schedule is a fixed interval one. Further, pay often is not really contingent on one's performance. The response needed to be rewarded is often attending work on pay day. Not only is pay often not contingent upon performance, but the fixed interval schedule is not given to generating a high response rate. In a creative article, Aldis (1966) suggested an interesting compensation program employing a variable ratio schedule. Instead of an annual Christmas bonus or other types of such expected salary supplements, he suggested a lottery system. If an employee produced above an agreed upon standard, his name would be placed in a hat. A drawing would be held. The name(s) drawn would receive an amount of money proportionate to the number of units produced during that period of time. This system would approximate the desired variable ratio schedule.

In addition to the prosperity of the owners of gambling establishments, there is some direct evidence that variable ratio schedules will be of use to those charged with predicting and controlling human behavior. A leading St. Louis hardware company,[1] although apparently unaware of the work of the operant conditioners, has applied an approximate variable ratio schedule of reinforcement to reduce absenteeism and tardiness. Although the complete data are not available, the personnel department has reported surprising success. A brief description of the system will be presented below and a more detailed study will be written in the near future.

---

[1] The author wishes to thank Mr. C. for making this information available and one of his students, Richard Weis, for informing him about this program.

Under the lottery system, if a person is on time (that is, not so much as ½ minute late) for work at the start of his day and after his breaks, he is eligible for a drawing at the end of the month. Prizes worth approximately $20 to $25 are awarded to the winners. One prize is available for each 25 eligible employees. At the end of six months, people who have had perfect attendance for the entire period are eligible for a drawing for a color television set. The names of all the winners and of those eligible are also printed in the company paper, such that social reinforcement may also be a factor. The plan was introduced because tardiness and absenteeism had become a very serious problem. In the words of the personnel manager, absenteeism and tardiness ". . . were lousy before." Since the program was begun 16 months ago, conditions have improved greatly. Sick leave costs have been reduced about 62 percent. After the first month, 151 of approximately 530 employees were eligible for the drawing. This number has grown larger, although not at a steady rate, to 219 for the most recent month. Although the comparable figures for the period before the program were unfortunately not available, management has noted great improvements. It would appear that desired behavior by organization participants in terms of tardiness and absenteeism can be readily and inexpensively developed by a variable ratio schedule of positive reinforcement. The possibilities for other areas are limited largely by the creativity of management.

The operant approach also has some additional implications for the use of money as a reward. First, many recent studies have shown money is not as important as other job factors in worker satisfaction. Herzberg (1968), among others, has said explicitly that money will not promote worker satisfaction. Undoubtedly, in many situations, Herzberg is correct. However, crucial factors of reward contingencies and schedules have not been controlled in these studies. Again, it appears that the important distinction that can be made between Herzberg's motivators and hygiene factors is that the former set of rewards are contingent on an individual's responses and the latter are not. If a work situation were designed so that money was directly contingent on performance, the results might be different. A second point has to do with the perception of money as a reward. Opsahl and Dunnette (1966) have recently questioned pay secrecy policies. They maintained that pay secrecy leads to misperception of the amount of money that a promotion might mean. The value of the reinforcers is underestimated by the participants' suggesting that they are less effective than they might otherwise be. Certainly, alternative rewards are likely to be "over chosen." By following policies of pay secrecy, organizations seem to be failing to utilize fully their available monetary rewards.

In addition to underutilization of money rewards, organizations seem to be almost totally unaware of alternative reinforcers, and in fact see punishment as the only viable method of control when existing reinforcers fail. What are some alternatives to a punishment-centered bureaucracy? Some, such as job design, improved scheduling of reinforcement, and a search for new reinforcers have already been suggested. There are other possible reinforcers, a few of which are discussed below.

The important thing about reinforcers is that they be made immediately contingent on desired performance to the greatest degree possible. The potential reinforcers discussed here also require such a contingent relationship, although developing such relationships may be a severe test of an administrator's creativity. One of the more promising reinforcers is leisure. It would seem possible in many jobs to establish an agreed-upon standard output for a day's work. This level could be higher than the current average. Once this amount is reached, the group or individual could be allowed the alternative of going home. The result of experiments in this direction would be interesting to all concerned. Quite possibly, this method might lead to a fuller utilization of our labor force. The individual may be able to hold two four-hour jobs, doubling his current contribution. Such a tremendous increase in output is quite possible, as Stagner and Rosen (1966) have noted, when the situation possesses appropriate contingencies. Certainly, the problems of industrial discipline, absenteeism, and grievances which result in lower productivity might be ameliorated. Another possible reinforcer is information. Guetzkow (1965) noted that people have a strong desire to receive communication. Rewarding desired performance with communication or feedback may be a relatively inexpensive reinforcer. Graphs, charts, or even tokens which show immediate and cumulative results may serve this function. Some of the widely accepted benefits from participative management may be due to the reinforcing effect of communication. Certainly the "Hawthorne effect" can be described in these terms. In addition, social approval and status may be powerful reinforcers. Blau's classic study described by Homans (1961) on the exchange of approval and status for help is but one example. People will work for approval and status. If these are made contingent on a desired set of responses, the response rate can be increased. At present, often social approval is given by one's peers, but is contingent on behavior which is in conflict with organizational goals.

In addition to these reinforcers, there are certain social exchange concepts such as justice, equity, reciprocity, and indebtedness which deserve attention. Recent research has demonstrated that an unbalanced social exchange, such as one which is inequitable or leaves one person indebted to someone else, may be tension-producing in such a way that individuals work to avoid them. In other words, unbalanced exchanges are a source of punishment. Relationships, such as those involving dependency, which result in such social imbalance can be expected to have the same latent consequences as punishment. Techniques which employ social imbalance to predict and control behavior can be expected to be less efficient in most respects than ones based on positive reinforcement.

The crucial variable in distributing any reward is contingency. Managers have been quick to point out that the problem with a "welfare state" is that rewards do not depend on desired behavior. This point is well taken. It is surprising that the same point has not been recognized in current management practices.

## Organizational Climate and Design

Important aspects of human behavior can be attributed to the immediate environment in which people function. The potential then exists to structure and restructure formal organizations in a manner to promote the desired behavior. Once this point is recognized and accepted by managers, progress can begin. The reaction of managers to this approach is often, "You mean my organization should reward people for what they ought to do anyway?" The answer is that people's behavior is largely determined by its outcomes. It is an empirical fact rather than a moral question. If you want a certain response and it does not occur, you had better change the reinforcement contingencies to increase its probable occurrence.

The first step in the direction of designing organizations on this basis involves defining explicitly the desired behaviors and the available reinforcers. The next step is to then make these rewards dependent on the emission of the desired responses. What are some of the implications of such reasoning for organizational design?

Already the importance of organizational climate has been discussed in connection with human development. Some additional implications merit brief consideration. A major one concerns conformity. Often today the degree to which people conform to a wide variety of norms is lamentably acknowledged and the question is asked, "Why do people do it?" The reasons in the operant view are quite clear: conformity is rewarded, deviance is punished. People conform in organizations because conformity is profitable in terms of the outcomes the individual achieves. In fact, Nord (in press) and Walker and Heyns (1962) presented considerable evidence that conformity has the same properties as other operant responses. If managers are really worried about the costs of conformity in terms of creativity and innovation, they must look for ways to reward deviance, to avoid punishing nonconformity, and to avoid rewarding conformity. Furthermore, the way in which rewards are administered is important. Generally, if rewards are given by a person or group of people, a dependency relationship is created, with hostility, fear, anxiety, and other emotional outcomes being probable. Dependence itself may be a discomforting condition. It is therefore desirable to make the rewards come from the environment. Rewards which have previously been established for reaching certain agreed-upon goals are one such means. Meaningful jobs in which achievement in itself is rewarding are another way. In general, to the degree that competition is with the environment or forces outside the organization, and rewards come from achievement itself, the more effective the reinforcers are apt to be in achieving desired responses.

A final point concerns the actual operation of organizations. Increasingly it is recognized that a formal organization, which aims at the coordination of the efforts of its participants, is dependent on informal relationships for its operation. As Gross (1968) noted,

> In administration, also, "the play's the thing" and not the script. Many aspects of even the simplest operation can never be expressed in writing. They must be sensed and felt. . . . Daily action is the key channel of operational definition. In supplying cues and suggestions, in voicing praise and blame, in issuing verbal instructions, administrators define or clarify operational goals in real life (p. 406).

More generally, what makes an organization "tick" is the exchange of reinforcers within it and between it and its environment. The nature of these exchanges involves both economic and social reinforcers. Many of these are given and received without explicit recognition or even awareness on the part of the participants. The operant approach focuses attention on these exchange processes. As a result, it may prove to be an invaluable asset to both administrators and students of administration and organization.

A final advantage of the operant approach for current organizational theory and analysis may be the attention it focuses on planned and rational administration. Gouldner (1966) noted "Modern organizational analysis by sociologists is overpreoccupied with the spontaneous and unplanned responses which organizations make to stress, and too little concerned with patterns of planned and rational administration (p. 397)." The Skinnerian approach leads to rational planning in order to control outcomes previously viewed as spontaneous consequences. This approach could expand the area of planning rational action in administration.

## REFERENCES

ALDIS, O., "Of Pigeons and Men," in R. Ulrich, T. Stachnik and J. Mabry (eds.), *Control of Human Behavior*. Glenview, Ill.: Scott, Foresman, 1966, pp. 218–221.

AYLLON, T., "Intensive Treatment of Psychotic Behavior by Stimulus Satiation and Food Reinforcement," in R. Ulrich, T. Stachnik and T. Mabry (eds.), *Control of Human Behavior*. Glenview, Ill.: Scott, Foresman, 1966, pp. 170–176.

AYLLON, T., and AZRIN, N. H., "The Measurement and Reinforcement of Behavior of Psychotics," *Journal of the Experimental Analysis of Behavior*, 1965, 8, pp. 357–383.

BIJOU, S. W., and BAER, D. M., *Child Development*, Vol. 1. New York: Appleton-Century-Crofts, 1961.

DALTON, M., "The Industrial 'Rate-Buster': A Characterization," *Applied Anthropology*, 1948, 7, pp. 5–18.

FLEISHMAN, E. A., "Leadership Climate, Human Relations Training, and Supervisory behavior," in Fleishman, E. A. (ed.), *Studies in Personnel and Industrial Psychology*. Homewood, Ill.: Dorsey, 1967, pp. 250–263.

"Free Records Given for E's, Pupils Report Cards Improve," *St. Louis Dispatch*, December 3, 1967.

GEWIRTZ, J. L., and BAER, D. M., "Deprivation and Satiation of Social Reinforcers as Drive Conditions," *Journal of Abnormal and Social Psychology*, 1958, 57, pp. 165–172.

GOULDNER, A. W., "Organizational Analysis," in Bennis, W. G., Benne, K. D., and Chin, R. (eds.), *The Planning of Change*. New York: Holt, Rinehart, and Winston, 1966, pp. 393–399.

GROSS, B. M., *Organizations and Their Managing*. New York: Free Press, 1968.

GUETZKOW, H., "Communications in Organizations," in March, J. G. (ed.), *Handbook of Organizations*. Chicago: Rand McNally, 1965, pp. 534–573.

HAMBLIN, R. L., BUSHELL, O. B., BUCKHOLDT, D., ELLIS, D., FERRITOR, D., MERRITT, G., PFEIFFER, C., SHEA, D., and STODDARD, D., "Learning, Problem Children and a Social Exchange System." Annual Report of the Social Exchange Laboratories, Washington University, and Student Behavior Laboratory, Webster College, St. Louis, Mo., August, 1967.

HERZBERG, F., "One More Time: How Do You Motivate Employees?" *Harvard Business Review*, January–February, 1968, pp. 53–62.

HERZBERG, F., *Work and the Nature of Man*. Cleveland: World, 1966.

HOMANS, G. C., *Social Behavior: Its Elementary Forms*. New York: Harcourt, Brace and World, 1961.

HULIN, C. L., and SMITH, P. A., "An Empirical Investigation of Two Implications of the Two-Factor Theory of Job Satisfaction," *Journal of Applied Psychology*, 1967, 51, pp. 396–402.

LINDSAY, C. A., MARKS, E., and GORLOW, L., "The Herzberg Theory: A Critique and Reformulation," *Journal of Applied Psychology*, 1967, 51, pp. 330–339.

MALTZMAN, I., SIMON, S., ROSKIN, D., and LICHT, L., "Experimental Studies in the Training of Originality," Psychological Monographs: General and Applied, 1960, 74 (6, Whole No. 493).

MASLOW, A., *Eupsychian Management*. Homewood, Ill.: Dorsey, 1965.

McGREGOR, D., *The Human Side of Enterprise*. New York: McGraw-Hill, 1960.

McGREGOR, D., *Leadership and Motivation*. Cambridge, Mass.: M. I. T. Press, 1966.

NORD, W. R., "Social Exchange Theory: An Integrative Approach to Social Conformity," *Psychological Bulletin*, (in press).

Northern Systems Company, "A Proposal to the Department of Labor for Development of a Prototype Project for the New Industries Program." Part one.

OPSAHL, R. L., and DUNNETTE, M. D., "The Role of Financial Compensation in Industrial Motivation," *Psychological Bulletin*, 1966, 66, pp. 94–118.

REESE, E. P., *The Analysis of Human Operant Behavior*. Dubuque, Iowa: William C. Brown, 1966.

ROY, D. F., "Banana Time—Job Satisfaction and Informal Interaction," in Bennis, W. G., Schein, E. H., Berlew, D. E., and Steele, F. I. (eds.), *Interpersonal Dynamics*. Homewood, Ill.: Dorsey, 1964, pp. 583–600.

SCHULTZ, D. P., "Spontaneous Alteration Behavior in Humans, Implications for Psychological Research," *Psychological Bulletin*, 1964, 62, pp. 394–400.

SKINNER, B. F., *Science and Human Behavior*. New York: Macmillan, 1953.

SKINNER, B. F., "The Science of Learning and the Art of Teaching," *Harvard Educational Review*, 1954, 24, pp. 86–97.

SKINNER, B. F., *Walden Two*. New York: Macmillan, 1948.

STAGNER, R., and ROSEN, H., *Psychology of Union-Management Relations*. Belmont, Cal.: Wadsworth, 1966.

SYKES, A. J. M., "The Effect of a Supervisory Training Course in Changing Supervisors' Perceptions and Expectations of the Role of Management," *Human Relations*, 1962, 15, pp. 227–243.

VINACKE, E. W., "Motivation as a Complex Problem," *Nebraska Symposium on Motivation*, 1962, 10, pp. 1–45.

WALKER, E. L., and HEYNS, R. W., *An Anatomy of Conformity*. Englewood Cliffs, N.J.: Prentice-Hall, 1962.

WOLF, M. M., Paper read at Sociology Colloquium, Washington University, December 5, 1966.

WOLF, M. M., RISLEY, T., and MEES, H., "Application of Operant Conditioning Procedures to the Behavior Problems of an Autistic Child," in R. Ulrich, T. Stachnik and T. Mabry (eds.), *Control of Human Behavior*. Glenview, Ill.: Scott, Foresman, 1966, pp. 187–193.

# Split Roles in Performance Appraisal*

## HERBERT H. MEYER, EMANUEL KAY, and JOHN R. P. FRENCH, JR.

IN MANAGEMENT CIRCLES, performance appraisal is a highly interesting and provocative topic. And in business literature, too, knowledgeable people write emphatically, pro and con, on the performance appraisal question.[1] In fact, one might almost say that everybody talks and writes about it, but nobody has done any real scientific testing of it.

At the General Electric Company we felt it was important that a truly scientific study be done to test the effectiveness of our traditional performance appraisal program. Why? Simply because our own experience with performance appraisal programs had been both positive and negative. For example:

1. Surveys generally show that most people think the idea of performance appraisal is good. They feel that a man should know where he stands and, therefore, the manager should discuss an appraisal of his performance with him periodically.

2. In actual practice, however, it is the extremely rare operating manager who will employ such a program on his own initiative. Personnel specialists report that most managers carry out performance appraisal interviews only when strong control procedures are established to ensure that they do so. This is surprising because the managers have been told repeatedly that the system is intended to help them obtain improved performance from their subordinates.

* Reprinted by permission from *Harvard Business Review* January–February issue 1965, pp. 123–29.

[1] Douglas McGregor, "An Uneasy Look at Performance Appraisal," *Harvard Business Review* May–June 1957, p. 89; Harold Mayfield, "In Defense of Performance Appraisal," *Harvard Business Review* March–April 1960, p. 81; and Alva F. Kindall and James Gatza, "Positive Program for Performance Appraisal," *Harvard Business Review* November–December 1963, p. 153.

We also found from interviews with employees who have had a good deal of experience with traditional performance appraisal programs that few indeed can cite examples of constructive action taken—or significant improvement achieved—which stem from suggestions received in a performance appraisal interview with their boss.

## TRADITIONAL PROGRAM

Faced with such contradictory evidence, we undertook a study several years ago to determine the effectiveness of our comprehensive performance appraisal process. Special attention was focused on the interview between the subordinate and his manager, because this is the discussion which is supposed to motivate the man to improve his performance. And we found out some very interesting things—among them the following:

1. Criticism has a negative effect on achievement of goals.
2. Praise has little effect one way or the other.
3. Performance improves most when specific goals are established.
4. Defensiveness resulting from critical appraisal produces inferior performance.
5. Coaching should be a day-to-day, not a once-a-year, activity.
6. Mutual goal setting, not criticism, improves performance.
7. Interviews designed primarily to improve a man's performance should not at the same time weigh his salary or promotion in the balance.
8. Participation by the employee in the goal-setting procedure helps produce favorable results.

As you can see, the results of this original study indicated that a detailed and comprehensive annual appraisal of a subordinate's performance by his manager is decidedly of questionable value. Furthermore, as is certainly the case when the major objective of such a discussion is to motivate the subordinate to improve his performance, the traditional appraisal interview does not do the job.

In the first part of this article, we will offer readers more than this bird's-eye view of our research into performance appraisal. (We will not, however, burden managers with details of methodology.) We will also describe the one-year follow-up experiment General Electric conducted to validate the conclusions derived from our original study. Here the traditional annual performance appraisal method was tested against a new method we developed, which we called Work Planning and Review (WP&R). As you will see, this approach produced, under actual plant conditions, results which were decidedly superior to those afforded by the traditional performance appraisal method. Finally, we will offer evidence to support our contention that some form of WP&R might well be incorporated into other industrial personnel programs to achieve improvement in work performance.

## APPRAISING APPRAISAL

In order to assure a fair test of the effectiveness of the traditional performance appraisal method, which had been widely used throughout General Electric, we conducted an intensive study of the process at a large GE plant where the performance appraisal program was judged to be good; that is, in this plant—

. . . appraisals had been based on job responsibilities, rather than on personal characteristics of the individuals involved;

. . . an intensive training program had been carried out for managers in the use of the traditional appraisal method and techniques for conducting appraisal interviews;

. . . the program had been given strong backing by the plant manager and had been policed diligently by the personnel staff so that over 90 percent of the exempt employees had been appraised and interviewed annually.

This comprehensive annual performance appraisal program, as is typical, was designed to serve two major purposes. The first was to justify recommended salary action. The second, which was motivational in character, was intended to present an opportunity for the manager to review a subordinate's performance and promote discussion on needed improvements. For the latter purpose, the manager was required to draw up a specific program of plans and goals for the subordinate which would help him to improve his job performance and to qualify, hopefully, for future promotion.

### Interview Modifications

Preliminary interviews with key managers and subordinates revealed the salary action issue had so dominated the annual comprehensive performance appraisal interview that neither party had been in the right frame of mind to discuss plans for improved performance. To straighten this out, we asked managers to split the traditional appraisal interview into two sessions—discussing appraisal of performance and salary action in one interview and performance improvement plans in another to be held about two weeks later. This split provided us with a better opportunity to conduct our experiment on the effects of participation in goal planning.

To enable us to test the effects of participation, we instructed half the managers to use a *high participation* approach and the other half to use a *low participation* technique. Thus:

1. Each of the "high" managers was instructed to ask his appraisee to prepare a set of goals for achieving improved job performance and to submit them for the manager's review and approval. The manager also was encouraged to permit the subordinate to exert as much influence as possible on the formulation of the final list of job goals agreed on in the performance improvement discussion.

2. The "low" managers operated in much the same way they had in our traditional appraisal program. They formulated a set of goals for the subordinate, and these goals were then reviewed in the performance improvement session. The manager was instructed to conduct this interview in such a way that his influence in the forming of the final list of job goals would be greater than the subordinate's.

### Conducting the Research

There were 92 appraisees in the experimental group, representing a cross section of the exempt salaried employees in the plant. This group included engineers; engineering support technicians; foremen; and specialists in manufacturing, customer service, marketing, finance, and purchasing functions. None of the exempt men who participated as appraisees in the experiment had other exempt persons reporting to them; thus they did not serve in conflicting manager-subordinate roles.

The entire group was interviewed and asked to complete questionnaires (a) before and after the salary action interview, and (b) after the delayed second discussion with their managers about performance improvement. These interviews and questionnaires were designed to achieve three objectives:

1. Assess changes in the attitudes of individuals toward their managers and toward the appraisal system after each of the discussions.

2. Get an estimate from the appraisee of the degree to which he usually participated in decisions that affected him. (This was done in order to determine whether or not previous lack of participation affected his response to participation in the experiment.)

3. Obtain a self-appraisal from each subordinate before and after he met with his manager. (This was done in order to determine how discrepancies in these self-appraisals might affect his reaction to the appraisal interview.)

Moreover, each salary action and performance improvement discussion was observed by outsiders trained to record essentially what transpired. (Managers preferred to use neither tape recorders nor unseen observers, feeling that observers unaffiliated with the company—in this case, graduate students in applied psychological disciplines—afforded the best way

of obtaining a reasonably close approximation of the normal discussions.)
In the appraisal for salary action interviews, for example, the observers
recorded the amount of criticism and praise employed by the manager,
as well as the reactions of the appraisee to the manager's comments. In
the performance improvement discussions, the observers recorded the participation of the subordinate, as well as the amount of influence he seemed
to exert in establishing his future success goals.

### Criticism and Defensiveness

In general, the managers completed the performance appraisal forms
in a thorough and conscientious manner. Their appraisals were discussed
with subordinates in interviews ranging from approximately 30 to 90
minutes in length. On the average, managers covered 32 specific performance items which, when broken down, showed positive (praise) appraisals
on 19 items, and negative (criticism) on 13. Typically, praise was more
often related to *general* performance characteristics, while criticism was
usually focused on *specific* performance items.

The average subordinate reacted defensively to seven of the manager's
criticisms during the appraisal interview (that is, he reacted defensively
about 54 percent of the time when criticized). Denial of shortcomings cited
by the manager, blaming others, and various other forms of excuses were
recorded by the observers as defensive reactions.

Constructive responses to criticism were *rarely* observed. In fact, the
average was less than one per interview. Not too surprising, along with
this, was the finding that the more criticism a man received in the performance appraisal discussion, the more defensively he reacted. Men who
received an above-average number of criticisms showed more than five
times as much defensive behavior as those who received a below-average
number of criticisms. Subordinates who received a below-average number
of criticisms, for example, reacted defensively only about one time out of
three. But those who received an above-average number reacted defensively almost two times out of three.

One explanation for this defensiveness is that it seems to stem from
the overrating each man tended to give to his own performance. The
average employee's self-estimate of performance *before* appraisal placed
him at the 77 percentile. (Only 2 of the 92 participants estimated their
performance to be below the average point on the scale.) But when the
same men were asked *after* their performance appraisal discussions how
they thought their bosses had rated them, the average figure given was at
the 65 percentile. The great majority (75 out of 92) saw their manager's
evaluation as being less favorable than their self-estimates. Obviously, to
these men, the performance appraisal discussion with the manager was a

deflating experience. Thus, it was not surprising that the subordinates re-acted defensively in their interviews.

## Criticism and Goal Achievement

Even more important is the fact that men who received an above-average number of criticisms in their performance appraisal discussions generally showed *less* goal achievement 10 to 12 weeks later than those who had received fewer criticisms. At first, we thought that this difference might be accounted for by the fact that the subordinates who received more criticisms were probably poorer performers in general. But there was little factual evidence found to support this suspicion.

It was true that those who received an above-average number of criti-cisms in their appraisal discussions did receive slightly lower summary ratings on overall performance from their managers. But they did not receive proportionally lower salary increases. And the salary increases granted were *supposed* to reflect differences in job performance, according to the salary plan traditionally used in this plant. This argument, admit-tedly, is something less than perfect.

But it does appear clear that frequent criticism constitutes so strong a threat to self-esteem that it disrupts rather than improves subsequent performance. We expected such a disruptive threat to operate more strongly on those individuals who were already low on self-esteem, just as we expected a man who had confidence in his ability to do his job to react more constructively to criticism. Our group experiment proved these expectations to be correct.

Still further evidence that criticism has a negative effect on performance was found when we investigated areas which had been given special emphasis by the manager in his criticism. Following the appraisal discus-sion with the manager, each employee was asked to indicate which one aspect of his performance had been most criticized by the manager. Then, when we conducted our follow-up investigation 10 to 12 weeks later, it revealed that improvement in the most-criticized aspects of performance cited was considerably *less* than improvement realized in other areas!

## Participation Effects

As our original research study had indicated, the effects of a high par-ticipation level were also favorable in our group experiment. In general, here is what we found:

1. Subordinates who received a high participation level in the perform-ance interview reacted more favorably than did those who received a low

participation level. The "highs" also, in most cases, achieved a greater percentage of their improvement goals than did their "low" counterparts. For the former, the high participation level was associated with greater mutual understanding between them and their managers, greater acceptance of job goals, a more favorable attitude toward the appraisal system, and a feeling of greater self-realization on the job.

2. But employees who had traditionally been accustomed to low participation in their daily relationship with the manager did not necessarily perform better under the high participation treatment. In fact, those men who had received a high level of criticism in their appraisal interviews actually performed better when their managers set goals for them than they did when they set their own goals, as permitted under the high participation treatment.

In general, our experiment showed that the men who usually worked under high participation levels performed best on goals they set for themselves. Those who indicated that they usually worked under low levels performed best on goals that the managers set for them. Evidently, the man who usually does not participate in work-planning decisions considers job goals set by the manager to be more important than goals he sets for himself. The man accustomed to a high participation level, on the other hand, may have stronger motivation to achieve goals he sets for himself than to achieve those set by his manager.

### Goal-Setting Importance

While subordinate participation in the goal-setting process had some effect on improved performance, a much more powerful influence was whether goals were set at all. Many times in appraisal discussions, managers mentioned areas of performance where improvement was needed. Quite often these were translated into specific work plans and goals. But this was not always the case. In fact, when we looked at the one performance area which each manager had emphasized in the appraisal interview as most in need of improvement, we found that these items actually were translated into specific work plans and goals for only about 60 percent of our experiment participants.

When performance was being measured 10 to 12 weeks after the goal-planning sessions, managers were asked to describe what results they hoped for in the way of subordinate on-the-job improvement. They did this for those important performance items that had been mentioned in the interview. Each manager was then asked to estimate on a percentage scale the degree to which his hoped-for changes had actually been observed. The average percent accomplishment estimate for those performance items that *did* get translated into goals was 65, while the percent estimate for those items that *did not* get translated into goals was about 27!

Establishing specific plans and goals seemed to ensure that attention would be given to that aspect of job performance.

## Summation of Findings

At the end of this experiment, we were able to draw certain tentative conclusions. These conclusions were the basis of a future research study which we will describe later. In general, we learned that:

*Comprehensive annual performance appraisals are of questionable value.* Certainly a major objective of the manager in traditional appraisal discussions is motivating the subordinate to improve his performance. But the evidence we gathered indicated clearly that praise tended to have no effect, perhaps because it was regarded as the sandwich which surrounded the raw meat of criticism.[2] And criticism itself brought on defensive reactions that were essentially denials of responsibility for a poor performance.

*Coaching should be a day-to-day, not a once-a-year, activity.* There are two main reasons for this: (1) Employees seem to accept suggestions for improved performance if they are given in a less concentrated form than is the case in comprehensive annual appraisals. As our experiment showed, employees become clearly more prone to reject criticisms as the number of criticisms mount. This indicates that an "overload phenomenon" may be operating. In other words, each individual seems to have a tolerance level for the amount of criticism he can take. And, as this level is approached or passed, it becomes increasingly difficult for him to accept responsibility for the shortcomings pointed out. (2) Some managers reported that the traditional performance appraisal program tended to cause them to save up items where improvement was needed in order to have enough material to conduct a comprehensive discussion of performance in the annual review. This short-circuited one of the primary purposes of the appraisal program—that of giving feedback to the subordinates as to their performance. Studies of the learning process point out that feedback is less effective if much time is allowed to elapse between the performance and the feedback. This fact alone argues for more frequent discussions between the manager and the subordinate.

*Goal setting, not criticism, should be used to improve performance.* One of the most significant findings in our experiment was the fact that far superior results were observed when the manager and the man *together* set specific goals to be achieved, rather than merely discussed needed improvement. Frequent reviews of progress provide natural opportunities for discussing means of improving performance *as needs occur,* and these re-

---

[2] See Richard E. Farson, "Praise Reappraised," *Harvard Business Review* September–October 1963, p. 61.

views are far less threatening than the annual appraisal and salary review discussions.

*Separate appraisals should be held for different purposes.* Our work demonstrated that it was unrealistic to expect a single performance appraisal program to achieve every conceivable need. It seems foolish to have a manager serving in the self-conflicting role as a counselor (helping a man to improve his performance) when, at the same time, he is presiding as a judge over the same employee's salary action case.

## NEW WP&R METHOD

This intensive year-long test of the performance appraisal program indicated clearly that work-planning-and-review discussions between a man and his manager appeared to be a far more effective approach in improving job performance than was the concentrated annual performance appraisal program.

For this reason, after the findings had been announced, many GE managers adopted some form of the new WP&R program to motivate performance improvement in employees, especially those at the professional and administrative levels. Briefly described, the WP&R approach calls for periodic meetings between the manager and his subordinate. During these meetings, progress on past goals is reviewed, solutions are sought for job-related problems, and new goals are established. The intent of the method is to create a situation in which manager and subordinate can discuss job performance and needed improvements in detail without the subordinate becoming defensive.

### Basic Features

This WP&R approach differs from the traditional performance appraisal program in that:

1. There are more frequent discussions of performance.
2. There are no summary judgments or ratings made.
3. Salary action discussions are held separately.
4. The emphasis is on mutual goal planning and problem solving.

As far as frequency is concerned, these WP&R discussions are held more often than traditional performance appraisal interviews, but are not scheduled at rigidly fixed intervals. Usually at the conclusion of one work planning session the man and manager set up approximate date for the next review. Frequency depends both on the nature of the job and on the manager's style of operating. Some times these WP&R discussions are held as often as once a month, whereas for other jobs and/or individuals, once every six months is more appropriate.

In these WP&R discussions, the manager and his subordinate do not deal in generalities. They consider specific, objectively defined work goals and establish the yardstick for measuring performance. These goals stem, of course, from broader departmental objectives and are defined in relation to the individual's position in the department.

## Comparison Setting

After the findings of our experiment were communicated by means of reports and group meetings in the plant where the research was carried out, about half the key managers decided they would abandon the comprehensive annual performance appraisal method and adopt the new WP&R program instead. The other half were hesitant to make such a major change at the time. They decided, consequently, to continue with the traditional performance appraisal program and to try to make it more effective. This provided a natural setting for us to compare the effectiveness of the two approaches. We decided that the comparison should be made in the light of the objectives usually stated for the comprehensive annual performance appraisal program. These objectives were (a) to provide knowledge of results to employees, (b) to justify reasons for salary action, and (c) to motivate and help employees do a better job.

The study design was simple. Before any changes were made, the exempt employees who would be affected by these programs were surveyed to provide base-line data. The WP&R program was then implemented in about half of the exempt group, with the other half continuing to use a modified version of the traditional performance appraisal program. One year later, the identical survey questionnaire was again administered in order to compare the changes that had occurred.

## Attitudes and Actions

The results of this research study were quite convincing. The group that continued on the traditional performance appraisal showed no change in *any* of the areas measured. The WP&R group, by contrast, expressed significantly more favorable attitudes on almost all questionnaire items. Specifically, their attitudes changed in a favorable direction over the year that they participated in the new WP&R program with regard to the:

1. Amount of help the manager was giving them in improving performance on the job.
2. Degree to which the manager was receptive to new ideas and suggestions.
3. Ability of the manager to plan.
4. Extent to which the manager made use of their abilities and experience.

5. Degree to which they felt the goals they were shooting for were what they *should* be.
6. Extent to which they received help from the manager in planning for *future* job opportunity.
7. Value of the performance discussions they had with their managers.

In addition to these changes in attitudes, evidence was also found which showed clearly that the members of the WP&R group were much more likely to have taken specific actions to improve performance than were those who continued with the traditional performance appraisal approach.

## CURRENT OBSERVATIONS

Recently we undertook still another intensive study of the WP&R program in order to learn more about the nature of these discussions and how they can be made most effective. While these observations have not been completed, some interesting findings have already come to light— especially in relation to differences between WP&R and traditional performance appraisal discussions.

### Perceived Differences

For one thing, WP&R interviews are strictly man-to-man in character, rather than having a father-and-son flavor, as did so many of the traditional performance appraisals. This seems to be due to the fact that it is much more natural under the WP&R program for the subordinate to take the initiative when his performance on past goals is being reviewed. Thus, in listening to the subordinate's review of performance, problems, and failings, the manager is automatically cast in the role of *counselor*. This role for the manager, in turn, results naturally in a problem-solving discussion.

In the traditional performance appraisal interview, on the other hand, the manager is automatically cast in the role of *judge*. The subordinate's natural reaction is to assume a defensive posture, and thus all the necessary ingredients for an argument are present.

Since the WP&R approach focuses mainly on immediate, short-term goals, some managers are concerned that longer range, broader plans and goals might be neglected. Our data show that this concern is unfounded. In almost every case, the discussion of specific work plans and goals seems to lead naturally into a consideration of broader, longer range plants. In fact, in a substantial percentage of these sessions, even the career plans of the subordinates are reviewed.

In general, the WP&R approach appears to be a better way of defining what is expected of an individual and how he is doing on the job. Whereas the traditional performance appraisal often results in resistance to the manager's attempts to help the subordinate, the WP&R approach brings about acceptance of such attempts.

## CONCLUSION

Multiple studies conducted by the Behavioral Research Service at GE reveal that the traditional performance appraisal method contains a number of problems:

1. Appraisal interviews attempt to accomplish the two objectives of (a) providing a written justification for salary action; (b) motivating the employee to improve his work performance.
2. The two purposes are in conflict, with the result that the traditional appraisal system essentially becomes a salary discussion in which the manager justifies the action taken.
3. The appraisal discussion has little influence on future job performance.
4. Appreciable improvement is realized only when specified goals and deadlines are mutually established and agreed on by the subordinate and his manager in an interview split away from the appraisal interview.

This evidence, coupled with other principles relating to employee motivation, gave rise to the new WP&R program, which is proving to be far more effective in improving job performance than the traditional performance appraisal method. Thus, it appears likely that companies which are currently relying on the comprehensive annual performance appraisal process to achieve improvement in work performance might well consider the advisability of switching to some form of work-planning-and-review in their industrial personnel programs.

> Wonders are many, and none is more wonderful than man.
>
> SOPHOCLES (495–406 B.C.)

# A Fresh Look at Management by Objectives*

## ROBERT A. HOWELL

DURING THE PAST FEW YEARS, a great deal of interest has been shown the "management by objectives" approach—in the pages of management journals, at management seminars, and in industry. Unfortunately, because of the benefits of the approach to the personnel functions in the area of performance evaluation and in part because of the recent surge in interest toward the thinking of behavioral scientists, I feel that many of the companies employing management by objectives are not even beginning to utilize its potential. In this article, I will try to show that:

1. Primary emphasis for using management by objectives has stemmed from the personnel function and behavioral scientists as an aid toward improving individual motivation and for providing a sounder basis for evaluating individual job performance.
2. This emphasis leaves much to be desired in terms of the overall usefulness of the concept to top management.
3. Management by objectives should be thought of as a top management planning and control approach, rather than as an aid to the personnel function.
4. When thought of in terms of this broader point of view, the effects on the overall organization may be very great. They would include a better integration of the objectives of the total organization, its subunits, and the individuals in the organization as to where the organization is going and how it is going to get there; emphasis on what is most important, not what is most expeditious, and thus the reduction of unnecessary work; and the elimination of overlapping responsibilities, reducing duplication of effort, interdepartmental misunderstanding, and conflict. All these would improve performance and boost morale.

---

* Reprinted by permission from *Business Horizons,* Fall 1967.

In addition to these four points, I will discuss several ideas that may be included in the management by objectives system to make it even more effective. These include peer objective setting, frequent performance review, and multiple performance evaluation.

## EMPHASIS ON THE INDIVIDUAL

Hardly a week goes by that I do not have at least one management article pass across my desk extolling the virtues of the management by objectives approach. After reading them I have drawn three basic conclusions.

First, articles and books are usually written by behavioral scientists interested less in the economic objectives of industry than in the health of the individual employee, or by personnel managers within industry interested in making their own jobs easier. [See, for example, Douglas McGregor, "An Uneasy Look at Performance Appraisal," *Harvard Business Review* (May–June, 1957); Rensis Likert, "Motivational Approach to Management Development," *Harvard Business Review* (July–August, 1959); H. H. Meyer, E. Kay, and J. R. P. French, Jr., "Split Roles in Performance Appraisal," *Harvard Business Review* (January–February, 1965).] These authors emphasize the importance of having the individual participate in setting his own work objectives and the resultant favorable effect on the individual's morale and performance. Little concern is given to the question of whether the individual's objectives relate directly to those of the organization. They emphasize the performance evaluation aspects of management by objectives—that is, by having the subordinate set objectives for himself, the superior is in a sounder position to evaluate his performance.

Second, the authors describe management by objectives as a "simple" process whereby the individual in the organization plans his work in terms of the objectives he has set by himself or with his superior's help, performs in accordance with the plans, and is subsequently evaluated in terms of the previously established objectives. This description is misleading and dangerous. As I will indicate later, the definition of an individual's role—that is, objectives—in the organization is not easy.

Third, the authors state that the individual and the personnel manager benefit from management by objectives. For the individual, benefits include: (1) knowledge as to what his superior expects to be accomplished, which assures that he directs his efforts toward what is most important; (2) an understanding on the part of each subordinate as to where he stands with his superior in terms of relative progress; (3) a better basis for performance evaluation than is possible through evaluation based on a list of personality traits (ability, initiative, integrity, judgment, health, and appearance); and (4) ultimate higher individual performance and morale.

For the personnel manager, the advantages include: (1) a reservoir of personnel data and performance information on a periodic basis for updating personnel files; (2) the determination of personnel development needs within the organization; and (3) a sound basis for promotion decisions and compensation practices.

In addition to articles and books, a number of management seminars also emphasize the importance of management by objectives for the individual. The following quotations illustrate some of the claims made:

. . . a workable tool for more effective planning and self appraisal.

. . . focuses attention on individual achievement, motivates individuals to accomplishment, and measures performance in terms of results.

. . . a managerial method whereby the superior and subordinate manager in an organization identify major areas in which the subordinate will work, set standards for performance, and measure results against these standards.

. . . effective alternate to the largely inadequate traditional approach to measuring results is a method that establishes definite results which the individual is to achieve in a given time frame. This is called management by objectives, goals management, or management by results.

## Effect on the Organization

We may question what effect the emphasis on the benefits to the individual has had upon the implementation of management by objectives within industry. I feel it has had much effect—unfortunately, not all favorable. Based on studies I have made over the past several years, I find the following to be typical of what is happening in many companies using management by objectives.

One company, a large U.S. corporation, has had a management by objectives system in operation since the early 1960's. All supervisory personnel participate in the program. Around mid to late November, the personnel managers in the various plants issue requests to all managers in their respective location asking them to begin formulating their objectives for the following year. The objectives are then forwarded to the manager's superior for approval and submitted to the personnel department for filing. All objectives are supposed to be approved and submitted before the beginning of the new year. Thus the individual manager has from three to five weeks in which to set his objectives. During the year, little emphasis is placed on evaluating performance; in fact, I could find no evidence of formal periodic evaluations. Toward the end of the year, again around mid to late November, another request is issued by the personnel manager asking each superior to evaluate his subordinates in terms of their established objectives and to encourage them to formulate new objectives for the ensuing period. This evaluation cycle is similarly short. The three- to five-week period is all that is provided for evaluating, counseling, and approving the new objectives of the subordinate manager.

## Shortcomings

Most of the benefits to be gained from using such an approach have been mentioned. In my estimation, there are also valid criticisms. *First,* top management plays a very passive role in this approach to management by objectives, with the personnel manager serving as the active agent. *Second,* the objectives of top management are not communicated downward in the organization to the subunits and individuals who also have objectives to set. *Third,* the objectives that do get set are not interwoven or integrated, and there is little assurance that major areas requiring attention have been covered or that other areas of lesser importance are not covered several times over. *Finally,* confusion exists as to where the organization is going, how it is going to get there, and who is going to do what; misunderstanding and conflict are the outcome.

## A BETTER APPROACH

### Top Management Involvement

My first recommendation is to put the management by objectives concept into the hands of top management where it can do the most good for the organization as a whole. This will require considerable effort on the part of both personnel and top management. Although personnel will still stand to benefit from the management by objectives system data regarding individual performance, it must look at the system primarily in terms of its usefulness to the total organization and, second, in terms of the usefulness to itself. Such restraint is always difficult.

Top management, meanwhile, must be willing to spend the time and exert the effort necessary to implement and maintain a management by objectives system aimed at improving overall performance and morale. This task, too, will be difficult. At the start of the year, for example, top management must spend the necessary time to define these objectives and the yardsticks by which performance will be measured. In turn, these overall objectives must find their way to the heads of the subunits and finally to the individuals. Only in this way can the objectives of subunits and individuals be integrated with the overall objectives.

One should not get the idea that what is being proposed here is *top-down autocracy.* At the same time that the chief executive and his staff are setting objectives for the company, the individual managers in the organization should be formulating their own objectives. When the objectives of the chief executive are disseminated to the organization and interact with the individual's objectives a reaction should take place that causes the individual to modify his goals to fit the organization's, or the organization to adopt some of the individual's. This is the key aspect of the whole objective-setting process. If this reaction does not take place, the potential effectiveness of the management by objectives system is drastically reduced.

Next to the lack of top management involvement, the failure to allow sufficient time for development is the major downfall of most objective-setting systems. To provide the needed integration of objectives throughout the organization—down, up, and across functional lines—requires considerably more time than just a few weeks. In fact, a preparation cycle of three to four months might be more appropriate.

The normal budget cycle in a typical organization starts with a projection of sales at estimated prices, and on this basis distribution and advertising expenses are tentatively set. From the sales projections in total and the demand spread over time, a production budget indicating the timing and quantity of production units and indicating material, labor, and overhead expenses is tentatively developed. Finally, budgets for such discretionary areas as administrative expenses, research and development, and capital additions are prepared.

The result is a first-cut plan, which is probably not acceptable to all functional areas or levels of the organization. Top management may not accept the projected profit performance. The chief executive may have a profit objective in mind, but because the marketing and production managers consider sales volume and product quality their primary objectives, the former may cut price to achieve his volume objectives while the latter may overengineer the product, both moves adversely affecting profits. The functional areas may be in conflict over what one ought to do and what another thinks it can do. Built-in cushions may have to be eliminated and disputes over perceived inequities resolved. The reason for the differences of viewpoint reflected in the first-cut budget is that schedules developed at one stage depend not only on information from prior steps but also on the information from succeeding steps. The first-cut budget, then, is a starting point; as many as a dozen trials may be necessary before a satisfactory budget plan is put together.

Just as the approved budget is the result of revisions and tradeoffs, so the objective-setting process is the result of compromise. Top management has some definite objectives for the organization—for example, in terms of profit and return, market share or growth, new product development, product quality, productivity, personnel development, and community relations. The interpretations of the chief executive's objectives may conflict with what the subordinate thinks can or should be done. Thus, complete acceptance of the top executive's objectives is probably impossible, just as complete acceptance of the initial sales objectives based on estimated prices is impossible. It is clear then that the objective-setting process must be a series of vertical tradeoffs between the objectives of top management and the objectives of the individual.

## Peer Goal Setting

The management by objectives process must also include lateral trade-offs similar to those made during the budgeting cycle when marketing, for example, sets quotas that are impossible to achieve given the existing production capacity, and marketing expectations must be relaxed to meet production limitations. Such lateral tradeoffs are just as important as the vertical tradeoffs if maximum integration of objectives is to be achieved. One worthwhile approach to this lateral understanding is peer goal setting.

Peer goal setting means that individuals at a given organizational level, whether it be the staff of the chief executive or peers at a considerably lower level, develop their objectives together. Two major benefits appear to result from such an approach. The first is that peers (managers, for example) may be in a position to give a particular manager unbiased viewpoints of those things to which he should be applying a major portion of his time, and they may be able to suggest solutions to recognized problems. The second benefit is the better understanding that should result between individuals in lateral relationships with the assurance that the objectives set by various individuals do not duplicate each other. The activity managers in the total organization, by working out their objectives together, may reach a better mutual understanding of how their various activities interrelate and how their efforts should be integrated for the good of the overall organization.

## Frequent Performance Review

One of the major faults of many of the existing management by objectives systems is that the objectives set at the beginning of a given time period remain fixed without any appraisal of progress or reevaluation of objectives. Such treatment casts doubt on how seriously the system is being utilized.

To get the most out of the objective-setting process, it is extremely important that a periodic evaluation (for example, on a quarterly basis) be made of an individual's objectives, and that the individual be informed by his superior of his progress toward the completion of the objectives. At this time new objectives should be set if the old ones are completed or otherwise need to be changed. When the individuals in the organization know that their superiors are going to be evaluating their performance formally on a frequent basis, it is highly unlikely that they will slough off the objectives by which they will be evaluated.

## Multiple Evaluations

The concept of multiple performance evaluations is similar to peer objective setting. The manager's performance will be evaluated not only by his immediate superior but by his boss's boss and a third party familiar with the particulars of his work efforts. This third party could very well be a peer involved with the individual's objective setting at the outset of the period. While each evaluation is made independently, the pooling of the information obtained should provide a multidirectional picture of the individual's performance with greater validity than any of the individual evaluations.

## The Superior's Role

Finally, emphasis must be placed on the individual superior and the importance of his role in assuring completion of several aspects of the program. He must be sure that:

1. Objectives developed by his subordinates contribute meaningfully to the objectives of the organizational unit and to the total organization.
2. Objectives are challenging and as specific and measurable as possible.
3. They must be reviewed periodically, and the individual must be counseled as to the progress he is making. The objectives are changed as conditions warrant.
4. Evaluations are based on the ability to meet or exceed the previously mutually-established measurable objectives. Evaluations distinguish between levels of individual performance.
5. The reward structure—promotion practices, training and development, recognition, and salary compensation—is a function of the explicit delineations of performance accomplishments.

## Advantages

Some of the advantages of management by objectives in terms of its usefulness to the total organization as a planning and control concept have been mentioned. Let us now look at these advantages a little more closely.

*Integration of Objectives.*   Under the approach to management by objectives that allows for a very short cycle of preparation there is little or no assurance that the objectives set by the individuals will be integrated and aimed toward the overall objectives of the organization. The proposed process of establishing objectives with the emphasis on top management objectives to be felt by lower management and vice versa, and peer objective setting, should provide for a much higher degree of integration. The result is that those objectives which the individual finally sets for himself are tied closely to the objectives of his immediate activity and to the objectives of the total organizaton, and, in fact, contribute directly to them. This provides for more potential efficiency than under the traditional approach to using management by objectives.

*Improved Communications.*  Top management gets involved in the objective-setting process and clearly defines and disseminates its objectives into the organization. This fact cannot help but have a favorable effect on the members of the organization in that they know the direction top management wants the organization to take. Then they are in a position to assist management in defining its goals and assuming responsibilities. Thus, the channel of communications is automatically opened by this concept of management by objectives in that downward dissemination of objectives is basic and upward suggestions are encouraged. The individual feels a part of the organization because he generates suggestions, as well as contributes to their realization.

*Emphasis on Significant Areas.*  The primary purpose of any objective-setting system is to highlight those significant goals that must be accomplished if superior results are to be achieved. Both the objective-setting approach aimed toward the individual and the approach described in this article aimed toward the total organization emphasize the significant, but in the former case the determination of what is significant is left exclusively to the individual and his immediate superior. In the proposed approach, those objectives deemed important for the individual are also important to the total organization.

*Less Duplication.*  Finally, the objective-setting process described here should result in the elimination of overlapping responsibilities and of the duplication of effort and misunderstanding common between groups within organizations. This change, too, leads to a potential increase in overall internal efficiency.

## Problems

It is naïve to think that the use of management by objectives, with its emphasis on direction from top management rather than from the personnel department, is a simple matter of implementation and maintenance. In fact, the approach takes a lot of work and has several associated problems that warrant attention.

*Getting Started.*  In my estimation, it takes three years of concerted effort on the part of a management to introduce management by objectives into an organization. Many managements want a quick solution and are not willing to spend this length of time. *First,* the individuals in the organization would write objectives for themselves in collaboration with their superiors. The superiors should in turn conduct frequent evaluations of their personnel. *Second,* the individuals would establish more measurable objectives for themselves and start the integration of objectives in the organization. During both the first and second year, I see performance evaluation as a strict supervisory responsibility. *Third,* the organization can start to employ peer objective setting, thereby achieving the lateral integration of desired objectives. It can also place further emphasis on periodic review and reestablishment of objectives, finally introducing the concept of multiple performance evaluation. At the end of three years, which to some managers is a long time to wait for results, the management by objectives approach should begin to have a strong, favorable effect on the organization.

*Time Involved.*    The objective-setting process described here is admittedly a time-consuming one; the proposed period of three to four months is as long as that allowed for an annual budget, and time is money. Yet the time involved or money spent is not wasted, for extensive planning should result in savings many times over from the deemphasis of time-consuming, low contribution effort, and the improved communications that result in the elimination of lapping responsibility and duplication of effort.

*Dynamics of the Firm.*    Business organizations are dynamic, and as a result the objective structure set at the beginning of an evaluation year may require frequent and significant revisions. But as the business is confronted by situations warranting a change in direction, it would seem logical that this change of direction be announced so that individuals in the organization can adjust their efforts accordingly.

*Measurability.*    With the help of their supervisors, individuals can set measurable objectives. It is my feeling that everyone in the organization, if he is going to contribute to it, should be able to state what he is going to do, when it is going to be accomplished, and how it contributes to the overall objectives of the organization. Each person, line or staff, should have a unique contribution that he can make to the organization.

*Comparability.*    Finally, there will always be the problem of comparability. This involves setting objectives throughout the organization that are of equal difficulty to the individuals in it and the evaluation of performance by supervisors whereby two individuals evaluated equally really are of comparable performance. The approach of using peer goal setting during the initial phases of the process and multiple evaluations in the end is aimed specifically at this problem, providing a means for cross-checking the difficulty of objectives set by individuals and the comparability of evaluations given by supervisors.

What I have attempted to point out in this article is the difference between looking at management by objectives as a performance evaluation aid and looking at it as a planning and control concept for top management. Until top management recognizes the distinction and takes positive action, they will miss many of the advantages to be gained from using management by objectives.

Top management must get actively involved in the process of establishing objectives for the organization and disseminating them downward; the individuals' objectives must be initially developed and subsequently modified so that the objectives of the individuals and subunits of the organization contribute to rather than detract from the objectives of the overall organization. The advantages to be gained from looking at management by objectives in this light include a commonality of purpose, an understanding as to what that purpose is, and an efficient use of the resources in the organization to achieve it.

# Performance Appraisal: Managers Beware*

PAUL H. THOMPSON
GENE W. DALTON

IN RECENT YEARS, we have seen the development of comprehensive performance appraisal systems. Technology-based companies, vitally concerned with finding ways to enhance the performance of their highly trained employees, have led in the development of these systems. The results, however, have often been the direct opposite from those intended. Consider this evidence:

The top management of a successful medium-sized electronics company became concerned about its system for administering the salary increases of engineers. There was a growing tendency, the executives believed, for increases to be given each year as a matter of routine, without appropriate emphasis on the meaning of the raises. Nearly everyone received an annual boost, and it seemed to the top executives that the engineers had come to regard the increases almost as cost-of-living adjustments, rather than as rewards for outstanding performance.

To restore the proper balance to the merit-increase program, the president proposed that, beginning in January of the coming year, these steps be taken:

1. The amount of money set aside for raises in the new year would be doubled.
2. High performers would be given their raises early in the year, with the expectation that the better the man, the earlier he would receive his increase.
3. When a raise was granted, the supervisor would highlight the relationship between the engineer's salary increase and the man's outstanding performance.

* Reprinted by permission from *Harvard Business Review*, January–February issue 1970.

4. The supervisors would let their employees know where they stood and would encourage them to continue to improve themselves.

The new program was made a main feature of the president's Christmas message to all employees, and everyone received the news with enthusiasm. However, by late spring, after a disappointing trial period, the managers and supervisors knew that something had gone wrong. Employees receiving raises often reacted with a sullen or dejected attitude, rumors were rife that several highly valued employees were actively looking for new jobs outside, and company morale was in a state of decline.

The electronics division of one large technology-based corporation deliberately took the same kind of steps that the first company had taken spontaneously. In this second company, the executives of the engineering department had become concerned that their supervisors were not discriminating sufficiently between high and low performers. Nearly all of the engineers, they found, were being given above-average ratings on the company's appraisal forms. Engineers sometimes complained that they could see no clear relationship between the ratings they were given and their salary increases.

Therefore, a special task force was created to develop a new system to handle performance appraisals and salary increases. After months of study, the committee recommended a comprehensive plan with these main provisions:

1. Each man would be rated on his performance rather than on his personality traits.
2. Salary increases would be tied directly to the performance rating which, along with his years of experience, would be used to determine his increase from a standard table of salary curves.
3. To prevent all ratings from clustering in a narrow "above-average" range, the ratings in each department would be spread out with each man's rating indicating his position on a normal distribution curve.
4. The supervisor's dual role of appraiser and counselor would be split. Each engineer would be interviewed at least twice each year. The first session would be on counseling and goal setting only. The second interview would be held three months later, and each man would be told the amount of his salary increase, if any. He would also be told where he stood in the numerical ratings, "to encourage the engineer and his supervisor to plan constructively for the engineer's personal development."

The engineering executives introduced the new program with the anticipation that a uniform and logical system for handling these important functions would help both the men and the company. Yet, a few years later, when we studied the corporation, we found that in this division—as in the medium-sized company earlier—both the supervisors and the men shared a deep dissatisfaction. Moreover, investigation revealed they felt that a large part of the widespread discouragement, the numerous instances of declining individual performance, and the distant relationship between management and the men could be attributed to the new performance appraisal system.[1]

## MISSING INGREDIENT

What do these two cases have in common? Why the wide gap between intentions and results in each instance? Had some important element been overlooked, or were both managements merely unlucky?

It is our opinion that there is a great deal of similarity between the events in these two companies and also that these events are being repeated in an increasing number of companies. Performance appraisal touches on one of the most emotionally charged activities in business life—the assessment of a man's contribution and ability. The signals he receives about this assessment have a strong impact on his self-esteem *and* on his subsequent performance.

Therefore, managers need to think through the human consequences of the procedures they set into motion. Good intentions do not suffice. In fact, if they serve as a substitute for the analysis required when dealing with human organizations, they may be detrimental. Performance appraisal can have negative as well as positive motivational consequences in the context of a complex social system. Surprisingly, it is this element which top management so often overlooks or misunderstands.

### Evaluation-Feedback Systems

The issue in both of the foregoing cases is the important process by which the organization evaluates the performance of its members and subsequently informs them of that evaluation. This process is expected by various members of the organization to fulfill a variety of functions:

1.  Top management wants a system which will motivate high performers to do even better and low performers to improve.
2.  Managers want a system which will identify those with high potential for advancement and those who are consistently low performers so that they may be encouraged to leave.
3.  Managers and personnel people want accurate and complete information for making decisions on salary increases, promotions, transfers, and so forth.

---

[1] Paul H. Thompson, *Performance Appraisal: Some Unanticipated Consequences.* Boston: Harvard Business School, unpublished doctoral dissertation, 1969.

4. Supervisors want an objective rating system to justify salary increases and to motivate their subordinates.
5. Subordinates want to know how they are viewed by their supervisors and what the future holds for them in the organization.

In many companies, just as in the two electronics organizations we saw earlier, there is growing concern that the existing evaluation-feedback systems are not performing these functions well. Executives are concerned that the supervisors tend to rate most of their men high and to award all of them fairly similar raises, thus failing to clearly distinguish between high and mediocre performers.

On the one hand, as a result of such practices, management complains that there is little employee incentive to improve performance, and that accurate information on which to base decisions on promotions and transfers is lacking. On the other hand, employees complain that they have little idea what their supervisors think of their performance, and many of the bright, aggressive young men become frustrated and leave.

Many companies experiencing problems like these are responding by making major changes in their evaluation-feedback systems. One method used to ensure that subordinates are evaluated and rewarded differentially according to performance is to use some form of performance ranking, an approach which has been gaining in popularity in recent years.

In the case of the medium-sized company, the engineers were ranked according to their performance, and then salary increases were awarded in the order of that ranking. The large corporation used a normal distribution rating system in its electronics division, forcing the average score to remain at the same level from year to year. Some companies prefer to divide their employees into quartiles based on performance and then use this rating as a major factor in determining salary increases. Still other companies accomplish the same thing by awarding raises according to performance and by making public the average increase in each salary grade.

In each of these evaluation-feedback systems the two main elements are (1) that management compares a man's performance and contribution against the performance of others at the same or comparable levels in the organization, and (2) that management somehow informs the man about how his performance compares with that of his peers.

## PEER-COMPARISON RATINGS

We have been describing evaluation-feedback systems that involve some type of peer comparison, which game theorists would say are zero-sum in nature. A zero-sum game is one in which any change for the participants adds up to zero. Thus, for example, if two men are playing cards and one wins $5, the other automatically has to lose $5, and the net result is zero.

Similarly, if there are ten men in a department working at different levels of effectiveness, by definition five of them are "below average." Thus if two of the below-average men leave, then one of the previously above-average men must fall into the below-average category.

The contstraint that such a system places on any efforts to increase the proportion of the group which excels is illustrated by a much-quoted gaffe uttered at a well-known eastern business school a few years ago. It was the first faculty meeting of the year and one of the assistant deans, full of enthusiasm for the potentialities of the entering class, suggested that the faculty members should all aim to "get more people into the top third of the class." The guffaws from the faculty were only partly aimed at the mixed metaphor, for the irony could not be missed. The only possibly way to achieve the dean's stated goal would have been to increase the size of the class. Better teaching has no effect where the measure of effectiveness is a peer comparison.

All purposive human organizations have both zero-sum and nonzero-sum characteristics. On the one hand, they are zero-sum in the sense that, like the dean's section, only $33\frac{1}{3}$ percent of the members can be in the top third. On the other hand, organizations are nonzero-sum in that they always have the potential to improve, become more efficient, produce more, become more profitable, and do things better than they have in the past. This is true both for the organization as a whole and for all individuals within it.

If one person finds a way to increase his effectiveness, it does not follow that another person's effectiveness will decrease by that amount. If anything, the reverse is likely to be true. The second person may learn from the first and become more effective himself. In this sense, there can be changes in which everyone wins.

Since both zero-sum and nonzero-sum characteristics are present in any organization, the fundamental question in evaluation and feedback is the extent to which each aspect is emphasized, for each has its own consequences. Referring once again to our earlier examples, we see that in the medium-sized company top management's action focused attention on zero-sum comparisons. Under the company's old system, the individual ratings and salary curves had been known only to the immediate supervisor and the salary administration group. No engineer had any direct knowledge of his own or his fellow workers' exact standings. Salary increases had been awarded at various times throughout the year depending on the time of a man's previous increase. The procedure had been followed for a number of years with little or no expressed dissatisfaction.

Under the new system, the engineers quickly recognized that those who were called into the supervisor's office on the first Friday of each month were receiving raises. Clearly, rewards were going first to those rated highest by management, and the men were finding out "where they stood" in relation to others.

However, before long it became evident that the new system was bringing about some unexpected—and unhappy—results. High-rated men were dismayed to find that certain others received raises before them. Older workers complained that the wives of younger men were talking about raises while their wives had nothing to say. Men rated average resisted the designation. The morale of those rated below average suffered substantially; work slowed while anxiety mounted. Even some of the supervisors became concerned when they had not received their own anticipated raises by April.

## The Vicious Cycle

The electronics division of the large technology-based company likewise directed attention to the zero-sum aspects by rating its engineers "on the curve." Under the division's new plan, each man received an annual numerical rating, indicating his placement on a normal distribution which ranged from 8 to 72. To ensure that the distribution did not become skewed upward by "inflation," the managers and supervisors were instructed that the average rating in each department (of about 50 engineers) was expected to remain at 40.

The supervisors in the electronics division, which had had its system in effect several years when we studied it, talked more about the effects on *performance* than did the supervisors in the medium-sized company, who spoke more about *morale*.

One of the division's supervisors described the problem this way:

Unfortunately, under the new Technical Performance Appraisal (TPA) system, we have to tell one half of our engineers that they are below average. After we tell a man his score is below 40, he won't do anything for a month. He stews over his low rating, and he may even take a few days' sick leave, even though he's not physically sick. After a month or two, we may be able to get him working again with the hope that he'll do better next year, but that's really a false hope. He won't get a better score next year, because the men above him now will still be above him next year, even if he does improve a little.

Another division supervisor said:

The effects of a declining rating are disturbing. If you give a man a rating of 35, he can't look himself in the eye. If you give him a 30, he goes numb; it's a terrible jolt to his pride. When a man's rating is lowered two points, his performance goes to pot. A few men will work harder if you lower their ratings, but most will give up. People need a pat on the back.

A number of engineers, even some with above-average ratings, reported that they became discouraged when their scores were lowered. They responded by reducing the amount of effort they were investing in the job, and a vicious cycle began.

One manager expressed the belief that low performers should be given low scores to encourage them to leave. However, it does not work that way. An analysis of the ratings of 60 engineers who had left over a four-year period revealed that almost all of them had above-average ratings or ratings just a few points below average. Thus it appeared that the engineers with very low ratings had lost confidence in themselves and had perhaps decided to stay with the company in the hope of attaining some measure of security.

Even when one of the division managers wanted to focus on some actual increase in performance, the corporation's TPA system made it difficult. One manager cited the experience of an engineer who had been told in a counseling session that his performance was improving, and who three months later learned that his rating had fallen. When he asked why, he was told that while his performance had improved, the performance of others had improved even more. Relatively, he had fallen backward. The logic was impeccable, but the man felt that he had been betrayed.

As a result of these kinds of experiences, the division's engineers became very cynical about the evaluation-feedback system. As one engineer said:

A man's TPA rating is not related to his performance. I know from experience. For example, this past review my rating dropped two points, but my supervisor admitted that he was stealing points from me. He said I'd done better work this year than last, and in spite of this he had to take two points from me to give to someone else. But it's not his fault—it's the system.

Caught between conflicting pressures, both the supervisors and the men found ways to cope with their difficulties, but almost always at a cost. One such practice often mentioned was the shifting of points from older men near the top of their salary bracket to younger men. Here is how one engineer described the rationale for the practice:

Because young engineers are very mobile, they can demand large salary increases or they'll leave. In order to prevent their leaving, management had to raise their ratings to get large salary increases for them. But the points given to the young engineers must be taken from someone else. That's where the older engineers come in; they are much less mobile, so management can take points from them without fear of their leaving.

### Management Constraints

Perhaps the strongest unrecognized effect of a zero-sum evaluation system is the impact on management's *thinking*. If a manager knows that he must eventually tell all his men what percentiles they fall in, he is almost forced to begin thinking about some of his men as below average or as bottom of the heap. Once he begins thinking this way about those men, they will sense it—and, in most cases, this will have a negative effect on their performance.

One engineer described the effect of such thinking in this way:

If your supervisor comes to believe that you are worth four points less and he begins to treat you that way, it's very hard to fight. You can tell yourself you are still a good engineer, but you've got to have a very strong ego if your supervisor tells you that you are 20 percent less effective this year than last. If he continues to lower your rating, sooner or later it gets to you.

The impact of the supervisor's rating continued even when a man was transferred to another group of section; the new supervisor would check on the man's most recent ratings and would treat him accordingly. At least one supervisor attempted to use this principle to his advantage. He described his group to us as his rehabilitation center:

Over the years, I've taken engineers who were castoffs and turned them into excellent performers. I've been able to do this by giving them challenging work, letting them know that someone cared about them, and making them feel a part of the enterprise. .

However, he worked under the same handicaps of the system as the other supervisors, and for every man he helped he had to disappoint someone else. He described one such experience as follows:

Recently, a man did a good job for me, and I told him I would raise his rating as a reward. But to raise his score I had to take points from one of my other engineers. When he found out what I had done, he was very upset and asked to be transferred.

*Single Number Values.* One of the chief arguments for using some form of zero-sum system for performance appraisal is that it supposedly "tells a man where he stands." In our opinion, this is a questionable assumption. An organization or even a group requires a carefully coordinated set of widely different technical and social skills and abilities to operate effectively. Each individual contributes a rich combination of these inputs in response to the needs of the task. A great many contributions are necessary, but none alone is sufficient to ensure the success of the joint effort. Yet the supervisor is asked to order his men's value along some single dimension. Can a single number, percentile, or decile reflect such important realities, for example, as these:

Arthur is invaluable as a detail man, seeing projects to completion, but he lacks the imagination to do the initial design work.

Bates, with his excellent training and enthusiasm, has great potential, but he still lacks balanced judgment.

Calhoun made vital contributions when the organization badly needed them in the past, but the most critical problems faced by his department today involve a technology he does not understand.

Dunmire and Ernst both made valuable contributions, but Dunmire's training is particularly marketable now, and if he is not given a high rating to justify a substantial raise this year, he may accept one of his many pending offers.

Is a zero-sum scheme useful in trying to tell any of these men "where they stand"? Does it even have the vital dimensions it needs? In our view, it oversimplifies a set of very complex relationships; in so doing, it introduces an unnecessary, and perhaps unrecognized, distortion because the number professes an accuracy which it does not in fact possess.

Most people do not deny management's need to form judgments about performance in order to make decisions about raises and promotions. They recognize that a number of subjective factors must be taken into account and that some shorthand methods must probably be used to represent their thinking. Management is usually implicitly trusted to make the judgments competently and fairly. However, it is when management attempts to emphasize *how* all the men are rank-ordered that its judgment is challenged.

By questioning the utility of valuing employees along some single number dimension, we are not advocating secrecy or damning attempts at candor. Rather, we are asking managers to recognize that there is often a spurious concreteness to any single number which attempts to represent a man's comparative value to the company.

*Invidious Comparisons.*  Zero-sum schemes also force a ranking of various tasks and assignments along some dimension such as "value to the company." If two men are equally competent but doing different tasks, which should be rated highest? An invidious comparison between tasks is required, and often a de facto policy is followed (e.g., "Give the men in design work higher average scores than other groups"). In engineering, is design work more vital to the company than coordination with manufacturing? Criteria can be found, of course, to make such a judgment, but when it is made obvious to the men performing the various tasks, the effect is to impose an unnecessarily unidimensional set of values on a complex and interdependent system.

In effect, management places itself in a position where it must say that the eye is more important than the hand, or that the shoulder is more essential than the foot. Before management's ordering of the various tasks is made known, it is possible for each man to say, with some justification, that his work is as vital as any other man's and that unless he does his work well, the company's operation will suffer. After such an ordering becomes known, a man in a middle- or lower-ranked assignment finds it harder to value his own effort. This entails some serious motivational costs.

*Impoverished Rewards.*  Interestingly enough, top management's efforts to design a system to demonstrate direct linkage between performance and rewards also tend to impoverish both management and employees in the kinds of rewards which are valued. In nearly all organizations, a number of things can be considered rewarding, such as challenging assignments, responsibility for large sums of money, recognition, opportunities to learn, promotion, and so forth. Potentially, each of these rewards signals to the recipient that he and his contributions are valued. But once a formal system is set up to publicize a direct link between performance ranking and rewards, the reward chosen becomes the only credible indicator of management's evaluation of individual performance.

Once again returning to our case examples, we see that in the medium-sized company the time of year when the general salary increase was given preempted all other rewards. The fact that larger raises were being given counted for little among those who felt they were getting their increases too late. In the electronics division of the large corporation there was likewise little satisfaction or motivation in the fact that the engineers were working on sophisticated technical programs, or that they were among the highest paid in their industry.

***Unintended Consequences.***  Finally, there is the assumption that the use of a peer-comparison system will have a positive, or at worst a neutral, effect on performance. The assumption is (a) that at most it will inspire the good man to work harder and improve his standing, and (b) that at least it will warn poor performers of their low standing and motivate them to either improve or go elsewhere. This assumption has not been borne out in the cases we have studied. The reason for this may best be understood by examining the findings of a study at General Electric:

Criticism had a negative effect on achievement of goals.

Praise had little effect one way or the other.

The average subordinate reacted defensively to criticisms during the appraisal interview.

Defensiveness resulting from critical appraisal produced inferior performance.

The disruptive effect of repeated criticism on subsequent performance was greater among those individuals already low in self-esteem.

The average G.E. employee's self-estimate of performance before appraisal placed him at the 77 percentile.

Only 2 out of 92 participants in the study estimated their performance to be below average.[2]

The probability is, therefore, that for 70 to 80 percent of all technical personnel a comparative ranking would be a deflating experience. Certainly, all would feel criticized, and those who asked for the reasons for their unexpectedly low rating would receive more specific criticism. Judging from the G. E. findings, this would have a disruptive effect on the performance of most of them. In addition, it would have a negative effect on their self-esteem.

---

[2] Herbert H. Meyer, Emanuel Kay, and John R. P. French, Jr., "Split Roles in Performance Appraisal," *Harvard Business Review* January–February 1965, p. 123.

Thus the combination of the two would be to increase the likelihood of lower ratings, as well as the vulnerability of the technical personnel to those low ratings in the future. As this cycle continued, it would be logical to expect increasingly lower ratings as a man grew older, which is precisely the pattern found in the electronics division of the large corporation.

*Binding the Supervisors.*    How does a per-comparison system for viewing employees affect the supervisors? Most such systems are, after all, supposedly designed to aid the first- and second-line supervisors in motivating their men. The systems introduced in the case-example companies seen earlier were, in fact, enthusiastically implemented by the supervisors. But, as we noted, many of the complaints in both companies soon came from the supervisors. They needed the all-out effort of their employees to accomplish the group objectives, and when they had to tell half of the men each year that their performance was below average (and that there was little realistic hope for a higher rating), they discovered that wholehearted effort was hard to obtain.

Under such circumstances, counseling and goal-setting, even when split into separate sessions, were often a farce. One supervisor, in the large corporation where counseling sessions were held three months before an engineer was given his rating and salary review, described the problem in this manner:

> The appraisal system is a very poor counseling tool. It's possible to evaluate a man's performance, but it's very difficult to write your evaluation down on paper and then defend it to the engineer. Therefore, in the counseling session, you try to anticipate how he'll respond to his rating three months later. If you think he will be dissatisfied and complain about it, then you only write down his faults. You don't tell him he's done a good job even if he has. In fact you don't counsel the man at all; you just try to build a case for the rating you will later be giving him.

## Motivation and Closed Systems

Defined broadly, an individual's relationship with an organization and the individuals within it can be described as a process of exchange. He invests his time and energies in exchange for economic and social rewards. But the level of his effort is usually less related to his current rewards than to his desired and anticipated rewards. We often speak of a person being "highly motivated" when he is working toward some objective, such as greater recognition, promotion, more challenging work, or any of a number of other things.

A high motivation or open system is one in which a large part of the members feel conditions are sufficiently open to their influence so that, if they perform well, they can look forward to certain rewards. Conversely, a low motivation or closed system is one in which only a small proportion of the members feel that high effort on their part will result in increased rewards.

Paradoxically, the zero-sum systems which are introduced as a means of increasing motivation often have the opposite effect. They focus attention on the zero-sum aspects of the work situation and create a closed system in which a high proportion of the men come to feel that regardless of their efforts they will remain outside the winners' circle.

## OBJECTIVE-FOCUSED APPROACH

Fortunately, peer-comparison ratings, with their emphasis on the zero-sum aspects of an organization, are not the only available methods for assessing and providing feedback on performance. A person's performance can also be contrasted against preestablished objectives and against his own prior performance. In 1954, Peter F. Drucker popularized the phrase, "management by objectives," which centered on the assessment of performance by contrasting it against goals.[3] Following his lead, many others have advocated a variety of specific methods which center on the establishment of goals and the subsequent contrasting of performance against these goals.

Our purpose here is not to describe or advocate any one of them, but to stress the point that an objective-focused approach provides an alternative for viewing and discussing a man's performance. Since each man has different tasks and different objectives, there is no reason why he cannot experience some success. Marked improvement in the performance of one person does not automatically require that someone else must slip backward.

Writers have advocated a management-by-objectives appraisal system for many reasons. Douglas McGregor, for example, favored it as a way to help a manager stop "playing God"—that is, judging the personal worth of his fellow man.[4] Alva F. Kindall and James Gatza were concerned about "quackery"—noting that under conventional performance appraisal, the manager was asked to diagnose personality traits. For them, concentration on target-focused appraisals assured a healthy emphasis on the task.[5] Herbert H. Meyer, Emanuel Kay, and John R. P. French were able to show that criticism had a negative effect on achievement of goals, and that performance improved most when specific goals had been established.[6]

---

[3] *The Practice of Management.* New York: Harper & Row, 1954.

[4] "An Uneasy Look at Performance Appraisal," *Harvard Business Review* May–June 1957, p. 89.

[5] "Positive Program for Performance Appraisal," *Harvard Business Review* November–December 1963, p. 153.

[6] *Op. cit.*

## Other Advantages

Our research prompts us to suggest several other advantages of an objective-focused approach:

1. *It is future oriented.* Rather than dwelling on the subordinate's past failures, it focuses attention on his subsequent performance. The past is examined for the clues it provides for future improvement. In addition, the focus is not on where the man stands relative to his peers (which in most cases is discouraging) but on what possibilities the future holds for him in the organization. We have found that it is anticipated rewards that motivate, rather than present rewards or past loyalties.

2. *It is an open, nonzero-sum system.* It is at least possible for all employees to experience positive changes when they are being compared with their own objectives, rather than with their peers. There is a chance for almost everyone in the organization to feel a sense of accomplishment, growth, and progress, and that his contribution to the organization is increasing. In zero-sum systems, only a small part of the members can have that feeling of improvement; the majority are led to believe they are staying the same or declining. Objective-focused systems avoid that pitfall.

3. *It is flexible.* Many of the peer-comparison systems are actually designed to reduce the freedom of the first-level supervisor to ensure that he tells his subordinates "where they stand" relative to their peers, and that he rewards them according to their merit. Objective-focused systems allow much more flexibility to both the supervisor and the subordinate; together, they can set goals which they feel are challenging but also realistic. They can explore together the changes which may be necessary to achieve these goals—that is, modifications in the subordinate's behavior, or even a change in the relationship between the supervisor and the subordinate. It is the supervisor's job to help his men produce and develop their abilities. He should be allowed to use his judgment concerning which kind of feedback might best accomplish those objectives.

Granted there are tasks—and engineering is one of them—where concrete, measurable objectives are often hard to articulate. But the increased effort it takes to make an objective-focused approach to performance appraisal work seems a small price to pay when compared with the high motivational costs we have observed in organizations when zero-sum evaluation schemes have taken their toll.

One of the most important features of a management-by-objectives approach to performance appraisal is the emphasis it places on the nonzero-sum aspects of organizational work life. Unfortunately, this has not been well understood. A failure to understand this point has led in some cases to the nullification of the effects of a goal-setting program by combining it with a zero-sum evaluation scheme.

As we saw earlier in the electronics division of the large corporation, the appraisal system included a session for mutual goal-setting and review. However, each session was carried on with the knowledge that three months later the supervisor would be giving the employee his comparative "rating." Thus the "coaching" role the supervisor was supposed to assume in the goal-setting and review session became a charade. Not only did both parties know that the supervisor was soon to reenter with his "judge's" hat on, but they also knew that the judging was to be a comparative ranking. In view of this, the so-called goal-setting session became only a ballet of careful sparring in anticipation of the announcement of the employee's ranking.

## CONCLUSION

In our study of the process by which a number of different technology-based companies handle the problems of performance evaluation and feedback, we have discovered that each company has its own unique circumstances, its own objectives, and its own history. We have seen certain methods of handling these important functions that have had results which were almost opposite from those intended by their initiators. Therefore, we should like to review a few rough guidelines which may help managers to steer around these particular shoals:

1. *Resist the temptation to devise one grand performance appraisal system to serve all management needs.* Managers do have to make decisions about assignments, promotions, raises, and layoffs, and they also have to discuss performance with each man. There are different and sometimes conflicting objectives in each of these activities; tying them into a single rationalized system may make the system less than useful for any one purpose.

Management's own needs for uniformity and consistency should not be allowed to impose a rigid system that makes impractical demands on the dynamic human organization. This does not mean that each of these activities should be planned in isolation. On the contrary, the entire method of handling performance, salary increases, promotions, and job assignments must be considered together.

2. *In providing feedback to the individual, use many kinds of feedback, and avoid zero-sum comparisons.* What seems fair and optimal at company headquarters may be totally inappropriate for a first-line supervisor trying to get the best work he can from each man. Supervisors can spend a great deal of energy trying to get around requirements they know will make their work harder. Moreover, there are serious questions about the validity of zero-sum comparisons as a representation of organizational realities. They inadvertently convey a spurious concreteness, and impose an artificial overvaluation on one type of reward, on one type of feedback, and on one

type of contribution. Perhaps more importantly, over time they produce widespread discouragement, cynicism, and alienation.

3. *Keep the company's approach to performance appraisal open and future-oriented.* Managers should not foreclose the possibilities for contribution and growth which are potentially available to almost everyone in the organization. An objective-focused approach will help to overcome the serious limitations of most performance appraisal methods, but only if it is administered by a management which appreciates the difference between an open and a closed system and the part management plays in determining that difference.

# Suggested List for Further Reading on Motivation and Control in Organizations

## I. Suggested Reading on Motivation Theory

ATKINSON, J. W. *An Introduction to Motivation.* Princeton, New Jersey: D. Van Nostrand Company, Inc., 1964.

BANDURA, ALBERT. *Principles of Behavior Modification.* New York: Holt, Rinehart and Winston, Inc., 1969.

BINDRA, DALBIR, and STEWART, JANE. *Motivation.* Baltimore: Penguin Books, Inc., 1966.

BIRNEY, ROBERT C., BURDICK, HARVEY, and TEEVAN, RICHARD C. *Fear of Failure.* New York: Van Nostrand-Reinhold Co., 1969.

HECKHAUSEN, HEINZ. *The Anatomy of Achievement Motivation.* New York: Academic Press, 1967.

HOMANS, GEORGE C. *Social Behavior: Its Elementary Forms.* New York: Harcourt, Brace and World, Inc., 1961.

McCLELLAND, DAVID, *et al. The Achievement Motive.* New York: Appleton-Century-Crofts, Inc., 1953.

MASLOW, A. H. *Motivation and Personality.* New York: Harper and Brothers, 1954.

REYNOLDS, G. S. *A Primer of Operant Conditioning.* Glenview, Ill.: Scott, Foresman and Co., 1968.

ROSENTHAL, ROBERT, and JACOBSON, LENORE. *Pygmalion in the Classroom.* New York: Holt, Rinehart and Winston, Inc., 1968.

SKINNER, B. F. *Science and Human Behavior.* New York: The Free Press, 1953.

STOTLAND, EZRA. *The Psychology of Hope.* San Francisco: Jossey-Boss, Inc., 1969.

WHITE, ROBERT W. "Ego and Reality in Psychoanalytic Theory," *Psychological Issues,* Vol. III, 1963.

For a rich source on Motivation, see the annual issues of the Nebraska Symposium on Motivation, University of Nebraska Press.

## II. Suggested Reading on Formal Control Systems in Organizations

ANTHONY, ROBERT N. *Planning and Control Systems: A Framework for Analysis.* Boston: Division of Research, Harvard Business School, 1965.

ANTHONY, ROBERT N., DEARDEN, JOHN, and VANCIL, RICHARD F. *Management Control Systems*. Homewood, Ill.: Richard D. Irwin, Inc., 1965.

BONINI, CHARLES P., JAEDICKE, ROBERT K., and WAGNER, HARVEY W. *Management Controls: New Directions in Basic Research*. New York: McGraw-Hill, 1964.

JEROME, WILLIAM T. III. *Executive Control—The Catalyst*. New York: John Wiley and Sons, Inc., 1961.

## III. Suggested Reading on the Relationship between Motivation and Control in Organizations

BLAU, PETER M. *The Dynamics of Bureaucracy*. Chicago: University of Chicago Press, 1955.

COHEN, HARRY. *The Demonics of Bureaucy*. Ames, Iowa: Iowa State University Press, 1965.

DALTON, MELVILLE. *Men Who Manage*. New York: John Wiley and Sons, 1959.

GELLERMAN, SAUL W. *Motivation and Productivity*. New York: American Management Association, Inc., 1963.

HERZBERG, FREDERICK, MAUSNER, BERNARD, and SNYDERMAN, BARBARA B. *The Motivation to Work*. New York: John Wiley and Sons, Inc., 1959.

LIKERT, RENSIS. *The Human Organization*. New York: McGraw-Hill, 1967.

LITWIN, GEORGE H., and STRINGER, ROBERT A., JR. *Motivation and Organizational Climate*. Boston: Division of Research, Harvard Business School, 1968.

MCGREGOR, DOUGLAS M. *The Human Side of Enterprise*. New York: McGraw-Hill, 1960.

MCGREGOR, DOUGLAS M. *The Professional Manager*. New York: McGraw-Hill, 1967.

MARCH, JAMES G., and SIMON, HERBERT A. *Organizations*. New York: John Wiley and Sons, Inc., 1958.

PORTER, LYMAN W., and LAWLER, EDWARD E. *Managerial Attitudes and Performance*. Homewood, Ill.: Richard D. Irwin, Inc., 1968.

ROETHLISBERGER, F. J. *Man-in-Organization*. Cambridge, Mass.: The Belknap Press of Harvard University Press, 1968.

ROETHLISBERGER, F. J., and DICKSON, WILLIAM J. *Management and the Worker*. Cambridge, Mass.: Harvard University Press, 1939.

SCHEIN, EDGAR H. *Organizational Psychology*. Englewood Cliffs, New Jersey: Prentice-Hall, Inc., 1965.

STEDRY, ANDREW C. *Budget Control and Cost Behavior*. Englewood Cliffs, New Jersey: Prentice-Hall, Inc., 1960.

TANNENBAUM, ARNOLD S. *Control in Organizations*. New York: McGraw-Hill, 1968.

WHYTE, WILLIAM FOOTE. *Money and Motivation*. New York: Harper and Brothers, 1955.

WOODWARD, JOAN (ed.). *Industrial Organization: Behavior and Control*. Oxford: Oxford University Press, 1970.

# Index of Cases